RETHINKING JAPAN
Volume I
Literature, Visual Arts & Linguistics

RETHINKING JAPAN

IN TWO VOLUMES

VOLUME I

Literature, Visual Arts & Linguistics

EDITED BY ADRIANA BOSCARO,
FRANCO GATTI & MASSIMO RAVERI

Japan Library Limited
Sandgate, Folkestone, Kent

RETHINKING JAPAN
Volume I
Literature, Visual Arts & Linguistics

© Japan Library Ltd

First published 1991 by
JAPAN LIBRARY LIMITED
Knoll House, 35 The Crescent
Sandgate, Folkestone, Kent, England CT20 3EE

Edited by Adriana Boscaro, Franco Gatti & Massimo Raveri

British Library Cataloguing in Publication Data
A CIP catalogue record for this book
is availble from the British Library

Set in Plantin Roman 10 on 11 point
Keywork by Ann Tiltman
Photosetting by Visual Typesetting
Printed in Great Britain by BPCC Wheatons Ltd, Exeter

Contents

PART II: Linguistics

List of Contributors

VOLUME I

AGEMATSU, Yuji	Tōkai University, Japan
BEFFU, Ben	University of California (Los Angeles), USA
CALZA, Gian Carlo	University of Venice, Italy
CHAMBERS, Anthony	Doshisha University, Kyoto, Japan
CHANG, Chia-ning	University of California (Davis), USA
DANLY, Robert Lyons	University of Michigan, USA
HARRIES, Phillip	University of Oxford, England
HIJIYA-KIRSCHNEREIT	University of Trier, Germany
INAGA, Shigemi	Paris
JACOB, Jeanne, R	Jerusalem
KAISER, Stefan	University of London (SOAS), England
KEENE, Donald	Columbia University, USA
KRISTEVA, Tzvetana	University of 'Kliment Ohridski', Sofia, Bulgaria
KUBOTA, Yoko	University of Venice, Italy
LaFLEUR	University of Pennsylvania, USA
Le NESTOUR	University of Lille, France
LIDIN, Olof	University of Copenhagen, Denmark
MELANOWICZ, Mikolaj	University of Warsaw, Poland
McCLAIN, Yoko	University of Oregon, USA
MONNET, Livia	University of Minnesota, USA
NAGASHIMA, Yoichi	University of Copenhagen, Denmark
OTTAVIANA, Giola	University of Rome 'La Sapienza', Italy
PLUTSCHOW, Herbert	University of California, Los Angeles, USA
PRONKO, Leonard	Pomona College, Claremont, USA
RADTKE, Kurt Werner	University of Leiden, Holland
RUCH, Barbara	Columbia University, USA
SHIMAMORI, Reiko	University of Lyon III, France
TAKAHARA, Kumiko	University of Colorado (Boulder), USA
TAKESHITA, Toshiaki	University of Bologna, Italy
TAKEUCHI, Lone	University of London (SOAS), England
TANATANI, Isao	Tōkai University, Japan
TESSIER, Max	Paris
WIENOLD, Götz	University of Konstanz
ZOLBROD, Leon, M	University of British Columbia, Canada

Preface

Why Rethinking Japan?

We felt it was the right moment to survey the situation in Japanese studies from as wide a perspective as possible.

Increasingly, a new mood, a new language could be identified in the work of Japanese and Western researchers. Diverse and significant new openings could be perceived emerging from their enquiries. Moreover, certain theories which for years had been accepted as sound and irrefutable had recently been brought back into the debating arena. One need only think of the reevaluation of the established views on the Tokugawa period. A new generation of scholars in the prime of their scientific maturity were now in the spotlight.

The idea of the Symposium therefore, was to put the American and Japanese worlds of study, which have been so active in these last decades, into direct contact with the more innovative tendencies in Europe, thus providing an opportunity to meet and reflect on how best to conduct our research and agree on both the objectives and the way ahead in our field. In other words, to redefine the meaning of Japanese studies today.

Ideally, we wanted to resume the discussions that had so animated the congresses and debates of the seventies on the characteristics of Japanology, on its real scientific possibilities and on its relationship with other disciplines based on comparativism.

Venice was possibly the ideal place for this. The city has a serene beauty which invites quiet reflection and which does not disdain irony's smile. It has a long tradition as a centre of international communications and as an intermediary between cultures, particularly between Europe and the East.

The Institute of Japanese Studies, which was founded 25 years ago at Ca' Foscari, was happy and proud to undertake this project which it saw as an important landmark in its scientific and didactic policy of openness and positive leaning towards international research.

The response was marvellous. Some 250 scholars from 19 countries met in Venice from 14-16 October 1987 to attend the Symposium, to read their papers, to discuss and to make plans for future meetings.

During the course of these three days and now reflected in many of the pages of these two volumes, this new mood was undoubtedly present. Judging from afar it is possible to affirm that if, in the human sciences much has changed, these changes have also been absorbed within the field of Japanese studies.

ix

Whether in the participation from the floor or in the discussions, one could note how the adoption of new methodological perspectives had overcome many of the old barriers that rigidly divided the various fields of research. A tendency to seek out connections between the different disciplines and a perception of a new order in cultural discourse clearly revealed themselves.

In the planning stage of the Symposium, we endeavoured to avoid rigid demarcations between the disciplines. And in order to encourage and support these innovating tendencies and to ensure that they continued to be creative and spontaneous we invited all the participants to forget traditional 'labelling' as far as possible.

Thus, in the discussions on the new demands of research, semiologists debated with specialists in classical literature, anthropologists spoke in front of economic historians, students of religion found themselves confronted with historians on common problems like, for example, the formation of ideology.

Many responded to our request, presenting their work in progress or the latest results of their studies and the debate concentrated on identifying underlying tendencies and new directions in our studies.

The results are presented in these two volumes. Volume I comprises the papers read at the sectional meetings of 'Literature and Visual Arts' (coordinated by Adriana Boscaro) and 'Linguistics' (Adriana Boscaro together with Yoko Kubota); Volume II comprises the papers read at the sectional meetings of 'Social Sciences' (Franco Gatti) and 'Ideology and Thought' (Massimo Raveri).

We hope that the publication of the Proceedings will encourage yet more new ideas and provoke the desire for further meetings in other countries which will continue the spirit of this initiative and develop the results of these reflections.

We take this opportunity to express our grateful thanks to our Publisher Paul Norbury for the painstaking work involved in getting these two volumes into print.

RETHINKING JAPAN ORGANIZING COMMITTEE
Adriana Boscaro
Franco Gatti
Massimo Raveri
January 1991

*These two volumes
are dedicated to Fosco Maraini*

Acknowledgements

We would like to express our deepest gratitude to the following Institutions for their very kind contributions to the organization of the Symposium and the publication of the Proceedings:

AISTUGIA (Associazione Italiana per gli Studi Giapponesi)

ASSICURAZIONI GENERALI

ASSOCIAZIONE ITALIA-GIAPPONE

AZIENDA DI PROMOZIONE TURISTICA DI VENEZIA

BANCA CATTOLICA DEL VENETO

BANCA COMMERCIALE ITALIANA

BANCO SAN MARCO

CAMERA DI COMMERCIO GIAPPONESE IN ITALIA

CONSIGLIO NAZIONALE DELLE RICERCHE (C.N.R.)

CONSIGLIO REGIONALE DEL VENETO

JAPAN FOUNDATION

TŌKAI UNIVERSITY EUROPEAN CENTER

UNIVERSITA' DEGLI STUDI DI VENEZIA

PART I:
LITERATURE
&
VISUAL ARTS

1

Abe Kobo's Internationalism

OLOF G. LIDIN

We live in the age of nuclear peace. No one is more aware of this situation than Abe Kobo, and our nuclear peace has been the subject of his two latest books, the novel *Hakobune Sakuramaru* (1984), The Ark, and a volume of essays, *Shini-isogu kujiratachi* (1986), The Whales. The background of The Ark is the imminence of the holocaust of an atomic tragedy. There is no question, it is only a matter of when. In his own dramatic fashion Abe points out in his more pessimistic passages that we are already in it. Perhaps the bomb has been thrown but has not yet fallen. The Iran-Iraq war is considered in The Whales as a prelude to what is to come, what must come, if we do not better our ways - and fast. This is therefore a very serious contention, which is underlined in The Whales, in which he discusses the same themes as in The Ark and presents his thoughts concerning the present world. The two works can profitably be read together.

The inevitability of the coming catastrophe makes Abe suspicious and critical of proposed measures to save at least part of mankind. The primary discussion in The Ark is about who is worth being saved in shelters and who is not. Just as Noah's Ark was a shelter at the time of the Flood, the Hakobune Ark is planned to serve as an immense Noah's Ark and its crew as a 'bank of genes' (*idenshi-banku*), and 'gene pool' (*idenshi-pūru*), at the time of the nuclear disaster. It is an enormous mountain cave to be launched as a Noah's Ark at the very same time that the nuclear war breaks out. The hero of the novel has made preparations for a long journey, dynamite charges are in place to be exploded, weapons are stored to be used against intruders, and he is looking for suitable members of the 'crew' when the novel begins, that is, for people who are to survive when the holocaust comes.

As the novel proceeds, however, it dawns upon the hero as it dawns upon the reader that the search for survivors is meaningless. What is survival under such circumstances? One has the impression that Abe is writing the whole novel as a parody, in order to show with all clarity the futility of trying to survive the nuclear holocaust that he feels is on its way, and he is no doubt right on this point. To survive in a shelter of any kind would only mean a brief respite, the postponement of an inevitable death sentence. A 'nuclear shelter' (*kaku-sherutā*) is likened to a prison

2

cell where a prisoner sentenced to death has had his execution postponed temporarily. In the novel Abe introduces two personalities, Sakura and his girl friend, both supposedly afflicted by cancer with only six months to live. In the same light he sees the whole crew of the mountain Noah's Ark. The cancer of nuclear radiation will reach them sooner or later, even if they are locked up for, say, six months in the Ark. 'What Ark can survive the flames of Hell?' Abe asks.

The hero leaves the Ark towards the end of the novel, abandoning at the same time his obsession with launching his Ark. He knows now that it is futile to save oneself at the time of nuclear war. With this new realization he steps out into the sunlight and finds that everything is transparent.

'Transparent rays of sunshine... coloured the city red. ...Facing the black-glass walls of the city hall, I set up my camera, using the wide-angle lens, and focused. I meant to take a souvenir photograph of myself and the street, but everything was too transparent. Not only the light but the people as well: you could see right through them. Beyond the transparent people lay the transparent town. Was I transparent too? I held a hand up to my face - and the town was seen through my hand. I turned around, and looked all around me; still, everything was transparent. The whole town was dead (alive), in an energetic, life-like way. I decided not to think any more about who could or would survive.'

On this note *Hakobune Sakuramaru* ends.

That Abe sees little hope for mankind in case of nuclear war is apparent. One can discern pessimism, even desperation, in a situation when man is preparing his own self-destruction. Shelters are not the answer, they only indicate the acceptance of nuclear war as inevitable. Abe states that the primary reason why he wrote the *Hakobune Sakuramaru* was to discuss the shelter and survival in face of a nuclear Armageddon. The shelter could have served a purpose in World War II, but it will serve no purpose in the next war. This he shows as clearly as Raymond Briggs does in *When the Wind Blows*. Raymond Briggs' work shows the futility of planning to escape from the nuclear war. *When the Wind Blows* has been described as a 'devastating black comedy' and as a 'grimly humorous and horribly honest book' and I think that the same can be said about *Hakobune Sakuramaru*. Raymond Briggs' book was first published in 1981, and although Abe's was not published until 1984, it was begun seven years earlier. There should then be no connection between the two works. Both end with the holocaust, Briggs' manifestly so, Abe's indirectly so. Briggs' does not discuss the coming of the nuclear war or the building of shelters; everything is just presented as matter-of-fact and the absurdity of the belief in the shelter is given in black pictorial humour. In *When the Wind Blows* the bomb is released and the tragic drama is described to its sad conclusion; in *Hakobune Sakuramaru*, the bomb 'is thrown before it has fallen', as the situation is described in *Shini-isogu kujiratachi*. There is thus a fatalistic view expressed about the present global situation in both works. Abe, for one, can see little that alleviates his fear. The bomb has been thrown but has not yet exploded; that is the world situation today according to him, it seems.

3

Abe's primary outlook is pessimistic, and he has a philosophical basis for his pessimism. He does not say that man is evil but he is close to saying so. He sees a cycle in man's life, a cycle which swings between a 'desire for destruction' (*hametsu-ganbō*) and a 'desire for renascence' (*saimei-ganbō*). There is nothing new in this view. We find cyclical thinking in Buddhism, in Hegelian and Marxist thinking, and also in the Chinese dynastic histories. Cyclical alternation does not differ fundamentally from dialectical alternation. Abe's thought can therefore be said to have both Eastern and Western roots.

If there is a difference, it can be found in the fact that Abe sees the 'desire for destruction' as the beginning and end of man. It is as 'inborn' in man's genes as evil is inborn in Christian thought. This tendency to wish for destruction under whatever circumstances is part of man's instinctive 'locked programme', his *tojita progurammu*. It is, however, always closely connected with the desire for renascence, which is again in a short time turned into the desire for destruction.

What Abe realizes is that cycles of destruction and revival have accelerated to occur closer and closer in time so that they today practically overlap and coincide. One can speak about a crescendo in world events from the time of Buddhist thought, when there were thousands of years between *shōbō* and *mappō*, until today when the periods of destruction come one after another in rapid succession. Only because we live in the age of nuclear peace, we have avoided the final holocaust, after which Abe sees no renascence. Therefore, he can also quote the Bible and say that 'The end of the world is near.'

Abe goes so far as to say, however, that the nuclear holocaust is not only imminent, but that it is under way. The desire for destruction still rules man, and he still stops short of nothing, not even total death, in order to satisfy his desire for death. Referring to the Iran-Iraq war, he sees it as a prelude if not the very beginning of the holocaust.

Is there then really no hope? Abe is certainly pessimistic in his latest two works, but there is also a glimmer of hope expressed - in the end. What frightens him more than anything else is modern post-war nationalism. After World War II nationalist feeling was at a minimum, but since then it has grown strong and dangerous. Abe finds this development ominous, and he would like both the nation state (*kokka*) and nationalism (*kokkashugi*) to be diminished, if not abolished. Nationalism comes only next to colonialism in Abe's catalogue of sins. They are twin brothers; when colonialism goes, nationalism takes over.

Abe is actually ambivalent when it comes to the state. He agrees with Marx that the extinction of the state is perhaps the only solution, but on the other hand, he realizes that the state is the necessary evil for a minimum of order. When the state is feeble, it ends up like Lebanon. But the state contains a latent cancer mechanism which thrives on nationalism.

International athletic events, as represented by the Olympic Games, Abe sees as the worst symbol of modern nationalism. They are an abomination when muscles are displayed and national anthems blare and flags flutter. The hero in the *Hakobune Sakuramaru* has a dream in which he establishes an anti-Olympic Games Movement, intended to disrupt the games. All ceremonies seem suspicious to Abe, all are means to collectivize man. Ceremonies make common activities sacred (*Gishiki wa zokuji wo seika suru*). A simple sexual act becomes communal when circumscribed by an official ceremony. It becomes socialized, as also births and deaths with other rites.

All the ceremonies surrounding man lead to greater and greater organization, and the epitome of all collectivized organization Abe sees in the armed forces, the military, which march for the nation state according to orders. No other animal does that, not even the wolf, which, after all, hunts in packs. The army is the very mirror of ceremony. The glorification of loyalty and the disparagement of disobedience are imprinted into men's minds and people are taught to march and to kill. Goose steps and uniforms are the ultimate of ceremony (*hochō to seifuku nanda yo gishiki no kyūkyoku wa*). Schools come next; they serve as centres for indoctrination and collectivization.

It can then be understood that Abe is against all national ceremonies. Japan is of course his starting point, and his memories of World War II constitute the background. He cannot forget the regimentation of the war years and what the Japanese people went through during and especially at the end of the war.

Inevitably, therefore, he is suspicious of anything that smells national and can lead to the same situation as during and before the war; equally, a national manifestation, such as at the Yasukuni Shrine, is anathema to him. If not controlled, the ceremonies at the shrine in honour of the soldiers who died during modern wars can easily become part of a rebuilt nationalism, which can be centrifugal rather than centripetal. What he reacts most strongly against is the fact that the prime minister and the cabinet take part in the ceremonies and give them national prestige. Just because it is on the national level and has official backing, it can easily become a drug that will poison the minds of the Japanese people yet again. It can be the national ceremony (*kokka gishiki*) which becomes the beginning of a national ideology (*kokkashugi*). Each such tendency must be fought, according to Abe, both on the national and international level. This may perhaps seem exaggerated and be difficult to understand for those of us who were not afflicted by the horrors and ideologies of World War II; but I can imagine that there are many, for example, here in Italy, who understand what Abe worries about and understand what he expresses. One is more nervously over-sensitive once one has had the experience.

It is, however, sport first of all that gives Abe the shudders. When a winner raises his fist slantingly upwards, Abe is reminded of Nazism and its raised arms. Sport is today the worst symptom of nationalism, and Abe points to world football games as one of the occasions when nationalistic feelings are displayed, in the same manner as at Olympic games. Abe happened to be in Copenhagen the day Denmark beat the Soviet Union 4-1 and witnessed the national hysteria resulting from the victory. He was visibly depressed.

Now Abe is an iconoclast. He behaves like a bull in a china shop not least within Japanese culture - more so than Japanese generally. He is suspicious of many elements within Japanese culture, and states openly that he hates others. The traditions are scrutinized and what he finds not up to standard, he criticizes and discards. In literature, for example, he finds *haiku* and *tanka* - perhaps poetry generally - too antiquated and traditional, without the force needed in our modern world with nuclear problems. Prose is the literary vehicle of this age.

Abe's iconoclasm does not stop with literature. He goes so far as to touch upon the most sacred areas of Japanese culture. He has a deep-rooted dislike for *matsuri* Shinto festivals (*tettei-shita matsuri-kirai*), a dislike which he himself finds unnatural. (He is Japanese after all). He dislikes the symbol of all Japanese symbols, the *sakura* cherry blossom, and he dislikes it although he finds it beautiful. Here he has an expressed reason for his dislike. *Sakura* has another meaning, an emotional meaning with roots deep down in the Japanese soul, a meaning it does not have for other people. Abe thinks it gives rise to the same emotion for the Japanese people as the word 'cowboy' does for the American people. These emotions connected with terms like *sakura* and *cowboy* are, according to Abe, the fulcrum and foundation of nationalism, and therefore he detests them. Nationalism feeds on them.

That Japanese supposedly love nature and the seasons more than any other people Abe considers to be nonsense. They have lovely theories about the seasons but no feelings for them. On the other hand, he finds that his countrymen are easily influenced by their emotions, prone to form collective groups and to be controlled by ceremonies. Individualism is normally not for them.

Customs and ceremonies (*shūkan and gishiki*) are found in all cultures. They are the necessary cement of the cultures, and as such Abe is not against them, as long as they are balanced by healthy individualism. Today, however, he is frightened by the growth of ceremonial forms which seem to crush all individual activity, especially when they tend in nationalist directions. Television is today the most custom-creating new mass-media device, and Abe is questioning its influence on the Japanese people. No earlier medium has had the ability to reach out to the whole people and create 'artificial ceremonial groups' (*gijigishiki*). The theatre and the cinema never had the power that television now has. Abe notes in this context that tears are a formidable means to create a togetherness mentality and group consciousness. Abe is generally against what smacks of 'group' and 'collectivity'. He even avoids going to concerts and prefers to listen to music alone - in bed with earphones on. What we have to watch out for is whether customs and ceremonies lead in the direction of patriotic passion and to nationalism, in turn leading to militarism.

Turning again to the desire for destruction (*hametsu-ganbō*), it acts both to annihilate existing ceremonies and to create new ceremonies. Abe sees this happening in religious movements, when old ceremonies are crushed only to be superseded by new ones. From religious movements the way is not far to political movements. Apparently, every new life situation brings forth new ceremonial forms. Also in The Ark, immediately a new power play and personal complications develop, which the hero leaves with evident relief at the end of the novel. Every group creates its definite forms of loyalty and obedience, and other rules needed for its everyday existence.

One must make a distinction between customs and everyday ceremonies and national super-ceremonies in Abe's thought. He accepts ceremonies which do not intrude upon man's individualistic freedom. They can even serve as an antidote to his desire for destruction. The line between the two categories, however, is nebulous and simple everyday ceremonies can easily lead to state ceremonies with political implications. Once having become political institutions, they have a capacity to snowball, and there is no return. We must be aware of the danger, but it makes Abe's hair stand on end when he notes how readily and meekly people accept the relentless growth of ceremonies.

It is an 'anti-ceremony campaign' (*han-gishiki-undō*) that Abe is conducting in his latest works. When he attacks ceremonies, he is attacking the state at the same time. No less than Marx, rather more, he wishes for the annihilation of the modern state, which he considers to be the threat to all humanity in our nuclear age. We can do without the state in most circumstances. If it is to remain, it is in order to be the vehicle of practical services for the people, nothing more.

The imaginative power of the nation is not to be taken lightly. In our century it has been successfully connected with racism and with various other 'isms'. All nationalism, however, is built on a lie. Yet people allow themselves to be drunk with nationalist feelings, to be driven to war for the 'nation', to kill for the 'nation', even to die for the 'nation'. Abe compares it with the Cheshire cat in *Alice in Wonderland*. Nationalism is, in the last analysis, nothing but a grinning Cheshire cat, with a grin but with no substance. But since the grin appeals to the emotions, and to the emotions of whole peoples, it is dangerous, even if it is only a grin. This is the irony of the whole matter: people allow themselves to be driven by empty feelings, directed towards empty ideals.

Abe probably considers the abolition of the nation (*kokka haizetsu*) as the only avenue to the abolition of the nuclear threat and the nuclear bomb (*kaku haizetsu*). He is, however, quite pessimistic on this point. He finds Mr Gorbachev as conservative as Mrs Thatcher, quoting him as having said that 'there is only the question of the good of the state' (*kokka no rieki ga aru dake da*). One understands that Abe is as disappointed with Communism, which he once supported, as with capitalism, which he never supported directly. Communism was on the right road with its international thought in its early stages with no frontiers accepted in the brotherhood of the proletariat, but the Communist states have become as national as other states. After 1946 frontiers were nebulous and the world was on its way to unity under the aegis of the United Nations, but since then the situation has hardened, the frontiers 'have become like gods', meaning that conflicts can easily develop, and have indeed developed. For Abe it is a crescendo that inevitably leads to holocaust.

Abe knows that he has taken on an almost superhuman task to combat the ceremonial jungle of Japan and the world. With some resignation he states that ceremonies and conventions seem to form some part of the evolution of life, ever striving for new forms. One cannot leave things passively at any time, without being overgrown by new thickets of ceremonies. One has at all times to keep watching and cutting away,

7

relying on man's open programme of *language and words*. Abe is on this point much influenced by Chomsky and his theories about man and language. At first glance, ceremonies seem complicated, but, on closer scrutiny, they are very simple. Even simple things, however, show toughness, even an amoeba, and likewise the simplest habit, once established, displays a magical tenacity.

Accordingly, there is a conservative element in ceremonies that makes them live on when they have lost their meaning and purpose. Abe points out, for example, the funeral ceremonies which meant much in the religious context in which they were born but mean less or nothing in a secularized society. They could be exchanged for something more timely, but they are not. A bloody revolution, as at dynastic change in China, is needed for ceremonies and bureaucratic forms to be eradicated, to 'be reduced to zero', as Abe puts it.

Abe draws a dark picture of despair. The future is bleak. If there is a glimmer of hope, it shines in the direction of a new internationalism which, crossing the frontiers, breaks through the parentheses of nationalism. One avenue he finds in the new literature which transcends the nations and which is written for the whole world and not for a single nation. The word is the weapon and the key to free man from the yoke of ceremonies and nationalism.

Such international literature which turns to the world with a new message, Abe traces to the Weimar era in Germany and then to the 1930s. The tradition begins with Jewish writers, who had to flee from Germany later and become refugee writers (*bōmeisha*). Brecht is mentioned first among them and Elias Canetti as a late exponent in our time. Abe adds Kafka as an earlier member of the Jewish group of modern *bōmeisha*. He writes in his latest book that he 'has come to like Kafka more and more' (*masumasu Kafka ga suki ni narimashita*). Garcia Marques is also mentioned among them, and others. This new literature was contemporary with Fascism, Nazism and Stalinism. Thus, at the same time as nationalism became extreme, culture acquired an international character (*bōmeisha bunka*). Abe concludes that culture is weak when confronted with politics, and the 1930s is evidence of this, as also the 1980s. However, even though this refugee culture did not mean much before the war, Abe thinks that it has exerted considerable influence since.

Paris became then the haven of refugee cultures. It moved, as it were, from Weimar Germany to France. There they assembled, avant-garde artists and writers, from all over the world, also from Middle and South America. (*Pari mo bōmeisha no tengoku datta*). It began in arts and film, for example, in surrealism, while it took longer for literature to mature.

Abe mentions a number of names among the Paris *bōmeisha*, among them also Picasso, but there is not a single Japanese. Why? He gives a reason in his essay about Garcia Marques. Japanese are too rational-digital in their mental set-up and in their approach to things, while a true *bōmeisha* needs to be irrational-analogue, first of all psychologically. Basing himself on Tsunoda Tadanobu, Abe finds that his countrymen are apt to digitalize their lives (they are left-brained), while they lack imagination, which, like music and the arts, belongs to the right side of the brain and is analogue.

8

This is all according to Tsunoda Tadanobu and his book *Nihonjin no nō*, 'The Japanese Brain', which theorizes about the left brain (digital) and the right brain (analogue). Abe apparently accepts it all without hesitation.

Abe does not mention any Japanese who *was* a member among the *bōmeisha*, but neither does he mention any Japanese who *is* a *bōmeisha* today. He is critical of most Japanese literature written today. It is local, parochial and *gishiki*-prone. It is national not international, and little of it is translated and read abroad. What about Abe himself? One must conclude that he makes true efforts to belong among the creators of a new world literature, and that he attempts to be analogue - and not only digital. He is also not understood by the Japanese reading public, which he of course explains by the digital predilection of the Japanese generally. For the same reason he finds that Garcia Marques is not much read, and that Canetti is not at all known in Japan, in spite of the fact that their works are translated in toto (digital work) and in spite of his own efforts to make them known. He admits himself that he had not heard of Garcia Marques until Donald Keene recommended his books, and that he had not heard of Canetti until he received the Nobel Prize. But then he was convinced in no time and has now read everything they have written, in Japanese, of course, and he puts them in the centre of today's prose literature and as forerunners of the world literature to come. It is the literature of the refugee writers that will show us the way across the borders into a universe where nationalism is diminished, if not annihilated.

The question is whether Abe can be counted among the *bōmeisha*. He certainly feels close to them and aims at the same universal goals as they do. Perhaps he also feels like at least a mini-*bōmeisha*, if not a full one. He had after all to flee from Manchuria, and he had to live the precarious post-war life in Tokyo while studying medicine at Tokyo University. Otherwise, however, he has not been on the run. But he has his refugee memories, and he feels close in intention and life with the runaway writers in Europe and America. And his novels, painstakingly written, reach out to the world and not only to Japan.

If there is hope for the world, Abe sees it in the cultural internationalism which these runaway writers, *bōmeisha*, stand for. Frontiers must be eliminated or at least perforated by cultural interpenetration and by cross-cultural concerns, and nationalism which grows increasingly threatening with more and more institutions and ceremonies must be exchanged for an internationalism of the spirit. If not, we can each one of us quote Indian wisdom together with Oppenheimer and say, 'I have become death, the destroyer of worlds.'

2

Rethinking Soseki's *Mon*

YOKO McCLAIN

Mon is not generally considered one of Soseki's masterpieces. It is said, however, that Soseki himself, in his later years, came to see *Mon* as his favourite work and expressed confidence in this novel.[1] Two points in particular seem to stand out in *Mon*. One is unusual warmth, which Soseki seems to have intentionally brought into the novel. By creating characters who are not intellectuals as well as by depicting the lives of these ordinary people, he made *Mon* unique among his works, since he usually presents the lives of a selected élite. He apparently followed a passage from his earlier work *Kusamakura*, in which he says, 'Approach everything intellectually, and you become harsh.'

Secondly, Soseki exhibits in this work the mastery of realistic writing. He was always interested in realistic writing, as shown in the long chapter 'Realism' in his book *Theory of Literature*. He seems to be particularly impressed by two elements of the realistic writing of Jane Austen, who he says always selected a simple subject as well as a simple method of expression.[2] In *Mon* Soseki uses like means and produces a sad but warm ambience surrounding a couple who rarely did anything special.

Mon is the third novel of a trilogy that begins with *Sanshiro* and *Sorekara*. Uncharacteristically, Soseki seems to have spent very little time preparing for *Mon*. In an advance announcement of *Sorekara* (22 June 1909, the *Asahi Shimbun*), Soseki listed his reasons for giving his forthcoming novel the title *Sorekara* (And Then): 'In this novel a strange fate befalls him [the protagonist], but nothing is said about what will "then" follow.'[3] It is apparent that even before the serial's first instalment, Soseki not only had a clear notion of how *Sorekara* would end, but also knew that he would write a novel to follow up *Sorekara*.

In the case of *Mon*, however, there is no evidence that he thought out the entire plot, particularly the latter part of the story, in advance. He apparently began writing the novel less than two weeks before the serial publication started. There seem to be several reasons for this lack of preparation. Within a week after completing *Sorekara* in mid-August, Soseki suffered an attack of stomach trouble, and did not recover for many months. His poor health, however, did not keep him from travelling through Manchuria and Korea for over a month, and writing a travelogue upon his return. He also took charge of the newly created *Asahi* literary columns in November of the same year.

When it was time for the *Asahi* to announce Soseki's forthcoming serial in February 1910, Soseki did not even have a title in mind. He asked Morita Sohei, one of his students, to think of a title and deliver it to the *Asahi*. Morita was flabbergasted that a writer would ask someone to devise the title for a novel he was about to publish, but he consulted Komiya Toyotaka, another of Soseki's students. Komiya opened up the Japanese translation of Nietzche's *Zarathustra* and found, at random, the word *mon*. The young students agreed that *mon* was a symbolic term and that any good writer would be able to construct a story around it. The title was announced on 22 February, the day after Morita delivered it to the *Asahi*, and reportedly even Soseki first learned of the novel's title through this announcement.[4]

Mon tells the story of how a man and a woman who defy society's laws have to live afterwards. Specifically it is the story of what happens to Daisuke and Michiyo after *Sorekara*. In *Sorekara*, Daisuke, the protagonist, gave Michiyo up to his friend Hiraoka, believing that it was the heroic thing to do, even though he loved her. But years later, when he found Michiyo unhappy with Hiraoka because of the latter's unfaithfulness during her prolonged illness, he decided to renounce his hypocrisy and ask Hiraoka to give Michiyo to him. The story ends with Hiraoka's consent.

There is no doubt that Sosuke, the protagonist of *Mon*, is the later incarnation of Daisuke, and Oyone, that of Michiyo. However, Soseki creates entirely different personalities for the two protagonists to fit each story. For instance, in the powerful, passionate *Sorekara*, Daisuke is a fighter. He is confident, believing that he and Michiyo need to be united even at this later stage because it is the will of heaven. Readers of *Sorekara* may admire Daisuke's courage to be true to himself, but his bold approach to his problems does not allow them to sympathize with him. On the other hand, Sosuke, in the gentle, sad *Mon*, is not capable of such a positive attitude. Even the way in which Sosuke acquires Oyone from his friend Yasui is not premeditated as in Daisuke's case. It was when Sosuke was still a student that he betrayed Yasui:

> 'A furious wind had blown up from nowhere and struck down
> the unwary couple. When they finally picked themselves up off
> the ground, they saw that they were covered with dirt from
> head to foot.... The world was without mercy holding them to
> account for their sin, but they themselves, before any
> recognition of moral guilt, wondered instead if they had been
> in their right mind at the time....'[5]

Sosuke is passive, and takes his present lonely fate as something he fully deserves. If Oyone ever says something consoling he reprimands her, saying that they do not have the right to hope.[6] Thus readers sympathize with him.

The novel opens in a dingy, rented house under a cliff. Sosuke is basking in the mid-afternoon sun on an Indian summer Sunday on the house's tiny verandah, with Oyone just a few feet away. She is sewing in the adjoining room, separated from the verandah by only thin *shoji* screens. Since these screens have glass insets in the middle, they can see as well

11

as talk to each other. Thus Soseki sets the tone of the novel at its very beginning. It is an ordinary scene of an ordinary couple. The season is late autumn, signifying that the two are already past their prime. It is a very calm afternoon, reflecting the couple's quiet life-style. The house is situated back on a small alley off the main road, isolating its residents from the outside world. Even though their house is dingy and damp, the tiny verandah Sosuke now occupies has the warm afternoon sun, implying that as long as the couple are together, they can find a warm spot no matter how harshly the world treats them.

Soseki intended to write about what happens to a man and a woman who wrong another person by breaking the laws of society. Ethically, then, he had to make them suffer, which he did to a certain degree. Sosuke and Oyone are forsaken by their families, friends and relatives. Sosuke, who once was 'a son of a man of considerable means... [and whose] character was worldly and inclined towards all kinds of extravagance'[7] is now a humble civil servant whose income is just enough to support him and his wife. They encounter misfortunes such as losing a child not just once but three times. The first one miscarries, the second premature baby has a brief life of only one week, and the third is stillborn after being suffocated by a twice-coiled umbilical cord. However, Soseki consciously avoids making the punishment more severe than necessary. Though Sosuke and Oyone's pain is deep and penetrating, it is not bitter. They suffer the consequence of their social sin together, and 'they learned to feel warmer in each other's arms.'[8] By tempering their suffering in this way, Soseki creates a strange irony surrounding a couple who are ostracized by society because of scandalous behaviour yet able to enjoy the blissful 'unchanging intimacy such as is realized by few married couples.'[9] Thus a gentle sadness permeates *Mon*.

The protagonist of *Mon*, Sosuke, is a lowly office worker who did not even complete his university training. He is a simple, uncomplicated man. Sosuke is the type of character one encounters every day but seldom remembers because he is so ordinary. The supporting characters also are quite ordinary. Their landlord Sakai is a cultured, educated man but is not a nervous intellectual like, for example, Ichiro in *Kojin* or Kenzo in *Michikusa*, both of whom are identified with the author himself. The characters in *Mon*, who are entirely different from those intellectuals, are thus a pure Soseki creation. At the time he wrote *Mon*, 'naturalism' was still thriving in Japanese literature. Soseki was against its basic tenet that a novel should slavishly copy real life. Soseki insisted that without the imaginative, fictional quality, the work would lose as a novel.[10] By creating characters who are not intellectuals, Soseki succeeded in bringing warmth to the novel.

Soseki made Sosuke and Oyone poor, but it is what McClellan calls 'genteel poverty'.[11] They live in a shabby, rented house, they do not have money to buy a new pair of shoes, and they are afraid of going to a dentist because it may cost too much. But poverty to this extent is not uncommon for an ordinary household. In other words, their life is not threatened by starvation. If he had made them literally destitute, he could have spoiled the ability of the common reader to identify and empathize with the characters. It could also have reduced the warmth the story emanates. Why did Soseki create such a sad but warm story instead of a harsh one with more severe punishment for the social outcasts? First, although he was a stern moralist on such issues as dishonesty, deceit and hypocrisy, he was always sympathetic to natural manifestations of genuine love between a man and a woman, even if sometimes the love might be considered socially unacceptable. This is evidenced by the relief rather than disapproval that readers feel when Daisuke in *Sorekara* finally confesses his love to Michiyo, his close friend's wife. In his personal memo of 1909 Soseki says, 'One who does not have any experience of love has a deprived life. True love makes one's life instantly rich.... One who tastes the moment of genuine love has led a long life, even if one's chronological life may be short.'[12] Love to Soseki is a serious and sacred matter. Almost all of his later works deal with love, though most are painful.

Second, Soseki may have created a warm story simply because he was not in the mood to write a harsh novel. On 2 March, the day after the first instalment of *Mon* appeared in the *Asahi*, Soseki's seventh child (and his fifth daughter) was born. Even though he jokingly laments to his friend over his undue burden of having to raise seven children,[13] his spirits must have been high with a healthy new baby in the household.

Finally, we have to consider Soseki's physical condition. It is now well-known that from time to time he suffered a serious neurotic disorder, and the violent rages it caused were often followed by a severe stomach disorder. According to his family, as soon as the stomach ailment replaced the neurotic disorder, Soseki became a caring and tender family man. While he was writing *Mon*, he was constantly plagued by the stomach illness. His condition actually became so bad that as soon as he finished writing the novel, he was hospitalized for an ulcer. Thus *Mon* must have been written in his psychologically 'softer' moments, which precluded his writing a sterner novel.

Sapped of energy and stamina because of his troubled stomach, Soseki did not exert himself to write a more profound work. His creation of a simple life of ordinary people who are not given to pondering metaphysical problems must have come more naturally. He wrote the story without affectation, which makes the novel more appealing than some of the others to which he applied much effort. By skilfully employing the technique of realistic writing, he produced a quiet yet convincing picture of a dull couple whose uneventful lives gave them little to talk about. When we think that at the time many Japanese writers still believed that 'unless the main characters become insane, commit suicide or adultery, the novels tend to become boring,'[14] his skill in creating a novel depicting the commonplace is noteworthy.

While the characters and their harmonious marriage are fictitious, Soseki used many scenes and common daily occurrences from his own surroundings to make the novel realistic. This is the only novel in which he elaborated on the location as well as the floor plan of the house. Both are given in such detail that one can visualize the muddy alley and the house at the end of it. We know where the entrance, the living-room, the kitchen, the drawing-room and the water-closet are in the house. He deliberately maps out the house in order to emphasize the ordinary life of ordinary people, since the floor plan describes a typical, small Japanese house of that time.

Everyday affairs are minutely recorded for both visual and auditory senses. In the days when labour came cheap, even a couple as thrifty as Sosuke and Oyone could have a young maid to do many household chores. Seldom going out, Oyone sits in the living-room and sews all day waiting for Sosuke to come home - a clear image of an ordinary housewife of the day. In one chapter Soseki devotes much space to describing how Oyone and her brother-in-law Koroku change the *shoji* paper, a common chore of every Japanese household. By doing so, he also portrays Koroku's personality, the relationship between Koroku and Oyone, and that between Sosuke and Oyone. For auditory images, Soseki uses the voices of the *natto* vendor early in the morning and the *tofu* vendor in the evening, typical sounds of the city in his day. The voices of the landlord Sakai's happy children are another common sound heard in the household. Their innocent giggles when at play echo happily in their home whenever Sosuke visits. The author's keen observation of his own children, the models for Sakai's children, is evident in these scenes of an ordinary family. By introducing various small insignificant incidents and scenes of a normal family life, Soseki successfully presents an ordinary Japanese daily life.

Strangely, after so carefully portraying Sosuke as an utterly ordinary man in an everyday environment, Soseki suddenly changes him into a religious man who seeks mental equilibrium at a Zen temple. Upon accidentally finding out that Oyone's ex-husband Yasui may visit Sosuke's landlord, who lives just above them, Sosuke is frightened of the encounter and completely loses his composure. Not wanting to worry Oyone, he does not tell her. He takes a short leave from the office and goes to a Zen temple in Kamakura with the pretence that he needs to rest. He stays there for a few days, trying to find peace of mind through meditation, but he does not succeed and comes home.

Soseki clearly made an error at this point. As already noted, Sosuke is Soseki's creation, and they have nothing in common. In spite of that, Soseki attributes to Sosuke his own experiences at a Zen temple, forgetting that he himself is a far more intellectual and introspective man than Sosuke. Sosuke's visit to a Zen temple is scrupulously described as Soseki himself had experienced it, and the scenes of actual Zen practice as well as his failure in attaining enlightenment are both unforgettably realistic. No one denies that the passage where Sosuke stands in front of the *Mon* to philosophize his inability to attain equilibrium is one of the most memorable passages in all Soseki's works. However, it is the voice of Soseki himself and not Sosuke that we hear. In other words, Soseki combined two incompatible elements into one story. He made this error, probably because, first, he had to force himself to utilize the given title *Mon*, and second, being extremely uncomfortable physically from his stomach trouble, he hastened to a conclusion without giving enough thought to his character Sosuke's probable response.

As mentioned earlier, in later years Soseki expressed his confidence in the work. There is evidence that at this time he yearned for a simple and ordinary life; thus, it is clear that in the early part of *Mon* Soseki accomplished what he was interested in - a warm, realistic portrayal of the ordinary lives of ordinary people. We are certain that it is the depiction of the quiet ordinary life that pleases him. *Mon*, being the combination of inharmonious parts, has flaws as a literary work. Soseki himself must have been aware of this weakness. Yet he liked the work, perhaps because he also knew that he had imparted a warm charm through his minutely detailed realistic writing, creating a work that succeeded in its primary aim and one genuinely unforgettable.

3

The Melancholy Flagellant or the Responsibility of Literature: Takahashi Kazumi and his Project for a Revolution

LIVIA MONNET

Le déprimé est nécessairement un habitant de l'imaginaire.
Julia Kristeva, *Soleil noir: Dépression et mélancolie*

Literature makes something happen...
Frank Lentricchia, *Criticism and Social Change*

'First thesis: We know a great deal. And we know not only many details of doubtful intellectual interest but also things which are of considerable practical significance and, what is even more important, which provide us with deep theoretical insight, and with a surprising understanding of the world. Second thesis: Our ignorance is sobering and boundless. Indeed, it is precisely the staggering progress of the natural sciences (to which my first thesis alludes) which constantly opens our eyes anew to our ignorance, even in the field of the natural sciences themselves. This gives a new twist to the Socratic idea of ignorance. With each step forward, with each problem we solve, we not only discover new and unsolved problems, but we also discover that where we believed that we were standing on firm and safe ground, all things are, in truth, insecure and in a state of flux.'
Karl R. Popper

However paradoxical it may seem, post-war Japanese literature makes out a curiously strong case for a history of poverty or absence. The writers' careers and works are liquid, elusive, blurring distinctions of style and group affiliation, frustrating attempts at precise labelling and description. Death imagery and a sense of powerlessness are ubiquitous. In recent years, literary quality has increasingly lost ground, and popular literature is usurping the place of serious literature. Excellent producers of fiction are, more often than not, undistinguished critics and literary theorists, and vice versa. Indeed, it seems easier to say what contemporary Japanese literature is not, or should not be, and gaps, betrayals, losses and distortions appear more manageable than masterpieces and transcending values. It is not that I am trying to disparage the overall achievement of this literature, or to 'decentre', in deconstructionist fashion, the voluminous batch of impressive, occasionally brilliant, even magisterial works we possess. It is just that we should not lose sight of the fact that 'rethinking' whatever fragment of the history of ideas is an enterprise necessarily entailing both laborious efforts and disheartening discoveries, and that this unfortunately holds true also for the development of post-war Japanese literature. Though there seems to be consensus, both in Japan and in the West, that we are at a turning point in intellectual history (needless to say, agreement vanishes when it comes to defining the nature of the particular crisis we are now facing),[1] and that 'reappraisals' should be carried out and 'new perspectives' obtained while there is still time,[2] how do we go about re-evaluating a phenomenon notorious for its heterogeneity, its dearth of exemplary cases and its stubborn autarkism? Given the no less notorious impermeability of Japanese academic criticism to 'winds of doctrine'[3] coming from Europe or the USA,[4] which analytical method and which interpretive tools will enable us to make valid re-evaluations?

The following remarks, therefore, are nothing more than tentative steps towards a reappraisal of post-World War II Japanese literature and, I hope, of the criticism, both Japanese and foreign, that has thrived upon it (the enormous self-confidence behind such titles as *Rethinking Intellectual History*[5] is to me paralyzing). Through a discussion of Takahashi Kazumi's life and works I hope to arrive at a platform of critical judgement that will enable me to make generalizations and, at the same time, to point to new avenues of interpretation. We shall look first at Takahashi's life, and second at his best-known novels and critical essays. The closing section of the essay deals with re-evaluation proper, although this, of course, will be anticipated in the preceding two sections.

I

Takahashi Kazumi (1931-1971) is to my mind one of the few exemplary cases of writers found in post-war Japanese literature (despite historical continuities I shall not refer here to the pre-World War II period). I call exemplary a writer who not only seeks to influence and transform the society he lives in both through eminently appealing works and through direct political action, but who also tirelessly strives for consistency in his writing, political activities and private life. Moreover, the exemplary writer is a firm believer in the catalytic, reforming ability of literature and constantly reflects on ways to increase its effectiveness as a means for social transformation. Hence the important place literary theory and criticism

16

(which may be accompanied by theoretical writing of a philosophical or historical kind) assumes in his career. Needless to say, the exemplary writer epitomises his time, which is the direct consequence of his conscious cultivation of a basic stance of broad-mindedness or openness. However, this openness is not unselective: since he advocates a *littérature engagée* (which, of course, does not necessarily imply left-wing), he is suspicious of the narcissistic, ritualized posture of avant-garde art and criticism. Whether he admits it or not, the exemplary writer is, by his own ironic choice, a traditionalist.

Compared to recent European and American literatures, from which a large number of exemplary writers may be cited (Sartre, Böll, Pasolini, Allen Ginzberg), post-war Japanese literature is surprisingly poor in this respect. Though the writers who have assumed an 'active posture' are, as Ōe Kenzaburo notes, legion,[6] there are only a few instances of exemplary careers as defined above. Beside Takahashi Kazumi I would mention Mishima Yukio, Noma Hiroshi and with certain reservations, Ōe himself (Ōe is an extremely complex writer, whose openness to change seems genuine and whose traditionalism is least noticeable).

Takahashi Kazumi was born on 31 August 1931 in Osaka. While in middle school he began to take an active interest in literature. The first American air raid on Osaka in March 1945 was for Takahashi a deeply traumatic experience he later recorded in his novels and essays. From 1951 to 1959 he studied Chinese language and literature at Kyoto University. He specialized in the literature of the Six Dynasties (222-589 A.D.),[7] on which he published several essays that were well received in the academic world. His B.A.-, M.A.- and Ph.D.-theses, dealing with Liu Xie (ca. 465-ca. 532),[8] Yan Yanzhi (384-456)[9] and Xie Lingyun (385-433),[10] and Lu Ji (261-303),[11] respectively appeared in *Chūgoku bungakuhō*. In 1954 he married Okamoto Takako, now the well-known writer, essayist and translator Takahashi Takako.

With fellow students at Kyoto University Takahashi brought out the literary magazines *ARUKU* and *Taiwa*. He was also a regular contributor to the literary coterie magazine *VIKING*.

During his student days Takahashi showed a strong interest in the activities of the Kyoto University cell of the Communist Party. In June 1952 he went on a five-day hunger strike in front of the office of the president of the University to protest the disciplinary measures concerning students who had signed the anti-war appeal to the Emperor on the occasion of his visit to this University in November 1951, or who had participated in the general strikes against the Anti-Subversive Activities Act.[12]

Takahashi's first full-length novel was *Sutego monogatari* (Tale of a Foundling, 1958). He established his reputation as a novelist with *Hi no utsuwa* (Vessel of Sin, 1962), which was awarded the Liberal Arts Prize in the year of its publication. In 1966 he was appointed associate professor of Chinese literature at Meiji University in Tokyo. In 1967 he took up the post of associate professor at Kyoto University. Concomitantly with his academic career he wrote several novels, a great number of short stories and novellas and essays in literary theory and criticism. He was one of the few writers who outspokenly supported the radical *zenkyōtō* (All-Campus

Joint Struggle Committee) movement during the nationwide student uprisings of the late 1960s.[13] In March 1970 he resigned his post at Kyoto University as a gesture accepting responsibility for the student disturbances.

Takahashi died of cancer on 3 May 1971 leaving two novels and a book of criticism unfinished.

Though this is not the place for writing yet another *sakka-ron* on Takahashi Kazumi,[14] I would like to single out three aspects of his life which might cast a new light on his personality and literary achievement: first, the exemplary fashion in which he responded to political and social upheavals of his time (the nationwide protests against the Anti-Subversive Activities Act and the student movement of the early 1950s, the movement opposing revision of the Japan-US Security Treaty in 1960, the Great Cultural Revolution in China, the Vietnam war, the student uprisings of 1968-1970, the revival of the anti-Japan-US Security Treaty movement in 1970).[15] Secondly, his peculiar stance, which might be defined as that of a 'melancholy flagellant:'[16] his taciturn, introspective attitude;[17] the 'Rodin's Thinker-Complex;'[18] protest and acceptance of responsibility in the form of either physical self-castigation (hunger strike, sexual abstinence,[19] deliberate cultivation of poverty)[20] or moral self-incrimination (the essays on the nature and function of the intellectual class found in the collections *Koritsu muen no shisō* (The Ideology of Helplessness) and *Ankoku e no shuppatsu* (Starting for the Dark) and the speeches Takahashi made during the student disturbances), or renunciation of social status and reputation (resignation from Kyoto University). Finally, Takahashi's romantic faith in the intellectual (especially literary) establishment as human society's sole repository of progress, coupled, despite repeated setbacks, with a persistent refusal to acknowledge that any project for social transformation based on the exclusion of the so-called non-intellectual classes is doomed to fail.

II

Takahashi Kazumi's literary career may be divided into three periods: a) 1950-1962, from the first literary experiments to the publication of *Hi no utsuwa*; b) 1962-1967, the period which saw the publication of his major novels; c) 1967-1971, from his appointment as associate professor at Kyoto University to his death.[21]

Takahashi's novels and short stories show an almost obsessive concern with three major issues: the nature and function of the intellectual class; defeat or fall from grace; the imperative of radical change (revolution). Needless to say, these themes are interrelated, and only rarely does anyone link in the triad appear without at least one of the other two. Moreover, failure and the attendant moods of gloom and despair loom so large in Takahashi's fictional world that he has been designated as the 'father of a (new) doctrine of spiritual torment' (*kunōkyō no shisō*),[22] and his novels characterized either as 'tales of destruction' (*hametsu monogatari*),[23] or as 'stories of discomfiture' (*haiboku shōsetsu*).[24] Was Takahashi indeed a prophet of destruction, and why did he repeatedly address himself to the same issues?

18

Hi no Utsuwa is the first-person tale of the downfall of Masaki Tenzen, dean of the Faculty of Law of X University and an authority on criminal law. Masaki, who is 55, commences an amorous relationship with his housekeeper, 45-year-old Yoneyama Miki, who also nurses his incurably sick wife. After his wife's death from throat cancer, Masaki continues to nourish Yoneyama's hopes that he will eventually marry he., or at least legalize their relationship in some form or other, while at the same time wooing another woman, 27-year-old Kuriya Kiyoko. Masaki eventually announces his engagement to Kiyoko, which provides Yoneyama with a legal reason to sue him for breach of promise. Masaki in his turn sues his former housekeeper for libel. As more and more of his past and present sins come to the surface and his egoism, callousness, dishonesty and cruelty are unmasked in rapid succession, Masaki becomes an object of public scandal and is eventually forced to resign his post at the university. He also breaks his engagement to Kiyoko. The novel ends with a pseudo-Faustian confession, in which Masaki not only acknowledges his secret pact with the Devil, but also projects a megalomaniac vision of himself as omniscient, infallible potentate, supremely contemptuous of humanity's piteous values and consciously going towards his ruin in the magnificent spirit of a Cesare Borgia.

'... Goodbye, Miss Yoneyama. Though I may also have to go back to the realm of the dead, and even if there is a life after death, we shall never meet again. You will die as a result of natural selection and, through the mercy of God, go to Heaven. You will settle in that Paradise teeming with reptiles, deep-sea fish, molluscs and other living beings which also died through natural selection a long time ago. In Paradise you will have nothing to do, just go on living a pleasant, uneventful life for ever. The men and women attending this trial, all the people now living on earth will also go to Paradise. The lawyer, the judge, Kuriya Kiyoko, my son Shigeru, my daughter Noriko, the students I have taught will all end up in heaven. Only I will not go. When I die there will be a fierce fight for my body and soul. Hordes of hungry demons will vie with one another to crush and tear me to pieces, and the hell I used to long for will finally become reality. More than for mercy I crave for rigour. I desire not slavish compassion, but the loneliness of a wild beast. I am the Power. I want to be the Power. I want to be above these pitiable men who keep craving for their ridiculous paradise. I want to cut myself off completely from their contemptible passions, their so-called good and bad deeds, their cowardly life and death, their happiness and unhappiness. Downing my cup of poison calmly and without blinking, I will laugh aloud. Hey, men. You pygmies down there, who live and die according to the laws of nature and to those you fashioned yourselves. Laughable creatures, persecuting your fellow men for your own pleasure, clinging to your laws as if they were the word of God itself, and not worthless scraps of paper. You monkeys, spying and distrusting one another, and doing your best not to encroach upon one another's lives within the cramped space you chose to live in. Don't you realize that you are being

19

inconsistent, that you are wasting your time in this madhouse you call a courtroom? Don't you see that your perverse reasoning and pretentious sophistries are incompatible with your claim to be masters of the universe? Wouldn't it be more reasonable to transform your tribunals into palaces of pleasure and steep yourselves in debauchery like your glorious ancestors, your Caligulas and Cesare Borgias? ....

Goodbye, Miki, Goodbye, Kiyoko. Farewell, my friends, all of you who will go on living. It's good to go, for, after all, you never meant anything to me.'[25]

Hi no utsuwa was undoubtedly intended as a novel of indictment. *Tenkō*, the ivory-tower, dehumanizing nature of academic research and the rigid, hierarchical structure of the academic establishment, the so-called classical stance of political neutrality of academics, any elitist conception of culture and progress are explicitly condemned. But what are we to make of Masaki Tenzen, a character so absolutely vicious, so fatally devoid of redeeming features as to appear hardly credible?[26] Can he serve as a viable 'negative model' in the sense envisioned by Ōe Kenzaburō?[27] Can the reprehensible university milieu and the occasional allusions to student discontent[28] in the novel serve as an incentive for rethinking, and eventually reforming Japanese university education? (Which is what Takahashi ultimately aimed at, though at this stage he formulated it less explicitly, and with less theoretical foundation, than in the essays written between 1968 and 1970).[29] I would say no. *Hi no utsuwa* is certainly well constructed, and the criticism it levels at the Japanese academic establishment is unquestionably valid. But it is also seriously flawed: not only Masaki, but also the three main female characters, Masaki's wife, Yoneyama Miki and Kuriya Kiyoko are grotesque, or at least become so under his influence. Masaki's wife is colourless, her most salient characteristic is the stench of putrid flesh she emanates (a victim of throat cancer, she slowly rots to death in her bed). The excerpts from her diary in chapter 31 reveal, if anything, Takahashi's appalling ignorance of feminine psychology. Miki and Kiyoko degenerate from women possessing, if not intelligence, at least sexual appeal, in Miki's, and beauty, youth and innocence in Kiyoko's case to mere bundles of lowly desires and ugly, selfish motives. (Whether this is a reflection of that aspect in Takahashi's biography I called self-castigation, or of what Nakayama Kazuko calls his 'dislike of sex'[30] remains to be demonstrated).

The style of the novel may be designed to match Masaki's character - dry, humourless, full of anachronisms and quotations from the classics, but it is, at the same time, the principal reason why this work makes anything but absorbing reading. The most serious flaw of the novel, from the viewpoint of the social function of literature, however, is one which is not immediately apparent and of which Takahashi himself, as far as one can judge from his discussions, both of literature in general and of his own fictional works,[31] was not aware: the paradoxical effect of the exaggeration of evil on the one hand, and of the fact that Masaki Tenzen, as a pessimist, a doubter and an anti-humanist is of necessity what Julia Kristeva calls 'an inhabitant of the realm of the imaginary' (*un habitant de l'imaginaire*),[32] that is, a prisoner of his own delusions about the academic establishment, language, sex, truth and the essence of life, on the other hand, is that *Hi no utsuwa* ultimately stands as a self-contained, unredeemable, carnivalesque apology for vice. (An example of the carnivalesque[33] in the novel is Masaki's Faustian inner monologue quoted above). This, needless to say, further invalidates the novel's status as a 'negative model' and an incentive for reform.

★   ★   ★

If *Hi no utsuwa* is an unintentional apology for evil, *Yūutsu naru tōha* (The Dismal Sect, 1965) and *Waga kokoro wa ishi ni arazu* (My Heart Is Not A Stone, 1967), are, by the same reasoning, apologies for defeat. Both novels delve further into Takahashi's favourite themes of the historical role of the intellectual class and of the necessity of revolution. *Yūutsu naru tōha* even brings into play another familiar issue, that of fictional literature as potential educator of the masses. However, both novels fail to convey any positive, constructive message, to present viable 'models for the present and of the experience of the future.'[34] What these works manage to get through to the reader amounts to little more than the rather trite truth that the present is a wasteland (post-war Japanese society as a moral, cultural and political disaster), and that there is no future (at least not for humanity's well-educated superstructure). Despite their ambitious scope (whereas *Yūutsu naru tōha* proposes to provide a handbook of Japanese history from Hiroshima and Nagasaki to the early 1960s, *Waga kokoro wa ishi ni arazu* attempts no less than a reassessment of the Japanese unionist movement from the late 1940s to the early 1960s) and their respectable literary quality, unquestionably superior to that of *Hi no utsuwa*, these novels stop short of accomplishing, in Gadamer's term, a 'fusion of horizons' (*Horizontverschmelzung*) which in modern philosophical and literary hermeneutics represents the essential precondition for a better understanding of reality (and implicitly, for transcending and transforming reality).[35]

Let me mention some of the reasons why *Yūutsu naru tōha* and *Waga kokoro wa ishi ni arazu*, read today and under premises that are certainly different from those of the readers of the 1960s, fail to generate that 'metaphorical meeting of minds'[36] that makes us feel the moral obligation to take an 'active posture' towards reality. First, there is the gap between the revolutionizing intent of both novels (vivid description of left-wing student activism in the early 1950s and the efforts of Nishimura Koichi, the protagonist in *Yūutsu naru tōha*, to resuscitate public interest in the tragedy of Hiroshima and its message for posterity; the unequivocal recommendation of a strong, unified labour unions movement as a forum of resistance against, and corrective of monopolistic capitalism's economic and socio-political strategies in *Waga kokoro wa ishi ni arazu*) and the extremely conventional, awkward love story scheme, smacking of catering to the sentimental, sensationalist needs of an undiscriminating reading public (the incipient love between Nishimura and the prostitute Yamanouchi Chiyo; the relationship between Shindō Makoto, the hero of *Waga kokoro wa ishi ni arazu*, and Kume Yōko). Secondly, one may point

21

to the vagueness of the definition of such crucial concepts as 'revolution', and the nearly permanent fog surrounding Nishimura's motives (in about three-quarters of the bulk of the novel Nishimura is guided, not by any clear-cut revolutionary impetus, but by 'a dark-brown, seething stream of anger' (*kasshoku no, nietagiru yōna gekido*) and an even hazier 'feeling of remorse' (*kōkai no nen*)) in *Yūutsu naru tōha*; and the interminable, inconclusive theoretical passages in *Waga kokoro ishi ni arazu*. Moreover, we come once again across the stance of the melancholy flagellant, which deprives both Nishimura and Shindō of the ability to judge, dispassionately and objectively, the errors of the past and the present, and to believe in salvation. Finally, I would mention the rigidity, coldness and slightly ludicrous pathos of the style, which, whatever its 'hard' or 'manly' virtues[37] provides very little in the way of a *plaisir du texte*[38] for the reader to partake of.

In terms of literary stature and philosophical depth *Jashūmon* (The Evil Faith, 1966) is unquestionably Takahashi's most impressive work. This difficult, voluminous novel[39] narrates in great detail the destiny of a fictitious religious sect, the Salvation Church of Hinomoto (*Hinomoto Kyūreikai*), from its founding in the first decade of this century until its total destruction in 1946. Leaving aside the question of the relevance of the sect's programme for 'changing the world' (*yonaoshi*) in the context of the late 1980s (though the 'epidemic' of suicides of Hinomoto believers at the end of the novel reads strangely prophetic of the recent mass suicides of followers of new religious sects in different parts of the world), one is obliged to acknowledge that *Jashūmon* stands as the most persuasive illustration of what may be called the latent subtext in Takahashi's entire corpus of fictional works: an unconscious fear that any revolution contains the seeds of its own destruction.[40]

As far as Takahashi's essays are concerned, I think it is safe to say that, with the exception of *Jashūmon* and perhaps *Yūutsu naru tōha*, he did better as a literary, social and political critic and theorist than as a novelist. His critical and theoretical writings show a constant preoccupation with the 'responsibility' and 'autonomy' of literature, with the 'historical mission' of the intelligentsia, with the substratum of historical continuity he detected in outstanding political events of his time. His views on literature may be summarized as the defence of an utopian, absolute concept of literature as a cultural phenomenon which, though participating in the life of the universe in accordance with the Buddhist law of 'universal mutual dependence' (*banbutsu sōi*) is, at the same time, an autonomous entity free of the contradictions and inequalities found in the material world and ideally capable of correcting them. The main 'responsibility of literature' (*bungaku no sekinin*) is to create values that may influence the 'basic perceptions,' and 'alter the consciousness' of the people.[41] Though an unequivocal partisan of *littérature engagée*, which he tried to accomplish in his own novels and short stories, Takahashi was at the same time an idealist who, through his insistence on language and on the autonomy of literature ('literature writing itself')[42] paradoxically anticipated structuralist and post-structuralist positions.

His stance as a political and social critic may be defined as 'non-sectarian, radical' left-wing.[43] A lucid, unsparing critic of contemporary society, Takahashi used interchangeably the perspective of the melancholy flagellant (which, however, is much less paralyzing in his political essays than in his novels) and that of what I would call 'the anxious thinker' (the intellectual bearing the weight of past and present history and worrying about the future).[44] His last essays, collected in the volume *Waga Kaitai* (Dismembering Myself, 1971) show an acuity of judgement and a depth of prophetic insight rarely found in theoretical discussions of other contemporary writers.

III

Takahashi Kazumi, then, was not a prophet of destruction, nor did he deliberately set out to advocate masochistic festivals of defeat and narcissistic self-pity as humanity's only way into the future. On the contrary, as exemplary writer endowed with an acute sensibility for the nodes of convergence of historical processes, he tried hard to point to ways out of the impasse he found Japanese society and culture was in. Through his writings and through direct political actions he sought to lead his contemporaries towards the realization that revolution was the only possible solution of that crisis, that this was an historical necessity (though not necessarily in the Marxian sense) and that the revolution of the future had to be prepared by way of a series of sweeping reforms (a new type of literature, a new type of intellectual, the revival of religion and of at least some of the moral values of the past, reform of the university education).

If his novels turned out to be paradoxical apologies for defeat that could not enlist the active support of large masses of readers for his 'revolutionary' programme during his lifetime, and that stand even more isolated today,[45] and if his critical and theoretical writings, after a brief spell of immense popularity in the early 1970s, seem to have irretrievably sunk into oblivion[46] it is not only because of their often forbidding density of thought and dry rhetoric, or because of a flawed construction, but also because of the problems I have tried to delineate in the foregoing discussion. To summarize these briefly: Takahashi's humourlessness and fundamentally pessimistic view of man and history, coupled with an impetus to hold himself (or, more broadly, intellectuals) responsible for whatever crises or impasses may arise and to exorcise the demons *(asuras)*[47] that brought about these crises by castigating himself, in short, the paralyzing stance of a melancholy flagellant; his delusions about literature and the intelligentsia, which he seems to have imagined as 'standing, uniquely and crucially, at the centre of the world and perhaps at the end of time[48]; a latent anxiety that revolution ultimately works for its own immolation; and finally, the belief that Japanese culture itself, due to what Takahashi called its ingrained 'suicide spirit' *(tokkō seishin)*, or 'craving for a heroic death' *(sange no seishin)* was due for the inferno of cultured civilizations.[49]

*   *   *

How are we to apply the foregoing remarks to our project for rewriting the history of post-war Japanese literature? Though I cannot claim to give any prescriptions for such a project (for who indeed can make such claims?), it seems to me that there are several things we can do. One way to get a grip on this unusually fertile and complex period would be to compare the careers of exemplary writers, first of Japanese writers, and, in the second stage, of exemplary Japanese with exemplary foreign writers (though several critics have suggested a comparison between Takahashi and Mishima Yukio,[50] no one, as far as I know, has yet made the two writers the subject of a detailed comparative study). Another way of reconsidering the problem (and this is meant for us, non-Japanese practitioners of an odd, hybrid art of interpretation, who never quite know which hobby-horse to ride) would be to integrate both more Japanese *sakkaron* and more relevant historical data in our discussions of particular works. Thirdly, to test the applicability of new literary theories, both Japanese and foreign, on the texts to be scrutinized, an experiment which should start from a workable synthesis of the tenets and premises of both Japanese and non-Japanese theories (which of course, is difficult, but, not impossible). Examples of such syntheses would be: Bhaktin and Nakagami Kenji, Maurice Blanchot and Yoshimoto Takaaki, Roland Barthes and Isoda Kōichi, Ōoka Makoto and Harold Bloom.

Finally, to do less violence to the texts, to squeeze them less into our models and patterns of interpretation, whatever the form and apparent usefulness of our ·'maps of misreading'[51] might be. This is neither a contradiction of my third recommendation for rewriting recent Japanese literary history, nor an appeal to resuscitate the (already dead, or at least moribund, as it seems) credibility of the Derridean assumption that there is 'nothing outside the text' (*il n'y a pas de hors texte*)[52]: it is just a low-keyed reminder that literature, whether or not it writes itself, has a right to speak for itself and that readers are equally free (and here Takahashi's idea of the 'reader's absolute right of choice' may prove very useful)[53]to take it as it is, or to use this rich material for creating their own 'maps of misreading' or 'erotics of art',[54] or for designing their own projects for a revolution.

Last, but not least, let me note that, however urgent the necessity of rewriting the history of post-war Japanese literature (or, of Japanese literature in general) may appear, such a project cannot be more than provisional, and our prescriptions for realizing it can only have a transient value. Literature, whether or not we mis- or re-read it, makes, and will continue to make, 'something happen',[55] and our efforts to extract from it universal truths or clues for a better understanding of the world will necessarily end in frustration, for, as Karl Popper remarked, 'with each step forward, with each problem which we solve, we not only discover new and unsolved problems, but we also discover that where we believed that we were standing on firm and safe ground, all things are, in truth, insecure and in a state of flux.'[56]

4

Abe Kobo's *'Ark Sakura'*

YOICHI NAGASHIMA

PREFACE

Abe Kobo's authorship has now been studied at the Japanese Section of the University of Copenhagen for more than 15 years. As a result of these studies, various papers on his works have been published in English, Danish and Swedish.[1] Abe has visited us twice in Copenhagen, giving lectures and discussing topics of current interest. Our relationship is fine and we have come to know him quite well. His imagination and ideas are fascinating and he has an insatiable interest in everything. This does not mean, however, that I am his spokesman or that I agree with everything he says.

As regards our research on his authorship, Professor Lidin concentrates on Abe's ideas whereas I have specialized in his fiction - his inventiveness and use of the language.

A BRIEF SUMMARY OF THE NOVEL *ARK SAKURA* (HAKOBUNE SAKURA-MARU, 1984)[2]

'I', the hero of the novel, is nicknamed 'Pig' or 'Mole', because he is enormously fat and lives underground. Not in a hole, but in a cave. He has converted a cave of an old quarry into a gigantic shelter preparing for a nuclear war he fears may break out. He has built the shelter, he believes, as a Noah's Ark in our times. At the start of the novel, the 'I', captain of the ark, looks for suitable persons to be taken on board. His huge ark is big enough for 385 passengers, but he must find at least 35 men to keep the ark in order and 'sail' safely. The first boarding ticket, called 'the ticket of survival', is given to a beetle-seller, who has sold the hero a queer beetle, 'Youp'ketcha' or Clock-beetle, in a department store. (Youp'ketcha can serve as a clock, because it eats its own excrement and completes a full circle on the same spot in one day.) But a mysterious couple who have worked for the beetle-seller as *sakura* or decoy, have run away with two boarding tickets and a spare key to the ark. When the hero, followed by the beetle-seller, returns to the ark, he finds that the couple have already broken into the ark despite many high security devices hidden at the entrance to the ark. The *sakura*-couple is accepted at last, and thus begins a collective life of the four people in the shelter - 1) Captain 'Pig', ex-fireman and allegedly professional photographer, 2) The beetle-seller, ex-soldier of the Self-Defence Force, 3) The decoy-man, cash-card swindler and pick-pocket, and 4) His coquette girl friend. These are the chosen people. A really dramatic setting.

*   *   *

Food and other necessaries of life are stored in the cave in considerable quantities. The ark is also well equipped with many useful and indispensable things such as a stool with strong hydraulic pressure - even weapons can be found on board. Meanwhile an uninvited guest or intruder appears in the cave, and then disappears leaving no trace. After this mysterious event, new characters are introduced into the novel: Pig's biological father 'Wild Boar' - Pig's mother was raped by him and thus gave birth to 'Pig'. 'The Broom Corps', a group of men with an average age of 75 who sweep the streets of the town and wear dark-blue uniforms. Another group are 'The Rout of Pot-boiled Wild Boars', juvenile delinquents who dream of building an underground utopia.

With the emergence of these rubbishy newcomers, life in the ark suddenly becomes busy and confusing and eventually unbearable for the hero. He has lost control over the situation in his own ark. By accident he falls into a toilet bowl and his left leg is sucked down by the vacuum mechanism which is so strong he cannot free himself. Unwillingly, he becomes a Youp'ketcha. In this tragi-comic predicament, he finally dynamites the passage which gives access to the surface in case of a nuclear war. As a result the pressure in the lavatory bowl is weakened and he is able to pull his leg out. He then tells a lie to the passengers in the ark, saying that A-bombs have exploded on earth, and then tries to escape from the cave, taking the decoy-woman with him. To the decoy-man he tells the truth, but the *sakura*-couple choose to remain in the ark. They have found their way of living (or dying) in the cave. They can be likened to criminals who voluntarily have chosen to stay in prison. They are imprisoned yet totally free.

The hero, too, has been dreaming of a self-sufficient and peaceful life as Youp'ketcha in the ark (not in the toilet bowl, of course). But when an adjutant of 'The Broom Corps' appears and introduces a fascist power-system in the cave, the hero has no choice but to escape from the nightmarish ark. With much effort and in spite of many difficulties, he manages to escape from the shelter. At last reaching the surface of the earth, the first scene that catches his eye is 'a transparent town' which is 'vital but dead'. (p. 333)[3] He returns to the place he has tried to run away from. The circle is now closed.

<h3 style="text-align:center">INTERPRETATIONS</h3>

I have given a summary of the novel without interpretation. Many reviewers in Japan have tried to interpret the novel, preaching their own intellectually one-sided, dogmatic views. A typical review of this kind has a well-known refrain, often something like this:

26

Fearing an outbreak of nuclear war, the 'I' has converted a huge ruined quarry into an 'ark'. But as soon as he has accepted other passengers, an embryo of a nation is taking shape in the cave and a relationship between the one who controls and the others who are controlled is established. The theme is clear, and Abe has treated it well...etc.[4]

Some of the reviews echo each other so much that one is led to believe that they were written by the same person, or that the reviewers have plagiarized each other.[5] Other reviews proclaim emotionally either that the novel is a masterpiece or that it is a fiasco, without explaining why.[6] If our only aim is to find the theme buried in the text by the author we had better read his essay in which he deals with the very same topic. It is much easier to discover the theme there. As for Abe, the theme concerning 'nation versus human being/individual' has been and still is his main concern. Whenever he is asked about his views on our situation today he will refer to this theme. We know his standpoint and his reasoning. A quotation from the novel can illustrate this:

'No stronger power than a nation's sovereignty exists. Whatever a nation does - and a nation can kill, steal or become rich by fraud - it can never be arrested or imprisoned. Never. It may happen that a nation is accused, it is never punished. This century is, in fact, the century of the sovereignty of nations.' (p. 290)

★   ★   ★

It is beyond doubt then, that Abe, both before and after the publication of the book, explained his own work chiefly from that point of view.[7] But I dare say that this was *his* interpretation of the novel among many other possible interpretations. To read a novel cannot just be an act of pulling out a message hidden among thousands of words in a text. If so, how can we get those unusual but exciting experiences while reading a novel? How can it be possible to forget oneself in the chains of evoking images? The sole purpose of reading a novel cannot be to find a theme or come up with the right answer. Abe's novel is neither a difficult question to be answered nor a mysterious riddle to be solved. It is rather a game, a game of simulation, in which he, by offering us a model of our world today, tries to decipher our present situation and ourselves.[8]

By the way, it is easy to find the central theme in *Ark Sakura*: - to analyze the romantic but also nihilistic philosophy of 'survival' (i.e. our hidden wish and hope to be selected as survivors in a shelter at the expense of others) in a nuclear age. The philosophy of 'survival' is considered an embryo to fascism. One of the characters in the novel actually says: 'Nuclear war has already started, although it hasn't begun yet.' (p. 328) And another says: 'We live in an age when we have to reset everything at point zero in order to find out who are worthy of survival and who are not.' (p. 222)

Abe has not written the novel to give us these messages alone. They are not modern *kōan*, either. We must not forget the simple fact that the novelist Abe supplies us with a well-composed text, 333 pages in all, written in a language of *fiction* (and not of daily life) introducing uncommon situations filled with maniacally precise descriptions of details.

For example, descriptions of the entrance to the ruined quarry are so fascinating (even though the place is in fact a dump) that they parallel those of the hole into Alice's Wonderland.

IMAGINATIONS

The essence of the novel, a *literary* work, is in short the development of the author's imagination, its flight through the fictitious world, supported by concrete and detailed descriptions of things. Abe even indulges himself in undreamed-of, queer things.[9]

Abe sharply outlines the images of Youp'ketcha and the stupendous stool - these two things are the starting-point in his novel. And then he finds an inner logic to their existence. In this particular aspect he is no doubt one of the most unique novelists of our age. His imagination is able to find an Abe-ish astonishing logic in everything. The reader should accept the Youp'ketcha and the over-sized stool as they are as well as other things and even the people who appear in the novel, *without* comparing them to things and people in real life, and *without* regarding them as symbols of something else or as caricatures of somebody. They simply exist and co-exist with each other, having no past, reason or necessity in their autonomous world.[10]

Events in the novel take place during the course of only two days, but the flow of time seems unnaturally slow. Even this, however, is controlled by the inner logic of the fiction. If you fail to follow the rules of fiction - the language game - you have no chance of enjoying yourself while reading. You may laugh at some of the slapstick scenes scattered throughout the novel.[11] But, by doing so, you still stand outside the fictitious world. What is required is the same strained and distorted fictitious laugh as that coming from the characters in the book placed in comical or embarrassing situations. Then you can hear the voice of the author, sitting somewhere outside the fictitious world, commenting and even explaining the events and the thoughts of the persons through the 'I', the hero.[12]

NARRATION

Almost all of Abe's major works are narrated by the 'I'. This type of narration gives the author the advantage of getting into and out of the hero's inner world so freely that we can form a life-like picture of the hero, and to some extent of the author, too. The hero sees and hears only what he himself can see or hear. He does not know anything that he has not had the opportunity to know.[13] Abe is an author who has fully mastered the technique of so-called 'narrated monologue' which gives his narration depth and expressive reality.[14] Relationships between the author, the narrator and the hero are intimately close, but they are neither identical nor fully differentiated. That is why the heroes in Abe's novels in a way resemble each other. They are all Abe's *alter ego* and speak his language, without being his incarnation, his double. Abe has lived their lives in his imagination and has tried part of their experiences in real life. We may surmise that Abe carefully structured the text in several levels, just like

28

the hero in the novel, 'Pig' or 'Mole', who constructed the ark in his morbidly sensitive and painstaking way.

LANGUAGE

Now, let us look a little more at the details, the language of the novel. As I have just mentioned, we can at times hear the author's comments in the course of the narration. Usually indirectly in the form of the hero's inner monologue, but also more or less emphasized by outer signs such as: 1) *Witty remarks* which are too witty for the hero, 'Pig'. 2) *Metaphors* which are too poetical for 'Pig'. 3) *Comparisons* which are too pertinent for 'Pig'. 4) *Typical Japanese proverbs and idioms* which are too bookish for 'Pig'.

These rhetorical devices have frequently been used in Abe's former novels too, but those in *Ark Sakura* are in general more down-to-earth and concrete, less sophisticated and abstract than those used in, for example, *The Box Man* (1973) and *Secret Rendezvous* (1977).

When we talk of Abe's choice of down-to-earth and concrete expressions, we have to mention his use of actual names of persons, companies and products: President Reagan, Subaru, BMW, Honda, Seiko, Mild Seven (cigarettes), Jintan (pills against foul breath) and Dentsū (advertising agency). These names and other items mentioned in the novel do remind us of this decade, but the purpose of using them is first of all to connect the fictitious world to real life, rather than to mirror our life in the fictitious world. Specification of things make the author's description vivid and 'touchable' without many explanatory words. But exaggeration is dangerous, because these descriptions cannot be understood by those who do not know the names of less famous persons or things.

In a similar way, we can regard Abe's frequent use of typical Japanese proverbs and idioms as inappropriate for readers abroad, because their connotation at times is almost impossible to convey to people who are reading the novel in translation. Comparisons or metaphors on the other hand *can* be explained and translated to some extent.

Proverbs and idioms are, by definition, deeply rooted in the cultural tradition and way of thinking of the people who have invented them. So they are not so easy to change once they are placed in the context of a novel. The use of specific proverbs and idioms often unveils the author's nationality and cultural background.[15] One further point. In *Ark Sakura* Abe has obviously used more *kanji* characters than ever before. *Jizura*, appearance of printed words on the pages in the novel is darker and more complicated. Many words which Abe used to write in *kana* are now written in *kanji*, and some of them are even supplied with *furigana*.[16] What has happened to his writing characters? As you may well have guessed, Abe has written, or more precisely, typed the novel using *wāpuro*, word-processor. With *wāpuro's* help you can write words in *kanji* quite easily, even when you have forgotten how to write them.[17] Abe has made good use of his word-processor, but some reviewers of the novel seem to have exaggerated this aspect.[18] In my opinion, Abe's word-processor has not changed anything essential in his novel, only the superficial *jizura*.

Even if he had written the novel all in *kana*, we still could recognize and enjoy his Abe'ish novel. This is especially true for his latest works. He is not one of the Japanese writers who appreciate and sometimes rely on *jizura* and the aesthetic value of characters. In translation all these conspicuous traces disappear. Only the story, its structure and style survive.

FINAL REMARKS

Generally speaking, Abe has returned to the fictitious world of *The Woman in the Dunes* 1962, as far as his way of story-telling and time-flow in the novel are concerned. The action and the time-flow in *Ark Sakura* is rather linear and straightforward, and we ask ourselves constantly: 'And then what?' or 'What happens next?' while reading the novel. Compared to a novel like *The Box Man* with its highly complicated circular structure, where the beginning can be an ending and an ending a beginning, and where an ending can be found in the main part and so on, the narrative structure in *Ark Sakura* is rather simple, although it contains a surprising and paradoxical ending which brings the hero back to the spot he started from.

Contrary to the hero in *The Woman in the Dunes* who eventually found a way out, 'Pig', the hero in *Ark Sakura* leaves the ark in despair. But despair, according to Abe, is a kind of hope (*zetsubō kibō*): So long as you are able to despair, there is hope, he says. In *Ark Sakura* Abe shows us a literary model of this despair in our model-less world today. His authorship cannot be confined within the realm of the exotic Japanese literature. New approaches are required.

5

The Socialization of Literature: The Idea and Prototypes of the Mid-Meiji Social Novel

CHIA-NING CHANG

A noted contemporary writer, reflecting on the literary mentality of his time, has the following to say about the imaginative vision of his country's fellow novelists:

> ...[Our] writers have lowered their sights. Novels are made smaller today - craftier, but tending not to grapple with the big political and social issues of our time.... When someone does a book that is socially ambitious, it's seen as a sort of aberration....
>
> The novelist has always tried to find a territory that's his own, but in trying to do this he's retreated, he's allowed himself

30

to be disenfranchised, or, to put it another way, he's come into
the house, closed the door and shut the curtains. Outside there
are wars, riots, sirens, screams. But he records life as a
whisper.... Writers, along with everyone else, have pulled
inward and miniaturized the significance of their lives.[1]

Although the writer who made these remarks was not a modern or
contemporary Japanese critic but Mr E. L. Doctorow, the author of such
works as *The Book of Daniel, Ragtime* and *World's Fair,* and although his
frame of reference is not the Taishō or early Shōwa literature but the
contemporary American novel, his words resonate with a haunting ring
to students of modern Japanese literary criticism *vis-à-vis* the twentieth
century Japanese novel and in particular with regard to the *shishōsetsu* or
the 'I' novel. Doctorow's critical remarks bear a striking resemblance, for
example, to Itō Sei's comparison of modern Japanese I-novelists to 'truth
seekers' (*kyūdōsha*) who complacently look at the world outside through
the windows of their monasteries.[2] Certainly, many post-war Japanese
critics have long been profoundly disturbed by what they consider to have
been a conspicuous lack of a tangible social dimension in modern Japanese
fiction. Indeed, even before the turn of the century prior to the rise of
the *shishōsetsu,* the tendency for many Meiji writers to eschew broader
social themes and considerations of the significance of social realism had
disquieted a wide range of writers and critics including Gotō Chūgai,
Takayama Chogyū, Uchida Roan and Taoka Reiun in the 1890s. Similar
lamentations over the social or political apathy of the Japanese literary
intellectual can be found in the writings of many late Meiji commentators
in one form or another. Shortly after the turn of the century, Nagai Kafū,
for example, in one of his more pessimistic moods around the time of the
notorious Kōtoku Shūsui Incident of 1910-11 and the subsequent
tightening of censorship control by the Meiji government, wrote satirically
in his essay 'Ruzan no rakudo' ('Paradise for exiles,' September 1910) on
what he called 'the extraordinary history' of the almost total demarcation
since the Edo period between the arts on the one hand, and the activities
of mainstream society in Japan on the other.[3]

Some of the most important works of Japanese literary criticism on the
shishōsetsu continued with Kafū's critical spirit, but the modern *gesakusha's*
detached sense of cynicism, mixed with more than just a trace of bitterness,
gradually gave way to a more serious mood of intense self-examination
and soul-searching. Considerations on the relative significance of the
integrity of the writer's private individuality on the one hand, and the
sociality (*shakaisei*) of his art on the other quite naturally became one of
the major preoccupations of late Taishō and early Shōwa literary critics.
In 1935, Kobayashi Hideo in his now classic 'Discussing the I-Novel'
('Watakushi-shōsetsu ron') already pointed out in effect that the notion
of the self - the 'watakushi' - in contemporary Japanese fiction had never
been nurtured in the kind of cultural and social environment to allow it
to become aware of its conflict or disharmony with nature or society.
Kume Masao's characteristic distaste for imaginative fictionalization,
tellingly expressed in his famous statement that Tolstoy's *War and Peace,*
Dostoevsky's *Crime and Punishment* and Flaubert's *Madame Bovary* were

nothing more than 'grand popular novels' (*idai naru tsūzoku shōsetsu*) was, as Kobayashi suggested, representative of perhaps the unconscious thinking of many contemporary Japanese writers. Many were convinced that fictionalization would unavoidably destroy the writer's 'sincerity,' presumably towards himself and to his readers, along with the true sense of reality in his works. The universality of fictional characterization as a literary technique seldom convinced Taishō or early Shōwa I-novelists of its authenticity or even plausibility. On the other hand, the integrity of raw experience and the writer's 'sincerity' could only be achieved, many felt, through the creation of the essentially non-fictional 'I', the undisguised resurrection of the writer himself, in what was known in popular terminology in the late twenties as *junsui shōsetsu* or the 'pure novel.' The Japanese self, then, to borrow Kobayashi's catch-phrase, has never acquired the qualities of a 'socialized I' (*shakaikashita watakushi*) as did the 'I' of men like Rousseau or Goethe.[4]

Post-war critics were of course not compelled to come to terms, in the same way as critics had been in the 1930s, with the dramatically polarized discourse of contemporary literary thinking, that is to say, the heavily-politicized imperatives of Kurahara Korehito's socialist realism on the one hand, and with the art-for-art's sake ideas of the Neo-Impressionists on the other, a fate that befell Kobayashi Hideo in the early Shōwa period. But they, too, have generally handed down harsh verdicts on the heavily autobiographical or confessional narrative style of the pre-war *shishōsetsu*, or on its narrow and idiosyncratic perception of truth and reality. Works ranging from Itō Sei's *Techniques of the Novel* (*Shōsetsu no hōhō*) in 1948 and Nakamura Mitsuo's *Discussions on the Novel of Manners* (*Fūzoku shōsetsu-ron*) of 1950,[5] to Hirano Ken's *Art and Real Life* (*Geijutsu to jisseikatsu*) in 1958[6] and Katō Shūichi's 'The Conditions of Contemporary Japanese Literature' ('Gendai Nihon bungaku no jōkyō') of 1962[7] continue to remind us of Taishō and early Shōwa's literary preoccupation with the trivial details of the writer's day-to-day living or with the slightest inklings of his private sentimentality. The central concern of any serious novelist to represent, to interpret, and to give imaginative vision to experience was replaced by another passion, the passion to reproduce, as much as possible, an undistorted, and hence unimaginative, record of daily living. Whether one chooses to call this 'one-dimensional depiction' ('*heimin byōsha*'), as Tayama Katai did, or, 'absolute absence of thought' ('*zettai mushinen*') in the words of Shimamura Hōgetsu,[8] or the 'anti-universal character' ('*hanfuhensei*') of Japanese literature created by a special group of literary *burakumin* ('*tokushu burakumin*'), as Itō Sei trenchantly characterizes it,[9] the result was that the creative vision was often trapped within the narrow confines of the writer's highly private self and his often gloomy personal vicissitudes.

This image of the post-Meiji I-novelists has long been captured by critical appellations and frozen into literary or intellectual prototypes. Nakamura Mitsuo, for example, tells us that I-novelists represent a kind of 'professional diarists' who sadly compensate the absence of a social dimension in their works by evoking an elitist consciousness of a chosen people free to present 'reports of their experiments with life.'[10] We also have Itō Sei's now classic paradigm of the *shishōsetsu* writers as *tōbō-dorei*, or runaway slaves from Japanese society and into that isolated but exclusive sanctuary of self-imposed exile otherwise known as the Tokyo *bundan* or literary world.[11] And few can forget Katō Shūichi's equally memorable characterization of the overall endeavour of the Japanese I-novelists as an exercise in excommunicating artistic imagination from the realm of fiction-writing, an exercise resulting in what he calls '*geijutsu no seikatsuka*,' or 'the domestication of art.' This is diametrically opposed to the presumably more admirable activities of the seventeenth-century Japanese tea master Ishikawa Jōzan, who instead had the good taste of turning his own life-style into an expression of art itself, or, in Katō's own words, '*seikatsu no geijutsuka*.'[12]

I wish to emphasize at this point that it is not my intention or purpose to challenge these thoughtful and deservedly acclaimed critical opinions on the nature of the *shishōsetsu*. But this characterization of the modern Japanese novel is at times so pervasive that we sometimes lose sight of other important trends of literary thinking and traditions, perhaps less powerful but nevertheless equally significant in the history of modern Japanese literature. I am not thinking at this moment about the rise of proletarian literature in the early Shōwa period, because it is a tradition with a very particular social and political dimension. However, I do wish to consider the validity of such a characterization of the modern Japanese novel when one moves away from the history of the *shishōsetsu*, and examines the literary landscape in the mid-Meiji period before the advent of Japanese naturalism and the rise of the *shishōsetsu* tradition. How, for instance, did Meiji writers and critics at the turn of the century formulate their views on the modern novel within the broader context of dramatic social and political changes in Japan in that period? Did they see literary creativity as an essentially intensely private endeavour, whereby the writer practises his craft in his study with its door tightly shut, both in the physical and symbolic sense, or did they cherish some degree of awareness of the social relevance of art, or of the responsibility of the modern artist in society? And subsequently, how did the cultural milieu in which they lived condition their perception of experience, their ideas on literature and creativity, and ultimately, their art? It is in this context that I wish to consider the question of the mid-Meiji social novel.

What then is the mid-Meiji *shakai shōsetsu* or social novel? What were the intellectual conditions and the literary thinking behind it that encouraged its emergence? What did critics mean when they said that a work was, or was not, a social novel? In other words, in what ways did they characterize, if not define, the *shakai shōsetsu*? And apart from theoretical considerations, what are the nature and salient characteristics of the actual Meiji social novel itself?

Before these questions are examined, it is important to note the formative literary atmosphere in Japan in the years after the Sino-Japanese War of 1894-95. The mid-Meiji period witnessed, in many ways, a dramatic clash of symbols and spirits of divergent literary sensibilities between the Ken'yūsha writers on the one hand, and their young and daring critics on the other. The works of Ozaki Kōyō, Yamada Bimyō and the other major

Ken'yūsha writers have long been scrutinized by Japanese critics. But the opponents of the backward-looking sensibilities of the Ken'yūsha school have, unfortunately, for a long time been relegated to the dustier corridors of Meiji literary history. It was not until the early 1960s that Japanese scholars first began to seriously assess their contributions to modern Japanese literature. Like Kitamura Tōkoku and Futabatei Shimei a decade earlier, these young detractors of the Ken'yūsha also shared an innovative passion in their attempt to bring a modern perspective to the aesthetic and intellectual qualities of modern Japanese literature. What they aspired to was a new literary purpose that gave public significance to their private creative impulse. What they tried to espouse was a more involved role for the literary man to play in his cultural milieu. Above all, their concern was best exemplified by their efforts at redefining the social relevance of art in a fast-changing society. While they differed in their critical standards, and their perceptions of the social and political conditions, this basic concern was the common denominator which characterized a wide range of writers and critics who welcomed the appearance of the social novel in the mid-Meiji period.

Both social and intellectual forces were at work to inspire these men to attempt this kind of intense soul-searching regarding the nature of their profession. Rapid industrial development led to the emergence of a new array of social problems which grew in both scale and seriousness in the few years after Japan's war with China. Deteriorating relations between labour and management, increasing labour unrest and strikes, harsh working conditions in factories and textile mills, the widening gap between the urban rich and poor, and the relative poverty of the rural areas all cast a dark shadow over the social scene.[13]

The intellectual response to these disturbing signs was quick and dramatic. The emergence of a variety of study groups for social problems all over the major cities demonstrated an increasing interest among writers, journalists and political thinkers in a wide array of social ideas ranging from Christian humanitarianism and pacifism to Utopian socialism.[14] The literary critic and novelist Gotō Chūgai in 1896 spoke for many when he remarked that the acute 'competition for survival' and 'life's miseries' made it difficult for writers not to reflect on their country's conditions and on the meaning of life in general.[15] The growing attention to the conditions of the poor and underprivileged found sympathetic expression in the moving works by Yokoyama Gennosuke and Matsubara Nijūsankaidō on the livelihood of the lower classes in large cities and the harsh working conditions in factories.[16] Yokoyama Gennosuke's *Nihon no kasō shakai* (*The Lower Classes in Japan* 1899), for example, is sometimes compared to Hosoi Wakizō's evocations of the lives of Taishō female textile workers in his classic *Jokō aishi* (*The Tragic History of Female Workers*) of 1925.[17] The new wave of social realism which fuelled the emotional intensity of the so-called *hisan shōsetsu* or *shinkoku shōsetsu* by writers such as Hirotsu Ryūrō, Kawakami Bizan and Izumi Kyōka also pointedly reflected a growing concern among writers after 1895 with the darker side of life.[18] In addition, the appearance of a number of new literary publications such as *Taiyō, Teikoku bungaku, Seinenbun, Mezamashigusa*, and *Bungei kurabu*

34

greatly extended the public forum for new literary ideas. They were instrumental in shaping literary taste and trends in the years to come.

The dramatic social transformation in the 1890s, inspired the new generation of writers and critics to acquire a degree of social awareness perhaps unprecedented in the history of Meiji literature. This new consciousness had an enormous impact on their literary ideas and prompted them to reflect upon the artistic standards of their time. Rising critics such as Taoka Reiun and Uchida Roan were particularly concerned with ways to integrate their social awareness with considerations of literary imagination. Taoka Reiun's essay entitled 'Karyū saimin to bunshi' ('The Lower Classes and the Writer,' September 1895), for example, notes the widening gap between the social classes in what was supposedly an age of enlightenment. Contemporary culture, he contends, exposes those above the middle strata of society to moral vices and drives the lower classes into the abyss of misery. A particular noteworthy passage in his essay reads:

> Is it not the business of poets and writers to sing the miserable fate of the lower classes and to depict their pitiful existence? Today when we have become fed up with delicately contrived love stories between young scholars and fair beauties or narratives about righteous heroes and virtuous heroines, when people are increasingly concerned with life's problems and wish to know the secrets of divine spirits, why hasn't any writer yet brought forth from his breast his swelling compassion for the miserable destiny of the poor.... Why hasn't anyone bemoaned and lamented on behalf of those ignored people and bravely brought their case before the eyes of the public?[19]

Efforts towards redefining social realism in literature were reinforced by increasing knowledge and keener appreciation of the works of many Western writers. The works of Dostoevsky, Tolstoy, Dickens, Ibsen, Victor Hugo, Edward Bellamy and a host of other Western writers were read with increasing passion by aspiring Japanese writers. For instance, to Uchida Roan, reading Dostoevsky's *Crime and Punishment* at the foothills of Mount Fuji in 1889 was like 'encountering a strike of thunder in the wild, open field, dazzling my eyes and deafening my ears.'[20] It was not until then, as he later confessed in his memoirs, that he realized what serious literature meant and how it differed from the frivolous spirit of the Bakumatsu *gesaku*.[21] Tokutomi Roka, in his autobiographical novel *Kuroi me to chairo no me* (*Black Eyes and Brown Eyes*, 1914) vividly describes how the young hero hungrily devours Victor Hugo's works,[22] and Taoka Reiun recalled some years later how, as a young student of Chinese literature at Tokyo Imperial University, he used to bump his head against sign boards or run into carts and wagons as he was deeply absorbed in reading Hugo on his way to school.[23]

This comparative perspective spurred mid-Meiji writers and critics to reflect on the conditions of their own literary world and to consider how the spirit of Meiji literature differed from that of other national literatures. Soon, important questions were raised about the adequacy of conventional literary techniques and motifs to capture new experiences in a fast-changing social milieu. Uchimura Kanzō as well as Uchida Roan and Taoka Reiun began to decry the existing state of Japanese literature and what appeared to them as its glaring flaws. Uchimura Kanzō's disappointment in the absence of 'great literature' (*'daibungaku'*) in Japan[24] echoed Reiun's lament over the lack of profound tragedies and pathos in the tradition of Japanese literature and his longing for the emergence of a Japanese Victor Hugo.[25] Roan's satirical attacks on the pre-modern *gesaku* literary mentality of his time[26] reinforced Miyazaki Koshoshi's trenchant criticism of Ken'yūsha writers' typical social apathy as a kind of *haisōshugi* or 'anti-ideaism.'[27] These were the unmistakable signs of a new awakening that provided the intellectual basis for the enthusiasm for socially-engaged literature from 1895 to the first decade of the twentieth century.

If many mid-Meiji writers and critics were convinced of the need for socially-engaged literature, how did they characterize the social novel? Some of the answers to this question can be found in a very spirited literary debate on the social novel (*shakai shosetsu ronsō*) which took place between 1895 and 1898.

The term *shakai shōsetsu* itself was not new to mid-Meiji sensibility. Already in 1887, Fujizawa Banshō and Ushiyama Kakudō had written a work called *Shakai Shōsetsu: Nippon no mirai (A Social Novel: Japan's Future)*, a kind of futuristic political novel depicting the workings of an idealized parliamentary system in Japan twenty years afterwards.[28] But it was not until Tokutomi Sohō's influential journal *Kokumin no tomo* announced its famous plan in 1896 to publish a series of social novels by some of the most well-known writers of the day (including Saitō Ryokuu, Hirotsu Ryūrō, Kōda Rohan, Gotō Chūgai, Saganoya Omuro and Ozaki Kōyō)[29] that writers and critics began to debate in the nation's most prestigious literary journals and newspapers on the nature of this particular mode of writing.

As the debate on the social novel unfolded, there appeared a series of attempts to characterize the genre. One anonymous *Mainichi* columnist, an admirer of Edward Bellamy's *Looking Backward, 2000-1887*, wrote in 1896 about his enthusiasm for novels that could make an impact on the current of thought in society.[30] Another writer for the journal *Gekkan: Sekai no Nippon (Monthly: Japan in the World)*, characterized the *shakai shōsetsu* as a novel that 'does not deal primarily with individual relationships, but captures and depicts the interaction between the individual and society.'[31] But any attempt to distinguish between the social novel and say, the psychological novel, is at best a thankless business, and confusion naturally arises as to where depiction of the individual ends and social portrayal begins. But to his credit, the *Gekkan* correspondent did not insist on a rigid individual *vis-à-vis* society dichotomy, nor did he deny the individual any important role to play in a novel which focuses on social conditions.

Then, an unsigned writer for the February 1897 issue of *Waseda bungaku* suggested that the term social novel was variously used by critics to refer to the kind of works which spoke for the poor and the working classes, or those which focused on the realistic depiction of the livelihood of the lower classes. In addition, according to the same writer, the terminology was also used by critics to refer to novels which gathered their material

36

from various facets of social life as a whole, or works in which society became the main focus of depiction, leaving the individual characters to assume secondary roles. The social novel, according to his last characterization, emphasized the importance of external phenomena of life rather than the inner worlds of individuals. Finally, he suggested that the term social novel was also used to refer to the kind of works which attempted to lead the currents of an age and to herald future social changes.[32]

Two months later, Shimamura Hōgetsu, who was to become one of the most powerful critics for naturalist literature in Japan, wrote in *Shinchō gekkan* (*New Writings Monthly*) that the term could be used to refer to works whose 'internal tension' ('*kattō*') derives not so much from the private arena of life but from the public dimension of contemporary society.[33] And Kaneko Chikusui, a lecturer at the Tokyo Senmon Gakkō, in an essay published in *Waseda bungaku* in February 1898, suggested that since novels are primarily concerned with '*setai ninjō no dōki*' or the motivations of social manners and human feelings, the social novel should primarily focus on what he vaguely calls '*shakai genshō no dōki*,' by which he probably means the motivations or perhaps the mechanisms of social phenomena.[34]

Were these efforts at defining the social novel useful? I think most of us would agree with Irving Howe that whether a novel may be categorized as a political or psychological novel, or, for that matter, a romantic or a social novel, is to a large extent simply a matter of convenience. While it seemed inevitable that mid-Meiji critics had to devise a literary category in their analysis and discussion of socially-engaged literature and commentaries on it, we must not think that they were obsessed with the business of turning a rather loose and imprecise literary term into a new distinction of form. Like Irving Howe in his discussion of the modern European political novel, men like Shimamura Hōgetsu, Kaneko Chikusui and the other commentators were 'concerned with perspectives of observation, not categories of classification.'[35] In their emphasis on the public dimension of the literary imagination, on their preference for social themes over highly individualized and internalized depiction, the ideas of these mid-Meiji critics undoubtedly represented a widespread awareness for new subject matter and fresh thematic emphasis in a new age of growing social complexity. And pointedly, it was also a significant reaction to the idea of the novel then prevalent in the literary world at the time.

During the social novel debate, attempts to give a more tangible shape to the elusive idea of the social novel so preoccupied mid-Meiji critics that they rarely bothered to integrate their ideas with the more intricate art of story-telling such as considerations of narrative techniques or methods of characterization. If politics in a work of literature can indeed be likened to 'a pistol-shot in the middle of a concert,' to use Stendhal's metaphor, practically no mid-Meiji critic paid any serious attention to the quality of the music afterwards. Lacking the modern tradition of socially-engaged literature that successfully synthesizes literary imagination and the writer's social and political sensibilities, the first few experiments with the social novel - such as Hirotsu Ryūro's *Hikokumin* (*Traitor*, 1897), Oguri Fūyō's *Seido* (*The Political Incompetent*, 1899), Tokuda Shūsei's

Namakemono (The Idler, 1899) had little to excite the modern reader.

As the Meiji social novelists continued to experiment with their craft, they continued to produce a number of interesting, if not entirely satisfying pieces of work. Uchida Roan's *Kure no nijūhachi nichi (28 December*, 1898),[36] a story highly rated even by post-war Japanese critics, is a study of the inner tension between high political romanticism and the constraints of moral responsibility in a middle-aged Tokyo intellectual. The protagonist, a writer by the name of Arikawa Junnosuke, is torn between his dream of building an Utopia in faraway Mexico with the politically-alienated members of his 'Animal Club' ('Dōbutsu kurabu') and his sense of obligation towards his unappreciative wife who harbours only suspicion and impatience with even the best intentions of her eccentric husband. But the treatment of Junnosuke's social or political discontent is at best cursory and at worst bafflingly elusive. What could in the hands of a master be turned into a moving and compelling portrait of the social rebel or a study of mid-Meiji marital strife often degenerates into the hero's narcissistic and emotional outbursts of protest against contemporary society and its supposedly helplessly corrupt politicians.

Another notable social novel at the turn of the century was Tokutomi Roka's *Kokuchō (Black Current*, 1902).[37] This full-length novel evokes the bitter conflicts between the social idealism of the Tokugawa Confucian political order and the crude pragmatism and moral decadence that dominated the political scene in the early Meiji period. What emerges from the juxtaposition of the personal tragedy of a former Tokugawa *hatamoto* and the dramatic turns of political events after the Meiji Restoration is an impassioned interpretation of both the private and public dimensions of the nation's recent spiritual history. Roka's novel was, as far as I am aware, the first serious full-length literary work in Meiji literature to probe the thinking and behaviour of Meiji political leaders, as well as their opponents, as its major theme. To Meiji readers of the time, its temporal immediacy must have been overwhelming. *Kokuchō* is not a historical novel which alludes to and satirizes the present under the disguise of an ancient setting; and its author has successfully incorporated the individual destinies of Higashi Saburō and the members of his family into the canvas of contemporary society, and painted them realistically as members of a lost generation.

However, there are many glaring flaws in the novel. Even granting the casual consideration given to structural control in the Meiji novel as a whole, *Kokuchō*'s narrative is exceptionally disjointed - the sub-plot and the main plot of the story are totally independent of each other. Roka's lack of understanding and knowledge of the intricacies of the political world and the personalities and behaviour of its politicians reduces his criticism of the Meiji political order to the level of what his biographer Nakano Yoshio correctly calls 'cheap journalistic taste' ('*shūkanshi-teki kyōmi*').[38] Prominent government leaders like Inoue Kaoru and Yamagata Aritomo appear on the scene not as rounded figures but somewhat lifeless puppets hanging loosely from Roka's artistic strings. After finishing the first volume of *Kokuchō*, Roka found himself totally drained of creative imagination to continue with his initial plan of producing an ambitious multi-volume work. *Kokuchō* as we know it today remains an unfinished work.

It was not until the so-called 'socialist' movement in the first decade of the twentieth century that a new impetus was given to the development of Meiji social literature. Kodama Kagai's poetry and Kinoshita Naoe's socially-inspired novels including *Hi no hashira* (*A Pillar of Fire*, 1904) crystallized the political vision and social perceptions of a few Japanese writers and poets at the turn of the century and infused Meiji social literature with a new political flavour. Kagai's *Shakaishugi shishū* (*A Collection of Socialist Poems*, 1903),[39] a collection of thirty poems written during the turn of the century, deserves attention not because it was the first collection of poems to be banned by the Japanese Home Ministry but because of his daring presentation of pressing social themes and the trenchancy of his social perceptions, often represented with shocking imagery. The characters that inhabit his poetic world are not Western-inspired individuals preoccupied with the liberation of the self, or refined men and women of taste absorbed in love or in their experience with nature. Instead, his poems celebrate Tokugawa peasant rebels and Ōshio Heihachirō, or the stoic heroism of a Chinese street peddler in Kyoto trying to earn an honest living amidst the humiliation he receives from his customers, or the tender feelings of a young female textile worker torn between her nostalgia for her home town and her suicidal impulses. We even find in one of Kodama's poems an impressively modern image of an old factory worker, a man painfully aware of life slipping away from him and whose only source of consolation is a kind of fatalistic, brutal self-mockery. Not until the late Meiji period do we find an equally striking image of modern alienation in the works of poets such as Ishikawa Takuboku.

Kinoshita Naoe's *Hi no hashira*[40] paints a vivid if idiosyncratic picture of the social scene in Tokyo before the Russo-Japanese War, complete with its stereotypical anti-war socialist-Christian heroes, self-serving religious leaders, labour union advocates, prostitutes, rickshaw-pullers, police spies, corrupt war merchants and decadent government officials. Even Itō Hirobumi appears without a disguised name in an outrageous scene in which he is depicted as 'having fun' with a young girl on his lap behind his wife's back. The social scope of the story is refreshingly extensive to allow Naoe to paint a broad cross-section of Tokyo society at the turn of the century, a vision seldom encountered in Meiji fiction as a whole. And it is not without considerable skill that Naoe depicts scenes of labour union meetings or the tense spectacle of police surveillance of anti-war rallies by Meiji socialists.

But again, the flaws of the story are many. The general predictability of plot and Naoe's one-dimensional characterizations aside, it is surprising that in this ambitious social novel, Naoe chooses to follow the mundane 'scholar-meets beauty' paradigm whose dramatic effectiveness seemed to have died a welcome death along with the political novels in the 1880s. To resurrect a motif used so profusely in popular love stories in a supposedly serious social novel is anachronistic in conception and incongenial in spirit. With its *gesaku*-like style and embarrassingly sentimental scenes, the story reads in part more like a Ken'yūsha love story than a product by a writer anxious to bring 'revolutionary thought' into his works. Yet despite all these shortcomings, one must give credit to *Hi no hashira* for carrying on the legacy of *Kokuchō* in giving Meiji literature a vibrant social and political colour.

The success of the Meiji social novel must finally depend on the profundity of its vision of the human condition and the manner with which it imparts that vision. All the theoretical considerations expounded by mid-Meiji critics, such as the relative significance of private or public themes, or the dialectical discussions on individual and social depiction, seem to offer little more than guidelines in the creative process. It goes without saying that no literary merit will ensue by merely adhering to these theoretical directions alone. Ultimately it is the craftsmanship of the artist that determines whether particular visions of society or politics might come to life in his interpretation of the human milieu.

Irving Howe characterizes the best political novel as one which 'generates such intense heat that the ideas it appropriates are melted into its movement and fused with the emotions of its characters.'[41] If we ask the question: Is the passion of the Meiji social novelist to offer us his interpretation of his social or political environment so intense that he is forced to let go of that impulse before he could bestow upon us, within the confines of his literary vision, something profoundly true about human nature, or as Howe has put it, 'some supervening human bond above or beyond ideas'[42] which, and which alone, would make his story meaningful to us? The answer to this question must be a qualified yes. But one must also note that from Taoka Reiun, Uchida Roan, Tokutomi Roka to Kinoshita Naoe and Kodama Kagai, the history of Meiji social literature offered modern Japanese writers a new literary vision and gave that vision a sense of public relevance. Its spirit compelled generations of writers and critics to reflect on their perceptions of the human condition in its never-ending dialogue with the social environment. Above all, it reminds them of the important fact that as creative artists, they were also thinking men in a cultural milieu that continues to condition their experience - and ultimately, their art.

6

Japanese Architecture Today

YUJI AGEMATSU

It is not easy to give a short report about contemporary Japanese architecture because there are so many kinds of architecture to be seen. It is as if the field was ablaze with a myriad of flowers. To begin with, therefore, I will describe some phenomena of contemporary Japanese architecture. Then I shall discuss certain characteristics of recent Japanese architecture. The buildings I mention are very recent. Even the oldest only goes back to 1980.

Casa Estrellita

First of all I will consider Casa Estrellita built in 1986 by the architect Osamu Ishiyama, born in 1944. This is a country museum in Izu peninsula standing next to Chohachi Museum which was built in 1984 as a memorial museum to the plasterer Chohachi by the same architect. In contrast to Chohachi Museum finished by the hand of the plasterer, Casa Estrellita was built in machine-produced steel and glass. Such a building conveys a kind of shock response and is representative of the context in which the Japanese architect works today. This 'hi-tech' tendency can be seen not only in Japan but also all over the world and especially at the original Pompidou Centre in Paris which had such an enormous impact on contemporary thinking. The history of modern architecture has already finished and post-modern architecture is developing also in Japan. Ishiyama represents the young Japanese generation.

Tsukuba Centre

The architect who represents Japanese post-modern architecture is Arata Isozaki, born in 1936. The Tsukuba Centre Building built in 1983 consists of hotel, community hall, concert hall, information centre, commercial street and plaza. When we see his plaza design created from variations of the paving pattern of Piazza Campidolio by Michelangelo, many people might well wonder why a Japanese designs such a plaza in Japan. Also in the vestibule of the concert hall we can see a painted Greek pediment. Isozaki excludes here any kind of Japanese element and intentionally breaks the rule and vocabulary of modern architecture. For the post-modern architect the historical quotation is of great interest. Therefore, it does not matter to him what he quotes from Europe or any part of the world.

41

Atrium

Next we have the rental apartments for 11 families called Atrium built in 1985 by Kunihiko Hayakawa who was born in 1941. Using the Gestalt theory, the architect wanted to give a dramatic character to the Atrium as ground in contrast to the residential part of the structure which is seen as figure. But the impression of the whole, so far as we can see, is much more American than Japanese.

Setagaya Art Museum

Setagaya Art Museum was built in 1985 by Shozo Uchii, born in 1933. The building is designed as a park museum so that the architecture harmonizes with the surrounding natural environment. We see the form of the architecture built low and horizontally, showing a strong influence from Frank Lloyd Wright.

These buildings have already received various awards and they represent quite well the Japanese post-modern architecture. There is a common problem not only for Japanese architects but also for architects all over the world. Namely, the modern architecture established in 1910 has since the 1960s begun to be seen very problematically. It was quite natural that the international style of architecture should be called into question. It would be quite strange if we could not find any differences between the architecture of New York, Frankfurt or Tokyo, although we know such buildings all over the world. Even in the case of modern architecture, the buildings in Italy must be Italian - as shown in the works of, say, Carlo Scarpa - and the architecture in Japan must be Japanese.

Naoshima Town Hall

Naoshima Town Hall by Kazuhiro Ishii, born in 1944, was built in 1983 by quoting the form of the Japanese traditional architecture Hiunkaku in Kyoto. This is a case of post-modern architecture making a historical quotation not from European architecture but from Japanese architecture. But if the architectural form of the past can appear so directly in the present age, we would like to ask what is modern architecture? Each age must have its own style and should not copy the form of the past.

National Noh Theatre

The National Noh Theatre in Tokyo was designed by Hiroshi Ooe, born in 1913. The structure, built in 1983, does not copy past architecture directly but revives the past wood construction, incorporating steel and concrete. Only the inside of the building was finished with wood. The roof is not covered with the traditional tile but with the square pipes of aluminium laid down like hurdles.

As we have seen above, the historical style becomes a challenging problem for architects not only in Japan but also throughout the world. The historical style is revived everywhere and replaces the dry as dust functionalism.

According to German art historian Heinrich Wölfflin there are three distinguishing art styles, namely, era, national and personal style. Era style refers to a style peculiar to each age or epoch. For example, the Renaissance era has its own Renaissance style and the Baroque era has its own Baroque style. National style does not mean any kind of political style but rather a style for each country and district. Personal style means a style special to each artist. If we take these three styles as a whole, we can say, for example, that the works of Filippo Brunelleschi demonstrated early Renaissance style, Italian and Tuscany style and his personal style which is different from that of Leon Battista Alberti.

These three styles are still applicable to current Japanese architecture. The architecture of the 1980s must have the style of the 1980s and modern architecture in Japan must have a Japanese style. Architects like Tadao Ando, Yoshio Taniguchi and Togo Murano have their own unique personal style.

The most difficult theme among the three styles would be the national style. If we are asked today what characterizes Japanese design, we Japanese ourselves are unable to give a clear answer. The problem has much to do with the theme of tradition and the present age in Japan. If we wished only to look after the old Japanese tradition, it would result in the conservation of Japanese culture and there could be no question of the creation of new culture. I have already indicated how wrong it is to bring the old traditional form directly into the present age. Real creativity is to inherit not the old traditional form itself but the principle, through which all the traditional form has come into existence. All forms of art must be new in each age but the principle is the same.

In the Japanese tradition there always exist two kinds of design principles. One originates from the Jomon era (2000 B.C.) and the other one from Yayoi era (200 B.C.). The Jomon principle expresses a dynamic and emotional world which can be seen in the straw-rope pattern pottery while the Yayoi principle expresses a static and rational world which can be seen in the simple pottery after 200 B.C. If we may use the concept of Friedrich Nietzsche, we are able to refer to Jomon design as being Dionysian and Yayoi design as being Apollonian. These two principles can be seen more or less in every Japanese art form. Sometimes, the Yayoi-Apollonian principle might be dominant and at other times the Jomon-Dionysian principle might be dominant.

In this way they are always competing with each other. To demonstrate these two design principles in Japan, the Katsura Palace can be said to represent the Yayoi-Apollonian design principle and the Nikko Toshougu to represent the Jomon-Dionysian design principle. Although we have a tendency to say there exists only the Yayoi-Apollonian principle in Japanese arts, we should not forget also the Jomon-Dionysian principle always pulsating behind them. Such design principles are still reflected in modern Japanese architecture.

Now we can continue our consideration of contemporary Japanese architecture. First of all, I would like to present examples of architecture as a machine which is peculiar to the present age. They do not belong to either Yayoi or Jomon design principles.

Wacoal Kojimachi Building

Wacoal Kojimachi Building was built in 1984 by Kishou Kurokawa, born in 1934. The structure is used as office and for storage by the clothing company. It looks like a large machine laid down in the urban space of Tokyo. The surface of the building is covered with aluminium plate. Kurokawa himself calls this architecture a 'pleasure machine'.

Bizan Hall

Bizan Hall was built by the female architect Itsuko Hasegawa who was born in 1941. The structure built in 1984, also represents architecture as a machine. This training institute consists of multipurpose hall and dormitory. The skylights of each dormitory make the main motif of the architectural design. Hasegawa herself calls this building a 'poetic machine' because this mechanical building has a poetic atmosphere through its light and shadow in the interior space.

Ark-Nishina Dental Clinic

Ark-Nishina Dental Clinic was built in 1983 by Shin Takamatsu, born in 1948. The building is used as a clinic and gallery and its mechanical design presents a world of new order. The details of the building are just like parts of a machine. Through the combination of such mechanical parts architecture as machine has reached its peak.

Tasaki Museum of Art

Now let us consider some buildings which follow the Yayoi-Apollonian design principle. Tasaki Museum of Art, for example, was built in 1986 by Hiroshi Hara, born in 1936. The Museum was created in the Karuizawa forest for the painter Hirosuke Tasaki who painted Japanese volcanoes like Mount Fuji, Asama, Aso etc. during his life. The outside of the building looks like a chemical institute, but the inside, including the courtyard, takes the surrounding nature into itself, so that the border between interior and exterior becomes uncertain.

'Spiral'

The building called 'Spiral' was built in 1985 by Fumihiko Maki, born in 1928. The structure houses the Wacoal Art Centre for performance and exhibition. The architect wanted to dismember the European rationalism and compose it again. The whole building is built by dividing, cutting and connecting the parts of square, grid, cube, column, cone, sphere, etc. In this way the work represents architecture as concept. The structure as a whole can be seen as the modern expression of the Yayoi-Apollonian design principle.

Mt Rokko Chapel

The chapel on Mt Rokko was built in 1986 by Tadao Ando, born in 1944. The building materials are limited to concrete, stone, steel and glass. Depending upon the Yayoi-Apollonian design principle Ando creates a modern church by simplifying the space and reviving the spirit of the

Romanesque monastery. The silent space composed with the simple materials appears through the sunlight.

Osaka Art Hall

The Art Hall of Osaka University of Arts was built in 1981 by Teiichi Takahashi, born in 1924. This is the concert hall which features the German pipe organ set in the front of the five stories void space. The design of the space made by the concrete shows the world of the condensed Yayoi-Apollonian principle.

Ken Domon Museum of Photography

Ken Domon Museum of Photography was built in 1983 by Yoshio Taniguchi, born in 1937. The museum was made for the photographer Ken Domon, who took many photos of architecture. In order to give focus to the exhibition of photographic works the space was designed in a quite simple way. Taniguchi attached importance to the correspondence with nature and connected directly with the Japanese traditional space composition by taking a form of circulation in the Japanese garden, so that he could reach a peak of the Yayoi-Apollonian design principle.

Tokyo City Hall

The New Tokyo City Hall by Kenzo Tange, was the winning design in the architectural competition held in 1986. The project, which reminds us of a kind of Gothic cathedral, won over all the other projects of tall office buildings. On the one hand, the project can be seen as the work of post-modern architecture supported by the high technology of our time. On the other hand, Tange wanted to connect with the Japanese tradition by using the oblong or lattice windows. Once the project is completed there is no doubt that it will be the newest architecture in Japan.

Japanese design is not confined to the Yayoi-Apollonian principle. Although this principle is dominant, we can see behind it another stream of the Jomon-Dionysian design principle.

Kushiro Marshland Museum

Kushiro Marshland Museum was built in 1984 by Kikou Mozuna, born in 1941. This is a kind of museum where a large marshland at Kushiro in Hokkaido can be observed and its materials can be seen. The inside of the building was designed from the image of the womb and connected with the Jomon-Dionysian design principle.

Kyusendo Forest Museum

Kyusendo Forest Museum was built in 1984 by Yasufumi Kijima, born in 1937. The structure was built as the exhibition hall for sightseeing and training to promote forestry in its district. The design of the building with seven domes inspired by the first Goetheanum of Rudolf Steiner has more to do with Jomon-Dionysian than with Yayoi-Apollonian principles.

Shinshukan

Shinshukan was built in 1980 by Team Zoo. The structure is used as Miyashiro Municipal Community Centre which contains a large and small hall, training rooms, restaurant, etc. Also in the exterior they designed an attractive plaza which can double as an outdoor theatre. The richness of the design shows more Jomon-Dionysian principle supported by native citizens than the Yayoi-Apollonian principle.

Tokorozawa Campus

Tokorozawa Campus of Waseda University was completed in 1987 by Yoshiro Ikehara, born in 1928. The architecture makes a spiral form in the surrounding environment and rises towards the tall laboratory building. The delicate design using the pleated walls has an intention more towards Jomon-Dionysian principle than towards Yayoi-Apollonian design principle.

Tanimura Art Museum

Tanimura Art Museum was built in 1983 by Togo Murano, born in 1891. The museum was planned especially for five Buddhist images by the sculptor Seikou Murata. Murano designed the exhibition space suitable for each sculpture. It means the architecture exists purely for the interior space as if it would envelop a man. We can see here how delicately the architect deals with the natural light. The work shows a peak of Jomon-Dionysian principle in contrast to Yayoi-Apollonian principle.

In summary, therefore, we have observed the mechanical tendency, Yayoi-Apollonian and Jomon-Dionysian tendency separately in contemporary Japanese architecture. But we cannot identify them as being purely from one side or the other because they often combine all these traditions. In this way the Japanese architects are struggling to find their contemporary, national and personal styles. It is extraordinarily difficult for architects to have their own personal style, national style and era style at the same time. In spite of the difficulty all artists in the world are on the way to seek their contemporary, national and personal styles.

7

Problems of Attribution in Japanese Art: The Case of Hokusai's Paintings

GIAN CARLO CALZA

Hokusai, who lived between 1760 and 1849, is certainly one of the greatest figures in world art history but strangely enough his paintings (as opposed to his woodblock prints) have been given little attention and are still little known in the West.

One of the reasons might simply be because he is such a star in the world of graphic art which has overshadowed the rest of his work: his Fuji series, for example, is certainly one of the most outstanding Japanese works of art. And it is my view that there is no other Oriental work of art as famous as his print known as the 'Great Wave.' It is also a fact that Hokusai is still thought of by most people only as a *ukiyo e* artist, while his pictorial output as a whole tends to be greatly underestimated.[1]

Yet if one starts looking into Hokusai's paintings, one is confronted by an almost overwhelming creativity over the long span of his productive life; at times one wonders how a single artist could have achieved so much. In an age, like ours, when artists tend to keep to one style once it becomes established, we are somewhat bewildered by the example of a man who abandoned a particular style as soon as he could master it; he also abandoned his art name as soon as it became well-known and used a different one.

As I went deeper into his superb but vast painting output, however, I became increasingly aware of the confused state of scholarship concerning it and of the large quantity of works, some of very poor quality, which were traditionally attributed to this great artist.[2]

In recent years there has been a general trend to reconsider many once firmly-established attributions or authentications in the light of new scholarship and many fresh discoveries. However, critical instruments and even methodology may still not look satisfactory at times. As a matter of fact, attribution scholarship in the field of Japanese art, or rather East Asian art in general, has not yet always, or at least not in all fields, reached the level of documentary evidence and accuracy of philological criticism it has in European art history. Academics as well as museum curators (not to mention auction-house experts) seem more reluctant than in the past to attribute works of art to the great Masters, preferring to use terms such as 'attributed to,' 'workshop of,' 'school of,' 'in the style of.'[3] The purpose of this paper, therefore, is to deal with some of these questions in connection with the study of Katsushika Hokusai's paintings.

No Japanese artist seems to have been appreciated in the West as much as Hokusai and in Japan as well he ranks among the most studied and cherished artists, yet so much love and study have so far failed to produce a single *Catalogue Raisonné*, the fundamental working tool for the study of any artist. Specific reasons are to be investigated as to the present situation regarding Hokusai's scholarship: little has been done with his paintings, less so with his prints[4] while far more with his illustrated books.[5]

CONCEPT OF FORGERY

In order to make myself clearer I shall add that the concept of forgery adopted here is the strictest one and includes any work which by way of signature or seal or other means was meant to be ascribed to Hokusai even though not actually painted by him. It is consistent with the approach whereby all workshop and pupils' works are considered forgeries if ascribed to the Master himself no matter by what expedient and without his hand in them. This is quite independent of the fact that they might have been produced during the Master's lifetime or later. Such works cannot be considered Hokusai's originals even though they are obviously a part of the *corpus* of paintings belonging to the pupil who produced them. As time passes and new works come to light, in Japan as well as in the West, it becomes more and more obvious that Hokusai is to be rated not only among the greatest painters in world art history, but also among the most forged. I therefore believe that it could be of some use to try and define certain categories of forgeries as well as to check the reliability of some of the most common criteria for establishing the authorship of Hokusai's paintings.

Paintings wrongly attributed to Hokusai appear to have been derived from various sources of inspiration and many have proved to be copies after existing or lost original work. An interesting example from this first category is a group of scrolls with a white snake[6] and *biwa*. Of course the themes of the white snake as well as the *biwa* are recurrent among Hokusai's paintings.[7] However, there seem to be no fewer than three such paintings with practically identical subject, same design and equivalent colour treatment. One of the pictures was recently exhibited and attributed to the Master in Ōbuse, near Nagano, at a Hokusai paintings exhibition arranged by the local Hokusai Kan. **Plate 1**. The painting which bears an inscription, signature and seal, is dated to the equivalent of 7 February 1845.[8] However, the colours are too flat and dull to be attributed to Hokusai and the line shows weaknesses typical of the copyist's uncertainty when drawing after an original painting or after another reproduction and frequently switching his eyes from his work in order to check what he is copying. Perhaps the copying was done from an almost identical painting in the British Museum, London, or vice-versa.

Plate 2. I said vice-versa as we find here similar types of mistakes as in the previous picture and it is impossible to tell which one might have been

48

taken after the other. This painting bears an identical signature, seal and inscription.[9] However, the same comments apply to it indicating that it is not Hokusai's production.

A third specimen, **Plate 3**, is housed in the Freer Gallery of Art, Washington D.C..[10] This painting appears to differ slightly from the previous two in some of the colouring, but not in the way in which the colour was applied nor in the shape of the *biwa* and the movement of the snake's middle part. The position of the script has been moved to the lower left side and bears a date of 4 June 1847.[11] However, it has obviously been taken from the same source of inspiration as the previous two.

The fact that we are confronted by no less than three fakes seems to point to the existence of an original painting which is now lost or has become untraceable.

A similar, interesting case, in this same category, is the well-known painting of a Chinese gardener and potted peony. **Plate 4**. This picture was first exhibited with a collection of Hokusai's paintings assembled by Kobayashi Bunshichi, shown at the 1900 Ueno exhibition and catalogued by Ernest Fenollosa a year later,[12] and has been housed in the Freer collection since 1903.

Eight years ago a copy, **Plate 5**, appeared at the Ōbuse exhibition already mentioned.[13] Substantial stylistic differences favouring the authenticity of the Freer's specimen are shown, as well as in the overall structure of the painting, the line and the colouring technique, by details like the head, **Plates 6, 7**. The Freer's head is a very fine example of Hokusai's ability to transmit human feeling. The gardener's expression is intense and full of love and admiration for the gorgeous flowers in the iron pan on the rock. In the copy, however, the intensity has disappeared, substituted by a stereotyped expression devoid of any feelings or warmth. The head itself shows signs of uncertain draftmanship. The left hand in the copy, **Plates 4, 5** looks unnaturally long and thin and awkwardly positioned when compared with the original and other authentic works of this period.[14] And the same last comment holds for the toes on the right foot. Unlike the previous examples in this case we are helped by the existence of the original painting.

STUDENTS' WORK

There are other paintings that fall into the category of forgeries and consequently have to be ruled out of Hokusai's production even though, from a certain point of view, it might be difficult to consider them fakes altogether. I am referring to workshop or pupils' paintings that by way of style, signature, seal, inscription or any other device are meant to be ascribed to Hokusai even though no part has been painted by him. It is, of course, consistent with this approach that all works falling into such a category should be considered forgeries if ascribed to the Master himself regardless of the circumstances, even though they have to be considered original works of the pupil who actually painted them.

An interesting example in this group, **Plate 8**, is the painting of a fisherman in the Metropolitan Museum of New York[15] which I believe to be a copy after a painting from the 'Warrior's Album' once in the Harari collection and now in the Pacific Asia Museum in Pasadena. **Plate 9**. By way of signature and style it was intended to be attributed to Hokusai, but the copy is by a talented pupil of his, possibly Taitō II. If it was indeed Taitō II who painted the Met's fisherman,[16] he seems to have disregarded some details that Hokusai would have never passed over and which become more noticeable when comparing the two paintings: the line of the left shoulder unnaturally covering part of the face which, nonetheless, shows through, the imperfection of the hand holding the pole of the net, and the general feeling that the fisherman is not walking on the muddy beach of the ebb tide, but almost unnaturally hovering above it.

One more problem is derived from the habit that Hokusai had of disposing of his many art names by passing or selling them to promising pupils. Let us take an example. One of his best known art names was the already mentioned Taitō, a name that he passed on to his pupil Hokusen in 1819. Hokusen thus became Taitō II even though he could very seldom be bothered to add *nidai* 'Second generation' to his new signature.... There is a painting in the MOA Museum of Art in Atami signed Taitō and long ascribed to Hokusai.[17] **Plate 10**. The style points to Taitō II (that is Hokusen) rather than Taitō I (that is Hokusai). But in addition to stylistic considerations, we are also comforted by an inscription: a *haiku* on cormorant fishing by Tani Sōgai dated 1820[18] a year after Hokusai had relinquished the name Taitō to Hokusen.[19]

SEALS AND SIGNATURES

Some scholars have shown of late the tendency to attach much importance to seals and signatures as a final means of ascertaining Hokusai's paternity of a painting. Others tend to reject them altogether due to their unreliability. We have already seen that we cannot safely and always trust seals even when right, since Hokusai would occasionally pass them on to someone else. And far from altogether denying their significance I believe, however, that the importance of signatures and seals is of little consequence in ascribing a painting to Hokusai. They can be considered only after all other means of authentication have been successfully satisfied.

Signatures were endlessly repeated by pupils as a part of the training in copying their master's work and seals were easy to reproduce when the actual master's seal was not available. I have found among the evidence to corroborate my theory **Plate 11** an interesting unfinished drawing in the Metropolitan Museum of Art, New York, showing a copyist's exercises with Hokusai's signatures and the KATSUSHIKA seal painted instead of impressed![20]

Uncertainty seems to surround not only signatures, but also seals. In the Saitama Kenritsu Hakubutsukan there is a well-known painting **Plate 12** with carp and turtles swimming in a pond.[21] It is not the aim of this paper to go into the problems of attribution that this controvertial and much illustrated painting poses. What interests us now is its inscription, dated 25 May 1813,[22] confirming the transfer by Hokusai of his seal KIMŌ DASOKU to a pupil.[23] According to Narazaki the painting itself was given by Hokusai to the same person at that occasion, but there does not seem to be firm evidence for such hypothesis.[24] This inscription is of no relevance, for the attribution of the picture since anybody, including Hokumei, could have conceived it for reasons of prestige or commerce and the authenticity of the script has not been proved yet. However, and in spite of whoever did it, it is an unquestionable document attesting to the mobility of Hokusai's seals.

'PHOENIX SCREEN'

An opposite example is offered by the 'Phoenix Screen' **Plate 13** that I discovered in 1987 at the Boston Museum of Fine Arts.[25] It is a large picture in tempera on gold-flecked paper showing a flying phoenix, its long tails elegantly flowing in the air, and it occupies the eight panels of an as yet unattributed screen. The phoenix is full of life and was painted so that feathers and floating tails, with their flowing, elegant lines, are moving as if in real flight. Their liveliness and freshness is such that they look as if they were alive, almost like independent creatures. But the head itself **Plate 14** is by far the most impressive part of the picture and in it Hokusai has transferred the best of his art. Like a bird of prey the phoenix has a powerful beak and the head is slightly bent to the side in a movement typical with birds. And there is something beyond the natural, as the eye of the bird throws a side glance full of wit and mockery. Once again and in tune with his own most characteristic style, the Master has managed to instil a touch of human expression in a creature with perfectly beastly features.

The screen appears to belong to the late phase of Hokusai's production and from stylistic grounds it should be referred to the Forties. As a matter of fact a small cartouche in silk is pasted on the bottom left side of the frame ascribing the piece to 1835 **Plate 15**. However, since the signature and seal do not appear to be totally convincing and Hokusai is known to have affixed his signature directly on paintings when he wanted it to appear, the cartouche must be considered a later addition by some dealer or collector. This fake and misleading inscription might be one of the reasons why the screen was never acclaimed.

In this case, therefore, we are confronted by a wrong inscription and seal on a perfectly original painting - actually, a great masterpiece.

There seem to be historical other than merely commercial reasons to explain the huge proportions of the Hokusai forgery phenomenon. In the first place Hokusai was widely acclaimed during his lifetime and had a large number of pupils who copied him for training reasons. The fact that Hokusai, unlike most *ukiyo e* artists, was as great a painter as a graphic artist made his drawings and paintings much sought after and copied. This fact, added to Hokusai's liberality with his seals and names, is today a reason of further chagrin for the specialist.

WESTERN DEMAND

A long and confusing story, that goes beyond the scope of this paper and therefore has to be omitted here, relates to Hokusai's incredible fortune in the West. Since the very birth of Japonisme, there seems to have been

51

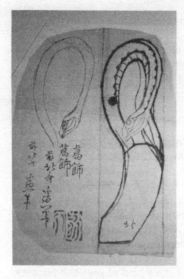

a belief that *ukiyo e* painting, in order to be really appreciated in Europe and America alike, had to be Hokusai's. One example will suffice for all.

The Bibliotheque Nationale in Paris[26] owns a yet unpublished series of paintings on silk in a squarish format probably formerly belonging to an album. The paintings were intended to be attributed to Hokusai as they are in fact signed and sealed in that respect. However, they are no less than copies after Hiroshige's most celebrated 'Tōkaidō' series reduced from rectangular to square size by trimming off the left and right sides of the images to adjust height and length to the desired proportions. I illustrate here the first, 'Nihonbashi' **Plate 16** which also carries Hiroshige's series title. As with all the other paintings it requires no further comment, so preposterous the attempted forgery appears to anyone with any sense except obviously whoever bought the series and brought it to Europe.

In this respect of the 'craze for Hokusai' one should not underestimate the impact of no less than three monographs written about him by 1914,[27] the only such case in the entire Oriental art history, I believe. Two of the authors were also two of the top writer-critics of their times, Edmond de Goncourt and Henri Focillon, and this fact must have had an enormous impact on Hokusai's fame in the Western world as much as proving a great productive stimulus for the Japanese artisans working for the Western market.

LACK OF DOCUMENTARY EVIDENCE

A major problem confronting the Hokusai scholars is the lack of documentary evidence. Genre painting was hardly prestigious enough to justify keeping any documentation about the commission to the artist and the usual clients were not from important families with private archives where students might nowadays search for evidence. There are exceptions as with the Ōbuse village, where the local Hokusai Association possesses

1

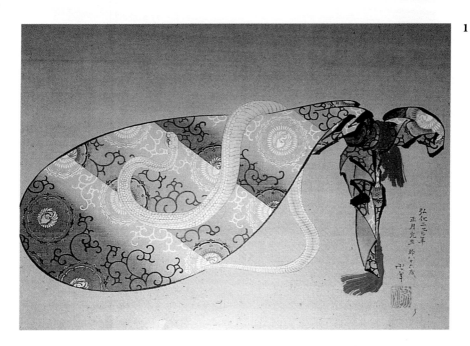

pl.1   AN., 'White Snake and Biwa', colours on silk. Courtesy, Hokusai Kan. Ōbuse, Nagano ken.

pl.2   AN., *'Idem'*, colours on silk. Courtesy, Trustees of the British Museum, London.

2

3

pl.3 AN., *'Idem'*, colours on silk. Courtesy, Freer Gallery of Art, Smithsonian Institution, Washington D.C.

pl.4 Hokusai, 'Gardener in a Chinese Robe and Potted Peony', ink and light colours on paper. Courtesy, Freer Gallery of Art, Smithsonian Institution, Washington D.C.

pl.5 AN., *'Idem'*, ink and light colours on paper. Courtesy, Hokusai Kan. Obuse, Nagano ken.

4

5

pl.6 Hokusai, *'Idem'* (det.). Courtesy, Freer Gallery of Art, Smithsonian Institution, Washington D.C.

pl.7 AN., *'Idem'*, (det.). Courtesy, Hokusai Kan. Obuse, Nagano ken.

8

10

9

pl.8 Taitō II (?), 'Fisherman at Ebb Tide', colours on silk. Courtesy, Trustees of the Metropolitan Museum of Art, New York.

pl.9 Hokusai, *'Idem'*. Courtesy, Trustees of the Pacific Asia Museum, Pasadena.

pl.10 Taitō II (attr.), 'Cormorant Fishing'. Courtesy, Museum of Art (MOA), Atami.

pl.12 Hokusai, (attr.), 'Swimming Carp and Turtles', colours on silk, Saitama Kenritsu Hakubutsukan.

pl.13 Hokusai, 'Phoenix Screen', colours on golden-flecked paper. Courtesy, Museum of Fine Arts, Boston.

pl.14 Hokusai, '*Idem*' detail of head.

pl.15 Hokusai, '*Idem*' detail of the cartouche.

pl.16 AN., 'Nihonbashi', colours on silk. Courtesy, Bibliothèque Nationale, Paris.

1. Casa Estrellita by OSAMU ISHIYAMA, 1986. 2. Tsukuba Center Building by ARATA ISOZAKI, 1983. 3. Setagaya Art Museum by SHOZO UCHII, 1985. 4. Atrium by KUNIHIKO HAYAKAWA, 1985. 5. National Noh Theatre by HIROSHI OOE, 1983. 6. Naoshima Town Hall by KAZUHIRO ISHII, 1983.

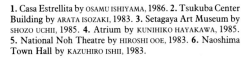

7

8

9

10

7.Bizan Hall by ITSUKO HASEGAWA,1984 8.Wacoal Kojimachi Building by KISHOU KUROKAWA, 1984.   9. Tasaki Museum of Art by HIROSHI HARA, 1986. 10. Ark-Nishina Dental Clinic by SHIN TAKAMATSU. 11. The Chapel on Mt. Rokko by TADAO ANDO, 1986. 12. Spiral by FUMIHIKO MAKI, 1985.

12

11

14

13

15

16

18

13. The Art Hall of Osaka University of Arts by TEIICHI TAKAHASHI, 1981. **14.** Ken Domon Museum of Photography by YOSHIO TANIGUCHI, 1983. **15.** Kushiro Marshland Museum by KIKOU MOZUNA, 1984. **16.** New Tokyo City Hall by KENZO TANGE, 1986. **17.** Shinshukan by TEAM ZOO, 1980. **18.** Kyusendo Forest Museum by YASUFUMI KIJIMA, 1984.

17

Mugai Nyodai

pl.1 *Gaki* section from the Kitano Tenjin engi

pl.2 *Gaki* section from Jikkaizu at Zenrin-ji

1. Théodore Duret about 1920, courtesy of the Kuroda family. 2. Kinoshita Mokutaro, 1917; courtesy, Iwanami shoten. 3. Kobayashi Kiyochika's 'Ryogoku Yakeato', Nishiki-e Oban, 1881.

some documents testifying to Hokusai's visits and work in 1842, 1844 and 1845.[28] The same goes for the famous watercolours supposedly ordered by von Siebold and De Sturler to Hokusai.

But with these exceptions still to be properly investigated and a few more, the rule is that we are left with extremely sparse documentary evidence. Nor is one much helped by the study of pigments and their chemical composition which have not been altered like in the West thus enabling the specialist to make useful comparative analysis.

It is therefore very important that some clarity be brought to this confused situation and it is becoming almost a moral obligation to this fine artist and his own real works to dissociate from his name a large quantity of paintings that have been falsely connected to it.

8

The Impact of Geographical Conditions on Japanese Creativity

ISAO TANATANI

In the context of the present world economy, Japan is involved in the greatest amount of activity she has ever encountered in her history. I believe, however, that this is not because the Japanese people and government alone wish to improve the economy as is commonly reported in newspapers and magazines.

Looking back in history, we can see that the economic and cultural base is constantly moving and that it never returns to the same place. I feel, therefore, that Japan's present condition is the result of certain organic dynamics taking place on a global scale.

Today, when we take a global perspective, we can see that the development of the present capitalistic economy began during the last two hundred years centred around the United States, and it is believed that this movement influenced Japan and other Asian nations. Japan especially in the past ten years, given her relationship with the United States, has been showing signs of a tremendous build-up of energy compared to the other parts of the world. This uncontrollable movement of organic energy is being activated somewhere - far away from the human dimension. The concentration of such energetic activity by Japan is now inviting world criticism. We Japanese who are in the midst of this dynamic process also notice that we are ourselves influenced by this torrent of energy.

Japan is facing more problems within the nation than the outside criticisms regarding her economic activities. These domestic problems include environmental problems, the problems of the budget allocation for culture and art and educational problems. At present, the Japanese economy is top priority and thus there is no room for improvement elsewhere. There are many museums being constructed and many international art exhibitions being held. However, these efforts are also considered part of the economic equation since they are treated purely as a consumer product with a limited life-span. This 'economic' creature that is making such massive advances and accelerating its combustion of heat energy, is threatening Japan. We artists are challenging this creature in an effort to think of ways of transforming this active energy in the direction of creation. However, once triggered towards a certain direction, a civilized society will continue its movement just as the sun continues its combustion until it burns itself out. The ruins of early civilizations and culture that we are able to see today are the results of the combustions of each time period. However, mankind is constantly forced to make decisions in the flow of nature and society. We have reached a point where we can make an important decision.

The development of social activity after World War II has centred around the United States. How did the wave of this vitality reach the small country across the Pacific Ocean? And how did this small country acquire this energy?

One of the conditions that greatly affected Japan is its unique environment. What is happening in this small country of the Far East? My interest lies in the topography and geography of nature. I also wonder how we could interpret and understand these phenomena in the context of history. A man must live his destiny within a limited geographical condition. Observing the formative senses and modes of living in Japan, we can see that the geographical position of Japan and the resulting factors are the important elements of Japanese uniqueness. I would like to discuss the creative senses of the Japanese from the viewpoint of environmental factors.

Japan's unique landshape was formed many thousands of years ago. It lies to the east of the Eurasian continent. The island is also adjacent to the largest ocean in the world, the Pacific Ocean. Japan is influenced by both of these geographical factors. From this point let us investigate the relationship between the value senses of the Japanese people and its geographical conditions.

Japan is like a tail attached to the Eurasian continent which can be seen as a gigantic elephant. In the next few paragraphs, I would like to discuss the features of Japan as a function of the tail of an animal. The tail is at the rear of an animal. Yet it is never isolated from the main body and always functions in conjunction with the body. However, even though the tail is made up of cells, blood and nerve systems just like the rest of the body, we can see from the functional features of a tail that it does not have a brain, heart, lungs and other organs of its own. A tail is given its life from the organs of the main body that it belongs to. A tail is not a subjective part of an organism and is more often regarded as an unimportant part of the body.

However, looking at an organism from the angle of the tail, we can see that the tail is closely connected to each part of the body in its actions. This nerve system at the end of the body is extremely sensitive to the changes that occur in various parts of the body. For example, by observing the tail we note that in calm periods it hangs idly and does not draw attention to itself. But when the main body is responsive and reacts to various stimuli, the tail also starts an action of its own linked to the reactions of the body. The tail is an antenna that catches the balance of the whole organism and it is also a regulator of the body. The tail acts keenly to regain balance whenever the body loses its balance. The main characteristic of the tail is that it does not have a function of its own but it responds quickly to the activities that occur in other parts of the body.

Japan, up to this present day, has been receiving civilizations and cultures from the main body, the Eurasian continent. Likewise, Japan functions as a reaction to an action rather than acting subjectively on its own. In this way the geographical background of Japan has been giving latent influences to the Japanese senses. Therefore, it is impossible to find the origin in the area of creation that is unique to Japan. Like the tail of an animal, it reacts to the stimuli of surrounding actions. But once it starts to function, the reaction is very keen. In some cases, the tail shows a flexibility similar to that of a whip. From these factors, we can conclude that a tail represents a style of action that is always equipped to react quickly to a given situation. Japan being a tail causes her actions to be linked with the world. It also causes Japan to react keenly to world movements and events.

Observing the geography of Japan, we can see that, unlike Korea, it is not contiguous to the continent. It should be clear at a glance how this condition caused the differences in culture and life-style of the two countries.

How does the geographical condition of being an island influence the senses of the inhabitants? An island limits the lives of the inhabitants within a specific range of activity and choice. Therefore, people living on an island must live within a finite world. These people are concerned with how to act life on a finite stage, the island. In the actual theatrical performances, the performer must act out an imaginary space within a limited stage where he becomes extremely conscious of the limitations and the psychological functions become very active to fabricate the world of imagination. This is the process of interpreting nature and material existence. And for the people, the island itself is a stage, small enough for them to be always aware of it. In daily life, people live inside specific facts and the people live their spiritual lives on a given stage. In the daily life of the inhabitants of the island, the island itself is their stage and thus they are always forced to act out their spiritual plays within a two-dimensional boundary. And by living so, they are hoping to join their world of performance with nature.

Observing this process, we can find a similarity between a stage being performed on and a space drawn on a painting. A world represented in a painting is always limited by a boundary. And this limitation resembles an island in the sense that the painting being expressed is always done within a limited boundary. In this respect, I believe that the spirit of the Japanese has something in common with the two-dimensional nature of graphic art.

Japanese senses do not seek a large-scale expansion for any kind of expression at an early stage. The senses first set a specific boundary before actually starting the process of expression. Japanese people aim at expressing as much infinite space as possible within a given finite space, and one must always endeavour to express the specific. This process is exhibited not only in the world of graphic art but also in the world of the martial arts, including the tea ceremony, and in Japanese gardens which represent a fantastic cosmic space within a very limited and specific boundary.

An island creates a closed society. Visually it is a 'point' which seems to possess a unique power of absorption. We can say that the Black Hole is the 'point' of the universe. Although points and islands may seem to be closed, they have the tendency to absorb the surrounding world to create a small world of their own inside. The unity of these small worlds may be the obstacles interfering with the understanding of the outside world. This may be the reason for the 'points' and an 'island' to be considered closed.

The island may also be regarded as a pot. Inside the pot, there is a constant unity of a number of microcosms. However, it is impossible to show this world in another container. A pot is always a container and can never be the content. It can hold things inside itself but it cannot become the content by itself. It can only hold and develop the microcosms that it absorbed inside itself. Once something enters the pot, it continues to develop just as wine would continue to ferment in time. Japan in her two-thousand-year history has developed the form of a pot and has taken in and developed culture and materials from the continent and the sea. Contemporary Japan is in the flow of new world currents, absorbing new materials.

Another geographical characteristic of Japan other than being just a 'point' is that it is an island located between the Asian continent and the Pacific Ocean.

In this connection I would like to discuss the characteristics of Japan by viewing it as a line that is drawn between a continent and an ocean. A line acts like a wall which divides a space. It is always swayed by the pressure from both sides and does not have an essence of its own. Its only active characteristic is the expression. The characteristics of the land and the ocean are entirely different. Due to the fact that Japan is located between a continent and a body of water, she is always influenced by both of these factors. And since both characteristics are in constant contention, Japan can never develop a subjective nature on her own. Japan is constantly being swayed by the wind from the continent and the wave of the ocean.

Japanese art has been extremely sensitive with regard to lines. Thus, various linear elements appear in Japanese forms of expression, especially in graphic art. This is due to the unique feeling of the Japanese towards a line, an aspect that reflects the geographical condition of Japan. The Japanese people value linear elements in their daily lives. Japanese calligraphy, which uses lines as means of expression is an example of this. The Japanese tendency to refer to 'a way' is another example of how Japanese people value a line.

From a linear point of view, Japan, being between two conflicting characters, has never been in a stable condition. And it seems that geographically Japan will always stay the way it is. The wave is always eroding the coastline, and the culture and materials continue to come in from the continent, like a wind. Japanese people have been reacting to these stimuli and up until the present time the nation has been able to function as a line. It may be similar to the destiny of a line which does not have an essence of its own, but we cannot help feeling a sense of resignation that the line will eventually be swallowed up by the surrounding nature.

Japan is surrounded by sea, and water is seen in various forms throughout the four seasons of Japan. Water is abundant in our lives and sometimes we even feel like aquatic animals.

The atmosphere, the materials and we ourselves are surrounded by moisture; as a result we feel more comfortable living in harmony with water rather than fighting it. Water does not have a shape of its own. The shape is determined by the container and thus water changes its form according to its circumstances. The passive character of the expressions of water is almost identical to the Japanese senses. This is how the Japanese senses can be observed in relation to the characteristics of water.

Throughout history the Japanese have developed and applied their unique senses towards materials and space determined by their geographical environment. Japanese people fear that one day, like a line, this land will be swallowed up by nature or the universe. Nevertheless, the spirit of the Japanese people is directed towards the unification of Japan with the universe by behaving like water. Although the last forty or fifty years of economic activity may have slightly stirred up the inside of the pot, the beauty of 'frailty' and the preference for a 'quiet presence' remain unchanged throughout its history.

9

Visions of Japan through Modern Films

MAX TESSIER

It is well known that the perception and appreciation of Japanese culture and society has often taken place through the medium of images, or pictures, from the first *Ukiyo-e* prints to other forms of the plastic arts, including western-style oil-paintings and Manga. But today's cinema has continued to be a witness of that complex society which is contemporary Japan, a unique mixture of ancient culture and extraordinary consumerism. And not only through the visions of great, universally-recognized directors like Kurosawa, or the late Mizoguchi, Ozu or Naruse, to mention but a few of the most famous names, but also through the less personal or original 'reading' of little known, sometimes almost anonymous film-makers of Japan's popular movies, now praised by the western intelligentsia. Those films and series (like the ultra-popular *Tora-san*, *Otoko wa tsuraiyo*, or the older *Zatoichi* and *Oryu Sanjo*) which were originally made for a specific Japanese audience, are now helping the happy western critic to penetrate the very substratum of the traditional Japanese mentality.

Following the post-war realistic approach to society through modern dramas like *Ikiru* (*To live*, or *Doomed*) by Kurosawa, hyper-realistic comedies like those of Ichikawa Kon or Kinoshita, or genre films like the 'shomin-geki' illustrated by films of Naruse and Gosho, a 'new Japan' has been born from its nuclear ashes, throughout the late Fifties and early Sixties, and especially after the pivot-event of the 1964 Tokyo Olympics. It was during those two decades that young film-directors, still in their twenties, started to rethink the basic realism of cinema, and deliberately gave their own interpretation of a society which was in the full flood of a major revolution of the economy.

The most radical change of attitude towards (social) realism was certainly exhibited by young Oshima Nagisa, whose second film, *Seishun zankoku monogatari* (*Cruel story of youth*), and his third, *Taiyo no hakaba* (*The sun's burial*) rocked the established visions of the youth phenomenon with a personal touch of nihilism. But the real 'revolution' of his cinematic language was made with *Nihon no yoru to kiri* (*Night and fog in Japan*, a title meant as a tribute to Alain Resnais) in which he introduced a totally new and theatrical way, with extremely long takes, of telling a complex story of the political events of 1960. Consequently the film was banned from the screens by the producing company, Shochiku, that was deeply shocked by a film that went totally against the home tradition of the Ozu/Kinoshita type films, with the result that Oshima nourished a deep rancour over that negative action.

During the same period, when the Japanese intelligentsia was deeply influenced by the new western trends of literature and cinema, especially the so-called 'nouvelle vague', other young directors went their own way, always trying to overcome traditional realism illustrated by the previous generation of the Fifties. Yoshida Yoshishige (born in 1933), a former student of French literature, influenced by Sartre and directors like Resnais and Antonioni, designed an inventive picture of post-war so-called democratic Japan, in *Akitsu Onsen* (*Akitsu spa*), through an intense love story running from 1945 to 1962. The extremely mobile camera goes frequently from one character to another, not only by aesthetic convention, but as a dialectical means of apprehending their secrets and relationships. Yoshida, the most gifted director of the Shochiku Cy with Oshima, went on in the Sixties with psychoanalytic essays such as *Mizu de kakareta monogatari* (A story written by water), until he totally gave up any realistic representation with his utterly radical *Eros + Gyakusatsu* (*Eros + Massacre*) in 1969 , originating from the life and death of the anarchist Osugi Sakae, killed during the Kanto earthquake of 1923 by a policeman. In this he boldly mixed past and present into two interconnected 'stories', one about Osugi and his women, and the other showing the nihilistic attitude of the young spiritual heirs of the sacrificed anarchist. Originally lasting 3 hours 40 minutes, the film had to be cut to under 3 hours because of a law-suit begun by one of the survivors, the mysterious Mrs K. (a living political figure). *Eros + Massacre* was probably the climax of experimental films distributed commercially and also marked the limits of hermetism from a powerful intellectual director who was soon to pay for this radicalism with a thirteen-year-long silence in the cinematic field, before his recent comeback.

Less radical, but a genuine explorer of Japanese social anomalies, especially through the portraits of low class women, was Imamura Shōhei (born in 1926), who was far from being intellectual. Having had a difficult youth in the post-war era, Imamura developed his own vision of Japan through his experience of the black-market, corruption, prostitution and odd jobs. This experience is reflected in one of his early films, *Buta to Gunkan* (*Hogs and warships*), where strange things happen around an American navy base at Yokosuka. The main character is Haruko, a young prostitute who has a relationship with a pimp, and thinks only of getting money from the men who use her services. Far from the usual decent portrayal of prostitutes or geisha in the traditional Japanese movies, Imamura stresses the animal vitality of this girl, as he would in later films such as *Nippon Konchiki* (*Insect woman*), or the even more remarkable *Akai satsui* (*Unholy desire*) whose heroine is a woman who falls in love, as it were, with her rapist. Whereas the vision of reality goes through crime and desire in Oshima's most characteristic films, and has psychoanalytic elements in Yoshida's films, Imamura's vision is in fact that of an entomologist who looks upon his characters as human insects who assume their natural cruelty. His approach is best realized in what may be regarded as his most personal film, the strange and fascinating *Kamigami no fukaki yokubo* (*Profound desire of the gods*), a deep insight into the natural wildness of a southern ludic society threatened by the northern Japanese industrial civilization, a mixture of colourful realism and ironical shots which really proves Imamura's love for those cast aside, on the margins of a society he deeply regrets to be forced to live in - as he expressed again in his recent version of Fukazawa's *Narayama bushiko* (*The ballad of Narayama*, 1983).

Not too far from that vision, perhaps because of *Suna no onna* (*Woman of the dunes*), was Teshigahara Hiroshi - the well-to-do son of the late Ikebana master Teshigahara Sofu. Originally a painter, Teshigahara (born in 1927) was soon linked with post-war surrealistic movements and groups, where he met the young writer Abe Kobo, also an adept of surrealism and experimental methods of writing. The two formed a fruitful team, who produced four independent films, the most celebrated of which is *Suna no onna* (1962). Again, humans are seen as kinds of insects, who find happiness in a remote village, far from the oppressing city, where inhabitants live as recluses: the hero is a lost entomologist who is kidnapped by dune-villagers, including a woman who has sexual power over him. The main theme, and that of the later films of this duo, is the desire to escape from society, also physically. In *Tanin no kao* (*The face of another*), the main character has a surgical operation in order to have a different face and be able to seduce his own wife; and in the even more mysterious *Moetsukita chizu* (*The burned map*), a detective hired by a woman to find her husband who has disappeared, not only does not find him, but eventually also vanishes in the odd circles of the society he explores. He loses his 'subjective identity' (as well as social identity), and is happy with its loss. Imamura himself made a documentary-like picture, *Ningen johatsu* (*A man vanishes*) in 1967, where, again, a woman tries to find her son through the intervention of the director and his crew: that direct intervention is at the same time a distancing element of the candid-eye type.

All these films, and several more of that rich creative period, underline the need to find a new identity in an economics labyrinth where man is forced to become more and more faceless in the crowd, and rebels against it. Unfortunately, after 1968/69, Teshigahara stopped his collaboration with writer Abe Kobo, apparently dissatisfied with the films he was not able to direct himself, and new economic difficulties appeared in the field of a cinema which was more and more desperately fighting against the mass invasion of television and video (which have now won the war). Thus, at the end of the Sixties, film was not merely a more or less faithful mirror of Japan and its limpid society, but more a reflection of troubled waters, sometimes muddy, in which all kinds of elements were used to make a meat-broth where everyone could take his pick.

In the meantime, major companies, which gave younger directors a chance because they thought mainly that sex and violence had appeal to a younger audience, kept making sequel films which, with their own codifications, enhanced the traditional group morality - the same as pre-war films which had been banned by the Americans in 1945. On the other hand, genre films, as opposed to the new 'immoral films' made by the above-mentioned directors, as they could be, and mainly produced by the Toei, Shochiku and Nikkatsu Companies, offered the masses simple heroes and morals, and a good deal of action, as in typical Hollywood thrillers or westerns. One of the most popular genre films, the Yakuza eiga, or outlaw film, was almost the monopoly of Toei, a very conservative company which has always managed to keep a popular audience. Originally a wandering outlaw, or rōnin, the Yakuza is a gentleman gangster who is ready to give his life and love for the sake of the clan, so as to proceed with an established social order. Based on the 'giri-ninjo' concept, a conflict between duty and human feeling, it represents exactly Japan's main dialectical contradictions: to do one's duty and build a unified country for the greatness of the nation, or to listen to one's own desire and make one's own happiness through a foreign (non Japanese) individualistic desire. In the Yakuza series, such as *Bakuchiuchi socho bakuto* (*Presidential game*) or *Abashiri-bangaichi* (*The men at Abashiri jail*), the hero, often played by the superstar Takakura Ken, or his colleague Tsuruta Koji, must make a moral choice between the right or wrong 'oyabun' (godfather) and comes to kill him to protect the clan from corruption. He tries to preserve the sense of 'Ninkyodo', or chivalry, which is threatened by bad elements influenced by foreign people and customs. Those films, which numbered by the hundreds in the Sixties and Seventies, are usually based on the pattern of the classical Kabuki (which has always had a great influence on traditional jidai-geki/period film, as opposed to the too noble Noh) and especially the classic of classics, *Chushingura*, known as *The Forty-seven ronin*, with a long introduction and development and most of the action concentrated at the end to resolve the previous contradictions. Classical Yakuza films are a typical antidote to the 'nouvelle vague' movies, which are generally critical of traditional values. Schematically, they represent the 'profound' ancestral, national Japan, which flourishes under the very superficial and sophisticated so-called 'westernized Japan'.

However, later in the Seventies and up to the present, some sequels have managed to show individualistic heroes who turn out to be pleasantly marginal. The most popular comedy series to date, usually directed by Yamada Yoji, is still *Tora-san (Mr Tiger)* also called *Otoko wa tsuraiyo (It's hard to be a man)*, starring comic actor Atsumi Kiyoshi, which has now gone beyond its 40th episode. Tora-san is a popular individualistic alibi to a gregarious society, and that may be why this vagabond story is so successful in Japan - but not much appreciated in the West, where it appears to be too mild compared with its foreign equivalents.

NEW VISIONS OF THE EIGHTIES

Now that directors like Oshima, Imamura, Yoshida and others are well-established, and Japan's triumphant economic expansion has apparently modified Japan's internal social mechanism (if not its very minds, which is another story), it seems that cinema as a form of art has greater difficulties in imposing itself, and that the new generation distances itself more from that very concept, while the linguistic expression of cinema seems to set back, as in many so-called 'developed countries', returning to an overall simplicity and desperate search for a simplified 'message', when there is one. Whereas the films of the Sixties and Seventies not only gave new visions of Japan, as a rapidly-changing society, but also showed a will to search for a new language and aesthetics, to create a new 'ecriture', most new Japanese films mark a setback from this point of view. The political film, once in the avant-garde, is now almost dead, maybe because economics have won over politics in Japan, and the 'figures de style' seem to be forgotten. Only a hard-headed experimental poet and film-maker like Terayama Shuji has, in his unique way, given a poetical and surrealistic image of Japan and his own childhood as a kind of exorcism, in films like *Sho o suteyo, machi e deyo (Throw the books away, and go into the streets)*, *Den'en ni shisu (Pastoral hide and seek)*, or *Saraba hakobune (Farewell to the Ark)*: he overcomes reality by splashing his own fantasies on the screen.

Otherwise, the main phenomenon is essentially that present-day Japan, as a social concept, seems of no interest any more to the great directors, even those who explored it a while ago. A 'living treasury' like Kurosawa has not made a single contemporary film since the 1970 *Dodes'Kaden* (which, rather characteristically, was a total flop in Japan), and his latest historical monumental epics (*Kagemusha* and *Ran*), which obviously show a profound scorn for the values of modern Japan, have been rejected by Japanese critics, and ignored in great part by local audiences, even though they were acclaimed in the West.

Oshima's latest powerful modern drama was *Gishiki* (*The ceremony*), the saga of a symbolic family, back in 1971, and since the worldly success of his scandalous *Ai no korida* (*In the realm of the sense*) set in 1936, he has made a cultural parable set in a Japanese war camp (*Senjo no merry Xmas/ Furyo*), and a very light comedy, set in the present day, but in Paris. Everyone expects him to make a new contemporary film in Japan, which seems to be more and more difficult. A more interesting development is that of Imamura, who, although less boldly than before, continues to give his own image of Japan, past and present, through parables: his interest for the ordinary and primitive people was confirmed in his unexpectedly successful adaptation of two essays by writer Fukazawa Shichiro (who died in 1987) in *Narayama bushi-ko* (*The ballad of Narayama*) mixed with elements of *Tohoku no zummutachi*, (*Men of the Tohoku*), in which he shows his own Japanese roots (a popular word in Japan a few years back), and more recently in *Zegen*, a sarcastic story of a Japanese 'Emperor of the brothels', who exploited the rapid expansion of Japan in South-East Asia at the beginning of the century. In both films, Imamura has an oblique vision of Japanese history unlikely to please the Japanese establishment of today. He even said, about *Narayama*, that to him, it was 'modern Japan which is a dream, and not the primitive one shown in the film'. One may wonder if Imamura is a prisoner of the modern nightmare.

It is finally Yoshida Yoshishige (or Kiju) who, after a long period of TV purgatory, has returned to the cinema with a strictly contemporary film, *Ningen no yakusoku* (*Promise*), in which he deals in his own way with the quite serious problem of the aged person in Japan today, where anybody who is unproductive is considered half-dead, or just sent away from the country. His bleak vision of the Japanese clean suburbs is almost like a documentary. So only younger, new independent film directors can give a real 'vision' of modern Japan, like Yanaginachi Mitsuo, who has a way of mixing realism and fantasy, in films like *Jukusai no chizu* (*The map of my 19 years*) or *Hi-matsuri* (*Fire-festival*), working with writer Nakagami Kenji. If one is interested in the actual problems of contemporary Japan, he has to view some militant documentaries, such as the *Narita* (*Sanrizuka*) series made by the Ogawa group back in the late Sixties and Seventies, or the Minamata disease series shown by Tsuchimoto Noriaki with very light technical material, outside the regular commercial distribution circuit. The Japanese tradition of the documentary has indeed survived and keeps exorcizing its past: the new film by Hara Kazuo, *Yuki yukite shingun* (translated as *The Emperor's army marches on*), produced by Imamura, shows an angry man going after criminals: a very impressive film on the demons of Japanese society, in spite of a basic ambiguity about the man, who is far from being a saint. The documentary is probably now the only field of cinema where first degree realism is still honoured. Otherwise, there are glimpses of reality in sequels like Nikkatsu's so-called 'roman-porno' films, a soft-core look at sex in Japan, which from time to time gives an interesting view on the life of young people.

However, the growing uniformity of present-day Japan, symbolized by the concept of 'Kintaroame machi' (an image given by a Japanese architect, which expresses the idea of uniformity, using the word Kintaroame, a candy that shows the same face of a boy wherever you cut it, and machi/city and quoted by Oshima) seems to involve the Japanese cinema itself. As everyone knows, the Japanese cinema is now called the 'sunset industry', as opposed to the rising suns of television and video systems: there is not much difference today between an ordinary Japanese film and a European or American film, in their increasing banality. Only a few individuals, as usual, carry on a tradition of cinematographic transcription of reality into a visual dream, a link with the concept of the 'floating world' (*Ukiyo*). These few people do not just copy reality, or escape from it, but transpose it to the level of their own reality, which becomes, in the best of cases, cinema.

10

Can Japanese Literature be Translated?

ROBERT LYONS DANLY

Can Japanese literature be translated? Let me begin to answer that by way of anecdote. A prominent American scholar of Japan working in the social sciences recently told me of an experience from his graduate student days twenty years ago. It is certainly, I think, one of the most amusing stories about learning - and translating - Japanese.

When he was still a tadpole in *Nihongo*, battling his way upstream against the torrent of *kanji* - using the Hibbett and Itasaka text for a sluice gate - his class was assigned to translate Akutagawa's famous suicide note. Our budding translator worked up a first draft, typed it neatly, and handed it in.

The weeks went by, and he passed second-year Japanese with flying colours. He had received a fellowship to study in Japan, and so, as soon as the course was over, he and his wife packed up their things and prepared to leave for the Far East. On the final day of packing, the tension was running pretty high. Tempers flared. They fought. He left in a huff, and went off to put the car in storage. While he was gone, amidst the rubble - a near-empty jar of peanut butter, the last of the instant coffee, an errant corkscrew, in the corner a dustpan, and everywhere stacks of cardboard boxes - his wife found his first-draft translation of Akutagawa's note. She was stunned. Their dispute had been vehement, but was the man she had married that thin-skinned? Was a little spat grounds for suicide? She read the note again. Filled with remorse, she began to call everyone who knew her husband, hoping against hope to catch him and prevent him from going through with it.

In the meantime, the translator had not gone very far when he realized that, given his agitated state, he had forgotten to bring the paperwork he would need to store the car. Returning to the apartment, he was surprised to find his usually robust wife collapsed in tears. This seemed to him a needlessly dramatic reaction to what had been, after all - when you put things into proper perspective - a family squabble. But there she was, trying to dial the phone through her tears and clutching Akutagawa's last testament to her bosom. And there he was! Alive! Her prayers had been answered, and the vile, tear-drenched words on the sheet of paper, which had ripped into her like a knife, seeming to destroy her whole world in an instant, were in fact nothing more than a piece of homework.

I would guess that, from the anecdotal evidence alone, most people's answer to the question 'Can Japanese literature be translated?' would be 'You bet!' After all, did not the translator's wife react to the translation precisely the way one might imagine that Akutagawa's wife had reacted to the original? It may have been an absolute novice who did the translating, a second-year student, but was not the original meaning, and something of the tone of the original, amply conveyed in another language? Is not this the goal of literary translation: to reproduce the meaning and effect of a text in a second language?

The answers to at least some of these questions, like so many questions in life, turn out to be both 'yes' and 'no'. The questions only raise further questions. To stay with the anecdote a moment more, why did not the translator's wife realize that the note could not have been from her husband, unless this future social scientist had a second life as a closet writer turning out novels under a pen-name? Akutagawa makes it pretty clear that the author of this note is a fiction-writer. And why did not the translator's wife realize that the financial situation of the man in the letter did not accord with that of her husband? Moreover, the original letter (I have not been privy to the translation, and I doubt it exists anymore) describes at some length Akutagawa's morbid comparison of the various means of committing suicide. Should he hang himself? Should he throw himself into the sea? Should he use a gun? Or a knife? Should he jump off a building? One might wonder why it did not occur to the translator's wife that their argument had only taken place that very morning. Would her husband really have had time for such deliberations - and time to write his four- or five-page missive - in between packing boxes? And of course, perhaps the biggest question: one wonders in what strange, contorted, artificial English this translation by a student still struggling to master Japanese must inevitably have been written. Could it really have sounded like her husband's voice? Could it have sounded like the voice of any native speaker of the English language?

All these questions raise further questions, and they are the ones I really want to talk about. We can leave the overwrought young graduate couple, alive and reunited - as they still are today: happy, eminent, and, so far as one can ever tell about such things, completely unsuicidal.

64

If anyone should be suicidal it is not the social scientist, but the poor soul intrepid enough to make belletristic translation his life's work. Look through the literature on translation, or translation theory, and what are you told? That translation is 'a legitimate form of plagiarism.' That it is, at best, 'a secondary activity' for the writer whose own originality and inspiration have temporarily deserted him - 'the best way to keep your tools sharp.' That translation is 'the skill of honourable deception,' that it is 'a transparent absurdity,' that it is 'a labour belonging to oblivion,' that it has about it 'a touch of treason... [where] hoarded dreams, patents of life... are taken across the frontier.' Even at its most successful, we are told that translation can only 'resemble a Persian rug seen from the back - the pattern is apparent, but not much more.' Nabokov's poem 'On Translating "Eugene Onegin"' offers its own well-known bit of discouragement:

> What is translation? On a platter
> A poet's pale and glaring head,
> A parrot's screech, a monkey's chatter,
> And profanation of the dead.

So the translator is likened to a spy, a traitor, a profaner of the dead, 'a beggar at the church door,' 'a bigamist' even - whose 'loyalties [are] split between native language and foreign tongue.' It gets worse and worse. We are told that anyone so depraved as to want to translate will finally end up in bed with his mother, at least figuratively. '[It is] *incest* that is at stake in the enterprise of translation. Through the foreign language we renew our love-hate intimacy with our mother tongue.' Having heard all this, one can no longer be terribly surprised to hear also that translation is 'linguistic castration.' I must say that before I ever attempted to translate a word of Japanese literature, the only risk I had heard of was that 'translators are men groping towards each other in a common mist.' I did not know that one of them might also be carrying a knife.

Why all this hostility towards an endeavour that even now, in our post-modern world, I suspect many people would consider a respectable, or at least harmless, pursuit?

Of course, the whole controversy predates the Western discovery of Japan. It is a perennial question whether in fact translation is possible. And it is a question whose roots lie firmly planted in ancient religious and psychological doubts about whether there ought to be any travel from one tongue into another. In the words of George Steiner, who summarizes this point of view quite succinctly, 'So far as speech is divine and numinous, so far as it encloses revelation, active transmission either into the vulgate or across the barrier of languages is dubious or frankly evil.'[1]

There is also, of course, a secular distrust of translation. It is based on the conviction that there can be no true symmetry between two different semantic systems. But even this mundane, linguistic view of translation shares the religious or mystical bias, the sense of depletion. Again Steiner puts it well. 'The vital energies, the luminosity and pressure of the original text have not only been diminished by translation; they have been made tawdry. Somehow, the process of entropy is one of active corruption. Traduced into French, said Heine, his German poems were "moonlight stuffed with straw".'[2]

One does not have to go very far in the study of the Japanese language, or the reading of Japanese literature, to realize that different languages, different cultures, structure reality in different ways. Does this mean that the reality thereby determined by a language, or culture, is fathomless to those outside the charmed circle? Or that only those languages close at hand - contemporary and directly across the border - are prudent objects of translation? If the graduate student had been translating the suicide note of a French writer, would his English-speaking wife have realized that it was not her husband's voice?

There are really two questions here. 'Is translation possible?' is one. And the second, 'Is translation possible only for cognate languages?' Anyone who attempts literary translation takes the affirmative answer to question number one as an article of faith. (And for faith to enter into the discussion is perhaps not inappropriate, given the early religious doubts about translation.) But what about those of us who must answer the second question? We are told by some philosophers of language that, since what passes for translation is really only a convention of approximate analogies, a makeshift contraption straining for similitude, the result will be just barely tolerable when the two languages, or cultures, are cognate. When they are not cognate - when a Japanese novel is being translated into English or Italian - both tongues and sensibilities are oceans apart, and the end product cannot but be spurious.

Let me at this point offer some personal observations as one who has attempted the impossible.

'The worlds in which different societies live are distinct worlds, not merely the same world with different labels attached.' Edward Sapir said that in 1949, and, the more I translate, the more I would be inclined to agree. But I would qualify the remark in several ways. This does not mean that we cannot move *between* worlds. All the evidence suggests the contrary. And to return to the question of cognate languages, or cultures, this 'distinct world' business is also a matter of degree. If two cultures have some relation, their customs and languages will clearly share an affinity, which cannot but simplify the translator's task. The real difficulty for the translator is more cultural than linguistic. The more distant the culture, in time and space, the more arduous the translator's agenda will be.

Indeed, eleventh-century Japan is a separate and distinct world from the America I grew up in. Finally, it is difficult for me to see myself falling in love with a woman who blackened her teeth. Or falling in love on the basis of a woman's handwriting, or the mere glimpse of her sleeve. But it is not difficult for me to see myself translating *Genji monogatari*, because, while the observation of aesthetic propriety was integral to the life of the Heian courtier, it is not really what *Genji* is all about. Fashions come and go, emotions are immutable. In all societies, people fall in love, grieve over death, know joy, fear, envy. All human beings have the same digestive tract.

In a certain sense, I would suspect that *Genji monogatari* might prove easier to translate than some other works in the Japanese literary canon. I refer precisely to those works where fashion and manners are much more central to the writer's purpose than they are in *Genji*. I have been toiling

66

recently in the Edo period. If ever there were a time in the history of Japanese culture when writers and artists concentrated their attentions on the ephemera of life - hairpins, the stripe of one's kimono, the curvature of the bowl on a tobacco pipe - it was Edo. Seventeenth- and eighteenth-century citizens of Japan may have been no more preoccupied with style than their counterparts in the eleventh century, but somehow the concern came closer to occupying centre stage in the literature of Edo. If that were the whole of it, one might not be particularly keen to render Edo literature into one's own language. In fact, such distinguished translators as Arthur Waley and Edward Seidensticker have not been the least bit interested.

And yet I cannot read the novels and short stories of Ihara Saikaku - taut, energetic, vividly detailed sketches of a new class of people in Japan, wily merchants and pugnacious townsmen - without feeling that I am peeking into a whole new world. A distant world, to be sure. A distinct world. But it is precisely that distinctness that fascinates me, that calls out in a way no modern Japanese novel can.

I have been to the world that Ōe and Abe Kōbō write of. It is too close to be very challenging. I can never travel to Edo, however, except via the text, via the imagination. The distinctness of Edo - and all the problems which that distinctness entails, both linguistic and cultural - becomes the lure. The translator is trapped. And I do not mean trapped in a fantasy, although I think the role of the imagination is crucial to any true act of translation. I am not proposing to invent my own seventeenth-century Japan, as one might say that Pound did with China when he conjured up *Cathay*. Nor do I mean to countenance the tendency we see among some translators, where the more remote the linguistic-cultural source, the easier it seems for them to achieve a kind of summary penetration, a glib transfer of signifiers. I mean rather the grappling with a text because it is remote - because the particulars of time and place, the capriciousness of idiom, the distant yet recognizable contours of the human situation are worthy not only of our curiosity but also of our respect. Once, in another country, things were done differently, and one might want to understand.

Difference, in the end, is what translation is all about. And I have come to feel that the greater the difference in the two languages, the two cultures, the greater the translator's chance for true achievement. Surely the authentic transfer of meaning (and beauty) between languages is possible. We have at one extreme the crude translation, as exemplified by the student's crabbed rendering of Akutagawa's last letter. Somebody somewhere is going to kill himself, and the note is in your husband's handwriting.

But we have at the other extreme translations that accomplish far more. They are renderings that not only attain a translucency of meaning, and perhaps critical exegesis. Imbued with the emotional and intellectual commitment of the original work, they indeed recreate the integral life of the original. But more, as translations that have only come into being because words in a distant world collided with one's own, they enhance the translator's native idiom, his own culture. What greater paradox is there than to find that in seeking to understand the distant, alien unknown, one has ended up mastering one's own tongue? It turns out to be exactly as translation's severest critics said, though the implication is, I think, rather different: in roaming the seas, one has in fact returned to mother.

11

A Sense of Tragedy: Attitudes in Europe and Japan

P. T. HARRIES

The view of tragedy presented here under the theme 'Rethinking Japan' seems only too obvious. Yet the possibility of tragedy as an essential element in Japanese literature seems largely to have been ignored as an aspect of critical study. To suggest that tragedy is pervasive in Japanese literature and furthermore that a corresponding term for it, at least at some points in its history, may be found in the Japanese *aware* or *mono no aware* does therefore involve a rethinking of our attitudes.

From the outset it must be made clear that there are two restrictions in the scope of this paper: firstly, I shall not deal with Japanese theatre, for I wish to avoid the still regrettably common generic concept of tragedy as a specific form of drama, and instead to follow modern criticism in emphasizing the wider concept of the sense of tragedy or the tragic vision, embodied in a variety of literary forms; secondly, for reasons of length, as well as from personal interest, I shall not go beyond the Heian and early Kamakura periods in considering Japanese works.

The origins of this paper go back to a time when I was translating the late twelfth/early thirteenth-century work *Kenrei Mon'in Ukyō no Daibu shū* and was faced with the word *aware* in the text. The author is describing the point in the Genpei War when the Taira nobility, including the author's own lover, flee the capital before the advancing Minamoto forces. She writes: 'Yume to mo maboroshi to mo aware to mo nani to mo subete subete iubeki kiwa ni mo nakarishikaba....' This was rendered: 'Whatever I may call it, dream, illusion, tragedy - no word can possibly describe it.'[1] When I proposed this translation, it did not go unchallenged. Yet, as I sought to justify both to myself and to others my choice of terms, I was convinced that this was a genuine case for the use of the term tragedy, not merely in its popular - we may even say debased - sense as a synonym for sadness or calamity,[2] but in its more basic sense; and moreover that the argument could be widened to treat of Japanese literature in general.

We have to contend with the fact that concepts of and attitudes to both tragedy and *aware* tend to be deep-rooted and rather rigid. Perhaps because of limitations in the critical concepts of the earliest commentators on Japan, there seems to have been no examination of the idea of tragic vision in Japanese literature and indeed an assumption that Japan did not have true tragedy. This can scarcely be accepted, even if we restrict our view to a narrowly defined species of drama. Still less can it be accepted when we view tragedy in the light of developments that have taken place in its conception and theory since the early nineteenth century.[3] It therefore behoves us to examine Japanese literature for ways in which it might embody the more widely defined sense of tragic experience or tragic vision. In fact, our instinctive reaction to much of Japanese literature is likely to be that it is deeply imbued with a sense of tragedy. But we must be careful to avoid use of the term merely to denote works with sad endings.

Here it is worth noting that in his book *The Nobility of Failure*, which he subtitled *Tragic Heroes in the History of Japan*, Ivan Morris suggested the pervasiveness of the tragic vision. He was surely right in his reading of cultural values, but his concern and his emphasis were historical, so he made no attempt to examine what we mean by tragedy or the modes by which it finds expression in Japan. It should not be forgotten that the essential vision of tragedy is literary: it is a literary response to the suffering of life, a way of forming our perceptions and attitudes, of bringing us to consciousness and self-consciousness through the specific medium of literature. Without literary embodiment or literary re-creation, historical figures and folk heroes, however pathetic they may be, are unlikely to become truly tragic figures. We need therefore to take Ivan Morris's example a step further into a specific examination of what it is that constitutes tragedy and look for those features in the literature of Japan.

Underlying the rigid attitudes to tragedy and *aware* is the fact that both terms are difficult to define. *Aware* in particular is a protean term with a wide variety of nuance, and it is no doubt the resonances of its many meanings, together with on the other side a rather narrow view of tragedy, that caused and may well still cause surprise at a linking of the two. I certainly do not suggest that they are exactly the same, but I do maintain that they are often *functionally equivalent* within their cultures. As far as *aware* is concerned, there is, it seems to me, a tendency in the West at least for the term to be sicklied o'er with the pale cast of Japanese delicacy. Do we not usually see it as a refined sensitivity, a gentle melancholy, a pervasive, somewhat limp pathos, especially in contrast to the vigour and robustness of tragedy? It may well be all of these, but in fact *aware* also embodies the profoundest and most powerful of emotions, in response not merely to the aesthetic norms of a courtly society and the changing seasons (which are themselves, of course, true matter for tragedy), but also to the most deeply sorrowful and desperate of human situations. For example, in the *Minori* chapter of the *Tale of Genji*, when Genji's consort Murasaki knows she is dying and sees some familiar faces for what she recognizes to be the last time, the description goes: 'kaodomo mo aware ni miewatasaretamō.'[4] A few lines further on, as she thinks of the brevity of all human life, but even more of the essential loneliness of death, the text reads, 'Mazu ware hitori yukue shirazu narinamu o oboshitsuzukuru imijū aware nari.'[5] It would be rash to suggest a 'correct' translation of such brief quotations, when a number of words for grief, sadness or tragedy offer themselves, yet all seem somehow flat and inadequate for this poignant scene.

The problem of choosing words brings me back to my starting point in *Ukyō no Daibu shū*. I had two reasons for using the word tragedy in that instance. The first is a mere matter of words: I could think of no other word of sufficient weight and strength for the context. Lady Daibu chose her words carefully, and at this point she used the most basic, most essential and all-encompassing term to represent the experience of suffering. The same had to be attempted in English. The second reason lies in the situation itself: here was a whole family driven to flight, ruin and death from the heights of power and glory. Can any other concept do for this? It is not mere sadness or pathos. It is the very stuff of tragedy.

To extend this discussion to a more general level involves two basic questions: does Japanese literature manifest the tragic vision as we understand it from the European tradition; and does the term *aware* encompass that sense of tragedy?

In response to the first question, we must examine - though all too briefly here - the essential features of tragedy. Again it must be stressed that these features shall not be specific to genre. The dominance of drama in the European concept of tragedy is in a sense accidental: the tragic vision reached mature expression in the masterpieces of Greek drama; Europe inherited the Graeco-Roman tradition, and the major works written in dramatic form have overshadowed much of our thinking. The drama may have certain advantages of intensity in the presentation of active suffering, but that is a matter of means and technique, not of the tragic vision itself. It can be, and is, argued that tragic drama has been in decline since the seventeenth century - a comparison of Marlowe's *Dr Faustus* with Goethe's *Faust* is instructive here - and some critics will maintain that tragedy has moved to the novel: 'In the nineteenth century certain of the novelists had the surest sense of the thing itself.'[6] In Japan, narrative prose developed earlier, and it was in this form that the tragic vision first appeared at its maturest and most powerful there. Therefore, we must not let purely historical factors determine our attitude to tragedy, and we must beware of mistaking specific requisites of drama, such as Aristotle's unities - in themselves controversial - for essentials of tragedy in general.

Yet despite the fact that Aristotle was addressing the tragic drama of his day, we find that he is still the bedrock of tragic theory, and the constituent elements of tragedy identified by him correspond, *mutatis mutandis*, with those of modern critics. These are: the centrality of suffering, with its combination of pity, fear and terror; catharsis; peripeteia, or change of fortune; anagnorisis, or the coming of awareness; the superior qualities of the hero; and the interplay of situation and tragic flaw, usually with a sense of inevitability. In some definitions, the elements are pared down even further, as in Oscar Mandel's, which essentially consists of a sympathetic protagonist, a serious purpose or action and necessary and inevitable suffering arising from them.[7] But such a definition seems almost too sparse, especially in its omission of anagnorisis; and the rather fuller list of constituents first given offers better scope for our discussion.

Of the elements enumerated, catharsis has proved the most difficult to define and understand. The most convincing modern theory of catharsis - proposed by Humphrey House - is that it refers not to a simple purging away or removal of emotion, but, as a metaphor taken by Aristotle from medicine, to a balancing of the humours, a return of the body or psyche and emotions to equilibrium and therefore health.[8] This seems to me to be a function of all good literature and one that affects the writer as well as the reader or audience, but it is the more noticeable in tragedy, with its particularly forceful, potentially destructive and certainly unpleasant emotions. It is clearly as much a part of Japanese literature as of Western tragedy, present not only in the acceptance and resignation that mark the diaries and the *Tale of Genji*, but also in the *waka*, perhaps most recognizably in the love poetry of the thirteenth and fourteenth centuries. We should note here that Hisamatsu Sen'ichi specifically lists balance as a feature of *aware*.[9] What he appears to have in mind, as far as I can judge, is a balance between the aesthetic pleasure of observation through elegant presentation and the potentially overwhelming effect of the pity and suffering itself. Milton in his *Preface to Samson Agonistes* (also quoted by House) says much the same things: '...to temper and reduce them [i.e. pity, fear, terror] to just measure with a hint of delight, stirr'd up by reading or seeing those passions well imitated.'[10]

But more than this somewhat elusive notion of catharsis, it is surely the presentation of suffering, pity and terror that is central to tragedy. These abound in Japanese literature: suffering and loss are the essence of *aware*. The main difference between Europe and Japan seems at first sight to be the degree of violence and naked terror involved. Where is the equivalent of the terror of Orestes or Oedipus, the blinding of Gloucester in *King Lear*, the wholesale slaughter of *Hamlet* or the plays of Tourneur? In fact, this violence is absent from much of European tragedy. As Racine comments in his preface to *Bérénice*: 'Ce n'est point une nécessité qu'il y ait du sang et des morts dans une tragédie.'[11] The tragic novel, with its emphasis on complexity of plot and character, tends to avoid violence and death - although we must acknowledge the prevalence of death in, say, the works of Thomas Hardy. The novel goes yet further and reduces the action from grandeur to a more everyday scale, and as Jeannette King says: 'Tragedy can arise from the trivial as much as from the important events.'[12] It is this sort of tragedy of everyday events that we see in the great diaries of the Heian period and in the *Tale of Genji*. Genji's real tragedy is not political or even social, it is domestic and personal. So is that of the authors of *Kagerō nikki* and *Sarashina nikki*. But the suffering, the loss and the waste are none the less real and significant for that, no less moving than in any tragedy of grand or violent action.

Yet suffering alone tends to produce pathos without tragedy. A vital element in the tragic vision is anagnorisis, the revelation, the sudden coming to knowledge, both by the hero and by the audience or reader. While the latter is usually in the ironic position of knowing or guessing beforehand what the hero will discover, it is the hero's plight that brings home the realization that the reader or audience too is caught up in the tragedy of the human situation. In the words of Clifford Leech: 'The "suffering" presented in tragedy is an image of something we intellectually

71

know is in store for ourselves but cannot in imagination properly anticipate.'[13] The same tragic effect may be found in lyric poetry. R. P. Draper says of *The Testament of Cresseid*, a poem by the fifteenth-century poet Henryson: '...the real concern of the *Testament* is with a moment of lyrical intensity when the prevalent condition of humanity is made feelingly known to a woman who has hitherto been essentially unaware.'[14] In the *waka* it is frequently this moment of awareness, the perception of our tragic position, that forms the core of the poem. It is the gradual self-knowledge and the ironic grasp of their own position that inform the Heian diaries and save the heroines of *Kagerō nikki* and *Sarashina nikki* from being merely self-pitying or pathetic and turns them into true tragic figures, as they contemplate the waste of their lives. This re-enacting and this contemplation awaken in the reader a fresh knowledge of what Gerard Manley Hopkins called 'the blight man was born for.'[15] This is the tragic vision, and in these two diaries, the unblinking stare of self-knowledge and the acceptance of a tragic fate are as powerful as we will find in any literature.

The fear too is there, not violent terror perhaps, but the slow creeping fear and horror of frustration, constriction, failure, a paralysis that affects not only the seemingly passive heroines but even Genji himself, as he awakens to the emptiness of life in the *Minori* and *Maboroshi* chapters, and that tightens round the whole of the Uji chapters. For most of us, this is the more real, more immediate terror of our situation, as we realize, in George Steiner's words, that 'the twist of the net which brings down the hero may be an accident or hazard of circumstance, but the mesh is woven into the heart of life.'[16]

Peripeteia, or change, can be taken to include plot, which is, of course, essential to the complexity of the tragic novel. It may also be taken to include that driving purpose or action which leads to the inevitable suffering. Heian works may seem lacking in plot and meagre in action, yet force of purpose and inevitable change are essential to them. Genji is driven by a purpose, a search, that leads inexorably to a fall, not a political or social fall but one that is personal and spiritual. The driving purpose and the potential for achievement in both Kaoru and Niou are turned to failure and frustration. We see not a sudden and dramatic reversal of fortune, but the slow yet certain march of fate from hope and promise to despair and emptiness, which is the true tenor of the tragic novel.

The novel form - not to mention industrial society itself - has had its effect on the nature of the tragic hero. The rise of the novel has seen a drop in the social status of the tragic hero. But what is still necessary is the hero's ability to engage our sympathy and goodwill and the presence of some exceptional traits of character, even if it is no more than the quality of endurance, which Jeannette King considers 'perhaps the greatest of the traditional tragic virtues, as exemplified by Oedipus and King Lear.'[17] Endurance stands out as a virtue of Japanese heroes and heroines. It marks so many of the women in the *Tale of Genji*, who are in their way just as much tragic figures as Genji himself. He, it need hardly be said, is a classic example of the outstandingly gifted, charismatic hero.

Prince Genji also exemplifies the concept of tragic flaws and their interaction with inexorable fate, as do the heroines of the diaries. Their suffering is in part due to circumstance, but it is intensified by aspects of their own characters: Genji's lack of self-control and his constant self-deception; the spite and anger of the heroine of *Kagerō nikki*; the passivity and timidity of the writer of *Sarashina nikki*. Their exceptional talents and position serve to make the loss and waste all the greater.

A major difference between these Japanese works and the classic tragedies of Europe is that their heroines and heroes do not suffer catastrophic social falls. Their suffering is more internalized, it is emotional and mental, it is the acknowledging of the fading and failure that is ineluctably our lot. However, the same is true of the great nineteenth and twentieth-century novels. Hardy's Jude dies young and unfulfilled, but it is his frustration in life that is the tragedy. Henry James's heroines endure and fight on in the knowledge of despair. In works of this sort, both literatures share the experience of quiet agony that pervades so much of our own age and was so much a part of the Heian world.

It seems, therefore, undeniable that the tragic vision is fully realized in Japanese literature, or at least in the Heian works I mention. Though at first sight the Japanese attitude may seem different, more quietist, more a sense of transience than the vigorous hubris and nemesis we associate with tragedy in Europe, it is perhaps our own European attitudes that need to be re-examined, to see how the essential tradition of tragedy has developed in the last two hundred years and embodies the same features as the tragic literature of Japan.

Finally, we return to the ticklish question of *aware* and its relationship to tragedy. This is not the occasion to attempt a definition of *aware*, with its wide range of meaning, from simple exclamation to sensitivity of soul, from love to deep sadness, merely to propose that there are points where it seems to embody features of tragedy. We should note, however, an important and potentially confusing difference: tragedy is used, as it were, from the outside looking in, of the observer's reaction, not of the suffering participant's consciousness, while *aware* is used both from within and from outside the experience itself, both to describe the sufferer's feelings and to characterize a scene. This is a matter of linguistic usage and does not nullify the fact that *aware* is used of situations where we would apply the term tragedy. This surely is the most profitable line of approach: rather than definition, what is significant is the function of both terms within their cultures. Both tragedy and *aware* are used as terms through which human beings can comprehend the pervasiveness, the inevitability of sadness and loss, the very texture of existence. This, it seems to me, was the vision that Saigyō was objectifying in his famous poem:

Kokoro naki	Even one
Mi ni mo aware wa	Who has denied emotion
Shirarekeri	Cannot but feel this tragic beauty -
Shigi tatsu sawa no	Snipe rise from the marshes
Aki no yūgure	Through the autumn dusk.[18]

What we feel here is the beauty and significance of the smallest, most trivial things set against their transience, the bleakness of the numinous beyond, the impossibility of escaping the net of tragedy. Here the general and the particular combine: the piercing beauty and the impermanence of the world reflect the personal tragedy of the poetic speaker, who, try though he might through priestly vows to escape, is caught as securely as any mortal in this life. Here too is recognition, self-awareness, that essential feature of tragedy. It can be no coincidence that *aware* was originally an exclamation of the deepest emotion, and then an acknowledgement of the grief which underlies all existence.

If we would cavil at equating *aware* with tragedy, we should ask what other term there is in the traditional vocabulary of Japan to express the tragic vision, this attitude to life that is basic to the literature of both Europe and Japan. For Japan, no less than Europe, felt the sense of tragedy, which enables human beings not so much to explain or rationalize suffering and the loss of what we deem most beautiful, most valuable and good, but to confront the experience and comprehend its inevitability, to share it and hence endure it.

12

Once More: On Problems of Literary Historiography

IRMELA HIJIYA-KIRSCHNEREIT

'Cold coffee' is what we in German call something stale, e.g. subjects of discussion that are thoroughly worn out by having been put on the agenda again and again, something, in short, that everyone is fed up with. If much of what I am going to say will make you think of cold coffee, I will have to be prepared to accept your reactions accordingly; but to be honest - it is cold coffee for me, too! Then why bother to serve it all over again, you may rightfully ask, and this is, I think, where I will have to start explaining my point.

Most of us in the humanities will remember that since the late Sixties matters of theory have become more and more important in various disciplines, a movement which resulted not only in radically questioning the meaning and raison d'être of many a branch within humanities, but which have themselves been continuously questioned and put to test in practical research. Nowadays, the scientific society in the humanities is much more oriented towards matters of practical concern, and the violent and seemingly endless discussions on methods and theories appear to be a thing of the past. Yet we can state that notwithstanding its excesses and fruitless phases of 'stewing in one's own juice,' a heightened sensibility towards the implicit presuppositions of one's work and towards the relationship between object constitution, method, and result counts among the more positive effects of those years of storm and stress.

Although Japanese humanities took notice of all these developments, they did not feel the necessity to engage in the discussion with comparable intensity. Obviously, they did not experience their crisis of legitimation, because, as may be inferred, their self-image and function within society differ to some extent from their counterparts in Europe and North America. Besides, the modes of discussion within the academic society in Japan are also considerably different from ours, another aspect which sets it apart and makes it difficult for us to grasp its points. Generally speaking, Japanese studies in the field of literary research have therefore avoided touching on these theoretical questions, and quite rightly they could point to the unproblematic state of affairs in Japanese humanities to justify their attitude. On the other hand, however, research is not done in a vacuum, and although we may rightly regard Kokubungaku, the discipline as it exists in Japan, as our 'mother discipline,' so to speak, we are apt to be confronted with problems in our practical work as long as we insist on remaining a part of our own academic society as well.

If we therefore deal with questions of theory at all, it is not out of a particular predilection to meta-criticism. Let it be clear that for someone deeply involved in practical research, these matters are rather a bothersome necessity and possess no attraction in themselves, but a necessity they are. They pop up one after another in the course of our work, and to ignore them is to take the line of least resistance but this may turn out to hinder new insights in the long run. Let me explain why I have come to think this way.

Since I began my own research in the field of modern Japanese literature in the early Seventies, I have paralleled the publication of some of the results with a series of papers and essays on various theoretical aspects as they turned up in the course of dealing with my sources. There was the question of evaluation, of mostly undefined but widely accepted though often contradictory norms in Japanese literary criticism.[1] This led to a more thorough study of the principles guiding *bungaku kenkyū* in Japan[2] and invited inquiries into further aspects such as the concept of tradition, a subject which I treated in a paper prepared for our EAJS conference in Florence,[3] and the question as to how matters of theoretical concern are dealt with in Japanese academia, exemplified by way of analyzing a recent *ronsō* between two literary historians.[4]

The writing of literary history poses a whole array of particularly complex problems, but we may well assume that they lie at the core of the study of literature as a whole, comprising those of the other two very popular - as a matter of fact, much more popular - 'genres' in *Kokubungaku kenkyū*, that are biographical studies labelled 'sakkaron' and textual analyses, so-called 'sakuhinron' which make up the bulk of the output.

Let us assume first of all a broad consensus on the necessity of literary history apart from or in addition to the study of single works or authors, and let us also try to define the objective of such a literary history as the attempt at describing the historical character of aesthetic structures, their functions in history and their relative autonomy as well as their development under the aspect of production, reception and impact (*Wirkung*) as part of the overall history of a 'culture.' This history can only be understood as an ensemble of elements which are mutually interdependent, and our aim is to recognize the ways in which individuals, society and culture interact.

On the other hand we must not forget that history, and literary history as well, is a construction which cannot be grasped empirically as a natural phenomenon but is constituted as a result of our scientific approach.[5] Strictly speaking, the object of our research comes into existence only in the process of it, but this process presupposes a model of cognisance.

What do these very theoretical-sounding statements mean in the case of Japanese literary history? First of all, they lead us to the simple observation that all the existing concepts, the so-called schools or *ryūha* as well as the diachronic groupings in the form of literary generations or other typologies, do not possess the status of facts such as the texts themselves but are constructs, so to speak, which structure our view of what we thereby learn to see as literary history. Take, as an example, the history of post-war Japanese literature which is commonly divided into a sequence of six or seven generations. Their labels are the 'First' and the 'Second Post-war Group' (*Dai ichiji, dainiji sengoha*), the 'Third New Generation' (*Dai san no shinjin*), followed by a grouping named after the title of a magazine, i.e. '*Ningen to shite*' (As a human being) or alternatively, after an edition of literary works under the title of '*Warera no bungaku.*' The fifth group carries the name of '*Naikō no sedai,*' the 'generation of introversion,' and the sixth one goes under the name of '*Kūkyo no sedai,*' the 'generation of the void.' Although there are some variations in the naming and some historians may insist on several sub-groups, the overall pattern of such a division into a quick sequence of generations is widely agreed upon. This may be astonishing in face of the fact that these labels in many cases were nothing more than convenient ad hoc constructions.

In his article in the January 1953 number of '*Bungakukai*' which introduced the '*Dai san no shinjin*' writers as a grouping to the public, Yamamoto Kenkichi frankly admits that he has no idea what this 'third' means but simply meets the wishes of the editorial committee who asked him to write about newcomers under this title.[6] Our astonishment at Yamamoto's compliance in accepting a label which apparently does not make sense to him will be modified when we regard the fact that this label was not only accepted without discussion by the contemporary public but meanwhile has advanced to be one of the most widely agreed-on groupings in the whole of post-war literary historiography. Practically no literary history dealing with this period dispenses with this name.

In the face of the diverse genesis and the casualness of these groupings, we should not be surprised at the severe contradictions and deadlocks which this periodization may lead to. I have hinted at some of the problems elsewhere,[7] but here I want to confine myself to the purely theoretical level of the problem which consists in 'comparing apples and pears,' to use another German idiomatic expression. The fundamental weakness of this periodization lies in the mixture of generic principles, of arranging some groups according to pure numerical succession (the first, second and third) and others according to media of publication or thematic criteria which were originally employed in a critical sense.

Should we then do away with this periodization altogether? This is a question which cannot be answered easily. We will surely have to ask ourselves what the descriptive value of this generational model is. Does it really enhance our understanding of the development of post-war literature or does it purely serve as a convenient system of drawers in which literary historians stow away each and every writer and work? Undoubtedly, there is a good amount of obsessiveness in many of these descriptive frameworks. Take for example the tendency throughout generations of critics to form triads, the so-called *sanpa teiritsu*, for which Tsuge Teruhiko furnishes a recent example by speaking of the 'troika in Japanese literature of the Eighties:' In my understanding, his three groups, which are 1) women writers of the Seventies, 2) male writers of *'Naikō no sedai,'* and 3) writers that were born after the war, clearly overlap,[8] and I see no immediate advantage of coming up with such a scheme. On the other hand, the necessity of finding common traits, of detecting structures and of abstractions cannot be denied, and this will naturally lead to giving names and constructing a framework of explanation. In doing so, however, we should always make sure that the criteria are compatible, so as to avoid comparing apples and pears, and at the same time be aware that every system and framework bears the tendency to shut out anything that does not seem to fit into it. We will therefore have to be sensitive enough to realize whenever our framework blocks our view instead of sharpening it.

Another problem of literary historiography is the question of terminology in general. Everyone who is acquainted to some extent with modern Japanese literature, which naturally includes a certain experience with Japanese presentations of its history, will have come across a fairly huge number of names for genres, sub-genres, schools and styles. These names seem to function as technical terms, but as such, many of them are problematic, being only loosely defined notions which may owe their formation to all kinds of coincidences. Again, one could argue that as long as these notions are accepted and circulate in Japan, there is no need to question them, but I should rather suggest that they are handled with a sound scepticism, too. The sheer amount of these terms, for one thing, nourishes the suspicion that their 'invention' was fostered, first of all, by a penchant for pigeon-holing on the part of the historian him- or herself who is victim to the illusion that one has a grasp on the matter once it is given a name. Yet we should not cease to ask whether generic terms such as *'madamu mono'* (stories of bar-hostesses) or *'byōsai mono'* (stories of sick wives), to pick random examples, really enhance our understanding of the phenomenon or whether they simply classify the obvious for classification's sake.

The case is easier when we are confronted with what I tentatively call programmatic terms, designations for literary groups or movements which originated in their very environment. Thus, *'Shirakaba-ha'* is a completely unproblematic term, and so is *'Shizenshugi'* for Japanese naturalism, a term which relates to the orientation of a number of writers at the beginning of this century towards what they understood as naturalism notwithstanding the individual differences in their interpretation and the distortions vis-à-vis the European concept. (But then we have to admit that naturalism in Europe is a fairly multi-faceted phenomenon, too). Problems only arise when 'programmatic' terms are paired with analytical or descriptive terms of a completely different genesis to form a comprehensive framework which subsequently functions as an explanatory scheme. We easily overlook that this screen may consist of partly incompatible elements insofar as these belong to different levels of speech or discourse.

I will cut short my rough sketch of problems of periodization and terminology here, prepared as I am to face the question as to why the discussion had to be so dry and theoretical. Why not do away with all this talk of methods and methodology altogether and stick to facts which are much more certain and reliable than windy theoretical stuff? The answer is that in our field, there are no given facts such as natural phenomena. Our objects only exist in the form of being interpreted objects. Thus, the questions which I touched upon are nothing but examples, surface phenomena, so to speak, of our subject which has much larger and more complex dimensions. I could have come up with other practical problems of historiography instead, for example, with the notion of literature, namely the question of what to regard as literature and what to exclude from it. (Recent Japanese research, possibly due to Western influence where this tendency can be observed since the late Sixties, has widened its notion of 'bungaku' to include a larger portion of mass-literature and of non-fictional genres than before). Then there is the problem of evaluation and of how to define the interrelationship between literature, society and culture in general. All these questions relate to each other on a more abstract level, and what makes them peremptory for us is the fact that we have to answer them before we start to write, or to be more exact: we are indeed furnishing our answers in the process of our work, whether we are conscious of it or not.

This observation is, of course, far from being new or original, and what is more - if Japanese Studies are a discipline situated on the crossing point between Japanese 'kenkyu' and the respective field in our own scientific tradition, then we are destined to be more sensitive to the unconscious decisions and the culturally bound presuppositions which inevitably colour research in the humanities.

Writing Japanese literary history, of course, means reconstructing the Japanese system of values and of anticipations in which the literary corpus is embedded and showing how it functions within the system of literary communication. I may sound paradoxical but it makes sense nevertheless that this form of literary history (which differs distinctly from that breathless enumeration of literary schools supplemented by short biographies of authors and summaries of works that make up the bulk of what is being treated as literary history at present) will greatly profit from this heightened consciousness on the part of the literary historian. The more sensitive we are towards the difference between our own criteria and the Japanese ones, the sharper our analysis can be, and only if we judge Japanese literature on its own terms without unconsciously mixing other, basically alien ones into it, can our analysis be insightful and fair. Our view from outside which makes us relativize both perspectives, that of the Japanese and our own, will, however, also make us more sensitive towards what I termed the 'hermeneutical innocence' of an opinion like the following one by a Japanese researcher who maintains that a major writer's position will never falter no matter how much new material may be detected about him or her.[9] No other historian should keep us from taking a new look for ourselves at seemingly well-known objects. Evaluations are, as we know, not given facts - they are subject to new evidence as well as to changing norms, and thus are part of history themselves.

Our outsider perspective may also lead us to propose new approaches to the description of Japanese literary history. The reconstruction of the system of literary communication and the role of the individual versus collective aesthetics, of conflicting norms and persisting values could be inspired by a closer analysis of *ronsō*, those literary feuds which have accompanied the development of modern Japanese literature in every phase. Other more sociologically inclined questions from *enquêtes* on reader response to research on literary prizes will also further our understanding of literary history if they are being related to the overall model of literary communication which forms the basis of our description. Needless to say, this focus will not do away with individual works and authors but will only help us to see them in the proper perspective. Again, the individual achievement can be judged better against the horizon of the collective performance.

The reason why I felt it meaningful to touch on these questions again, or to serve cold coffee, so to speak, has to do with a recent development in our field. Japanese literary studies are increasingly absorbing new Western approaches and their vocabulary. This, too, is nothing new as they have always done so, but as the Japanese mode of reception tends to be accumulative rather than exclusive, we must be prepared to meet even more layers of new discourse alongside the traditional concepts of description and analysis. At the same time, non-Japanese scholars have begun to apply new approaches, theories and methods to the study of Japanese literature, and it seems that at long last research in and outside Japan is beginning to coincide to a greater degree than ever before.

In the face of this welcome new development, we should, however, remain alert towards the dangers of eclecticism. Applying new methods from structuralism down to deconstructivism can be really exciting, and if reverberations of these theories are even reflected however faintly in the Japanese critical discourse, we may feel euphorically safe and sound. Let us remain critical, though, towards all conceptions no matter where they originated while applying them with good scholarly common sense. Only then will we be able to handle not only the many theoretical pitfalls that are waiting along the way, but also be prepared for a meaningful dialogue within the field, across the border that has so far separated the study of Japanese literature inside Japan, or '*kokubungaku*,' our 'mother discipline,' from our *Nihon bungaku kenkyū*.

13

The Problem of Time in Japanese Literature

MIKOLAJ MELANOWICZ

In 1985 I saw the original of Kurosawa Akira's film *Ran,* which is not easily rendered into French or English. In Japanese the word *ran* means 'disorder', 'turmoil', 'destruction', as well as 'chaos' or 'war'. A few days later I went to admire paintings by Roberto Matta in Paris. One of the works by this great surrealist is called 'Les puissances du desordre', or 'The Powers of Confusion', and depicts an irrational force driving things towards confusion, towards decomposition, destruction. 'Matta's space is the space in constant movement, bifurcation, decomposition. The ejecting, plural space. The space with traits of time: it flows away and gets incessantly divided into subtle particles' - wrote the Mexican poet Octavio Paz in 'Vestibule', the text accompanying the exhibition.

These observations by Octavio Paz bring to mind a well-known painting by Pieter Bruegel entitled 'The Triumph of Time', saturated with symbols of the passing of the confused, somewhat chaotic present moment.[1]

In *Ran* Kurosawa utilizes a dimension that is a unity of time and space, a *sui generis* 'time-space'. In a very precise manner he constructs two such 'time-spaces', namely the dimensions of harmony and order among people, and also between people and nature. This part of the film is followed by the presentation of the process of transformation and reaches the 'time-space' stage of destruction; time is inseparable from space. Both parts of the film are aspects of the same phenomenon, adequately named by the Greek-rooted word 'chaos'. It is monistic dimension, merging qualities of time and space into unity.[2]

* * *

The Japanese approach to the concept of time can in no way be isolated from the South-East Asian cultural sphere. It was soon after Christ - if not before his time - that Japan became part of the area strongly influenced by the cultures of India, China and Korea. Japan received and accumulated values and impulses from foreign cultures but had no way of conveying them farther. The Japanese archipelago was receiving human achievements in their transformed state: Indian influences, for example, were being

80

remoulded in China, and often once again in Korea, before they reached Japan.

In India, more so than in China, the interests were focused on the spiritual sphere, first of all the so-called philosophical fiction. Both currents of thinking about the world, that is both types of human attitudes, the Indian and the Chinese ones, were confronted at the dynamic moment when Buddhist writings were translated from Sanscrit into the old Chinese. Buddhist canons along with elements of the old Indian culture were reshaped in the process of translation - Chinese realities were taken into account, thus allowing Chinese intellectuals to adopt the new religion.

The next stage of transmission to Korea in the fourth century and then to Japan in the sixth century would not have come about without the role of translators, or in fact their contribution; their inventiveness was indispensable to create new terms and epithets. They stemmed from a different understanding of similar phenomena, or from trying to fit foreign and not always clear texts into their own world and experience.

The extent to which Buddhism changed on Japanese soil has become a testimony to the existence of Japanese characteristics, of national characteristics, of the national character, i.e. ways of thinking and feeling about the surrounding realities and foundations of evaluation, of hierarchies. However, how does one tell the original Japanese from the imported Chinese or Korean elements of the approach to time? Perhaps one should first define the concept of time in the Indian Buddhist sense, then in the Chinese and Korean ones, and also in other religious and philosophical systems that influenced Japanese thought. It would be a tedious undertaking.

In order to describe the Japanese treatment of time, one ought to consider various intellectual trends, not forgetting interrelationships and interdependencies like the combination of Buddhism and Shintoism in the so-called *ryōbu shintō*. It is next to impossible now to reconstruct the attitude towards time in the pre-Buddhist era.

Therefore, we shall begin searching for the specifically Japanese understanding of time as found in literature of the court culture in the tenth and eleventh centuries. Then we shall proceed to a philosophical and religious treatise written by Dōgen (1200-1253), a master of Zen. Both the novel and the works by Dōgen and other Zen masters had a paramount importance in the formation of Japanese patterns of thinking and experiencing the world, and the Japanese concept of time.

★　　★　　★

In *The Tale of Genji*, considered to be the most representative work of the matured culture of the court aristocracy, one fairly frequently comes across the word *aware*, in various word clusters. Less often the noun *kaisō* (memory, recollection) is found. Both of these words or, more correctly, the emotional states evoked by them, are linked with the concept of *mujō* - the instability or impermanence of things. The notion dominates the characters' attitudes. It unambiguously defines the heroes' interpretation of time.

The above terms stand for basic units, mutually dependent and describing various aspects - or perhaps degrees and stages - of the perception of the world. Having the right idea of the meaning may help to reconstruct the concept of time in aristocratic circles of tenth century Japan. Let us recall how *aware* was explained by Ivan Morris, author of *The World of the Shining Prince*:

> The gamut of its use in Heian literature is extremely wide.(...) its most characteristic use in *The Tale of Genji* is to suggest the pathos inherent in the beauty of the outer world, a beauty that is inexorably fated to disappear together with the observer. Buddhist doctrines about the evanescence of all living things naturally influenced this particular content of the word, but the stress in *aware* was always on direct emotional experience rather than on religious understanding. *Aware* never entirely lost its simple interjectional sense of 'Ah!'[3]

The term often appears in the phrase *mono no aware*, which is roughly an equivalent of *lacrima rerum* (the pathos of things). Nevertheless, it does not mean sad feelings only. '*Aware* is born when man can tell a difference in the sense of things and knows their essence. Therefore, *mono no aware* is impossible unless the person faces "the essence of existence". With this in mind, *mono no aware o shiru*, or gettong to(know) *mono no aware* signifies the ability to realize the essence of existence (of things) in the process of experiencing.'[4]

What, then, is this 'essence' of existence? The characters in *The Tale of Genji*, when facing a landscape, things that surround them, or other people, not only perceive the beauty of the world but also give way to reminiscence. Seeing the moon in a certain quarter, a flower of wistaria or a bindweed they return to the past. Autumns and springs keep coming back, but moments and events lived through become more and more distant and they cannot reappear with a new season. They can only be recalled in memory (*kaisō*) and exist in the present moment, right in the middle of now (*nakaima*), here and now. Quiet musing, contemplative immersion in this unique moment, the awareness of change in man's life and surroundings - in spite of the natural periodicality - are indispensable conditions for the emergence of emotions which in *The Tale of Genji* are called 'the pathos of things ' or *mono no aware*. Recollecting the past usually implies melancholy. In this sense recollection, or memory (*kaisō*) is activity containing grains of emotional ecstasy, that is to say, *aware*. The point is that '*kaisō*-memory' is not just reaching back to the past - it is directing the past to the present. It all takes place in the mind of man, wandering between the recalled past and present. The past makes it possible to look at the present in a new way. The present sheds new light onto the past. The hero of *The Tale of Genji* perceives - in this process of wandering between the past and present - and almost painfully feels the passage of years and months. His sigh ('ah,' 'oh,' 'aware') transforms into other words, in *mono no aware*. Therefore, *aware* accompanying reminiscence is an act of realizing time as an outflowing dimension, vanishing, never to come back. In the world of the senses and nature the time is revealed in movement, in changes and transformations. One may then say that *aware* is awareness of the constant volatility of life.

This eternal repetition, the seasonal nature of natural phenomena allows the characters in *The Tale of Genji* to see the new aspect of time, reflecting the changes in things and people. They experience deeply and directly the changeability inseparable from the irrevocable passing of things. The realization of this truth is not a matter of a moment; it spreads over a period of time. Simply, the moment of contact with an object gives rise to the feeling that attaches man to this particular fragment of reality, and causes that man to experience the moment which also contains memories, as if beyond the natural passage of time. This is the moment of breaking the psychical ties with the cycles of time, with the seasons and seasonal rituals. In *The Tale of Genji* this happens when a relative or friend goes away for good. The acute sorrow after the death of a beloved person makes the living ones lose touch with reality. The hero's sight actually gets blurred after the death and funeral of Murasaki, or the loss of the friend, Kashiwagi. There is a break, a lack of contact with 'natural' time. When the pain subsides, the hero returns to 'natural' time. And then he painfully notes the speed of the days' passing.

The peculiar relationship between the 'natural' and the 'human' time brings us to the concept of *mujō* - 'impermanence' - and *mujōkan*, the feeling of impermanence as a *sui generis* philosophy of life.

Literally, *mujō* means 'im-permanence', 'in-durability', and more or less the same as *tsune nashi* ('it is not so that anything is for ever, always'), *sadamenashi* (there is no constancy), *hakanashi* (ephemeral), or even *tsuyu* (dew).

In turn, *mujōkan* is the feeling of impermanence of things and people. It is doubtless a Buddhist term. Quickly adopted, it covered the whole range of emotions concerning impermanence experienced by the Japanese before the sixth century. That is, before the Buddhist books were known. *Mujōkan* became a key word used to define and describe the essence of existence, and in the late Middle Ages, in the thirteenth and fourteenth centuries, it was a philosophical, ethical and aesthetic category. *The Tale of Genji*, though, is the first literary work to show how this concept of impermanence of being influences the attitudes of characters. The concept of *mujō* provides philosophical background to the emotional way of experiencing the world, that is expressed as *mono no aware*.

Reading Genji we notice that everything that was said before comes into the clearly defined sphere of man's work and emotions. This sphere is *miyako* - the space created by man. In this sense the space is artificial. Nature was brought to the city of Heian, it was shaped and tamed there and only then its beauty and 'tenderness' were admired as natural. It was believed there was harmony between human life and nature so formed.

Along with this 'artificial nature ' there existed the 'artificial' time brought into being by way of human conventional activities, like annual celebrations. The natural, physical time was so abstract that it was never noticed.

What the hero of *The Tale of Genji* perceives very clearly, and what he thinks important, are the seasons (*shiki*). The seasons are observed through the facts of cherry's blossoming, birds' singing or cicada's chirping. However, the deepest sense of the passage of the seasons is rendered by the participation in traditional, ritual or aesthetic acts. That is how the heroes remember the past seasons. This 'time-space' is the place for the drama of passing, for the ecstatic performance evoked by the beauty of the impermanent world. So, in *The Tale of Genji* time is a current of emotional experience of the volatile show of life, and the process of contemplation of 'impermanence' as the fundamental category of being. In both cases it happens at a particular moment of the present time, sometimes involving past events. It is characteristic that the future is of slight interest for the hero.

*   *   *

The thirteenth century brought about political changes. The aristocracy lost its position and the samurai came to power. Among them, the Buddhist meditative teachings were gathering disciples. Most of them were attracted to Zen. At the same time, a new ethos was shaped from the processes of recognizing concrete reality, with a conscious contribution to life. The masters of Zen never forgot about *mujō*-impermanence, and this notion was vital for the world outlook of monks, the samurai, aristocracy, and probably other social spheres, too. The Zen thinkers also kept in mind the basic thesis of *The Tale of Heike*, as pronounced at the beginning of the book:

> The sound of the Gion Temple bell
> resounds with things' impermanence,
> and the shara tree, blossoming,
> heralds this in the colour of its flowers:
> that whatever flourishes
> is destined to decay.[5]

Master Dōgen in one of his poems expressed the rythm of the passing of cyclical time:

> In spring the flowers
> in summer the cuckoo
> the moon in autumn
> and snow in winter
> bright and cool.

Dōgen did not present any new approach to time. He only spoke emphatically about what had always been the crux of Japanese time-oriented rites and reflections.

Nevertheless, the meditative sect of Zen, best represented by Dōgen, was conducive to more thorough analysis of time as a dimension entirely contained in the present. Even before, in the court period, the present - as a frontier between the past and the future - was a subject of reflection and the tenor of expression of the experience of the present, mingled with the elements of the past. In the Middle Ages the Zen philosophers saw salvation - *satori*, enlightenment - as dependent on man's own effort of searching for the Truth. They never suggested counting on any help from the outside, as was the case with those who worshipped Amida.

Since so much depends on man's own activity, the significance of the present is also enhanced. The activity of work always takes place here and

84

now. Thence, man has nothing but time - writes Dōgen - and only upon the condition that he makes creative use of it. As opposed to other religious sects and Buddhist intellectual currents, Dōgen's vision of the state of Buddha, that is the State of Enlightenment, is not static but goes with human endeavours. Life, then, is just activity, and Zen is a discipline of creative work.

According to *Shōbō genzō zuimonki*, or 'Notes In Keeping With What Was Said' - Collection of Teachings for True Law, Dōgen once quoted the following anecdote, relating to time:

> An ancient master said:
> we should not waste time.
>   Therefore, I ask you: does the saving of time lead to stopping its passage? Or is the passage of time uncontrollable? One must understand that it is not time that elapses in vain, but people simply waste it. The words by the ancient Zen master warn us not to waste time and encourages us to improve our way to Buddha. Therefrom comes but one conclusion for us - we should enter this Way of Enlightened Buddha.[6]

Dōgen writes about the so-called *yūji* (*aru toki*), or 'the time that is.' And he says: when cherry flowers blossom, the spring comes; not the other way round. The cherry does not blossom because of spring. When the flower blossoms, the world comes into being. It is the moment of the flower blossoming, of the wind blowing, the moon shining over a bay, green pine twigs swinging. These are instances of becoming and acting, of emergence of the things and phenomena. They are instances of the act of creation of things. All this is also the creation of time. This concept of time identifies it with the symptoms of movement and activity. For man, it exists only if it is filled with action, work. Perhaps, this is the most valuable seed of the Japanese concept of time.

Both in artistic and philosophical thought, and in literature, the only aspect of time that is treated seriously is 'this moment,' or the present. 'Now' is most essential. As early as in the *Record of Ancient Things* (*Kojiki*, 712) we can find the ideogram for the abstract notion of *nakaima*, or 'the middle now,' 'in the middle now,' or maybe the Elliotan 'this moment in time': let us add 'the time of today.' In this connection Yamada Takao[7] develops the philosophy of *nakaima* - this 'now as the middle.' He even uses this concept in an educational paper commissioned by the Ministry of Education during World War II. It was entitled '*Kokutai no Hongi*, 'The Real Meaning of the Fundamental National Traits.' Yamada goes as far as saying that 'down in the roots of our history flows the eternal now.'[8]

The dozen or so centuries of the history of Japanese thought shaped the concept and the social attitudes towards time as first of all the present, tantamount to action. In this sense the Japanese were forerunners of 'the philosophy of the present' (cf G. H. Mead, *Philosophy of the Present*) and now they are becoming the first in this epoch to sustain such a consistent attitude. They now enjoy the results of their efforts, the efforts without which time does not exist for either individuals or society.

14

Chaos or Coherence?

SATŌ HARUO'S NOVEL *DENEN NO YŪUTSU* AND
YU DAFU'S TRILOGY *CHENLUN*[1]

KURT W. RADTKE

The title 'Chaos or Coherence?' does not only refer to problems of novelistic structure and plot, but also to the central theme of both novels, the state of mind of an alienated hero.

It is true that both novels do not easily fit simplistic concepts of novels with a 'coherent plot.' The evaluation of novels that *seem* to lack a 'coherent' plot has always been problematic. It is a problem that faces us not only when dealing with non-Western literature, when we cannot presume acceptance of Western genre definitions.[2] It is a problem that also exists within traditional European literature where Russian novels, for instance, have enjoyed a reputation for having a weak plot. As P. Waddington observed:

> For Turgenev - as for most great Russian writers - characters were more important than plot. He chose his subject, related it to realistic characters, and allowed the situations to develop naturally in his mind as he elaborated the setting in which he would place them.[3]

Likewise, Yu Dafu ranked 'mood' before plot and character.[4] This is how Lee Ou-fan described Yu's short story *Caishi ji* (The Cliff of Coloured Rock):

> The story is typical of many of Yu's short fictional works, with its multilayers of past and present woven into one impressionistic whole, its lingering invocations of mood arrested in time, its fragmentary threads of memories which undulate with the slow progression of the plot - or non-plot - and finally its very anecdotal and incomplete quality.[5]

'Chaos or coherence?' is also a way to describe the mental state of the protagonists in our two novels, and furthermore, it is an apt way to refer to the intellectual climate of both China and Japan in the period following the intrusion of European powers and the United States in the affairs of East Asia since the middle of the nineteenth century.

> The petroleum... started burning. It burned nervously. The way it burned resembled the state of excitement of a man like himself - without any mental unity whatsoever.[6]

86

Anticipating one of my conclusions I believe that the true focus of both writers is not merely on the history of psychological disorder of the protagonists or even their inability to establish 'normal' human relationships throughout these novels, the breakdown of the stable social order of the past keeps lurking in the background, the breakdown of a traditional value system that caused anguish and anxiety both at the individual and the national level. While it is fairly easy to demonstrate this point for a novel like Yu Dafu's *Chenlun* it is perhaps not so obvious in the case of Satō's novel *Denen no yūutsu*.[7]

Guren shuo de bu gu, bi you lin.

> Our ancient forefathers said that he who maintains moral values will never be isolated, and he will have somebody next to him. These days, however, it is the opposite way. Those who urge others to cease warring for the sake of peace are thrown into prison. Those who expose justice on behalf of the workers for a morally just order are sentenced to hard labour. Those who oppose the unreasonable legal system of the state are burned.[8]

Yu Dafu focuses on the general breakdown of value systems in China: Confucianism is not relevant any more; Christianity is hardly a viable alternative. Yu Dafu's attitude towards (Christian) religion is at best ambiguous, but among the foreign (or native) belief systems referred to in *Chenlun* Christianity occupies a predominant position.[9] Rather than claiming that Yu Dafu leaves it to the reader to apply moral judgement to the action of protagonists in his novels it seems more appropriate to say that his novels illustrate a conspicuous lack of a firm moral, philosophical or religious framework in Chinese society of those days. This is one of the sources of 'alienation' in Yu Dafu's novels. Throughout *Chenlun* we find a lack of sincerity in the character of the protagonists which precludes a serious discussion on the merits and demerits of one or the other value systems.[10] Satō Haruo's novel, *Denen no yūutsu* likewise focuses on 'alienation', and despite obvious differences it is in this respect that both novels become truly comparable. Both novels take psychological disorders, the result of alienation and disturbed human relations, as the central theme.[11]

The alienation of the central figures in both novels is closely linked to changes in the social, political, economic and cultural fabric. These changes did not only bring chaos to society as a whole, they were also reflected in the state of mind of individuals. We should guard against the simplified view that such alienation is simply the result of 'Westernization', and therefore quite similar. One of the main topics in *Denen no yūutsu* is the chasm between 'original nature', 'nature transformed by man' and modern 'man-made' society; nature is perceived indirectly through art, but nature does not offer the salvation sought. For Satō, nature is not a refuge, nor the 'home' (*furusato*) to which one yearns to return like the archetypal Urashimatarō. The increasing mental problems of the protagonist lead us to doubt the healing forces of nature. Right from the beginning of *Denen no yūutsu* there are also various hints about the destructive forces in nature. [12] The lack of a *moral* order in nature appears more reminiscent of Taoist ways of thinking than the moralistic Confucian approach.[13] In *Chenlun*, too, the hero seeks consolation in nature, but in vain. We may add that a comparison of both novels is also interesting because of the relative closeness of *Chenlun* to the Japanese taste which has made it quite well known in Japan.[14] From the point of view of literary history, finally, it seems necessary to consider a reevaluation of these novels that, for various reasons, have been consistently underestimated by most critics of Chinese and Japanese literature. Although Lu Xun's 'lyric short stories' *Guxiang* (Home) and *Shexi* presented a veritable breakthrough, Yu Dafu's novel *Chenlun* published in October 1921 was the first *novel* after China's modern 'literary revolution'.[15] Like Yu Dafu's trilogy *Chenlun*, Satō Haruo's novels, in particular *Denen no yūutsu* have been frequently ignored in surveys of modern Japanese literature.[16] In the case of Yu Dafu this is probably the result of the attitude of Chinese critics who are not prepared to tolerate deviations from a narrowly defined path of political and moral demands.[17] *Denen no yūutsu* is all too easily identified with clichés such as 'romantic' and 'poetical' (after all, the novel has been called a poem in prose *sanbunshi*.[18] The importance of Yu Dafu's novel as a pathbreaker in modern Chinese literature, and the question of Japanese influence, in particular that of *Denen no yūutsu*, is one of the reasons for a thorough reevaluation of both novels in Asian literary history.

There are thus some good reasons for a comparative study of *Chenlun* and *Denen no yūutsu*. We may also refer to Yu Dafu's admiration for Satō's novels, and also the existence of direct influence. Yu Dafu greatly admired Japanese writers of the I-novel such as Kasai Zenzō and in particular Satō Haruo.[19] Let us once more return briefly to the question of the breakdown of the traditional order in Japan and China. First of all 'Westernization' - or, to use a term I prefer 'modernization' - proceeded in quite different ways and under different conditions in Japan and in China, and, at least equally important, these changes took place at quite different speeds (we may recall that such differences are partly responsible for different social and political developments in European countries as well.)

Secondly, we should keep in mind that the pre-modern value systems of Japan and China were not identical, despite the common Confucian heritage. If used uncritically terms such as 'Confucianism' can obscure, rather than elucidate specific characteristics of various 'Confucian' Asian societies. With regard to national literatures we should also keep in mind that differences in the social position of the writer versus society also influenced the attitude of writers, and by the same token the shape of their literary works.

China's modern literature was truly creative when her writers acted and behaved not as slaves of one or the other political master, but as guardians of the moral conscience of the nation. Such an attitude need not be reflected in literature that was outright 'political,' as long as it remained relevant to the chaotic changes occurring in China. The Chinese writer lived in a society that was irrevocably being destroyed. The same cannot be said of the Japanese writer: while the early Meiji period was also dominated by the mood of 'chaos reigning' he was surrounded by a society which despite all turbulence and rapid social changes preserved more than just a bare minimum of social coherence and cohesion. It is true to say that altogether Japanese literature has an a-political tendency, a penchant towards escape from politics,[20] but this does not necessarily imply that writers are *not* aware of social and other changes, or that such changes are not reflected in their writings. The penchant towards *relativism* in such a period easily reinforces latent traditional Buddhist tendencies to view values and 'aims' as essentially void.[21]

'Alienation' is a constant phenomenon in any dynamic and changing society; the 'quality' of this alienation cannot be viewed in isolation from the context in which it is produced, from the past, the present and also the apprehension that accompanies vague fears about an uncertain future. By the end of the nineteenth century, 'traditional' feelings of anxiety and frustration characteristic of European romanticism were being replaced by an awareness that the values that had inspired - and had lent sanctity to - the often suicidal fate of the romantic hero were also becoming irrelevant.

> 'Ach,' sagte die Maus, 'die Welt wird enger mit jedem Tag, Zuerst war sie so breit, dass ich Angst hatte, ich lief und war glücklich, dass ich endlich rechts und links in der Ferne Mauern sah, aber diese langen Mauern eilen so schnell aufeinander zu, dass ich schon im letzten Zimmer bin, und dort im Zimmer steht die Falle, in die ich laufe.' - 'Du musst nur die Laufrichtung ändern,' sagte die Katze und frass sie. (Kafka) [Mann, *Deutsche Literaturgeschichte*, p. 546].

The sphere of a narrowing and threatening world is not unique to Kafka, a European Jew; with all necessary reservations I do see parallels to the narrowing world of the protagonist in *Denen no yūutsu* whose world is scattered and destroyed by increasingly severe mental disorders. I should like to recall once more that the character, and the speed of social developments that formed the background for German and French romanticism differed significantly from developments during the Meiji period in Japan; for this reason alone it seems inappropriate to expect Japanese writers who give themselves labels such as 'naturalistic' or 'romantic' to merely copy certain Western literary currents; the same caution is required in tracing the influence of modern Japanese literature on Chinese writers.[22]

Rather than attempting a 'one by one' comparison of *Denen no yūutsu* and *Chenlun* I wish to illustrate a few selected aspects of these works. According to Xu Zidong there is one decisive difference between *Chenlun* and *Denen no yūutsu*, the fact that Yu Dafu has not 'closed off' the protagonist from his social surroundings (as did Satō in *Denen no yūutsu*). At the same time Satō did influence Yu Dafu in the choice of the topic, literary techniques and a certain similar 'mood' (*qingyun*). Perhaps surprisingly, the influence of 'Japan' on Yu Dafu's trilogy *Chenlun*, *Nanqian* and *Yinhuise de si* does not seem to go much beyond the fact that all three of them are set in Japan.

> It appears that Yu Dafu did not obtain much from Japan, but that he obtained much during his stay in Japan.... The Japanese I-novel sharpened his sensibility.[23]

What else did he learn during his stay in Japan? It is striking to notice that those Chinese writers who went to Japan were much more likely to be infected by 'Western romanticism' than those who were educated in England or the United States.[24]

It is quite questionable to what extent Yu Dafu was consciously aware of the scope of changes to be confronted by China:

> Coming from a country village, he was painfully naïve and ignorant of the hybrid culture in China's large treaty ports.[25]
>
> While times were changing and China was in the jerky process of 'modernization,' Yu Ta-fu's mental world remained traditional. It was only during his years in Japan that he developed a certain 'modern' outlook and imbibed strongly Western literary influences.[26]

Further on we will return to some of these questions in greater detail. Unfortunately, the scope of this paper cannot take in a more detailed discussion of other novels and writings by Yu Dafu and Satō Haruo, in particular Satō's *Tokai no yūutsu*, which in spite of its status as a 'sequel' to *Denen no yūutsu* is quite different, both in its narrative technique and its subject matter, from the latter. *Denen no yūutsu* rarely makes use of devices such as 'interior monologue,' for instance. In fact I am inclined to compare its style to traditional 'surface description' (*heimen byōsha*).[27] There is likewise insufficient room to deal in detail with imagery, symbolism and narrative technique in these novels.[28] I intend to make up for these omissions in an elaborated version of this paper which will be included in a more comprehensive study on changes in modern Chinese and Japanese culture and society.[29] The wholesale importation of Western poetic forms, for example, was made difficult by the relative lack of poetic prosodic patterns such as rhyme.[30]

How should we approach the products of modern Japanese and Chinese literature? Do we have to rely on the 'native' critic - who is obviously better equipped to grasp the value of these works in an intuitive way, based on his literary experience? Do we have to follow the Chinese critic who tends to demand an explicit social and political commitment?

> With modern Chinese writers the task of exposing and reforming glaring national ills assumes such importance that by contrast the exploration of the deeper reaches of the mind can only appear an idle game.[31]

Should we refrain from cold logical analysis in judging Japanese novels? It may be remarked that not only Japanese, but also quite a few French critics exhibit a deep-seated aversion against Anglo-Saxon academic criticism with its threatening array of footnotes. To present a short answer I have no scruples in expressing my own preferences and judgement even on products of a literary tradition that is far removed from my own. On the other hand I would be foolish not to listen to 'the native critic.' At any rate, I do not believe that literary critics should mistake art for science and present their own views in the cloak of scientific truth.

It is perhaps encouraging to remember that we ought not even to feel compelled to take the word of the writer himself as final wisdom. In his later years Satō Haruo commented on *Denen no yūutsu* and claimed that:

This work should be seen as one with a traditional theme deriving from indigenous Eastern literature expressed with literary techniques from contemporary European literature.[32]

Conceptually speaking, Satō here follows an approach that has been very popular in Japan and in China since the middle of the nineteenth century. In essence he returns to the often quoted distinction between a time-honoured 'unchanging' Eastern 'substance' which is aligned with, but not essentially changed, by Western 'techniques'.[33] As will become apparent later on, this assertion by Satō turns out to be quite untenable - we should not even exclude the possibility that the theme of Satō's novel is much more modern than he himself cares to admit.

Likewise, we should not feel constrained by Yu Dafu's own interpretation of *Chenlun*. In his preface to the trilogy *Chenlun* Yu Dafu pointed out that the conflict between the different demands of mind and body (*ling - rou*) is at the centre of the novel. A contemporary critic, Cheng Fangwu discussed this point with Yu Dafu and commented:

> After the appearances of *Chenlun* there were quite a few people who claimed that this work described the clash between mind and flesh (*ling - rou*), I haven't heard anybody until now uttering a different opinion; but is it really a description of a clash between mind and flesh? I have serious doubts about it.... [That the fate of the hero is tragic is] because he demands love, a love that cannot possibly be realized, and definitely not because of some clash between the flesh and the mind.... The other two novels - *Nanqian* and *Yinhuise de si* are also similarly coloured.
>
> I remember when I was in Tokyo, I discussed this observation of mine with Yu Dafu, and it seems he agreed with me. When this book was subsequently published Yu Dafu - I don't know why - wrote in a preface that it was a description of the clash between mind and flesh and sexual demands. Did Yu Dafu put this in on purpose to mislead? Or did he honestly think that way at the time? It's something I don't know. But as far as my [previous] observation is concerned I think that I would be able to obtain this approval.[34]

In contrast with Yu Dafu's novels it is quite striking to observe that sex plays virtually no role in *Denen no yūutsu*. Despite the heavy emphasis on 'psychology', or perhaps more appropriately, the mental state of the protagonist in *Denen no yūutsu* we are hardly told anything about this aspect of the life of the protagonist. This seems to underline that Satō is not so much interested in tracing the complete make up of an individual psyche, but rather a particular phenomenon, in this case alienation. The only dichotomy which is vaguely reminiscent of the typical Western concept of the division between 'mind' and 'body' is in the following reference:

> He [i.e. the protagonist] was a youngster who had the sagacity (*richi*) of an old man and the emotion typical for a youngster, and the willpower of a child.[35]

In an important passage Satō Haruo elaborates on this theme and alludes to an image from the first pages of the novel, the image of the tree that receives its life-sustaining power from nature around it:[36]

Kare jishin no gotoku, hotondo nai to itte ii hodo ni ishi no chikara no otoroete iru mono no ue ni, ishi no chikara no yori tsuyoi ta no ningen no, arui wa kono kūkan ni hishimekiatte iru to iu fukakensekai no supirittotachi no ishi ga, jibun jishin no mono no ijō ni, chikarazuyoku hatarakikakeru to iu koto wa ariubeki koto to shite, kare wa sore o mitomezaru o enai yō ni omotta. seimei to iu mono wa, shūi ni aru subete no mono o kokukoku ni seifuku shi, sore o kutte, sore no naka no chikara o jibun no naka ni kyūin shite, shikamo sore o jūbun ni tōitsu shite iku aru chikara de aru. nikutaiteki ni wa akiraka ni sō de aru. ryōteki ni datte, seishinteki ni datte sō ni chigai nai. sō shite ima ya, ta no mono o kyūshū shi tōitsu suru sayō o motta shinpi na chikara wa, kare kara dandan to otoroete ikitsutsu atta. mushiro kare wa ima made motte iru jiko jishin o kokukoku ni hassan shite iru nomi de atta. kare ga, yami to iu mono wa nani ka sukima naku hishimekiau no mono no atsumari da, sore ni wa jūryō ga aru to kizuita no mo kono toki de aru. konna fū ni shite, kare no kidoairaku ya kyōfu wa, gensekai ni seison shite iru ta no hitobito no sore to wa, mattaku kyōtsū shigatai nanimono ka ni natte itta. kodoku to mui to kono kyōdai wa, jitsu ni kii na chikara o motte iru mono de aru. moshi jibun ga tada, shūdooin ni iru to shita naraba? to kare wa aru toki sō kangaeta.[37]

This similarity is however quite superficial. In a beautiful passage Satō further elaborates on this point:

Sō shite inaka ni mo, tokai ni mo, chijō ni wa kare o yasuraka ni suru rakuen wa doko ni mo nai. nani mo nai. [Tada banyū no tsukurinushi naru kami nomi kokoro no mama ni....] to sonna koto o itte miyō ka. keredomo kare no kokoro wa, kesshite uchikudakarete iru no de wa nakatta. tada shinobite iru dake de aru.[38]

The loss of identity, the absence of meaning in life are presented not as the particular personal problem of the protagonist, but given a wider, philosophical, if not religious dimension.

From another point of view, one might approach both novels as yet another literary treatment of the topic of psychiatric disorders. Satō's interest in this aspect is supported by a passage in *Denen no yūutsu*.[39] The topic as such is interesting precisely because we cannot simply assume that psychiatric disorders, or even 'normal' psychological problems, are structured in the same way in Japan, China, Europe or the United States.

Kato... goes on to discuss a common condition which is designated as 'anthropophobia,' the literal meaning of which is 'fear of people.' The actual meaning of the term, however, is 'fear' that one may give a poor or unpleasant impression of oneself to another person, so that one's relationship may be disrupted, or one will lose another person's favour. 'It is the general opinion of Japanese psychiatrists that the incidence of this condition is significantly higher in Japan than in the West.' '... The non-separation of emotion and intellect, unlike the situation in the West, where a sharp dichotomy can be observed between reason and feeling, or the intellect and emotion.... Nevertheless, the traditional and at times irreconcilable separation of reason and emotion in the West may have predisposed modern man to find it difficult to separate the sexual act from human closeness.'[40]

It is open to debate to what extent the intrusion of Western concepts contributed to the emphasis on 'sex' and the inability to entertain normal human relations in *Chenlun*, and whether the absence of 'sex' in *Denen no yūutsu* might perhaps be simply explained by the fact that Satō does not attach great importance to this factor in the relational problems of the protagonist of *Denen no yūutsu*. As in *Chenlun* Satō's hero is unable to communicate because he is unwilling and unprepared to confide in others.[41] His inability to relate to others is expressed, for instance, in his penchant to view the human face as something ugly.[42] There is no suggestion how the protagonist might be released from his tragic situation, and the novel ends on a dark note. In *Chenlun* the hero is clearly suffering from his self-imposed isolation and yearns for love, but it is questionable whether he always realizes clearly that purely sexual contacts will not solve his problems:

> I don't need knowledge, I don't need fame, I only need a 'heart' that can comfort me, understand me...[43] What I require is love from the other sex![44]

Despite the obvious interest and importance of a detailed comparison of the psychological state of mind of the protagonists in both novels such a comparison goes far beyond the scope of the present paper. Suffice it to say that one of the important differences between them is the relative absence of feelings of self-reproach and guilt in *Denen no yūutsu*, so important in *Chenlun*.[45] It is interesting to speculate that this difference is mainly due to the intrusion of Christian and other Western concepts, not just with respect to Yu Dafu's personal world, but also due to Christian influence among the Chinese élite in general. Whatever the case may be, the fact that the protagonists suffer from psychiatric disorders also affords the writers considerable freedom to lead the readers through a fantastic, allegorical world, which is reminiscent of the role of dreams in Western writers such as Kafka. Although Satō himself had suffered from nervous disorder it is not quite clear whether the history of progressive disorder depicted in *Denen no yūutsu* is due to his personal experience, and his imagination and knowledge derived from the reading of belletristic literature,[46] or whether he was aware of the introduction of Western-style psychiatry in Japan.

> In the West, the individual as represented by 'I' is more of a constant, and is expected to act as such; while in the East, the individual is relatively speaking a function of his human nexus and of nature. Such tendencies result in characteristic personality features which contribute to positive as well as negative consequences in daily life.[47]

Let us suppose for a moment that this statement does in fact apply to writers such as Satō Haruo and Yu Dafu; we might then conclude that a rapidly and drastically changing environment would tend to influence their mental world more thoroughly than in the case of a more 'constant' 'Western' individual. On the other hand, an 'Eastern' individual may react to such changes in a more supple and flexible way. Even if we do not follow this argument we should keep in mind that Japanese and Chinese writers may react to social, cultural and other changes in ways that differ from those experienced in Europe and elsewhere.

China and Japan were confronted with a chaotic array of foreign influences: writers had to cope with an influx of foreign ideas - romanticism, nihilism, symbolism, socialism - that entered their minds through a variety of different channels. It is quite easy to compile impressive lists of foreign writers and literary and philosophical currents that are thought to have influenced our two writers: Rousseau, Turgenev, Tolstoy, Dostoevsky, Wordsworth, Heine, Gissing, Goethe, Tieke, Arnim, Sturm, Nietzsche, Blake, Romanticism, Christianity - it would not be difficult to expand this list considerably. New narrative techniques were studied, images and symbols acquired new functions. The new literature was not born in a void: literature - and especially poetry - is unable to free itself from the past completely, and it would become incomprehensible if it would do so. Ekkehard May has correctly pointed out that the break with tradition in the modern Japanese novel was certainly not a complete one,[48] and this applies to modern Chinese literature as well.[49] It would be difficult to trace in detail how a particular writer was influenced, and to what extent such influence shows up in his works. As in the case of Russian literature, modern West European literary developments were transmitted to other traditions in sometimes quite a circuitous way:

> Only very few of the Russian symbolists had any considerable first-hand acquaintance with the work of their French godfathers, and Edgar Allan Poe had certainly a wider and deeper influence than any single French poet.[50]

In his essay on *Denen no yūutsu* Shimada traced Satō's description of landscapes to D'Annunzio:

> The river that runs in front of the house, the flowering blossoms, the wind, trees, clouds and the living creatures are depicted in detail and shape the *Grundton* (basic mood) of this story (*monogatari*): this kind of nature is neither merely conceptual nor symbolic, its vision has been enriched with sparkle and exhilaration, and that is something that Satō learned from the poetic style of this Italian poet.[51]

While I would not deny the possibility of such an influence, the relative lack of explicit comment on the background scene in *Denen no yūutsu* is quite in consonance with Japanese literary conventions,[52] and contrasts with the accurate description of locality, time, etc. so characteristic for Chinese traditional literature and for *Chenlun* as well.[53] Yu Dafu owes much to traditional techniques in his orderly, clear description of the traditional Chinese desire for 'veracity' and a concern with locality which ought to be seen as a reflection of popular geomantic beliefs that survived until the present day.[54] The way Satō's images acquire symbolic value can perhaps best be compard to techniques known to us from other Japanese writers, such as Nagai Kafū's *Sumidagawa*.[55] Certain groups or 'classes' of images are indicative, sometimes in quite an abstract (but not simply symbolic way) of the state of mind of the protagonist: there are repeated

94

occurrences of images that reinforce the sentiment of 'undefinedness, limitless' such as rivers, streams and 'lines' in landscapes.

> Yu Dafu did not imitate or follow all sorts of literary currents that kept appearing and disappearing, but absorbed and assimilated [various elements], beginning with the tone of the early I-novel and ending with Satō's melancholy and his attitude towards beauty.[56]

Turning to Yu Dafu's description of landscapes in *Chenlun* I would likewise argue that it owes much more to traditional Chinese techniques than to Turgenev and other European writers.[57]

> Yu Dafu knew that the soul of the I-novel lies in its psychological dimension (*xinjing*).... Therefore, it was reasonable for him to neglect aspects of plot and structure. His knowledge of classical poetry led him quite naturally to air his anguish in a relatively limited world of 'scenery' (*jing*) and 'protagonist' (*ren*), 'sentiments' (*qing*) and 'social background' (*shi*), searching and striving for what Kasai Zenzō had called 'an extremely subtle balance between the subjective and the objective.'[58]

Less successful seems Yu Dafu's sometimes chaotic use of quotations from, and allusions to, foreign literature: quotations are frequently used out of context. One cannot avoid feeling that Yu Dafu consciously sought to impress his readers,[59] and that Yu's style is a direct reflection of the transitional and hybrid character of Chinese culture at that time.[60]

Satō Haruo's use of allusions and quotations appears much more controlled.[61] One may in the first place refer to Satō's adoption of the 'Western' image of the 'rose' ('if it is a rose it will flower'). The image of the worm-eaten rose is said to have derived from Blake.[62] It may be correct that Satō's image of the worm-eaten rose is taken from Blake, but the treatment of this image is neither Goethe's nor Blake's.[63]

'Influence' is however not merely limited to the incidental use of allusions and quotations.[64] In some ways *Denen no yūutsu* reminds us of the world of Baudelaire's correspondences:

> La nature est un temple où de vivants piliers laissent parfois sortir de confuses paroles; l'homme y passe à travers des forêts - de symboles qui l'observent avec des regards familiers.

Sōshite, sōbi no iro to kaori to, sate wa ha mo toge mo, sorera no yūshū na musū no shiku no hitotsu hitotsu o hiryō to shite onore no naka ni kumiage suikonde - sorera no utsukushii moji no maboroshi o onore no haigo ni kagayakasete, sono tame ni eda mo tawawa ni naru yō ni omoeru hodo de aru. Sore ga sono hana kara hitoshio no bi o kare ni kantoku saseru no de atta. saiwai de aru ka, iya mushiro hanahadashii fukō de arō, kare no seikaku no naka ni wa kōshita ippan no geijutsuteki inshuu ga hijō ni nebukaku kokoro ni ne o hatte iru no de atta. kare ga jibun no jigyō to shite geijutsu o erabu yō ni natta no mo kono kokoro kara de arō. kare no gejutsuteki na saibun wa konna inshū kara umarete, hijō ni hayaku mezamete ita. ...sorera no koto ga, yagate muishiki no uchi ni, kare o shite kaku made sōbi o aisaseru yō ni shita no de arō. shizen sono mono kara, shin ni seishin na bi to yorokibi o chokusetsuni tsumitoru koto o

95

shirienakatta koro kara, sorera geijutsu no inshū o tōshite, kare wa kono hana ni nomi wa kō shite fukai ai o sasagete kite ita.[65]

And further on the link between 'paroles' and the poet:

> Sono kawari ni wa, hitotsuhitotsu no kotoba ni tsuite wa iroiro na kūsō o yobiokosu koto ga dekita. sore no rei o, iwayuru kotodama o ariari to miru yō ni sae omou koto mo atta. sono toki, kotoba to iu mono ga kare ni wa iishirenai fushigi na mono ni omoeta. ...sorera kotoba no hitotsuhitotsu wa sore jishin de sude ni ningen seikatsu no ichi*DANPEN* de atta. ...Kare wa sono jisho no naka ni aru komaka na sashie o miru koto ni yotte, mada mita koto mo kūsō shita koto mo nai uo ya, jū ya, kusa ya, ki ya, mushi ya, gyorui ya, aruiwa kateiteki na iroiro no kigu ya, buki ya, kodai kara zainin no shokei ni mochiirareta samazama na keigu ya, fune ya, sore no ho no harikata ni tsuite no shuju na kufū ya, kenchiku no bubun nado ni tsuite shiru koto o yorokonda. sorera no kibutsu nado no sasai na katachi ya, dōbutsu ya shokubutsu nado no naka ni wa samazama na *ANJI* ga atta. nakanzuku, ningen jishin ga kufū shita samazama na mono no naka ni wa kotoba no genrei no naka ni aru mono to mattaku onaji yō ni, jinrui no shisō ya, seikatsu, kūsō nado ga michimichite iru no o kanjita - sore wa sugoku *DANPEN* teki ni de wa atta keredomo. Sōshite, kare no kokoro no seikatsu wa sono toki chōdo sorera no *DANPEN* o kangaeru ni sōshita dake no chikara shika nai no de atta.[66] [emphasis added].

The frequent emphasis on a 'fragmentary' way of conceiving the world may lead us to assume a reference to an 'impressionistic' view of the world; it is an approach akin to the one taken by Ishikawa Takuboku:

> ...a poem should be a strict report of events taking place in one's emotional life (for the want of some better term) - a straightforward diary. This means it has to be fragmentary, it can't have unity or coherence.[67]

And yet, there seems to exist a mysterious life-force that promises unity behind apparent chaos. *Denen no yūutsu* thrives on images that express a force of life that exists in the universe, sounds that refer to another reality:[68]

> (The sounds he heard) produced something that was a sort of pleasure, one might be able to call it feelings of lust, which was both instinctive and spiritual (mental) at the same time. Should it have happened in a monastery people might have called it 'bliss' (*hōetsu*).[69]

Let us briefly refer to Hartley's summary of Baudelaire's universe:

> If [the poet] could not change the world around him he would create new worlds from language, worlds that should be no less than the tangible one and that should, indeed, correspond to the most secret rhythms of the universe. ...It follows that when the poet uses a metaphor or even when he simply names an object, he is involving something real. His use of the language is magical, his poems are spell-binding, since they have a reality which comes from their real correspondence with the objects described. The universe has a mystical unity. ...The idea (which was so popular with Baudelaire and other poets in the nineteenth century) of the unity of the arts and also of

the sensations (synaesthesia). The equivalence of colours and sounds of music and poetry, which was to play so large a part in the discussions which went on around the Symbolist movement....[70]

Despite these fascinating parallels between the world of Baudelaire and Satō Haruo we should not overlook the fact that the character of the medium 'language' - which after all is so central to the whole idea of symbolism - is quite different for the French and the Japanese poet. One of the serious problems in adapting romantic and symbolist modes of expression to the exigencies of the Japanese language is its totally different prosodic background, especially when we keep in mind the important role played by 'sound' in European symbolist (and romantic) literature:

> Its vowels are so few in number and variety that they are not suitable for creating rhythm; its pitch is obscure, lacking accent; its words when pronounced are not clearly distinguished from one another and their individual beauty cannot be appreciated; the definitions of the words lack clarity; its vocabulary is limited; and the sounds of the words are such that they do not sufficiently express complicated human emotions.[71]

One is tempted to refer to Japanese food which, at least to the uninitiated foreigner, appears to have a similarly 'weak' taste. Rather than arguing this point on the theoretical level I should like - by way of contrast - to quote Blok's poem 'Na pole Kulikóvom' with its 'heavy' rhythms:

> Na póle Kulikóvom
> Reká raskinulas'. Techót, grustít lenívo
> i móet beregá.
> Nad skúdnoj glínoj zhóltogo obrýva
> v stepí grustját stogá.
> O, Rus' mojá! Do bóli
> nam jásen dólgij put'!
> Nash put' - strelój tatárskoj drévnej bóli
> pronzíl nam grúd'.[72]

Another reason for choosing this poem is to recall the fact that the nationalist undercurrents, or national consciousness that are so much part of *European* romanticism, have hardly a place in the portrait of a 'weak' hero like the protagonist in *Denen no yūutsu*.

> Thus, neither in the countryside, neither in the city, nowhere on earth is there a paradise that would grant him feelings of ease. There is nothing 'only a god [kami] who is the creator of everything [is free to] follow his mind...' he attempted to say. But his heart was definitely not smashed and broken. It was merely withered.[73]

The protagonist in *Chenlun* appears at first to be much closer to the typical European romantic hero, and some critics have indeed drawn a close parallel between the death of Werther in Goethe's *Die Leiden des jungen Werther* and the protagonist in *Chenlun*.[74] In contrast with the 'true' West European romantic hero whose tragic fate is closely linked to his frustrated aspirations both protagonists in *Denen no yūutsu* and *Chenlun* have few genuine aspirations:

Werther's death is his rebellion against despair, for him defeat is more important than an existence by compromise, and here lies his heroism; Yu Dafu's 'hero,' however, surrenders to fate surrounded by feelings of shame and self-pity.[75]

It is the lack of willpower perhaps more than anything else that makes for a similarity in the character of Turgenev's Rudin and the heroes of Yu Dafu and Satō Haruo.[76] Numerous critics have noticed certain similarities with the 'superfluous man' (*lishnij chelovek*) so often portrayed in nineteenth-century Russian literature.[77] Quite apart from the fact that we can hardly imagine this type of 'superfluous man' to appear outside the specific context of Russian society, it is simply incorrect to claim that Turgenev's novel *Dnevnik lishnego cheloveka* (The Diary of a Superfluous Man) aims at describing such a 'type':

Turgenev's chief preoccupation is not, after all, with a 'superfluous man', so much as with an unhappy personal relationship.[78]

This, however, is not identical with the inability of our protagonists to entertain human relationships. Lack of willpower is one aspect; there are other concepts of European romanticism which would be difficult to adapt to the Japanese context:

This attribution of a value to the flow of life is the basic element in romanticism, and Baudelaire pushed it to a greater extreme than it had been carried by the poets more properly called Romantics.[79]

Satō's concept of a force of life appears already on the first pages of *Denen no yūutsu*. It is true that elsewhere Satō has his protagonist refer to Goethe's Faust,[80] and in the passage quoted, by implication also to Goethe's view of such a force. I have, however, doubts whether we may identify Satō's concept with that of Goethe. First of all, we repeatedly encounter references to the 'uselessness' of certain creatures and plants, and also to nature's 'impartiality' which owes much, if not all, to Taoist philosophical concepts.[81] Secondly, nature itself (and not a force 'outside' nature) is portrayed as essentially arbitrary and violent; it is the task of the human mind to superimpose an order on this chaos. In *Denen no yūutsu* this is more clearly expressed in numerous references to the efforts of a gardener who will never 'beat' nature, and who can impose his own order only for as long as he is able to care after his garden.[82] In the mind of the hero in *Denen no yūutsu*, nature is seen in increasingly violent, disruptive and chaotic terms which is also a reflection of the state of mind of the protagonist: he argues that nature (or life) can be tackled only if the human mind superimposes order on it.[83] The divergence of views on nature and 'life force' between *Denen no yūutsu* and the works of Goethe, Baudelaire and others is too pronounced to be ignored.[84]

Both in *Chenlun* and *Denen no yūutsu* nature is initially presented as a safe haven to which one may retreat, where one may find 'salvation'.[85] In both novels the search for salvation in nature ends in utter failure. Also, we should not identify the 'nature' as the idealized opposite of the modern city, which in the modern literature of many countries has given rise to the contrasting images of the modernized (if not Westernized) corrupt urban society and the 'healthy' traditional countryside.[86]

In both novels the image of the 'peasant' appears, and from the repeated references we may infer that the 'peasant' is viewed by both writers as the symbol of traditional patterns of life, still unaffected by the anxieties of modern society.[87] In a passage in *Chenlun* the hero is described meeting a 'peasant' on his walks in the mountains; the hero imagines himself to be Zarathustra, addressing words of Zarathustra to the peasant in his imagination. The important point is, however, that the hero is still compared to the Chinese hermits of the past.[88] Yet the hero in *Chenlun* should definitely not be confused with the traditional recluse, and he is certainly not identical with the figure of a Qu Yuan (or his epigones) who withdrew from society as a sign of (political) protest.[89]

Let us return once more to the topic of alienation, in particular its psychological dimension. Looking at the reasons for the progressive alienation of the hero in *Chenlun*, but also in *Nanqian*, several factors come to our attention; first of all, there is the 'personality factor':

> His parents and relatives all blamed him for lack of constant character.[90]

Secondly, there is the 'family factor': in *Denen no yūutsu* we do not hear much more about the father. His parents reappear only in a short reminiscence towards the end of the novel.[91] In *Chenlun*, the hero consciously severs all existing bonds with his family, apparently in protest against what he feels is the neglect shown to him.[92] He is clearly obsessed with finding a mother figure.[93] In *Nanqian* the loss of the father, lack of love by his mother, and the fact that he received love only from his grandmother is given as the reason for his unbalanced character.[94]

Of particular interest for our discussion is the fact that alienation is not a purely 'accidental', individual predicament; it has not only a psychological, but also a cultural dimension. In *Chenlun*, the sexual obsessions of the hero may at least be partially due to the oppressive and anti-liberal foreign religious school.[95] His cultural background is not merely a mixed Chinese - foreign one; his favourite readings are mainly foreign books by writers such as James Thomson, H. Heine, Leopoldi and Ernest Dowson.[96] In the passage from *Nanqian* quoted above the protagonist is acutely aware of the breakdown of the traditional moral framework. Moreover, the protagonists in *Nanqian* are either unwilling or unable to fulfill the high moral demands of Christianity, an imported foreign creed.[97] The hero's attitude towards sex is, however, also heavily tinged by the traditional Chinese portrayal of women as a treacherous and corrupting force, so noticeable in the novel *Water Margin* (*Shuihuzhuan*), and also referred to in Lu Xun's short story *Ah Q*.[98]

Megalomania, contempt for other human beings and an all-pervasive suspicion against fellow human beings make the hero in *Chenlun* a very unlikely candidate as a forerunner of spiritual and sexual liberation.

While sex plays a central role in Yu Dafu's novel, it seems to have hardly any place in Satō's novel. It should be noticed, however, that virtually all human relations between the protagonists and others described in both novels are contacts with persons of the other sex.[99] Putting it in psychological terms, we may guess that the hero in *Denen no yūutsu* has apparently few, if any problems in separating sexual acts from human closeness, quite in contrast with Yu Dafu's hero who is unable to build up relationships of human closeness due to his overriding obsession with sex.

> ...it is the general opinion of Japanese psychiatrists that the relative incidence of homosexuality is significantly lower in Japan than in Western nations. ...The same observations were noted in Hsu's study of traditional Chinese society.... The reasons for this lack of concern about homosexuality are multiple. But one reason may be the non-separation of emotion and intellect, unlike the situation in the West, where a sharp dichotomy can be observed between reason and feeling, or the intellect and emotion.... Nevertheless, the traditional and at times irreconcilable separation of reason and emotion in the West may have predisposed modern man to find it difficult to separate the sexual act from human closeness.[100]

It has often been claimed that:

> the real theme of the story is Yu's feeling of sexual guilt as connected with national and racial humiliation.[101]

There is a clear tendency - especially by Chinese critics - to interpret *Chenlun* as a political allegory, as a novel of political protest:

> We can observe in his works the social and economic situation which leaves no room for the young generation.[102]
> The search of the hero of *Chenlun* for love cannot at all be separated from his failure in politics, from his concern for the fate of his country.[103]

The central question in interpreting *Chenlun* is whether the protagonist's (unsuccessful) search for love may be taken as a parable for China's equally unsuccessful search for nationhood. It is an interpretation which might be justified by China's long tradition of putting political comment and criticism in the form of stories or poems on unrequited love.[104] There are, however, several indications that such an interpretation may be only partially - if at all- justified. To my mind, the protagonist's psychological problems are to such an extent 'personalized' that an allegorical interpretation seems farfetched.

> The nationalism of Yū Ta-fu in Japan was therefore personal and psychological, not exclusively political or ideological, as has been alleged by some Communist scholars.[105]

It is highly significant that Yu Dafu wrote *Chenlun* during his stay in Japan, and that the hero of *Chenlun* is likewise a student in a foreign country, and that all his girlfriends are Japanese. My interpretation seems supported by the way Yu Dafu portrays the (Japanese) female protagonists in *Chenlun*.[106] Close reading of *Chenlun* reveals that the role of Japan in the novel is mainly that of an alien setting, which contributes even further to his alienation. This is another fact that points to individual alienation as the basic theme of the novel.[107] Most importantly, few critics seem to have paid proper attention to the fact that an essential ingredient in the unfolding plot of *Chenlun* are the progressively increasing mental problems of the hero.[108] It is also highly significant that his illness commenced before his arrival in Japan.[109] There are hardly any hints that the origin of the protagonist's psychiatric problems is specifically connected with political or historical events, as should be expected if the novel were allegorically intended. In one of the few comments on the hero's behaviour it is said in *Chenlun* that his *Chinese* friends thought that he had been affected by mental illness.[110] His suicide is the result of utter alienation, and this is the way his final outcry should be understood.[111] In addition, Yu Dafu's protagonists are unlikely candidates for nationalistic heroes since they are portrayed as looking *UP* to foreign cultures in a way typical for semi-colonial societies. This is not to deny that Yu Dafu felt a genuine concern about and commitment to the fate of China,[112] although he could never bring himself to unquestioning submission to leftist or communist organizations.[113] In addition, one may point out that there is hardly any ideological debate except for two references to religion, mainly in *Nanqian*.[114]

Compared to Yu Dafu's novels *Denen no yūutsu* has a much greater artistic coherence. At the risk of overstating our case we may say that Satō uses a coherent style to express 'disorder,' whereas Yu Dafu's novels reflect the chaos in China's cultural world in the apposition of many incongruous elements. In both cases the theme of 'disorder' is a reflection of processes of fundamental transformation and disorientation that have dominated the history of modern East Asia.

Towards the end of *Denen no yūutsu* Satō refers to the - in origin Buddhist - image of waves spreading in circles, and the idea of a temporarily disturbed water surface recalls Bashō's famous haiku 'kawazu tobikomu.' But rather than suggesting that the hero has rediscovered his peace of mind this image is another step in the direction of ultimate self-deception: the traditional image is broken.

> [Looking at the water in the well he saw that] From this disturbance
> little waves spread silently over the whole surface, the water quivered
> and returned to its former tranquillity. Silence, silent silence. Limitless
> silence.[115]

15

Unheeded Voices; Winked-at Lives

BARBARA RUCH

INTRODUCTION

In re-examining Japanese cultural history, how are we to deal with 'absence'?[1]

Over the past decade it has become increasingly clear that pre-modern history in Japan, not unlike Japanese court poetry, has been written from a now canonized list of pre-selected,privileged topics. Not only traditional predilections favoured over the centuries, but modern arthritic habits of scholarly attention and an academic vocabulary frozen by class, gender and status preclusion have led to a preference for certain topics of research, and a denigration of other features. For example, the professions and activities pursued exclusively by men, such as the Gozan institution of Zen monks or *sarugaku* Noh performers and repertory occupy a privileged place in Japanese history, whereas those professions and activities pursued exclusively by women, such as the Gozan institution of Zen convents run by ecclesiastical women, or the *kugutsu* and *asobime* sororities of *imayō* performers have been systematically excluded from standard and official histories. As women, therefore, major cultural leaders and prominent creative talents have been wholly ignored in the pages of our histories. Such institutionalized bias in our profession skews methodology and calls into question current interpretations of Japanese cultural, literary and religious history.

Within the constraints of these few pages let me introduce just one major cultural leader who was a woman and one female creative talent, both of whom have remained unheeded, indeed have been treated with virtual programmatic neglect. Restoration of these persons to their proper place in history should help us to 're-think Japan.' May their lives and activities stand as examples of some of the directions we must take here [at the Venice Symposium] as we attempt to re-examine Japanese history and our own obligations as scholars.

MUGAI NYODAI

Scholars of art history for years have done careful and interesting research on the Japanese sculpture genre known as *chinsō*, those large realistic

102

wooden or clay portrait-sculptures of Zen priests made as stand-ins to convey the essence of the master to his disciples after his death. One day, leafing through a book filled with photographs of *chinsō*,[2] all of them depicting illustrious Zen masters dressed in Buddhist robes and with shaved heads, I was astonished to find one that proved to be the figure of a thirteenth-century female Zen master. I was riveted by this statue-portrait, the first I had ever seen of a medieval Japanese abbess. Intrigued by what I then naïvely considered an anomaly in Japanese religious history, I pursued her story.

It turned out that her religious name was Mugai Nyodai and she lived 1223-1298. The intimate realism of her superb statue-portrait reveals a serious woman in her seventies with life-worn face and meditative posture whose glimmering eyes of crystal emanate a sense of great power and life force. During the past decade this statue has been studied carefully and it has been designated an 'Important Cultural Property.' But neither the woman it depicts nor the important religious association of Zen convents she founded has received any serious academic attention whatsoever.

The simplest of my probes into the standard Japanese references on Buddhism or cultural history revealed at once our woeful state of current research on ecclesiastic women in Japan. Few sources mention Mugai Nyodai at all and each that does perfunctorily assigns her a different father and husband. Some Japanese reference works are so blatantly casual as to attribute to her a husband who proves upon investigation to be thirty-five years her junior. One assigns her a father who was born eight years after she was and another twenty-five years after![3]

Scholarly irresponsibility and neglect of this sort is due in no way to any failure on Mugai's part to be worthy of historians' attention nor to any lack of her social status or accomplishments. She was an extraordinary woman; most likely, in my view, if we study birth and death dates carefully, she was the daughter of Adachi no Kagemori, and she would appear to have been the first wife of Hōjō (Kanazawa) Sanetoki. Highly educated in both Chinese and Japanese she studied Zen in Kamakura under Mugaku Sogen (1226-1286) who had come from China in 1279 at the invitation of the regent Hōjō Tokimune to head the temple Kenchōji there. It was Mugaku Sogen who recognized Mugai Nyodai as heir to his teachings and gave her the character '*mu*' from his own name. She became the first woman in Japan fully qualified as a Zen master and she became the founder and abbess of Keiaiji and its more than fifteen sub-temples in Kyoto. Mugai's Keiaiji headed the then-developing network of Zen convents known as the Niji (Amadera) Gozan or Five-Mountain Convents Association, a parallel institution to the well-known and well-studied Gozan monasteries for male priests. Shortly after her death the Five-Mountain Convents expanded beyond Keiaiji and its sub-temples to include Tsūgenji, Danrinji, Go'nenji, Erinji and their respective sub-temples as well as a parallel five convents in Kamakura: Taiheiji, Tōkeiji, Kokuonji, Gōhōji and Zemmyōji.

I am still amazed that after almost thirty years of professional study of Japanese literature and cultural history I had never been taught, nor had I heard or read a single word about this considerable female side to medieval

Zen, nor have I ever seen any references to this aspect of the lives of eminent medieval women. To this day I still have not found a single scholar anywhere who has researched and written on the Five-Mountain Convents, despite the fact that, without doubt, it was an extensive economic and political power in both Kamakura and Kyoto and is one of the most important manifestations of institutionalized Buddhism in medieval Japanese history.

I feel compelled to recount here, for the record, that when I recently questioned such an enormous gap in our concern for and knowledge about this aspect of medieval Japanese religion, a well-known and respected scholar in Japan told me that Japanese scholars (most of whom are male) 'are embarrassed (*hazukashii*) to do research on institutions that deal essentially with women.'

Given the dismal perception of the writing of Japanese religious history that Mugai Nyodai's case represents, it is heartening to keep in mind that, after centuries of neglect in the West concerning the history of women ecclesiastics in the Christian tradition, concerted scholarly efforts over the past decade have produced a rich harvest. The writings of numerous women theologians have been re-discovered and translated for the first time into modern languages. Histories of the Christian Church Fathers are now being balanced by soundly researched pages about the Mothers of the Early Church. The same can surely be the case for Japan. 'But there is probably no documentation to be found in Japan,' say the sceptics. To whom one must reply, 'Where are the research projects designed to survey Japanese Convents and seek out such documentation? It is a wide open field.'

This indeed is the time to integrate the study of medieval Japanese ecclesiastic women into a world context. Since 1982 a major computer-supported survey of European convents and religious communities of women from Italy to the British Isles has been under way; in due course, it is planned that years from 500-1500 will all be surveyed. The parallels with medieval Buddhist Japan are obvious and enlightening despite the theological differences in the faiths that motivated the women East and West. Reporting on this research project in the Catholic West, Mary McLaughlin outlines a situation that could as well describe medieval Japan in Mugai Nyodai's day.

> Women associated with religious life... belonged to families at nearly every level of medieval society from royal and aristocratic to those of decidedly lower status in towns and countryside. By no means all of them were professed nuns; many communities also included... female servants and sometimes lay 'boarders'.... Further extending the social range of women associated with the religious life were houses of repentant prostitutes established in many late medieval towns and cities. Still another category... especially numerous in England, were those who abandoned the world or monastic communities for the solitary life of recluses and anchoresses.[4]

Several of Mugai's successors were tonsured empresses or members of the imperial family. At the same time, McLaughlin's narrative reminds us of the author of *Towazugatari*, Lady Nijō (1258-1305?) who, after taking the tonsure and setting out on pilgrimages around the country, encounters several nuns who previously had made their living as prostitutes, one a former brothel owner.[5]

In the Muromachi period *monogatari* called *Shichinin bikuni* are depicted the lives of seven nuns. One is particularly illustrative of several of the life-styles of medieval Japanese nuns and yet is also remarkably similar to the description of cloistered nuns, mendicant nuns and solitary recluses in the McLaughlin report. *Shichinin bikuni* reads:

> (She)... cut off her hair, and changed her flower-like appearance to that of a nun. In linen robes, carrying a mendicant's bag, her make-up gone, her natural complexion revealed, she wandered through the provinces as a tattered beggar.... She decided to go to Zenkōji. There was a sub-temple to one side, the abbot of which was greatly revered as someone who obtained enlightenment. She felt this was the kind of place she had been looking for and stayed in the area for two years. Sometimes she secluded herself in mountain valleys; sometimes she begged with other mendicants.[6]

There are even more striking parallels to be found between the Christian West and Buddhist Japan during the early years when these religions were first developing. Japanese women faced a situation with the importation of Buddhism that was very much like the plight of their Greek and Roman counterparts for whom Christianity was also an import. In both worlds a religion imported by men was growing and being domesticated in a religious environment of ritual and thought organized by males into male institutions, with only satellite places for women. The ascetical male writers of the Christian Church voiced themes that sound exactly as if they could as well be quoted from an orthodox Buddhist text: 'Virtue properly pertains to men, but through grace, women are also capable of being elevated to manhood.'[7]

Yet Mugai Nyodai was born at a moment in Japanese history, short-lived though it was, when radical new ideas were emerging. Dōgen had travelled to China the year Mugai Nyodai was born and introduced Sōtō Zen thought in Japan when she was just four years old. His treatise *Shōbōgenzō* was uncompromising in its assertion of the complete equality between the sexes in religious matters.

> What is so sacred about the status of a man?.... The four elements that make up the human body are the same for a man as for a woman.... You should not waste your time in futile discussions about the superiority of one sex over another.... Learning the Law of Buddha and achieving release from illusion have nothing to do with whether one happens to be a man or a woman.[8]

The fact that Mugaku Sogen, founder of Rinzai Zen in Japan, named Mugai Nyodai as heir to his teachings is clear indication that he, too, believed that religious enlightenment was genderless.

Although in the pages of Japanese history Mugai Nyodai seems to appear out of nowhere and for the moment is alone on the horizon, we dare not treat her as an anomaly. An anomaly is harmless; it surprises and entertains us but it need not concern us in fundamental ways. Mugai, however, shows us how fundamental our misconceptions have been. No understanding of medieval Zen, its values or practices or even medieval society itself begins to approach reality until it reflects Mugai's presence in it. On the other hand, if we simply categorize Mugai Nyodai as 'woman' or as 'nun' we will have merely substituted classification for meaning. Mugai Nyodai must stand not only for herself but for all the unstudied founder-abbesses of Japanese history. Indeed she also stands for all those women who took the tonsure and thereafter moved not only to the cloister but out into the world of commerce and the arts: merchant nuns, artist nuns too played a fundamental role in the creation of Japan's emerging national culture.

In the year 1498 Keiaiji burned to the ground. Mugai Nyodai's *chinsō* was rescued and removed to one of Keiaiji's sub-temples in Kyoto, the cloister Hōji-in, where it remains today,[9] a continuing power and presence in the lives of the nuns who live there. Nonetheless, for all of us, this 'Important Cultural Property' remains an important cultural challenge, a powerful reminder of that other side of gender, of those voices from the past we scholars have left unheeded for so many generations.

OTOMAE

Let me move on to another woman who took the tonsure in old age but who had led a life radically different from that of Mugai Nyodai - a woman as famed in her own day, maybe more so, than Mugai was in hers. Yet she too has been so overshadowed in history by her male associates that few Japanese today have even heard her name.

Otomae was a *kugutsu*[10] singer without peer in early twelfth-century Kyoto. Her repertory was the best the centuries had to offer of *imayō* songs, which by her day had become almost classical in form; and she was master of more than twenty variant types. Like the German *lied*, the Japanese *imayō* was a deeply-moving combination of words and music - a universal story told with deeply culture-bound nuance.

Already retired and known as 'the Gōjō Avenue nun,' Otomae was in her early seventies when Emperor GoShirakawa, then just entering his thirties, called her to court in 1157 and apprenticed himself to her so as to learn her repertory. That great collection of songs of past centuries, the *Ryōjin hishō* (Secret Selection of Songs that Make the Rafter-dust Dance), is traditionally thought of as Emperor GoShirakawa's work.[11] It was of course his passion for these songs that led him to study with Otomae, collect these songs in repertory, and commit them to writing to preserve them. It would perhaps be better, however, to refer to the *Ryōjin hishō* as Otomae's songs. As a *kugutsu* singer her professional lineage can actually be traced back, matrilineally, through at least three generations of female *imayō* masters: her own teacher and adopted mother was Mei,[12] who was the disciple of Shisan, who in turn had been the adopted daughter and disciple of the *imayō* master Nabiki.

From about age 12 Otomae had devoted her life to learning, performing, and no doubt adding to the repertory, and then teaching those songs. GoShirakawa was, we should not forget, her devoted student and amanuensis. In a very real sense he was her final disciple. Although Otomae

106

had a daughter to whom GoShirakawa refers several times in his anecdotal accounts about the *imayō* world, she is never named and is never mentioned as a singer or possible heir. She attends *imayō* gatherings and seems an astute listener and critic, but we must assume she lacked the vocal talent (or will) requisite for public performance.

GoShirakawa was a passionate enthusiast for the popular vocal music of his day as well as for the great body of songs that had by then become the favourite classics in the repertory of professional performers. GoShirakawa was a dedicated, even fanatical student. His own account of his practice sessions reveals a man who practised long hours daily without fail, often in all-night sessions to the annoyance of his neighbours who found the percussive beats of the accompanying hand-drum hardly conducive to sleep. He lost his voice numerous times from sheer vocal fatigue, so assiduous was his pursuit of mastery.

Determined to preserve these beloved songs and to assure their transmission for future generations just as *waka* poetry had been preserved in collections and adorned by interpretive treatises, GoShirakawa committed himself to learning Otomae's entire repertory. And so overwhelmed was he by Otomae's talent, even in her seventies, that he re-learned from her all the songs he had learned before from others, so as to reproduce faithfully her words and musical interpretations.

Some ten years later when Otomae was in her eighties and had fallen ill, GoShirakawa sat at her bedside and sang the thirty-second song from the collection which concerned Yakushi Nyorai, the Healing Buddha, a song whose power was believed to invoke a cure for the most serious of illnesses. Within months of her death he had taken the tonsure and by year-end completed all but the conclusion of the *Ryōjin hishō* collection he had been copying down for so long since Otomae first came into his household as mentor.

Historians transform life that has been lived into narrated life, and in this sense they are not unlike novelists. By selecting, focusing and retelling they inevitably reshape. By focusing on GoShirakawa, the aristocrat, the Emperor, scholars have been able to justify their study of the *Ryōjin hishō* collection of songs and to enjoy it. In the selective re-telling, however, Otomae, the source and the star, but after all the lowly, winked-at, *kugutsu* singer-entertainer, was deposited into the footnotes and now finally has been lost to national memory.

That was certainly not GoShirakawa's intent. His *Kudenshū* is filled with his admiration and awe of her, with his record of her critical remarks, with his dreams of this elderly nun after her death in which she returns from the next world and continues to teach him. He is straightforward: he has received the complete transmission of Otomae's art and has dedicated himself to preserving it for posterity.

But Otomae is not alone in her neglect. GoShirakawa was not merely a passionate disciple of the one he considered the best; he was a connoisseur of the best voices of his day. He mentions specifically by name more than twenty other professional *kugutsu* or *asobime* singers in the *Kudenshū*.

Needless to say the most accomplished and influential of female artists have not fared well in the pages of history. They have generally been swept

107

into the easily dismissable anonymous category of 'entertainer' or even 'prostitute,' and their names are subsumed and obscured under the glowing fame of their élite male patrons. The great *shirabyōshi* dancers such as Ishi and Kamegiku, for example, have been lost to the modern consciousness; no one recognizes their names. When Zeami wrote his famous treatises on Noh plays in the fifteenth century he put *shirabyōshi* dancers such as Iso no Zenji, Ishi, Kamegiku and Shizuka on the same level of artistic accomplishment as such Heian poetesses as Lady Ise and Ono no Komachi.[13]

But history is not written by great artists about other artists. Scholars, heavily influenced by Confucian thought, simply dropped these women from their list of appropriate subjects for research. The problem was not simply one of gender but of sex. Entertainers who also provided sex for a living, or those who did not, but who in the course of life had lovers and patrons, all seemed most easily classified as 'prostitutes.'

Japanese *kugutsu* and *asobime* singers and *shirabyōshi* dancers suggest many parallels with the professional hetaerae ('female companions') from fourth century B.C.E. Greece. They were skilled entertainers; lived fashionably alone or in small all-female groups; ranged in origin from slave to free professional; were patronized for their arts and conversation by wealthy men; were hired to perform at state and family events; and were taxed by the government. They may also be fruitfully compared to the religiously-sanctioned performer-prostitute of South India, the Devadasis, who go back also to the fourth century B.C.E.

GoShirakawa mentions several times employing *asobime* from Eguchi and Kanzaki as well as *kugutsu* from Aohaka and Sunomata in Mino to take part in the fifth-month Buddhist flower dedication ceremonies at court. Indeed at least one of GoShirakawa's long-time consorts and mother of one of his sons was Tamba no Tsubone, an *asobime* whose mother too had been an *asobime*.

Because women professionals such as shamans, *kugutsu* and *asobime* singer-entertainers and *shirabyōshi* dancers were each and all husband-less, independent, often living (and if itinerant, travelling) in small self-regulating groups and were matrilinear in lineage, mother to daughter or female adept to adopted daughter-disciple, observers throughout history have tended to see them all as of a kind and to expend little effort in determining the differences among these very different artists and their groups. Since none of these groups was maintained by the court or the Buddhist temples as had been male professionals like *bugaku* and *gagaku* troupes and *sarugaku* players, virtually every female entertainment artist in pre-modern Japanese life, therefore, was outside the institutional structure.

Due to gender bias the label 'prostitute' hangs heavily over the history of women entertainers, not only those who did engage in selling sex but all of these several types of husband-less, independent, medieval female artists (even those who were virginal and ascetic) in a way it does not hang over the lives of male artists who were, likewise, like Zeami, involved sexually with their patrons.

It is important to realize that we *have* no conceptual framework in which to consider the historical activity of sex commerce. The modern term 'prostitution' is virtually useless. Leah Otis' recent study of prostitution in twelfth to sixteenth-century France makes it clear that 'it is not possible, in studying the history of prostitution, to rely... on the social sciences for a set of assumptions or constraints.'[14] As she points out, prostitution in the modern sociological literature is seen as 'deviant' behaviour, and therefore the investigator is invariably more interested in determining motive and recruitment than in establishing analytical models that might be useful to the historian. The profession as an urban phenomenon with its considerable commercial importance and complex tax structure has been largely ignored by economists, dismissed as a 'non-productive' activity.

From the highest ranking élite and powerful ecclesiastics like Mugai Nyodai to the greatest of performing artists in the capital like Otomae, and those who as yet remain nameless in our annals of history, all of these women were orthodox constituents of the medieval Japanese social order. Whether they have been winked at patronizingly or wholly ignored by early scholars who set the tradition, the fact is that they have been aborted from the pages of official history.

Theodore Bestor, in his commentary on a recent 'Workshop on Gender Issues in the Study of Japan,' reports that as of the 1970s when gender studies as a field was in its infancy, the impact of such gender considerations on research about Japan was virtually nil.[15] Once gender studies gained momentum in American academia, however, a reverse phenomenon occurred: numerous studies suddenly emerged taking as their object of research topics that narrowly focused on women treated as phenomena separate from mainstream Japanese culture and society. In short, women were no longer absent from the research agenda, but they were segregated within it (i.e. studies of 'women politicians;' 'women poets;' etc.). Our goals must be the integration of knowledge about *all* the influential actors on the stage of history when we attempt to reconstruct the past.

Japan has not one past, but many pasts, all of which are indispensable to our knowledge of the whole. As we [at this Venice Symposium] attempt to 're-think Japan,' it is not enough merely to expand the limits of historical discourse - that is to say, merely to incorporate more of the actual world into our studies. When we include individuals and groups traditionally excluded from the historical and literary narrative we are incorporating new social territory as well. Old maps will not do.

New methodologies, new sources, new forms of presentation will be necessary. There is no way, for example, that we can write the history of ecclesiastic women simply by taking old histories of monks as models. Nor does current research on Zeami, for instance, provide a functional framework for the study of Otomae. Yet both the old and the new will be enriched by taking new approaches that incorporate all actors on the stage of history irrespective of gender. Therefore, as I urge here the recovery of lost histories of neglected groups I am not advocating further segmentation of scholarship. Rather I suggest that our search for the larger synthetic patterns in literary and cultural history will fail if half the lights are out.

109

16

Yūgen: Aesthetics and its Implications in Global Communication

BEN BEFU

Japan today, with her burgeoning economic success, has been thrust into a position of unexpected leadership in the international community. Her mounting trade surplus has put the Japanese in an uncomfortable situation of having to explain their success and what they plan to do about the excess dollars. And the Japanese are not doing it well, for various reasons; it seems from our vantage point across the sea that they have gone into a frenzy with *kokusaika* (internationalization), an identity crisis with regard to the international community.

Suzuki Takao explains Japan's predicament as one of 'xenophygia' which he defines as "'always fleeing from foreigners," or "avoiding foreigners as much as possible."'[1] According to him, the Japanese have always been very receptive to foreign ideas but have felt uncomfortable with the physical presence of foreigners among them[2] and as a result of the historical accident of isolation '[the Japanese] apparatus for reception is very extensive and well-developed, but we have no transmitting systems.'[3] The Japanese are poor communicators in more than one sense. The Japanese do not argue well partly because of the perceived unseemliness of heated arguments; certainly it is not in their culture to engage in sustained give-and-take discussions and as a result the Japanese are poor practitioners of well-articulated arguments that proceed step by step.

There is, of course, that other Japanese mode of communication, *haragei* (visceral communication), which lies very near the end of the spectrum of non-verbal communication. As Robert C. Christopher explains it:

> The essence of haragei is that because of the racial homogeneity and almost identical social and cultural conditioning of the Japanese people, it is often possible for one Japanese to determine the reaction of another to a particular situation simply by observing the second man's facial expressions, the length and timing of his silences and the ostensibly meaningless grunts he emits from time to time. Among Japanese of the same generation and occupation, this process can become so sophisticated that words are expended only on courtesies and badinage, and the art of direct verbal communication almost atrophies.[4]

There is no place for articulated discourse in this type of communication. Nakamura Hajime has gone so far as to claim that 'neglect of logic is one of the salient features of traditional Japanese ways of thinking.'⁵

Certainly, as Edwin Reischauer points out, the Japanese do have a suspicion of verbal skills, a penchant for non-verbal understanding, an eagerness to avoid personal confrontation and refrain from frankly expressing their views.⁶ Robert C. Christopher cites an example of a Harvard-trained Japanese cultural anthropologist who wrote an article on how straight talk disturbs the typical Japanese and confessed in a footnote that even to write about it openly made him uncomfortable. In an effort to examine the nature of the Japanese taciturnity, I should like to turn our attention to the medieval aesthetic concept, *yūgen*, and then consider an aspect of the Japanese language.

Yūgen, usually rendered 'mystery and depth,' is one of the most important of a group of poetic ideals that emerged in the twelfth century and came to be associated with Fujiwara Shunzei (or Toshinari, 1114-1204) and his son Teika (or Sadaie, 1162-1241). Robert Brower and Earl Miner refer to it as 'the crowning poetic ideal in any discussion of the aesthetic of the age.' For an illuminating discussion of the concept I shall defer to and refer you to their *Japanese Court Poetry*.⁷ Let me simply point out that one of the earliest to attempt an explanation was Kamo no Chōmei (1155-1216). In his poetic treatise, *Mumyōshō*, he wrote in answering the question as to just what was *yūgen*:

> Since I do not understand it at all well myself, I am at a loss as to how to describe it in any satisfactory manner, but according to the views of those who have developed the skill necessary to penetrate its mysteries, the qualities deemed essential to the style are overtones that do not appear in the words alone and an atmosphere that is not visible in the configuration of the poem (sen wa tada kotoba ni arawarenu yosei, sugata ni mienu keiki narubeshi).⁸

The essence then, in short, was overtone: a quality that is suggested but not stated in words. One of the classic examples of this ideal is the well-known poem by Teika:

Miwataseba hana mo momiji mo nakarikeri
    Ura no tomaya no aki no yūgure
I gaze into the distance
    Looking neither for cherry blossoms
        Nor maple leaves:
A grass-thatched hut
    In the deepening autumn dusk.   (*Shinkokinshū* 363)

What is sought here is not the conventional beauty associated with the gaiety of colour but rather a subdued beauty represented by the monochrome vista that evokes a sense of loneliness. The quality of mystery and profundity informs this poem because attention is directed not simply to the absence of colour but to an absence of colour in a context where it was contrary to expectation; and thereby raises a question. The idea was to imbue the poem with more than what was made explicit in words. To return to Chōmei:

It is only when many meanings are compressed into a single word, when the depths of feeling are exhausted yet not expressed, when an unseen world hovers in the atmosphere of the poem, when the mean and the common are used to express the elegant, when a poetic conception of rare beauty is developed to the fullest extent in a style of surface simplicity - only then, when the conception is exalted to the highest degree and 'the words are too few,' will the poem, by expressing one's feelings in this way, have the power of moving Heaven and Earth within the brief confines of a mere thirty-one syllables, and be capable of softening the hearts of gods and demons.[9]

I do not suggest that overtone or *yojō* was synonymous with *yūgen*. Yet, as we have observed, for Chōmei, it was at least an essential part of it. And, at the risk of over-simplifying the case, it may be said that, for Shunzei and Teika, tonal complexity typically achieved by means of overtones was a most highly regarded quality.[10] The essence of *yūgen* was, again in Chōmei's words: 'When one gazes upon the autumn hills half-concealed by a curtain of mist, what one sees is veiled yet profoundly beautiful; such a shadowy scene, which permits free exercise of the imagination in picturing how lovely the whole panoply of scarlet leaves must be, is far better than to see them spread with dazzling clarity before our eyes.'[11]

Seven centuries later we find Natsume Sōseki (1867-1916) expressing the same sort of preference for the misty and vague. In his *Kusamakura* (Pillow of Grass, 1906) he describes an unexpected encounter with a nude woman, glimpsed only through the steam of a hot-spring bath:

> She stood there surrounded by swirling eddies of mist into which the gentle light suffused a rose-tinted warmth.... Wave upon wave of steam rolled upwards refracting and diffusing the late spring light, and filling the entire room with a warmly scintillating rainbow.... Such complexity yet unity of structure was surely unique. It would be impossible to find a shape so natural, so soft, so lacking in resistance and yet so unobtrusive.
>
> It was not in fact thrust flagrantly into view like the average nude, but being only dimly visible in the midst of a strange aura of enchantment which lent mystery to all within it, gave no more than a subtle hint of its full beauty. There was about it that same artistically perfect combination of atmosphere, warmth and sense of the ethereal that exist in a picture in which the artist suggests the presence of a horned dragon merely by dotting a few scales here and there in an inky black haze.[12]

Masao Miyoshi notes, in his *Accomplices of Silence*, how the painter hero, lying in the hot water, comes to realize the painting of Ophelia was attractive to him because of the sense of detachment and it is at this moment that the woman in the nude makes her appearance. The mist through which she is seen plays a crucial role in the painter's perception of her as a beautiful artistic object. Masao Miyoshi makes an acute observation that there was a need for distance between the body and viewer; and at the climax of this encounter 'just as he, and we, are about to close the distance and see her face to face,' she turns around and disappears.[13] This is interesting because Kubota Jun, to whom I am indebted for the conceptualization of this paper, has published a highly original analysis of *yūgen* based, *inter alia*, on the role that distance plays in the poems Shunzei associated with *yūgen*.[14] Also, I would add here that Thomas Rimer's analysis of *Kusamakura* that this was a *haiku*-novel akin to *haibun* ('haiku prose') in which Sōseki was attempting 'a working out in modern prose of traditional Japanese aesthetics'[15] takes on additional significance when viewed in this light.

Another writer known for his predilection for and reliance not only on themes and techniques of traditional Japanese literature but traditional Japanese aesthetics as well was Tanizaki Jun'ichirō (1886-1965). His celebrated essay, *In'ei Raisan* (In Praise of Shadows, 1933-34) needs no introduction.[16] It is a nostalgic essay expressing an unabashed adoration of the richly suggestive beauty drawn out by the old, the dark, the shadowy and the dimly lit. In Makoto Ueda's words, 'the main reason why he admired shadows so much was that they breed fantasies,' and again 'Tanizaki's literary aesthetic centres on the beauty of half-light, of dusky visions that vibrate in the imagination.'[17] They allow imagination its full play to those inclined to savour the riches that can be had. *In Praise of Shadows* obviously lies in the main stream of the *yūgen* tradition.

But this is no essay in the usual sense of the word. It is an essay only in the traditional Japanese sense of *zuihitsu* 'following the brush,' albeit with a central theme. It is a piece of writing wherein the writer wanders from topic to topic, often with the most tenuous of transitions and seemingly without design. Thomas Harper who, along with Edward Seidensticker, did the translation of *In Praise of Shadows*, offers this explanation in his afterword:

> One of the oldest and most deeply ingrained of Japanese attitudes to literary style holds that too obvious a structure is contrivance, that too orderly an exposition falsifies the ruminations of the heart, that the truest representation of the searching mind is just to 'follow the brush'.... It is not that Japanese writers have been ignorant of the powers of concision and articulation. Rather they have felt that certain subjects - the vicissitudes of the emotions, the fleeting perceptions of the mind - are best couched in a style that conveys something of the uncertainty of the mental process and not just its neatly packaged conclusions.[18]

Indeed it is a style that agrees with Tanizaki's subject matter and, as well, one that is particularly suited for expressions of the ruminations of the heart that so characterizes Japanese thought. It is also a form of writing made to order, one might say, for those who abhor straight talk. Which brings us to another point: ambiguity. Tanizaki, according to Makoto Ueda, felt that a writer should take advantage of the fact that the Japanese language is not very 'grammatical' and cultivate ambiguity for the sake of elegance. To Tanizaki, a passage written with no ambiguity was like rudely exposed thighs and knees.[19] This is calculated ambiguity for stylistic purposes, consistent with the *yūgen* tradition.

We have observed that the Japanese have traditionally shown a predisposition for the hazy, the misty and the suggestive as a literary ideal, and in modern discourse an active distaste for clear and unambiguous communication. There are some who would claim that Japanese is a language in which it is impossible to make clear, logical statements. Others, like Edwin Reischauer, insist that 'there is nothing about the Japanese language which prevents concise, clear and logical presentation, *if that is what one wishes to make*' (italics added).[20] The problem is that the Japanese so often choose not to do so, for a number of reasons. In the case of the *yūgen* ideal it was for aesthetic reasons. In the case of the *zuihitsu* it may very well be for stylistic reasons. In the case of verbal give-and-take it may be to avoid confrontation or to avoid committing oneself to a hard and fast position. In any case, it would be safe to say that the inclination to avoid clear communication is a deeply ingrained matter. The fact of the matter is that the Japanese have developed a system of communication wherein suggestions instead of statements often rule. In this peculiarly Japanese culture people have become experts at decoding highly cryptic remarks.

Contributing to this situation, undoubtedly, is the nature of the Japanese language. The absence of the subject and even the object in a given sentence is all too well known:

A. Ageta no? (Lit., Gave?)

B. Un, yatta yo. (Lit., Ya, gave.)

The precise interpretation of this exchange would depend on the known facts surrounding the event. Given a context, anyone proficient in Japanese would understand it without a moment's hesitation. But it does require a lightning speed assessment of just what the known facts are at the time of the exchange. The principle of such a linguistic operation is not unique to Japanese; it is just that, in Japanese, the demand for the operation is greatly multiplied. As a result, and coupled with other cultural factors, the Japanese are supreme practitioners of the art of assessing the situation and reading between the lines. Naturally, the operation works both ways: the speaker is well aware that he need not provide complete information. He knows he can depend on the listener to do the decoding.

John Hinds, in a recent study, has proposed a linguistic typology based on speaker and/or writer responsibility as opposed to listener and/or reader responsibility.[21] In a language such as English the speaker or writer has the desire and accepts the responsibility to write or speak clearly. In English, the speaker or writer considers much more carefully than a Japanese would how he is going to make the presentation in a logical fashion, with introductory remarks, perhaps outlining the plan of presentation, and then proceeds with the talk; he would likely conclude with an appropriate summary. In public speaking, Hinds notes, there is the aphorism: 'Tell 'em what you're going to tell 'em, tell 'em, then tell 'em what you told 'em.'[22] In Japanese culture such plain talk might well get a negative reception, possibly as lacking in intellectual rigour, or possibly as an insult to the intelligence of the audience, or both.[23] Hinds states, 'In Japan, perhaps in Korea, and certainly in classical China, there is a different way of looking at the communication process. In Japan it is the responsibility of the listener (or reader) to understand what it is the speaker or author had intended to say.'[24]

Hinds confines the scope of his analysis to how speaker and reader responsibility operates with respect to unity in expository statements. He states:

> For English readers, unity is important because readers expect, and require, landmarks along the way. Transition statements are very important. It is the writer's task to provide appropriate transition statements so that the reader can piece together the thread of the writer's logic which binds the composition together.
>
> In Japanese, on the other hand, the landmarks may be absent or attenuated since it is the reader's responsibility to determine the relationship between any one part of an essay and the essay as a whole. This is not to say that there are no transition statements in Japanese. There are. It is only to say that these transition devices may be more subtle and require a more active role for the reader.[25]

In other words, the Japanese writer operates under a set of rules under which it is accepted and expected that the reader will participate in the process of comprehension to a degree far beyond the situation in English. The Japanese writer will encounter no serious problem as long as he is writing for the Japanese. When, however, he addresses an audience in a different part of the world where listener responsibility is inoperable, frustration and misunderstanding are likely to be the result, if the necessary adjustments are not made.

Let me relate what I believe to be a concrete example:[26]

> In May 1987 the Japanese government announced what it called an Emergency Economic Package involving some $43 billion. The package was designed to expand domestic spending, increase imports, and contribute to the international community. All of this was calculated to improve the imbalance of world trade and ease pressures on Japan.
>
> Among other things, the programme would reduce Japanese taxes by $7 billion (thus stimulating spending for consumer goods), launch a large public works programme, promote housing investment, create 300,000 new jobs, reduce consumer prices and open up markets to foreign goods.
>
> Recognizing the importance of its action, the Nakasone government issued a series of news releases. The problem was they weren't news releases at all. They were fact sheets. Only if one were determined enough could one get through the verbiage and find out what it was all about.
>
> From all that I can gather, Japan expected its action to make quite a media splash in the U.S. The expectation was natural in view of persistent American carping about Japan's economic success, particularly since the emergency economic measures were an impressive response to criticism.
>
> But what happened? Not much, not much at all. The economic papers, like the *Wall Street Journal*, carried fairly comprehensive stories. *Time* magazine had a line or two. Local newspapers all but ignored the news....

So the Japanese government missed a golden opportunity to reap some public relations gain.

When a text is translated into English, a skilful translator will fill the gaps and supply the missing transitions to the best of his ability but the result is often less than satisfactory. Fixing problems of this nature requires not simply a competent translator but an editor-translator who not only has the required expertise but the authority or carte blanche to adapt the text as he sees fit.

I have touched on the Japanese cultural distaste for straight talk, the cultural background for the Japanese disinclination for clarity in communication, the traditional cultural preference for the misty and the vague and suggestive, the literary significance of *yūgen* and the notion of overtone, and an aspect of the language as contributing factors for the lack of clarity in Japanese writing. I believe the issue is not only deeply ingrained as a cultural trait but reinforced and exacerbated by the nature of the language that requires listener or reader participation in the communication process. When the Japanese direct their communication to the international community, it is suggested that they take due cognizance of these factors.

17

Recognizing and Translating Covert Irony in Japanese Literature

ANTHONY H. CHAMBERS

The subject of irony in Japanese literature interests me for two reasons. First, as a translator, I have been fascinated by irony as a persistent rhetorical problem, and second, as a reader of the writings of Tanizaki Jun'ichirō (1886-1965), I have been trying to define what it is about his style that appeals to me.

In this preliminary discussion, I shall limit myself to what Wayne C. Booth calls 'covert irony' and use his description of it: 'regardless of how broadly or narrowly he defines irony - and the problem of definition is by no means a simple one - every reader learns that some statements cannot be understood without rejecting what they seem to say.'[1] (Booth distinguishes covert irony from 'overt irony,' which proclaims itself with phrases like, 'It's ironic that...,' and from 'irony of event,' in which the outcome - but not the rhetoric - is ironic. An example that illustrates both overt irony and irony of event is, 'It's ironic that Murasaki never had any children of her own.') A reader encountering covert irony has to reject

116

the surface meaning of the ironic statement and 'reconstruct' another, incongruous meaning.[2]

Perhaps the most famous example of covert irony is *A Modest Proposal*, in which Jonathan Swift offers a plan for 'Preventing the Children of poor People in Ireland, from being a Burden to their Parents or Country; and for making them beneficial to the Publick'[3] by fattening Irish children and selling them to butchers, thereby alleviating the burden on their families and, at the same time, providing an additional source of nourishment for the general public. Few readers will have any difficulty recognizing the irony of this proposal or reconstructing an alternative meaning. Further, most readers will enjoy the process. As Booth says,[4] covert irony implies a tacit relationship between the author and the reader: the author assumes that the reader will recognize and appreciate the irony; the reader is flattered by this assumption and gratified by his or her own ability to perform the needed reconstruction. Here, then, lies part of the answer to one of my initial questions: why do I find Tanizaki's writings appealing? Because Tanizaki is constantly taking me into his confidence by sharing covert ironies with me.

How do I know that certain Tanizakian passages are ironic? Well, I just know, as we all know that Swift's proposal is ironic. If pressed, I would say that my confidence is based on a feeling, acquired over time, for Tanizaki and his works. Covert ironies are not always as obvious as Swift's,[2] of course, and even Swift's were not always obvious to his contemporaries.[5] The question 'How do I know?' is a complex one. Booth deals with it at far greater length than space permits here. I would like to focus on the fact that a reader's recognition can be delayed or impeded by cultural differences: Have Japanese writers in various periods had an ironic sense comparable to Swift's? That is, are there statements in Japanese literature whose surface meanings must be rejected before the statements can be understood? Can a modern Japanese writer assume that a Western reader will recognize Japanese irony? Can a Western reader be sure that what looks like irony in a Japanese work is not simply a reflection of different cultural assumptions? To put the question in terms of specific texts: Why are ironic passages so much more numerous in Seidensticker's translation of the *Genji* than in Waley's, and how much of Seidensticker's irony is present in the original? Why do some readers see no irony in, for example, Tanizaki's *Bushūkō hiwa*, a novel that I find deliciously ironic?

It could be argued that the importance Japanese culture attaches to the virtue of *makoto* ('sincerity') might preclude the use of covert irony by Japanese writers or its recognition by Japanese readers. The conclusion of Ihara Saikaku's *Nanshoku ōkagami* (1687) should refute that notion right away:

> Because there is female love, the foolish human race continues to thrive. Would that the love of boys became the common form of love in the world, and that women would die out and Japan become an Isle of Men. Quarrels between husband and wife would cease, jealousy disappear, and the world enter at last into an era of peace.[6]

Much as this wish might appeal to some, it is impossible to believe that

Saikaku really wanted to abolish women - though doing so would surely bring about universal peace. This passage is the clearest example of covert irony I have been able to find in a hasty review of Japanese literature. We would no more offer Saikaku's suggestion for world peace to Mr Reagan and Mr Gorbachev than we would offer Swift's modest proposal to Mrs Thatcher.

Here is a more gentle example of covert irony, this time from the *Kokinshū* (number 84):

Hisakata no	On a day in spring
hikari nodokeki	When the light throughout the sky
haru no hi ni	Warms with tranquillity,
shizugokoro naku	Why is it with unsettled heart
hana no chiru ran	That the cherry flowers fall?[7]

The reader's reply - or reconstruction - might be: it is not the flowers whose heart is unsettled, but the poet's, and ours.

More often, however, it is difficult to know whether an irony is real. I have struggled over Narihira's famous '*Tsuki ya aranu*' (Kokinshū number 747), and still am not sure whether it is ironic. Booth offers several reasons for readers' failure to catch ironies: ignorance, prejudice, inattention, lack of practice and emotional inadequacy.[8] 'Ignorance' is exacerbated by cultural and chronological distance, which is probably our greatest obstacle when dealing with Heian texts.

Marian Ury has scrutinized Seidensticker's *Genji* and found that the translator 'is such a master of ironical statement that his techniques are worth cataloguing.'[9] She concludes that some of Seidensticker's ironies faithfully reproduce ironies in the original *Genji*, and that others are questionable. Here is an example of an authentic *Genji* irony. Ury sets the scene: 'Higekuro's first wife is mad; she has just poured the contents of a brazier over her husband's head: [Seidensticker translates:] "It was all so horrible. Had he not known what an essentially gentle creature she was, he would not have been able to endure it so long."[10] The original text reads: '*Makoto no kokorobae no aware naru o mizu shirazuba, kō made omoisugusubyō mo naki keutosa kana....*'[11] As Ury says, 'It is exactly the fact that Higekuro's rationalization proceeds in such specific terms ('essentially gentle creature' for *makoto no korobae no aware naru*) that makes us realize how remarkably kind this man is to himself.'[12] This realization constitutes the reconstruction called forth by the irony. (As Ury notes, Waley missed the irony here.) In some other passages, Ury finds Seidensticker's ironical treatment inappropriate. She gives this example: 'Aoi is newly dead; Genji "had for some time had his eye on one Chūnagon, but for the period of mourning had put away amorous thoughts. It seemed most civilized of him"... *Aware naru mi-kokoro kana to mitatematsuru*. In the case of Higekuro's wife, *aware naru* was "essentially gentle," here it is the sneer of "most civilized." For Seidensticker to read hypocrisy into this moment of feeling seems unnecessarily unkind.'[13]

Ury knows Heian Japanese well enough to second-guess Seidensticker, but what are less knowledgeable readers to do? First, I would say that the *Genji* is, by its nature, a profoundly ironic text. Northrop Frye's observation that the novel is a realistic parody of the romance applies perfectly to the *Genji*, particularly to the later chapters.[14] In a Heian romance, the hero finds a beautiful lady in an unexpected place, as Narihira does in *Ise monogatari* and as Genji does in *Wakamurasaki*. In a realistic parody (and parody is a form of covert irony, in Booth's definition),[15] the hero finds a homely lady (e.g. Suetsumuhana), instead of the conventional beauty, or the 'hero' misses his chance by being neurotically indecisive (e.g. Kaoru). When read this way - as a realistic parody of Heian romantic conventions - the *Genji* is full of potential for rhetorical irony as well.

How are we to know whether a particular irony is Seidensticker's or Murasaki Shikibu's? As a translator myself, I am perhaps not the best person to respond, but I would say that the reader has no choice but to give a reputable translator the benefit of the doubt. Just as we must rely on our own judgement as readers when we think we have spotted an irony, I think we have to trust the translator's judgement, as well, unless there is good reason not to.

I would like to conclude by discussing a passage from Tanizaki's 1935 novel *Bushūkū hiwa*, which I have translated as *The Secret History of the Lord of Musashi*, and Professor Atsuko Ricca Suga as *Vita segreta del Signore di Bushu*.[16] In Book IV, Terukatsu (the title character) has found a tunnel under the toilet of his master's wife. A samurai named Daisuke has been there before him. Here is my translation:

> We may assume that the excavator, after finishing the tunnel that Terukatsu discovered, was killed, thrown to the bottom of the shaft, and absorbed into the earth forever with the lady's excrement. What happened to Daisuke?...[W]e are told that... [for] four months... Daisuke lay doubled up inside a cave-like cavity that had been specially dug near the top of the shaft. Never taking a step into the outside world, he subsisted there on rice balls provided by the lady and his mother. From ancient times there have been numerous examples of men who sacrificed themselves for the sake of their masters, their parents or their brothers; but there cannot have been many who endured the hardships suffered by Daisuke, secluded for four months beneath a toilet. The reader must not confuse Daisuke's behaviour with the shameful conduct of a pervert or sex maniac. He was motivated by uncomplicated loyalty and filial piety. And probably, when this faithful, courageous youth realized that he had fulfilled his mission as far as he was able, he fell nobly on his sword, cast his body into the same darkness that had received the excavator, and *literally sank into his grave* [emphasis added].[17]

The passage is full of irony and culminates in a gloriously ironic pun, which I have failed to translate adequately. In Japanese the last clause reads: *shin ni mojidōri kanbashii saigo o togeta no de arō* ('truly, he must have met a literally *kanbashii* end').[18] Surely Tanizaki uses *kanbashii* ironically. It is worth remembering that the author was not of samurai stock, but was a member of the Tokyo *shitamachi* merchant class, and as such was perhaps readier than some of his compatriots to view the samurai class ironically. Further, the readers of the magazine in which the novel was first serialized - *Shinseinen* - were prepared to expect, or at least to be alert to the possibility of, irony, because of the magazine's reputation for sophistication, much as readers of *The New Yorker* have learned to be on the lookout for irony. As Booth says, 'No matter how much biographical or historical information we need or use in making our reconstructions [of ironic passages], they are finally built into patterns of shared literary expectations - the grooves of genre, the trajectories of aroused expectations and gratifications [p. 100].' *Kanbashii* can mean 'praiseworthy' or 'honourable,' and these would perhaps be the first senses to occur to a Japanese reader, given the context. The primary meaning of the word, however, is 'fragrant.' The irony arises from the interplay of both meanings. In this setting (a toilet), 'fragrant' can be understood only ironically; and death in a 'fragrant' toilet, even under the most honourable circumstances, can be called 'praiseworthy' only by someone with an ironic turn of mind. With one devastating word, then, Tanizaki has characterized Daisuke's end as both fragrant, which it was not, and praiseworthy, which it also was not. The words *shin ni* ('truly') and *mojidōri* ('literally') serve to call attention to the irony.

In fact there is a third dimension to the pun. *Kanbashii*, when it means 'fragrant,' connotes 'blossom', *hana*, which in turn reminds the reader of the other *hana*, 'nose.' No one who has read the novel needs to be reminded that noses play a significant role, and in fact the pun on noses and blossoms occurs explicitly in the following chapter.

Puns can rarely be translated effectively, and I am far from satisfied with my rendition of the phrase in question. The problem is that I was unable to find an English word that means both 'fragrant' and 'honourable.' Consequently, rather than translate *kanbashii* in either of its meanings, I invented an English play on words to suggest something of Tanizaki's playfulness. I might have said instead that 'Daisuke went out with a splash,' or that 'he died in good odour,' but neither of these vulgar efforts captures Tanizaki's irony or wit. Professor Suga's translation is better, though even she has not been able to reproduce the whole effect: 'incoronando una breve vita con profumi letteralmente imcomparabili' ('crowned a short life with literally incomparable fragrances.)[19]

Apparently some readers - even Japanese readers - do not see any irony in the passage. Booth is helpful in this connection. In discussing 'prejudice' as an obstacle to recognizing ironies, he writes, 'ironies that touch too close to sacred objects are almost certain to be misread' [p. 226]. This may explain why the Japanese military never (to my knowledge) objected to a novel that, to this American reader, looks like a savage parody of the samurai ethic.

In conclusion: covert irony, as defined by Booth, occurs in Heian, Genroku and modern Japanese literature, and there can be little doubt that it provides its distinctive spice to any number of works from all periods. Western readers and translators are not necessarily impervious to its pleasures; Japanese readers are not necessarily sensitive to them. A translator, therefore, must be alert to the possibility of covert irony in a Japanese literary text and trust his or her own judgement, being ever careful not to impose new ironies on an innocent passage. The reader who wants to be certain can only be advised to keep studying Japanese.

18

The Eccentric Tree: *Kami* and *Gaki* in the Botanical Imagination of the Medieval Japanese

WILLIAM LaFLEUR

The 'enchanted forest' is a nearly universal theme in literature and folklore: out on the edge of man's cities and villages, the forest - or at least a portion of it - has often been regarded with a mixture of fear and fascination. Personalized as something which intends to draw into itself the unsuspecting human being, such a forest - especially in the lore of Europe - is often presented as a locus of considerable danger. It is so either because it can disorient those who happen into it or because it can include malicious animals or humans which seem to be merely waiting to prey upon the unsuspecting. Children's stories are, of course, replete with this theme.

Sometimes, however, it is the individual tree that stands out from its fellows by being numinous or the object of wide, public circumspection. In this essay I focus on this individuated type of enchantment and apprehension rather than on the collectivity in which it stands. That is, I hope in this brief space to reverse the old precept about not seeing the forest for the trees - even if in this instance it is a tree of the enchanted or sacred variety that will receive attention.

Japan, of course, gives even the casual visitor ample opportunities to see and encounter individual sacred trees. They can be easily found in parks, groves, in the midst of deep forests, and, of course, in shrines. They will almost invariably be marked off from the others - girdled by the rope and tassels referred to as *shimenawa*. Beyond that we can often note other physical features of such trees that make them unusual. Extraordinary height, stateliness, or girth may characterize such a tree. An unusual deformation is, however, also quite common. Sometimes the *shimenawa* may encircle nothing more than a hollowed-out stump or the decayed hulk of something long past the prime of its botanical life-span. We realize, of course, that such trees have been singled out for respect and awe because within that complex of religious sensibilities often collectively called 'Shinto' they were and are thought to be inhabited by invisible *kami*. When people wish to describe Shinto they almost without fail call attention to these trees and how they are regarded. Along with the rock that has been girdled with a *shimenawa*, the tree regarded as a

121

kami is about as basic - and important - a representation of Shinto as one may find.

We can, moreover, be certain that the respect for such special trees derives from Japan's archaic period. From antiquity they were commonly regarded as those in which a *kami* would dwell. Carmen Blacker is certainly correct in defining the kind of things in which *kami* habitually reside:[1]

> These objects usually by their very shape proclaim that something numinously 'other' lies hidden within. A camphor tree of unusual age and hugeness, for example, a cryptomeria tree of vast girth, a pine tree with its roots twisted into peculiar contortions, a stone of unmistakably phallic shape - all these are clearly vessels through which an inherent numinous presence shows as though from another world.

There are several points deriving from this which I think are especially worth nothing.

The first is the clear nexus between a given tree's irregularity or eccentricity and the fact that it is commonly assumed to be indwelt by a *kami*. There is a connection between where *kami* choose to dwell and a perceptible oddity about the tree itself. Something about the *kami*-indwelt tree sets it off from most of its fellows: age, shape or even being 'disfigured.' That is, as Mary Douglas has shown in her widely-influential *Purity and Danger: An Analysis of Concepts of Pollution and Taboo*, the 'sacrality' of things can be directly correlated with the fact that such individual things, at least in comparison with their fellows, are perceived as anomalous. And they are also dangerous to the extent that they are anomalous and eccentric. And that element of danger will mean they are treated in special ways.

The *shimenawa* around the sacred tree of Shinto is a clear sign of that. It signals that the human community has noted something unusual about the tree, refers to it as indwelt by *kami*, and will treat it with a mixture of respect and fear. It is the perceived unusualness and danger that are important - rather than matters of aesthetics. Extremely aged trees may be reduced to little more than a hollowed and weather-beaten stump - but still be girdled by a *shimenawa* and revered. Likewise, the gnarled, bizarrely shaped and dessicated can qualify; beauty is not the criterion.

I call attention to these features of phenomenological eccentricity and perceived danger in such *kami*-dwelt trees because recognition of them can, I believe, assist our grasp of what happened in medieval Japan when Shinto notions and practices were fitted - either happily or not so - into the more comprehensive and powerful Buddhist paradigm that characterized that era. What I wish to demonstrate here is that there was conceptual and imaginative bridgework between the archaic, Shinto notion of *kami* in trees and the medieval, Buddhist one of *gaki* or hungry ghosts in certain eccentric individuals in the botanical world.

The attention to trees within the ethos of Shinto is well known. What is comparatively unknown, however, is that at a point fairly early in the history of Buddhist presence in Japan a keen interest in botanical life - and its religious significance - also exhibited itself. A hypothesis I have been pursuing for some time now is that by tracing the lineaments of this problem we can learn a great deal about the historic interaction between

Shinto and Buddhism. Although the theories of *honji-suijaku* dominated the medieval discussions of the relations between Shinto and Buddhism - and had a profound presence in the arts of the period,[2] conceptions of botanical life were not unrelated. In an earlier study I traced the Buddhist philosophers' disquisitions on the question whether or not 'trees and plants attain buddhahood' (*sōmoku jōbutsu*), a topic on which there was considerable discussion in Japan already in the Nara period; it was one that attracted considerable public attention, especially on the occasion of the 'great debate' formally held under imperial auspices in the year 963. Those matters will not be rehearsed here. It is, however, at least important to note that although the discussion of this problem began in China, the Japanese seem to have entered into it with a special degree of enthusiasm. They also concluded the matter almost unequivocally in the affirmative: to them it seemed almost inconceivable that trees and plants would *not* have Buddha nature.[3] The point to be drawn from this, I suggest, is that in the minds of the Japanese the status - even as objects of religious attention - of trees was not a matter of indifference. Undoubtedly reflecting archaic Shinto sentiments, the learned Buddhist philosophers of the late classical and medieval periods concluded that trees are not only capable of being enlightened but, in all probability, are already more enlightened than most human beings.

My focus here, however, is upon a slightly later phase in the Buddhists' incorporation of botanical life into their concerns and, specifically, on things that at first sight might seem to be minor sections of a few medieval works of pictorial art. Holding that the close analysis of even seemingly obscure details can often provide an angle of sight into fairly large historical developments, I will try here to look at certain documents which purport to show what were called 'hungry ghosts in trees.'

* * *

'Hungry ghost' is the common but somewhat inadequate rendering into English of what the Japanese called *gaki* (*preta* in Sanskrit, *o-kuei* in Chinese.) Depicted as everlastingly famished, this figure appears already twice in the *Man'-yōshū* poetry collection of the eighth century. In one instance the concept seems to be used in semi-jest by the poet Ikeda Taritsugu to taunt another person named Ōmiwa Okimori:[4]

teradera no	A temple-hopping
megaki mōsaku	female hungry ghost asks
Ōmiwa no	to mate with
ogaki tabarite	Ōmiwa and make offspring
sono ko umahamu	looking like them both

There is a somewhat less levity in a poem by Kasa no Iratsuhime (Lady Kasa), an eighth century woman poet who, for the intensity of the passion in her verse, is often considered a precursor of Ono no Komachi:[5]

aimowanu	Longing for someone
hito o omouwa	who does not return one's love
ōdera no	is just like bowing
gaki no shirie ni	in a temple to a hungry ghost
nugazuku ga gotoshi	icon's backside

Later, however, when the Japanese had entered deeply into their medieval period the *gaki* seems to have been taken with total seriousness; by then it was not something that ordinary people, especially if there were Buddhist practitioners, would be quite so likely to treat in jest. There is overwhelming evidence, both textual and visual, that the *gaki* were in that period taken as real, although usually invisible, beings. According to orthodox Buddhist teaching the *gaki* constituted a differentiable category within the basic six (*rokudō*) that comprise the 'hierarchy of being' within the Buddhist taxonomy that originated in India - the scale on which individuals will be born, will die and will be repeatedly reborn according to karma's law.[6] Hungry ghosts were the epitome of craving and were classically defined in the Buddhist literature as creatures with enormous appetites but lacking the physiological wherewithall to satisfy such desire. The incompatibility between their appetites and their capacity for satisfaction was in the Buddhist sutras represented by portrayals of them as having 'stomachs the size of Mount Sumeru [the cosmic centre of the Buddhist cosmology] but throats as thin as needles.' Moving beyond mere frustration, the *gaki* were viewed as beings in perpetual pain.[7]

Although, as noted, *gaki* appear already in the *Man'yōshū*, it is really in later literature and art that they can be found in great numbers. And inasmuch as in the later classical and medieval periods that literature and art became more and more self-consciously Buddhist, it is natural that we find more extensive and intensive presentations of the hungry ghost therein. In fact, two outstanding, extant artistic works of the medieval period are the *Gaki zōshi* or 'Hungry ghost scrolls' which today are housed in the National Museums of Kyoto and Tokyo.

I have elsewhere analyzed these materials in an attempt to show that the hungry ghost was far from being a minor or quaint figure in the intellectual, religious and artistic landscape of the medieval Japanese but, on the contrary, an important cog in the machinery of the medieval mind.[8] My specific concern here, however, is not with the general theory of *gaki* in this period but with what seems to have been a sub-species of these pitiable creatures - namely, what should be called 'hungry ghosts in trees.' Two instances are chosen here for an exploration of what this involved in medieval Japan. The first is from the *gaki* section of the 'Kitano Tenjin engi,' the original of which is dated to 1219.[9]

Aside from one green-bodied demonic figure in the lower left of this segment, the rest of the creatures portrayed are brown-bodied hungry ghosts. Most have enormously bloated stomachs although one has a mid-section consumed by flame. A *gaki* in the upper right eats children and one on the lower right consumes flame - in accord with scriptural statements of what such creatures are apt to do in futile attempts to appease their insatiable hunger.

In the lower centre section, however, is what purports to be the withered bole of a tree. I think it important to note that the parts of this tree, when seen compositely, take on a humanoid form. The limbs extending upward from its mid-section resemble arms. There is also a perceptible distinction between a 'trunk' and a 'head' in this figure. Finally, the placement and shape of the black cavity in the upper portion is obviously meant to resemble a gaping mouth. In the hollowed-out 'stomach' portion of the tree is painted an indistinct figure that looks somewhat like a brown homunculus. In some sense this represents the *gaki* within the tree, yet it would be equally accurate to say that the whole tree constitutes a hungry ghost in vegetational form. It looks like a tree in pain. Its widely opened 'mouth' suggests both a condition of starvation and an orifice from which a cry of anguish comes forth. It is clear that the artist showed an impressive imaginative scope and ingenuity in this portrayal of how a tree-form *gaki* might appear in the world we see with our own eyes. Each of the above features of the tree, if considered separately, would not deserve mention; collectively, however, and in concert they add up to a vivid representation of a humanoid, hungry and suffering tree.

The second illustration of this kind of being is found in a scroll now at a temple known as Zenrin-ji in Kyoto. It appears in a type of Buddhist painting known as 'jikkaizu' and dates from the late thirteenth century.[10]

A *jikkaizu*, it should be noted, is literally a diagram of 'ten worlds' or categories of being. The more typical Buddhist taxonomy was one of 'six paths' - beginning at the bottom with the creatures of hell (Japanese, *jigoku*), then upwards through the hungry ghosts (*gaki*), the animals (*chikushō*), bellicose titans (*ashura*), human beings (*ningen*), and the deities (*kami*) at the top. Tendai Buddhism later added four additional, specifically Buddhist, categories: the direct auditors of Sakyamuni (*shōmon*), self-enlightened beings (*engaku*), bodhisattvas (*bosatsu*) and Buddhas (*butsu*).[11]

It is this total of ten that forms the conceptual framework of the *jikkaizu*, which in its totality is a painting of groups of figures representing each category.

The group of *gaki* is, then, only one portion of the whole painting belonging to Zenrin-ji. In it these creatures are engaged in various activities traditionally associated with them, especially eating fire and consuming smoke. The two on the right edge of the insert are most probably eating infants - since the perpetually starved condition of the hungry ghost compelled it, we are told, to try to consume anything within reach and one's little children are often close at hand. All, of course, are portrayed with horribly distended stomachs, nearly skeletal frames and thin throats.

At the centre of the *gaki* section is, of course, a tree - one that in its lower half seems to be literally fused together with the brown body of a hungry ghost. The execution of this coalescence is so clever that two downturned 'limbs' of the tree are simultaneously an arm and a leg of the humanoid ghost which seems to be sitting inside the base of the tree. To the bottom right and on the two upper limbs of the tree are the inverted tree scars left where other limbs had come off. However, inasmuch as it is the concept of hungry ghost that is meant to shape our understanding of the specificity of this particular tree, those scars can readily be seen as multiple orifices - in fact, as a series of gaping mouths. The third irregularity of this particular tree is the distension of its bole on the lower left. This part of the tree, obviously by design, looks alternatively like the protruding stomach of a *gaki* and like a gargantuan tumour that has developed on this part of the tree.

What the artist has executed with such skill is a provision of humanoid limbs, mouths and a stomach for this tree. The result is a visual puzzle, a 'now it's this, now it's that' kind of doubled image. And, to be sure, the Buddhism that shaped the intentionality of this kind of medieval painting was one which made much of the fact that our perceptions of reality are fundamentally unstable. Since one of the operative notions in Buddhism is that the real world is usually not all that it seems within the constructs of our multiple illusions, this was the kind of visual puzzle that would fit in well with Buddhist philosophical and religious suppositions. It is not difficult to imagine a medieval monk pointing to it to illustrate a sermon on the theme of the difference between appearance and reality.

We can quite easily trace the textual basis for trees like these. For Japanese Buddhists the *locus classicus* for hungry ghost representations in the canon was in the Chinese text *Cheng-fa nien-ch'u ching*, a Buddhist work translated from a Sanskrit original in the sixth century. That work listed thirty-six sub-species of *gaki* and the third from the last in that list is the kind of 'hungry ghosts that live in trees.'[12] Closer in time to the twelfth and thirteenth centuries Japanese painters, however, was Genshin's *Ōjōyō-shū* and its mention of *gaki* that inhabit trees. That important Japanese source says:[13]

> There are hungry ghosts that get born within trees and suffer greatly
> by being squeezed within the trunks of such trees like *tokusa* worms.
> People who in their present life cut down the cool forests, groves or
> the trees in temple precincts are reborn this way as karmic retribution.

The immense authority of Genshin's work made its pronouncements into models for Japanese of the medieval period and certainly a text which served as the basis for a good deal of literary and pictorial art.

To trace the textual origins of this kind of art, however, does not yet explain how it 'worked' within the medieval Japanese mind - that is, how and why people believed it as something which made sense to them. To attempt an explanation of how it 'worked,' however, a contextualization of the matter is needed.

In order to do this I am forced to present a hypothesis which, I realize, tends to fly in the face of a commonly accepted view. That is, a fair amount of scholarly and popular writing - especially in Japanese - about Japan's rapid and ready acceptance of Buddhism attributes that acceptance simply to a kind of endemic national impressionability and a naive, ready acceptance of everything exotic: a 'simple' and unquestioning people pursuing and embracing what for them was the latest foreign import. One cannot, of course, deny an element of this.

Yet, this explanation may itself be overly simple. We need to note, for instance, that it has become increasingly clear that the process of Buddhism's acceptance was considerably more protracted, complex, uneven and difficult than the theory of 'a people of simple impressionability' assumes. While the process of acceptance of Buddhism in Japan was easier than it had been in China - where what Erik Zürcher called a 'conquest' was needed - it nevertheless was one which required the presentation of arguments, apologies and defences. Research in recent decades has made that increasingly clear.

To that I wish to add the following. When we look at the materials involved in the Buddhist apologists' attempts to convince the not-yet-persuaded (as distinct from intra-Buddhist debates), it appears that much of the Japanese Buddhists' argumentation for the viability of their paradigm focussed on its use in explaining the whys and wherefores of a wide variety of totally terrestrial, observable phenomena. That is, they pushed their view often as not as the latest 'science' rather than as what we today identify as 'religion.' They often treated and tried to establish Buddhism's credibility first of all by giving 'explanations' within a relatively broad range of smaller but puzzling things about which the Japanese of that period were naturally bound to be curious. The area of 'proof' of Buddhist teaching often was played out first in the realm of phenomena of the observable world - proximate rather than ultimate concerns, matters of 'science' rather than soteriology.

Once that point is recognized, the epoch as a whole becomes newly interesting. In fact, it leads directly to the observation that during the classical and medieval periods of their history the Japanese demonstrated a great deal of curiosity about natural things, anomalous phenomena and problems of causality. It is important to recognize that the cause-effect nexus, at that time articulated as the Buddhist principle of *inga*, is the subject of multiple documents originating from this epoch. Moreover, what is striking is the unusual number of paintings and artistic representations that deal with causality. It is the explicit topic of certain picture scrolls (*emaki*), especially the *Kako Genzai Inga-kyō* and the *Jūni Innen Emaki*. In addition, we have abundant evidence to show that precisely during the epoch under consideration - that is the twelfth and thirteenth centuries - the Japanese demonstrated a good deal of curiosity about what we today would call medical pathologies. This, too, they carried over into the forms of art. In this context it is worth remarking that exactly contemporaneous with the Hungry Ghost Scrolls and medieval paintings such as the *jikkaizu* considered here was produced another type of painted scroll that explicitly details the phenomena of a whole set of physical ailments. Dating from the late twelfth century, the *Yamai no zōshi* or 'Scroll of Illnesses' depicts with striking vividness what people of that era clearly saw as physiological or psychological oddities in human society.

The significance of the *Yamai no zōshi* and its intrinsic connection with other documents of the era have not received the attention they deserve - at least by persons other than art historians. This scroll, well known to the historian of art, portrays a variety of human illnesses and anomalies. Examples are: a white-haired albino girl in a public place evoking gales of laughter due to the irregular features of her body; a court lady suffering from acute insomnia and lying wide awake in a room where other women are sleeping soundly and 'naturally'; an indoor scene of a family whose three children all clearly have the same abnormal 'black nose' as their father whereas the mother does not - thereby showing curiosity about congenital defects; a woman suffering from extreme obesity and requiring cooperative assistance from a group of 'normal' women in order even to walk; a woman whose eye has been pecked by a rooster - thought to be a proffered etiology for human 'night-blindness' by way of contagion from fowl, which were obviously recognized as lacking the ability to see in darkness. Since the Edo period it has been common to group the 'Scroll of Illnesses' with the 'Hungry Ghost Scroll' (*gaki zōshi*) and 'Hell Scroll ' (*jigoku zōshi*); modern art historians concede the stylistic similarities and the fact that all these clearly date from the last decades of the twelfth century. Reflecting the deeper significance of this consensus, Miyeko Murase correctly notes that the Illnesses Scroll:[14]

> ...must have been intended to represent the pains and sufferings that characterize existence in the Realm of Human Beings within the Buddhist scheme of the *rokudō*, or the Six Realms of Reincarnation.

This point is important - and important precisely because it can be employed to tell us what the '*gaki* in trees' were all about. There is no reason to assume that the medieval Japanese person's curiosity about physiological and psychological anomalies - so patently present in the *Yamai zōshi* - would not have extended also to the asking of questions about 'oddities' within the non-human world as well. My point is that unusual forms of botanical life would have been the subject of exactly the same curiosity and concern. The artists, no doubt reflecting the concerns of their patrons and appealing to the eventual viewers of their work, seem to have been intensely interested in *anything* that showed itself as anomalous. The concern for anomalies extended, of course, to attempts to provide explanations as to how they came about. And that is the area in which the text-mastering Buddhist 'doctors' can be expected to have wanted to prove themselves as authorities, the persons with ready-to-hand theories that could give the 'real story' and demonstrate once again the explanatory power of the Buddhist paradigm. These doctors were the masters in matters of cause-and-effect, the scholars whose religion was also the best available science of the day.

It was noted above that art historians have come to see the 'Illnesses Scroll' as itself part of the comprehensive explanations offered by the Buddhist theory of the *rokudō* or six paths of being. This means that there seems to have been an intrinsic connection in the medieval mind between 'illness' perceived as anomalous types and the karmic causality scheme that was the conceptual engine for the *rokudō* system. Botanical disease, then, would be fitted into the same scheme: the unusually shaped tree which we today might explain in terms of disease and/or dessication could within the confines of this medieval 'science' be explained on what might be called 'the hungry ghost hypothesis.' Their shape was forced upon them by the presence within them of invisible *gaki* which, as the result of karmic patterns, had taken up residence there. The argument makes an appeal to a 'see-it-for-yourself' kind of quasi-empiricism; it is intended to 'convince' even though it is circular. By using the Buddhist notions of karma and hungry ghosts to 'explain' why it is that certain trees are quite unusual, those visibly contorted trees seem to have been used, in turn, as a witnessable 'proof' of the existence of the *rokudō* system and of the workings of karma.

The key to this is the simple fact that all human beings at one time or another have seen trees very much like these. The first function of the trees in the scrolls would seem to be to remind us of phenomena we have already seen in nature. A tree such as the one in the *Kitano Tenjin Engi* is, although slightly exaggerated in the painting, basically none other than one that has become severely dessicated. Its trunk has become a hollow cavern and it has gaping holes on its surface. Likewise, the tree in the *Jikkaizu* is characterized by disease; some of its limbs have broken off - leaving scars - and a portion of its base has an excessive development of cells in the condition known as 'edema.'

In many ways, of course, culture changes at a more rapid rate than nature does. We have, therefore, every right to assume that the medieval Japanese saw basically the same botanical world that we see today - and could readily notice the difference between basically healthy trees and those which were either withered or diseased. The difference between them and us, however, is that our pathology for such anomalies is defined in the scientific terms of a botanical language whereas their 'explanations' were drawn from Buddhist texts.

Of course this was didactic art - but no less impressive or artistic for being so. Part of its intentionality was to make slightly more patent what the naked eye can 'see' if pushed in the right direction by the art as medium of sight.[15] Likewise, because this kind of argument was basically circular, such trees themselves, then, must have become a kind of 'proof' that the phenomenon of the *gaki* had empirical, visible, referents in the real world. The effect can be easily imagined. If the notion of the *gaki* could be employed to explain such trees, those same trees in turn did their part to lend credibility to the total explanation being promulgated by the Buddhists. By providing an explanation for less than ultimate matters, the Buddhist clarification of ultimate things gained a wider receptivity. In a medieval age religion and 'science' often occupied a similar space in the intellectual landscape. In such a context art of this type played a very crucial role; in its very concreteness it mediated between the doctrine - for instance about *gaki* in canonical texts and an entire range of things about which ordinary people would tend to be naturally curious. The texts, the art and common curiosity were brought together in this way.

That the Japanese artists paid attention to finessing the details of 'hungry ghosts in trees' to make them look both fascinating and credible was not, I think, incidental. On one level the Buddhist 'doctors' could in this way explain not only such trees but also why from archaic times the Japanese, under the aegis of what we call Shinto, had already long had a profound respect for certain trees. The medieval Buddhists, precisely in striving to provide a more *comprehensive* paradigm - or 'theory' at a higher level - had to explain not only details of the world but also why the older paradigm had long had a hold on the mind - that is, why on its own level it had 'worked.'[16]

Within Shinto there had been a pre-history of imagining certain trees as having *kami* somehow present within them; respect, awe and a measure of fear vis-à-vis such trees had been, as noted above, the corresponding practice from antiquity. Buddhists then augmented that with theories about some of these trees, theories that aspired at least to be 'scientific' and up-to-date based on the latest texts from continental Asia. The tree

129

seen as inhabited by a hungry ghost became a tree that served as an intellectual/religious structure that was complex and worked out in considerable detail. My argument is that the medieval period seems to have accepted the Buddhist interpretation of such things not necessarily *because* it was complex, overwhelming and 'metaphysical' but because on many levels it seemed - at least on the basis of the state of knowledge at the time - to sharpen the understanding of natural processes and the causality behind natural forms. The widely accepted view is that Buddhism made an impact merely by being exotic and mystifying; the alternative suggested here is that, on the contrary, in many areas Buddhism tried to explain certain mysteries - and gain credibility via its power to explain. It often 'worked' then because it seemed to function like science, not because it was touted as what modern man classifies as religion or metaphysics - especially if by 'religion' and by 'metaphysics' are meant mere mumbo-jumbo and mystification.

*　　*　　*

The modern world, of course, explains things differently. Ironically it is, I suspect, easier for people today, both within and outside of Japan, to feel a certain attraction to Shinto's relatively simple and straightforward notion of natural forms as worthy of respect and, perhaps, even as 'sacred.' Our ever more rapid and aggressive depletion of our world's forests makes us feel there is real 'reasonableness' in the archaic Shinto respect for such natural phenomena. Medieval Buddhism, I have here suggested, did not, however, so much lay a foreign and 'metaphysical' imposition on such things as try to explain in a new vocabulary more exactly why the archaic view was one of value. If anything Buddhism seems to have extenuated and ethicalized the element of danger already present in the archaic respect for such trees. A lesson was drawn. The Buddhists claimed that *karmic* consequences are operative when there is human interaction with nature. Trees - and, by extension, whole forests - could not, the Buddhists said, be misused with impunity. The *Ōjōyō-shū*, it should be recalled, combined its description/explanation with a hard-hitting moral lesson:

> There are hungry ghosts that get born within trees and suffer greatly by being squeezed within the trunks of such trees like tokusa worms. People who in their present life cut down the cool forests, groves or the trees that grow in temple precincts are reborn this way as *karmic* retribution.

Today it may be more the morality rather than the 'science' in this that looks to find a ready receptivity in our world.

19

A European Eye on Japanese Arts and a Japanese Response to 'Japonisme' (1860-1920)[1]

A Transcultural Interaction between Visual Arts and Critical Discourse

INAGA SHIGEMI

I

One of the first champions of the Impressionists, Théodore Duret (1838-1927) is also known as one of the first 'japonisants' or amateurs of Japanese arts. His authority was based on his experience. As a matter of fact, he was one of the first French civilians to visit Japan.[2] This privileged position is worth noting principally because it was Duret himself who affirmed as an eye-witness the Japanese influence on French Impressionists. In one of his essays entitled 'Critique d'avant-garde' (1885), we see Duret advance an analogy between Japanese Ukiyo-e prints and Impressionist paintings.

> Il a fallu l'arrivée parmi nous des albums japonais pour que quelqu'un osat s'asseoir sur le bord d'une rivière, pour juxtaposer sur une toile un toit qui fût hardiment rouge (...) et de l'eau bleu. (...) Ces images japonaises (...) sont d'une fidélité frappante. (...) Je regarde un album japonais et je dis: oui c'est bien anisi, sous son atmosphère lumineuse et transparente, que la mer s'étend bleue et colorée (...) aussi a-t-il fortement influencé les Impressionistes. / L'oeil japonais, doué d'une acuité particuliere, exercée au sein d'une admirable lumière (...) a su voir dans le plein air une gamme de tons aigus que l'oeil européen n'y avait jamais vue et (...) n'y eût probablement jamais découverte (...). Claude Monet, parmi nos paysagistes, a eu le premier la hardiesse d'aller aussi loin qu'eux [les Japonais] dans ses coloration.[3]

In the years that followed Duret continued to make this comparison. Interesting as it may be, the assertion is rather problematic, for it is beyond verification. Nevertheless, Richard Muther's *Geschichte der Malerei in neunzehenten Jahrhundert* (1893-94, in three volumes) does suggest the authority Duret enjoyed in his day. Respecting Duret's conception of an evolution in European modern painting, the author of this monumental book was obliged to insert a chapter on Japanese art between 'Realismus' and 'Impressionismus' in order to explain the gap that would otherwise remain open between the two. A curious and heteroclite mixture from our point of view, for Impressionism would be a bastard or a mutant, rather than the legitimate son of European painting tradition if we would not admit, with Duret and Muther, the legitimacy of Japanese insemination!

II

We should recall a passage of the Goncourt brothers' *Manette Salomon* (Ch. XLVII), to make the point that this vision of Japan as a world without shadow and filled with bright and transparent sunshine was a sort of 'constant' for that generation of French 'Japonisants,' and that they believed this 'pays féerique, un jour sans ombre et qui n'était que lumière' to be transmitted with complete fidelity by Japanese ukiyo-e prints.[4]

This French optic clearly appears when we examine how Duret perceived the historical evolution of Japanese colour prints:

> En ce qui concerne le coloris proprement dit, au commencement du XIXe siècle, il consistait en tons pâles et comme atténués, mais à mesure que l'art se développe, il s'accentue de plus en plus. C'est dans l'oeuvre de Kouniyoshi et Toyokouni II qu'il atteint enfin son maximum d'intensité et arrive à un degré d'éclat qu'il serait impossible de dépasser.[5]

Duret, therefore, dates the apogée of the ukiyo-e polychrome prints in the middle of the nineteenth century. We can readily understand why Duret came to this view; and while we can no longer share his view, the fact is it was widely accepted as authentic by French 'Japonisants' circles at the time. In the same way he considered Impressionist painting to be the result of a liberation from the conventional academic chiaroscuro and a step towards open air aesthetics; he also believed that the vivid colour of the Japanese ukiyo-e prints had reached the peak of perfection in its own evolution.

This exaggerated preoccupation with crude colours in late ukiyo-e prints was to be replaced in the 1890s by a more sophisticated preference for the attenuated colours of the eighteenth century prints. A native art dealer, one Tadamasa Hayashi (1856-1906) seems to be largely responsible for this fundamental change. During this same period French amateur painters no longer recognized any kind of climacteric in the use of primary colours of the nineteenth century Japanese print but rather began to see in it a sign of decadence.[6]

Interestingly enough, this aesthetic shift coincided with the so-called Impressionist crisis. A curious coincidence, indeed, because it was precisely when the French amateurs began to regard the late ukiyo-e prints with their crude colours as decadent work, that French aesthetics was also dominated by 'Decadentisme.' Significantly, Stephan Mallarmé's collection contains only a shoddy 'pacotilles' of the so-called 'bariolage' of late Japanese prints. Rather than to ascribe this to a 'mauvais goût' of our great poet, it would be more appropriate to say that this decadent poet justified himself by his own 'decadent' Japanese prints collection.[7]

The apogee or the decadence, that is the question; which of these incompatible interpretations of the late Japanese prints is the right one? Rather than make a choice between the two, we should try and understand how and why such a divergence took place in the aesthetic judgements of the second half of the nineteenth century European appreciation of Japanese prints.

Divergent as they are, both of these hypotheses are based on the then prevailing organic theory of social evolution. The 'phase difference' between the two stems only from a psychological complex inherent in any cultural exchange. As a matter of fact, did not the Japanese disdain the occidental amateurs for their one-sided appreciation of the so-called 'decadent' Japanese prints? By so doing the Japanese could declare, if not ostensibly, a superiority of ukiyo-e prints over Impressionist painting. It would indeed have been quite infamous for the Europeans to learn that the new world vision achieved by Impressionism reflected nothing but a decadent tendency in Japanese ukiyo-e prints. Moreover, we should not forget, here, that the famous 'bariolage' of late ukiyo-e prints was largely due to the chemical pigments imported from Europe. Before the Impressionists, it was therefore the Japanese that suffered from the so-called 'indigomania,' to use the expression of J. K. Huysmans.[8] Did the decadence of ukiyo-e, then, come from the decline of Occident?

In short, it is one thing that cultural exchanges amplify artistic experience; it is another thing if this exchange serves as a criterion for any quality judgement.

III

Now let us return to the Japonisme thesis which regards Japanese prints as the origin of Impressionism and let us examine if the hypothesis was relevant in Japan or not. For, if Impressionist aesthetics had been unconditionally accepted in Japan, it would have justified Théodore Duret's claim, but the historical fact was much more complicated.

As we know, during the Meiji period, when Japan 'imported' European oil painting techniques, there was a conflict between the option of the 'Bitumen' School ('yani-ha') and the 'Violet' School ('murasaki-ha'). In other words, there were incompatible positions in Japan as to how the European oil painting technique should be applied. The 'Bitumen' School represented a tendency of the Barbizon School transmitted by Antonio Fontanesi (1818-1882) to Asai Chū (1856-1907); whereas the 'Violet' School reflected a moderated impressionist tendency imported to Japan by Kuroda Seiki (1866-1924), a disciple of Raphael Collin (1850-1916).[9] It would be useless to try to judge which of them was better suited to represent Japanese nature or 'local colour.' Much more important for us is to recognize that such a conflict between the Bitumen School and the Violet School did exist in spite of the impressionistic world view for which Japan was par excellence an ideal model of the Violet School. We can deduce here that such an impressionistic interpretation of Japan, advanced by Duret and other Japonisants like Louis Gonse had no realistic cognitive base at all.[10]

IV

This fundamental ambiguity of Japanese nature in face of the Impressionist aesthetics gave birth to a more complicated situation in the next generation.

It is no longer an empirical question but rather an ideological and theoretical conflict. In 1909, Yamazaki Nobuyoshi presented a clearly impressionistic painting to the official Salon Bunten, which provoked a vivid discussion. The Shirakaba School members enthusiastically applauded this painting, saying this canvas was equal to Claude Monet's 'La Gare St Lazare' in its achievement. On the contrary, Oda Kazuma (1882-1955), painter and engraver, harshly criticized this work. Oda could not admit the painter's irresponsible imitation of Claude Monet because, by such an imitation, the painter violated the local colour typical to Japan. In other words, Oda did not accuse the painter of plagiarism but of infidelity to the spirit of Impressionism which, according to him, consisted of respecting the sensation the painter feels in front of Nature. Oda maintained: 'If Impressionism was born in the French climate, a painter respecting the Japanese climate would naturally get a different effect of nature from that of French Impressionists. So the painters in question were not at all faithful to Japanese nature which is much more sombre, calmer and more sober than French nature. It was therefore quite natural that Impressionism should not develop in Japan.'[11]

In this way, Oda vigorously argued the inadaptability of Impressionistic coloration to the Japanese landscape. A declaration which completely contradicts the naive hypothesis of Thaodore Duret. This refutation is all the more symbolic as it was developed by a painter-engraver who, during that period, reestablished the tradition of Japanese prints not by returning to the past but rather by renovating it according to the modernist demands of the epoch. In short, what was 'avant-garde' to Théodore Duret in Japanese prints was nothing but a fossil of past feudalism for a Japanese contemporary artist.

Opposing Oda's view was Takamura Kōtarō (1883-1955) a famous poet and sculptor who defended Yamazaki's impressionistic painting. Paradoxically, however, this plea contradicts the Impressionist aesthetics he should have defended.

> In our present artistic world in Japan, most people believe that it is important to respect local colour. It is as if to say that the destiny of oil painting in Japan depends on its capability of finding a compromise with the local colour proper to Japan. As for us, we want to ignore such local colour; even if somebody wants to paint the sun with green pigment, I would not condemn him.[12]

Kōtarō speaks as if he were repeating the Impressionist principle of negation of local colour, but as a matter of fact, he rejects at the same time all that represents Japan. In this way, Kōtarō refuses to admit that the painting transmits any impression proper to its environment. He thus transgresses the limits of Impressionism. Moreover, with his incantation of the green sun, he opens up to Impressionism. Just as in Germany with Kandinsky or in England with Roger Fly, the delayed reception of Impressionism in Japan was inextricably mixed up with the artistic reaction that Impressionism itself had occasioned at the end of the nineteenth century.

We can now see that the affinity Duret pretended to have found between Japanese art and Impressionism was nothing but pure fantasy. But far from being negative, this fantasy was rather productive. Thanks to this 'idée-reçue,' a Japanese critic in the Taishō era could discover a forgotten old Japan; Duret tried to regenerate this Japanese tradition in the heart of the modernity Japan was experiencing. Kinoshita Mokutarō (1885-1945) was initiated to the forgotten world of ukiyo-e prints in about 1913 by European critics like R. Muther and Théodore Duret, and later he looked back upon this experience: 'Without any comparison with Impressionism we could hardly truly appreciate either the Japanese ukiyo-e prints of the Edo period nor the atmosphere they emanated.'[13]

Here we can see one case of reverse movement in Japonisme. This return of Japonisme to Japan makes it evident how complex cultural exchange is; for it reveals to us a kind of 'inverted synthesis' of the European misinterpretation of Japanese art, on the one hand, and the refusal of Impressionist aesthetics in Japan, on the other.

Guided by the Impressionist aesthetics, Mokutarō turned his gaze to ancient Japan and discovered about 1913 a forgotten 'artisan' - one Kobayashi Kiyochika (1847-1916). A disciple of Kawanabe Gyōsai (1831-1889), considered then by Europeans as the last personification of the disappearing Hokusai School, Kiyochika was at the same time one of the students of Charles Wirgman (1832-1891), special correspondent and painter for the *Illustrated London News* in Japan, who served as the first instructor of European painting techniques in Japan. Kiyochika was also interested in the photography being applied for the first time in Japan by Shimooka Renjō.[14]

In a series of Kiyochika's woodcuts 'Tokyo Meisho Zue,' executed between 1878 and 1881, Mokutarō found an unknown beauty, really impressionistic features 'avant la lettre.' What is significant here is the fact that this series was called 'kōsenga' or luminous images.[15] But contrary to what would be expected by a Théodore Duret, these 'plein-airist' images did not come so much from the tradition of Japanese ukiyo-e prints. Paradoxically, this singular expression of light effect came rather from the strict application of European academism's chiaroscuro technique. Moreover, this imitation of a European technique was undoubtedly exploited for its European export prospects. Of course these commercial tactics failed, because at the time the Europeans were earnestly looking for old Japanese prints and were no longer interested in contemporary art.

If Duret discovered in the ancient Japanese ukiyo-e prints a world filled with sunshine and transparent limpidity which he pretended he had really seen during his stay in Japan, the originators of these ukiyo-e prints, generally speaking, continued to ignore what was light and consequently what was shadow. It was not before they learned light and shadow from the Europeans that they recognized the existence of these factors in Nature. Thus, can we really suppose that the crude coloration of ukiyo-e prints truly reflects the 'limpid light' of Japan, as was declared by Duret?

If the Impressionists recognized the unknown light effects in the

Japanese traditional prints in which the Japanese noticed nothing of the sort, Kiyochika, in his turn, acquired in the rudimentary European academic technique of chiaroscuro, the ability to render the 'plein-airist' effects in his own 'modernist' woodcuts. It would certainly be a paralogism to call his discovery impressionist, as these unknown effects would not have been obtained without European Academism. Nevertheless, the result was quite 'impressive,' if not 'impressionistic.' Was not this double-misunderstanding the origin of a better mutual understanding and further communication between Eastern and Western aesthetics?

VI

It must be noted, finally, that just as the fantastic critical discourse of a Théodore Duret was necessary in order to retain and consolidate the Impressionists' interest in Japanese art, so the introduction to Japan of Impressionist aesthetics as theory was indispensable in order that the forgotten Kiyochika woodcuts should be exhumed from oblivion and rehabilitated. Indeed, thanks to Mokutarō the work of this Japanese 'Impressioniste avant la lettre' who had abandoned his 'kōsenga' thirty-five years earlier and was about to die, was saved. Sadly, he died without fully appreciating that a next generation had begun to reappraise his forgotten prints.

Here closes a complex link of aesthetic exchange. It was only at the end of this double negation between Europe and Japan that the Impressionist's view of Japanese art formulated by Duret was ratified in Japan. This vision had been grasped by a Japanese artist who did not know anything about Impressionism, but only the academic technique Impressionism disdained; and then this same vision was recaptured, only retrospectively, by a young critic who was indoctrinated, indeed for the first time in Japan, by Impressionist aesthetics, yet his appreciation of the new aesthetics was only through black and white reproductions!

Ultimately, nobody can say if it is legitimate, or not, to call Kiyochika an Impressionist. For it is no longer a question of an a-historical legitimation but of a historical recognition of legitimacy. It was exactly in this dynamism of paradoxical encounter between cultures, in this mutual determination between visual art and its discourse, or in this dialectical movement between words and images that Mokutarō recognized the real adventure of critical aesthetic discovery.

From that moment, the Impressionism imported to Japan was no more an artificial amalgam of Eastern Tradition and Western Modernity. Instead of imposing itself under the name of Europe, as was feared by several Japanese like Oda, Impressionism, from now on, was to contribute to further research in the Japanese aesthetics from which it had been inspired. At the end of this 'transcultural' voyage, we can recognize that the 'Impression: Soleil levant' of Claude Monet is finally justified in the 'Empire du soleil levant.'

20

Communitas, Equality, Anti-structure:
Reading Buson's Painting and Bashō's
Prose Poem, 'The Broken Hammer'

LEON ZOLBROD

Among the surviving pieces of poetry, calligraphy and painting attributed to Bashō (1644-1694) and Buson (1716-1784), the two most famous classical Japanese haiku poets, there is an ink drawing and calligraphic scroll known as 'The Broken Hammer' (*Kine-no Ore*).[1] The text is attributed to Bashō. The scroll, with Buson's signature and seals, is preserved in the Itsuō Art Museum, Osaka Prefecture. It is dated the sixth month, An'ei 6 (1777).

As an example of Buson's haiku painting and calligraphy and as one of the pieces that has helped to make Bashō a god-like figure in Japanese poetry, literature and art, 'The Broken Hammer' not only exemplifies one kind of beautiful object but the text may also be read as suggesting a kind of traditional Japanese social equality, which may be conveniently related to the anthropologist Victor Turner's concept of communitas.[2] The ideology of the text may be traced to earlier Japanese literature. The meaning points to an aspect of Japanese society often overlooked when people emphasize the rigid and hierarchical side of Japanese social life. Turner's concept of anti-structure matches the idea of social movement from high to low, as well as the reverse, which 'The Broken Hammer' enunciates. Besides the ideological and visual aspects of the pictorial and calligraphic representation of the text, a performance dimension may also be extracted from 'The Broken Hammer.' The mixed poetic and prosaic form known as *haibun*[3] may be projected by means of the recitative style of Noh chanting, which like haiku poetry was pervasive during the Tokugawa period.

In theoretical terms it is possible to explore text as idea, text as visual artifact and text as performance. All three features of 'The Broken Hammer' underscore the need to re-think traditional categories and disciplines and to reconsider the epistemological consequences of modes of representation that transcend ordinary boundaries or generic entities. Thus Japanology itself may be seen as a challenge to Western modes of organizing knowledge.

In English translation the text of Bashō's prose poem, 'The Broken Hammer' reads as follows:

'This object, called the "Broken Hammer", is treasured by an eminent person. It is one of the rarities of our land.

'Broken Hammer, what mountain were you born on? What lowly person in what village used you for pounding? You used to be an ordinary hammer, but now you are called a flower vase. Renamed as you are, your place is over the head of a noble person.

'It¯is the same with people. When you are in a high position, you must not be haughty. When you are lowly, you must not be envious. It is best in this world to be an ordinary hammer.

> 'What was this hammer?
> Was it once a camellia
> Or was it a plum?'
> (*Kono tsuchi no/mukashi tsubaki ka/ume no ki ka.*)[4]

The capping verse of the above text was first published in 1701, seven years after Bashō's death.[5] Then half a century later, in Hōreki six (1756), in a collection of Bashō's posthumous writings, *Bashō kusen shūi*, the complete text of the Japanese original appeared in woodblock type.[6] In a movable type edition of this text there are 149 graphemes. Some twenty years after this time, in An'ei six (1777), according to the surviving inscription, the poet-painter Buson rendered a calligraphic scroll in nine lines of text consisting of 151 graphemes together with a simple, almost diagrammatic, representation of a cylindrical instrument suggestive of a broken hammer or mallet of the kind once used in traditional China and Japan to pound stiff cloth on a *kinuta* or 'fulling block,' to make it more supple.

Below and slightly to the right of the capping verse of the text of 'The Broken Hammer' in three Japanese graphemes, is written 'Ha-se-wō', or Bashō, the name of the poet. In the lower right-hand corner of the scroll in two lines of text is an inscription that may be translated, 'By Shunsei, on the full moon of the sixth month, in the year of fire and the cock,' which corresponds to An'ei six by traditional Japanese chronology, or 1777 in the Western calendar.

'Shunsei' denotes Buson, and two seals that the poet-painter frequently used lend credence to the ascription. Scholars writing about 'The Broken Hammer' have never questioned either the attribution of the *haibun*, or prose-poem, to Bashō or the calligraphic rendition and sketch to Buson. Nonetheless, late in the summer of 1987 in Tokyo in private discussion with a distinguished Japanese scholar of Bashō and Buson, Professor Ogata Tsutomu, the question of authenticity arose. Such matters demand utmost tact and caution, and for purposes of the present paper it should suffice merely to report that room for doubt exists both for the ascription of the text to Bashō and the sketch and calligraphy to Buson.

Yet, despite the measure of uncertainty that remains, the text itself is part of the pre-modern legacy of Japanese poetry and deserves to be analyzed as such. Likewise, the painting is typical of the asymmetrical and abbreviated technique of Zen art,[7] which found abundant expression in haiku painting of the seventeenth to nineteenth centuries, as well as in modern times. Each line of the sketch presents a contrast. Thus, the

138

handle shows a thin line on the left parallel to a thick one on the right. The top end is thin and slightly concave, and the bottom end is wavy. The calligraphy itself is in an informal running style appropriate for haiku. It strikes one as typical of Buson's manner, which may be described as wobbly knees but strong backbone. Buson's work, it may be added, ever since his own day, has been particularly valued for his calligraphy.

The prose-poem, or *haibun*, itself contains a message. In musical terms, it begins on a high note, mentioning a treasured rarity. Then it descends to two low notes, telling of a humble tool in a mountain village and of a lowly person using it for pounding. Then a high note is struck again in referring to a flower vase, one of the appurtenances of the tea ceremony, which were often given poetical names, although it is impossible to know how the 'broken hammer' looked like a flower vase. A similar pattern of high, low, low, high may be found in the remaining part of the text, beginning with, 'It is the same with people.' First comes the idea of high but not haughty. This is followed by that of low but not envious and of its being best 'to be an ordinary hammer.' Then in the capping verse 'camellia,' in terms of a hierarchy of flowers in Japanese poetry and culture, is relatively low, like dandelion, for instance, and 'plum' is high, like cherry blossoms. The complete prose-poem, therefore, in musical and semantic terms consists of two brief movements or segments, high, low, low high; high, low, low, high.

Presumably Bashō had been invited to participate in a tea ceremony or to enjoy hospitality in the company of someone who practised and patronized the way of tea. Then afterwards Bashō may have been asked to 'pay' for the hospitality by contributing some memento. Conceivably this could have been the source of the prose poem, from which the verse of 1701, the woodblock text of 1756, and the calligraphic scroll dated 1776 were derived.

By itself the text strikes the reader as being somewhat didactic,[8] preaching how high-born and low-born people should behave and concluding that it is better to be lowly. The text is saved from becoming a tiresome sermon in part by the cryptic capping verse at the end, which evokes the common nature of the camellia, as opposed to the elegance of the plum, yet another instance of highness and lowness and of an imaginary or poetic confusion.

In the context of increasing interest in the normative function of Tokugawa period ideology[9] and of the *kine* as a normative tool in its own way, the text of 'The Broken Hammer' may be read as an example of traditional Japanese social equality, which can be conveniently related to Victor Turner's concept of 'communitas'. Likewise, as if foreshadowing Turner's ideas, which developed out of his fieldwork in Africa, the Japanese-American scholar, Ryusaku Tsunoda, wrote of the idea of haiku as evincing a 'democracy of poetry'.[10]

More recently, in Japan, Hirakawa Sukehiro, taking a cue from another scholar, Watanabe Shōichi,[11] has discussed similar ideas in the context of an older form of traditional Japanese poetry, *waka*, and in the texts of Noh plays, known as *yōkyoku*. To put it briefly, a message of equality emerges from a number of passages in Noh, and underlying such Japanese group-oriented activities as *waka, renga* (linked verse), and tea, to say nothing about the martial arts and other endeavours as well, an implicit assertion may be found that people are all in the same boat and that distinctions of rank and class are minor and superficial. In 'The Broken Hammer,' therefore, an aspect of an ideology involving ideas that run contrary to the accepted notions about Tokugawa society thereby emerges. This may be thought of as a counter-ideology, which downplays distinctions of rank and sex and emphasizes a populistic social levelling.

Bashō wrote a number of prose-poems besides this one, some sixty to seventy items in all, ranging in length from one hundred to 1,500 graphemes. A number of these texts, including 'The Broken Hammer,' allude to earlier literary works, such as *yōkyoku*, the *Heike monogatari* ('Tale of the Heike'), and the *Genji monogatari* ('Tale of Genji'). Specifically, in the Noh play *Atsumori* the travelling monk, Renzei, who as the warrior, Kumagae, had killed the teenage warrior, Atsumori, in battle and now in remorse revisits the site of that action, hears from the ghost of his former adversary words to the effect, 'Do not envy those who surpass you, and do not despise your inferiors.'[12] This message indeed echoes the opening passage of the *Tale of the Heike*.

Besides 'The Broken Hammer' there is also a parallel text ascribed to Buson himself, entitled 'Kuwa no jigasan' ('In Praise of the Hoe'),[13] although it is not known when he executed it. Likewise, there may be doubt about the surviving example's authenticity. Caption and illustration, at least in scroll form or early-modern woodblock text, have disappeared from public view since the 1930s. The text, however, has regularly appeared in movable-type editions of Buson's writings. No scholar has publicly questioned the place of the text in the canon of Buson's writings. The basic message of the text is that ever since the age of the gods the hoe has not changed. It was good enough to settle the country and serve the home. With it one can dig for mushrooms in the snow, or for gold. The capping verse states in effect that, 'In the fields it is better to have a good hoe than a wishing-hammer.'

Essentially, the hoe, like the hammer, is a normative tool. The two implements may be seen metaphorically as expressing in parallel fashion the theme on which this paper focuses, namely that in pre-modern Japanese society, along with the rigid and hierarchical side of social life, on which researchers have long focussed, there exists a reverse side, roughly equivalent to Victor Turner's concept of anti-structure, which points to an abiding belief in a concept of equality. Further research in this direction shows promise for helping people, both in Japan and in the Western world, better to understand the ideological underpinnings of modern Japanese social ideals, business practices and industrial organization. For people who are also interested in matters concerning poetry, art and aesthetics it may be an additional bonus that close reading and creative interpretation of texts such as 'The Broken Hammer' lends substance to such a thesis.

21

Japanese Diaries

DONALD KEENE

The three best-known masterpieces of Heian diary literature, the diaries of Murasaki Shikibu and Izumi Shikibu and the Sarashina diary were translated into English of a kind in 1920, and a German translation of the Izumi Shikibu diary was made as early as 1885. The choice of these diaries reflected Japanese preferences that had evolved over the centuries.

The high reputations of these particular diaries stemmed in part from their intrinsic literary qualities, but the fame of Murasaki Shikibu and Izumi Shikibu as people, quite apart from their diaries, undoubtedly imparted a special cachet to the diaries, and it is possible that even if the content of these diaries had been noticeably less interesting than that of others of the period, the same choice would have been made; curiosity about the author of *The Tale of Genji* and about the poet so conspicuously represented in various court anthologies would have given their diaries additional weight and importance.

With respect to the *Sarashina Nikki* the case is somewhat different. We cannot be sure that the author of this diary wrote anything else that survives, but she is still credited by some scholars with various works of late Heian fiction such as *Yowa no Nezame*, and perhaps such attributions influenced its selection when Fujiwara no Teika, or another connoisseur of literature, decided that copies should be made of *Sarashina Nikki* rather than of some other diary.

When we leave behind these three examples of diary literature, only one other was an obvious choice for preservation, *Tosa Nikki*, the diary of the great poet Ki no Tsurayuki. Its importance was recognized in its time, as we know from the recent discovery of a tracing of the original manuscript by Teika. But the other survivals may have been mainly accidental. The unforgettable *Kagerō Nikki* may have attracted the attention of some early chronicler of Heian court life. The opening words of the diary indicate that the author was writing this account in order to leave a record of what the life of a woman of the upper classes was really like (as opposed to the fantasies of the story-tellers). It is conceivable that the mother of Michitsuna left the manuscript with a relative or friend as a testimony to the life she had led. But this diary is not so often quoted by later literary men, and we are fortunate that it was not lost, along with many other manuscripts, in the conflagrations that accompanied the numerous civil wars.

The remaining literary diaries of the Heian period - that is, diaries

141

written in Japanese, usually including poetry, and usually by women - seem to have survived mainly by accident, and they have not been accorded anywhere near the careful attention extended to the diaries I have mentioned. *Jōjin Ajari Haha no Shū* is my favourite among the as yet untranslated diaries. It is the account by a woman in her eighties of the misery she suffers because her son, the *ajari* Jōjin seems indifferent to her. He has decided he must go to China to study Tendai Buddhism at its source, but his pious intent gives her no pleasure. She has long looked forward to her last hours, when Jōjin and her other son, who is also a high Buddhist dignitary, would be in attendance, one on either side, and she interprets Jōjin's decision to go to China, where he may find himself when she dies, as a malicious act intended to deprive her of the long-awaited pleasure of dying with a son on either side. Or, she reasons, perhaps Buddha himself hates her and that is why he makes her suffer so. She wonders why she, who was so delicate as a child, should have been obliged to live for so long, only to have this terrible calamity befall her. She is quite unreasonable in her attitude, but there can be no doubting her love for her son, who (though he is in his sixties and a most distinguished man) is still the child who would weep when anyone else touched him but smiled when she took him in her arms. Jōjin is unmoved by his mother's complaints. He is sure that study in China will help them both to be reborn in paradise; the short separation on earth is of no importance when compared to the eternity of bliss in the other world. The diary, though written in deadly earnest, is bound to make us smile as we recognize in its pages attitudes typical of mothers the world over. The special relationship between mother and son in Japan, far more important (at least in works of literature) than that between father and daughter, is given an extreme statement in *Jōjin Ajari Haha no Shū*.

Another striking example of the mother-son relationship, this one from the Kamakura period, is found in *Kaidōki*. An unidentified man who lives in Kyōto avails himself of an opportunity to go to Kamakura. His description of the journey is interesting, though marred by an overly literary style with many Chinese allusions. Hardly has he reached Kamakura, however, than he feels compelled to return immediately to Kyōto. We gradually realize from hints in the text that his decision to travel to Kamakura was motivated not so much by reports he had heard of the splendour of the Shogun's capital as by a subconscious desire to get away temporarily from his mother. She has entered second childhood and it breaks his heart to see her in this state. But as soon as he arrives in Kamakura he feels guilty over his escape, and he rushes back to his mother, though he knows that this can bring him only unhappiness.

Kaidōki has never been as popular as *Tōkan Kikō*, which also describes a journey from Kyōto to Kamakura. This, however, is no more than an account of the journey, without the self-analysis and the total commitment we find in *Kaidōki* and other diaries that still have the power to move us. *Tōkan Kikō* influenced later diaries, notably those by Bashō, and that gives it some importance, but next to the neglected *Kaidōki* it seems inconsequential.

Perhaps the most affecting of all the Kamakura diaries is *Utatane*, the

142

youthful diary of Abutsu-ni, whose *Izayoi Nikki* is far more celebrated. It is baffling why a work of such appeal has been so seldom studied and, for that matter, why the boring *Izayoi Nikki* ranks as a classic. The girl who wrote *Utatane* moves us by the intensity of her love for a man who, we are sure, is unworthy of her; the battle-axe who travels to Kamakura to demand justice for her son is not endearing. Two other diaries of the period are often treated as a pair, *Ben no Naishi Nikki* and *Nakatsukasa no Naishi Nikki*. The standard opinion is that the first is cheerful, the second dark and brooding. Ikeda Kikan went so far as to describe Nakatsukasa no Naishi's diary as the record of a woman who suffers from a split personality; 'she makes us see the misery of human suffering for which there is no remedy, writhe and gasp as one may.' I find this diary an exceptionally attractive account of life at the court, by a happy woman who did not doubt its glory, and who never ceased to marvel at each new moment of beauty. My interpretation, so at variance with that of a distinguished scholar, may be mistaken; but at least it is worth investigating how two such different interpretations are possible.

When we come to diaries of the Muromachi period, the numbers are greater, and there is considerable variety, ranging from grave accounts of monks on pilgrimages to sacred places to the uninhibited *Sōchō Nikki* with its salacious poems. Striking by their absence are the diaries by women which, from the early Heian period, constituted the mainstream of diary literature. This, of course, reflects the changed position of women in society. The Kamakura and Muromachi periods are often lumped together as the Japanese Middle Ages, but in terms of literature, especially the diary literature, there is a far greater gap between Kamakura and Muromachi than between Heian and Kamakura. When we read the description by Nakatsukasa no Naishi of the pleasures of life at the court we have trouble in accepting the established view that the court, deprived of all power after the foundation of the shogunate in Kamakura, had fallen into neglect. Even *Towazugatari*, written towards the end of the Kamakura Period, describes a court which, though deplorably lacking in morals, was well provided with luxuries. But the emperor's court hardly figures in Muromachi diaries. The chief appeal of the Muromachi diaries is what they tell us about such important literary figures as Shōtetsu, Sōgi and Sōchō. The dispersal of cultural life into the provinces as the result of the destruction of the capital during the Ōnin War is well-known to every student of the period, but the diaries supply concrete details that make the events more striking and memorable than in history books.

The end of the Muromachi period, the era known as Momoyama, is described in various diaries, notably those that relate to the war in Korea. Although these diaries possess relatively little literary value, they provide intriguing sidelights on a particularly exciting period of Japanese history.

The diaries of the Tokugawa period, though numerous, have rarely been given the benefit of commentaries or other scholarly notice, with the notable exceptions of the diaries by Bashō and Issa. None of them can be called a literary masterpiece, but these diaries surely deserve more extensive attention than having been included in the *Teikoku Bunko* some ninety years ago. Diaries by women, though not as numerous as those by men, reassume some of their old importance. The authors range from the wives of shogunate officials down to prostitutes, and vary in style from an archaic pseudo-Heian diction to the anonymous manner of the male diarists of the same period. It is surprising how seldom these diaries have been utilized even by scholars concerned with the lives of women of the time.

The true diary - that is, a journal kept day by day - had existed even in the early Heian period in the form of the *kambun* diaries kept by officials at court, but it is only in the Tokugawa period that a similar kind of diary, kept in Japanese rather than *kambun*, becomes frequent. By the time one comes to the end of the Tokugawa period, a mountain of diaries, most of them never printed, awaits the intrepid explorers of this genre of literature. Among the printed diaries of special interest are the four volumes of *Bakin Nikki*; the fifth volume, an index, has not yet appeared although it was promised fourteen years ago. *Iseki Takako Nikki* (in three volumes) has attracted surprisingly little attention, considering that the author has been praised by some as having been the Sei Shōnagon of the bakumatsu period. Common to both the Bakin and Iseki Takako diaries is the woeful scarcity of notes.

Diaries of the Meiji period and later are too numerous ever to be fully recorded. Many of the major writers of the Meiji period kept extensive diaries, notably Masaoka Shiki, Higuchi Ichiyō, Ishikawa Takuboku and Nagai Kafū. There are also diaries of great interest which describe their travels abroad by persons who may or may not have had literary ability. Some diaries, notably those by Shiki and Takuboku, seem even superior to the poetry and other literary compositions by the same writers. Other diaries are sometimes disillusioning, the prejudices expressed revealing unpleasant sides to the characters of respected authors; I find Natsume Sōseki's diaries especially disagreeable. Some diaries are so striking that we have no choice but to look at their authors with new eyes. I doubt that anyone who has read Tokutomi Roka's *Omoide no Ki* or knows of his journey to Russia to meet Tolstoi will be prepared for the startling frankness with which he describes his sexual life in his diary. Roka, incidentally, is one of the few authors who actually burnt his old diaries, though many authors have left word on their deathbeds that their diaries are to be destroyed. Fortunately, such commands are rarely obeyed.

During the Pacific War Japanese soldiers and sailors were regularly issued diaries on New Year's Day, and they were expected to keep them faithfully. No doubt the diaries were inspected from time to time to ensure that the writers were inspired by the proper sentiments, but once the writers were cut off from their units the tone often changed abruptly, as genuine emotions - as opposed to approved ideals - were voiced. These war-time diaries, with a very few exceptions, have never been printed, though they possess almost unbearable intensity and could certainly inspire books. Even their whereabouts are uncertain, assuming they have not been destroyed.

Keeping a diary is still a normal part of every Japanese schoolchild's life, especially during the summer vacation, but (needless to say) few of them are of even historical interest. But the habit of keeping a diary seems deeply ingrained in the Japanese, perhaps because of this early training.

144

Scholars of diary literature sometimes divide diaries into two categories - those written solely for the diarist himself, and those written with readers in mind. This is a fair division if one is trying to separate engagement books from diaries, but it does not apply to most of the surviving diaries from the past. The implication is that a diary written for other readers will be more literary, make a greater effort to keep the attention of the reader than a work intended for oneself alone, but before we can accept this view it will be necessary to find out the circumstances of transmission of diaries. The kind of diary about which we know most, the court chronicles kept in *kambun* by officials, are impersonal and suggest that they were intended to be read by all persons concerned; but again and again one finds the notation that a particular diary absolutely must not be shown to anyone else. The importance of such a diary to the person who kept it was its record of court precedents and usages, and the diary itself was passed down from father to eldest son as his most precious possession; an accurate knowledge of precedent would enable the son to declare with authority that five reigns earlier such-and-such a procedure was followed. This knowledge enhanced the man's position at court. Should such a diary be considered as public or private?

The literary diary, on the other hand, may originally have been a diversion for ladies of the court, and not necessarily tied to the events of a particular day or year. No one would have consulted such a diary for information about precedents, but it would have been read for pleasure. The 'private' diary, in which the author described highly personal reflections, was therefore more likely to be read publicly than the 'public' diary in which the author carefully noted precisely which member of the court was entrusted with the opening of a door in the palace when the Emperor went to attend a ceremony. The concept of 'public' and 'private' may not be appropriate. Perhaps the only safe division is between diaries kept in Japanese and those kept in *kambun*, but such a division is not illuminating. The diary of Minamoto no Ienaga has been dismissed as an aberration because although it was written by a Heian courtier, it is in Japanese instead of *kambun*. Its reputation has accordingly suffered, but it is a work of considerable literary interest, if read without prejudice. In the end, the only division that makes much sense is between diaries that have the power to interest us and those that are at best of only historical value.

The later diaries offer the greatest possibilities for making discoveries, though the diaries in *kambun*, as yet little translated, undoubtedly possess more interest than their reputations would suggest. 'Rethinking Japan' in terms of diaries would involve a fresh look at such works.

22

Towards a Definition of *Tama*

HERBERT PLUTSCHOW

The term *tama* is often translated into Western languages as 'soul', 'spirit' or other equivalent words. An investigation into its use and meanings, however, reveals that this translation, if it is not qualified, is inadequate. *Tama* is a far more complex concept than the Judeo-Christian 'soul', and whenever we translate it as 'soul,' we must account for the differences between the two. This essay is meant to be a modest contribution towards defining *tama* by taking into account the nature of the sources we use in our investigation and the context in which it appears in them.

The earliest texts which use *tama* are such eighth-century works as the *Kojiki* (Record of Ancient Matters) of 712, the *Nihon Shoki* (Annals of Japan) of 720, the *Fudoki* (Geographical Surveys) of 713, the undatable *Norito* prayers and the songs compiled in the mid-eighth century in the first Japanese anthology entitled *Manyōshū*. Should we try to define *tama* according to these sources alone, we must recognize that we are in fact limiting our investigation to the eighth century and its surviving oral traditions, to the nature and language of transcriptions applied in these texts and to the culture and preconceptions of the preservers. This awareness presupposes the possibility that the word *tama* may have been used variously in a culture that was perhaps far from being as homogeneous at that time as it was later. Such differences appear when we compare the belief systems attached to the modern *tamashii* in various regions of present-day Japan.[1] Yet these variations are not documented in early Japan, and even in the *Fudoki*, which deals with local cultures, the term appears in accordance with the cultural background of those people who observed and recorded local customs and belief systems. Nevertheless, deep differences between the modern *tamashii* and the ancient textual *tama* do not appear to the extent that we would face serious problems when limiting our investigations to the texts reflecting the then consolidating imperial authority, culture and language. Through other sources, we realize in fact that the imperial and local cultures did not hold such widely divergent views of life and death as to render them distinct or even conflicting cultures. We must be aware, however, that one possible cause of their seeming homogeneity may stem from the kinds of observation and recording that took place and from the possible Chinese influences upon them. We find for instance such influences in the recording of the myths of the imperial family indicating that not only was Chinese language used but also, quite often, the cultural concepts behind that language.

146

The ancient Japanese texts, as we shall see in the next section, illustrate the term *tama* and its attendant belief systems.

The term *tama* appears as a singular noun, but also in compounds such as *tamagaki* (*tama*-fence), *tama-arare* (*tama*-bail), *tama-kushi* (*tama*-comb), *tama-matsuri* (festival for the dead), *tama-mono* (gift), *tama-ya* (funerary house). It is often used with prefixes: *ara-tama* (rough, dynamic, restless, ill-behaved *tama*), *sachi-tama* (luck *tama*); and suffixes: *tamashii* (dynamic, floating *tama*). It appears in *makura kotoba* (pillow words or epithets) such as *tamahoko* (*tama* staff), used as the epithet for travel road and village exit. It appears in the names of shamanesses such as Tamayori-hime (lit. Approaching *Tama*-Girl). It appears in verbs such as *tamau* (a superior gives to an inferior), *tama-waru* (ibid.), *tama-yobau* (call back the *tama* of the dead), *tama-jiwau* (keep a *tama* inside), *aratamu* (to renew the year, renew). *Tama* is used for animals, plants and things, especially ritual implements. Also meaning 'jewel,' it is used as an embellishing element in certain compounds and epithets.

As applied to persons, *tama* appears as a complex set of dualities which deserve close scrutiny. *Tama* and *tamashii* (tamashihi) is such a set. *Tama* stands for the life essence of man; *tamashii* is its dynamic aspect, meaning literally '*tama*-effectiveness.'

Another *tama* duality is *aramitama* and *nikitama*. *Ara*, like *tamashii*, is the dynamic aspect of *tama* whereas *niki* (also *nigi* or *niko*) is its peaceful one. The *nikimitama* of the deity Ōkuninushi, the deity of the land of Izumo, appears in the *Nihon Shoki* as a kind of guardian spirit floating towards the deity from the outside.[2] Though it is no doubt part of the deity's spirit, Ōkuninushi while in an *ara* state apparently fails to recognize it as part of himself; hence his *nikimitama* needs to reveal its own identity.[3] We find the term *nikitama* in the *Norito* entitled 'Izumo no Kuni no Miyatsuko no Kamuyogoto,' another text related to Izumo, as applied to 'pacified' deities, that is, deities that have accepted imperial overlordship. The opposite term, *araburugami*, which appears in the same text, refers to the still-unappeased deities; that is, deities who have not yet accepted and are resisting imperial authority.[4] The following story appearing in the *Izumo Fudoki* adds a further dimension to this duality of *ara* and *niki*.

A fisherman of Izumo, not unlike Captain Ahab in *Moby Dick*, seeks revenge upon a shark which has killed his daughter. In order to effect his revenge, he asks the deities to engender the duality in him, beseeching them to create their *aratama* to help him successfully hunt the shark and their *nikitama* to protect him during the hunt. The myth suggests that the father must divide his *tama* into two opposites: *ara* - his dynamic, vengeful spirit - to carry out the hunt, and *niki* - the guardian spirit - to protect him from dangers and to ensure his safe return home.[5] *Ara* and *niki* are opposite aspects of the same personality, accompanied by radical behavioural differences. Both aspects are identified with *kami* (deities), indicating perhaps the union of these split-off aspects, a union which combines not only human and divine behaviour, but also the human and natural environment. *Arano* (wasteland, wilderness) and *niki ni shi ie* (palace, house) support the assumption that, in *ara* and *niki*, we deal in fact with a totality of *tama* and the world.

147

The story of Ōkuninushi introduces a notion of *tama* which is important for our understanding of the term. It suggests belief in a 'floating' *tama*, a *tama* that can leave the body and return to it, and, furthermore, a split of personality or behaviour so radical that one kind of behaviour cannot recognize its opposite as part of the same ontic self and personality. Although the Ōkuninushi myth suggests that it is the *nikitama*, the guardian spirit, which can leave and return to the body, it seems that both can do so. To support this assumption, let us look at the myth of the Empress Jingū in the *Nihon Shoki*. As she was preparing to wage war against the Korean kingdom of Silla, an oracle told her: 'Let your *nikimitama* guide you and protect your life. Use your *aramitama* as your spearhead and let it guide your warship.'[6] This suggests that both aspects can be externalized. As aspects of a floating *tama*, they both seem extensions of the ontic *tama*.

When her campaign ended, the Empress was told to worship both aspects, perhaps because, like in the story of the shark-hunting father, this division of her *tama* is also a division of the deities and the external world. Though she paid her respects at separate places, this worship was aimed perhaps at laying to rest the duality, restoring a unity of peace and harmony. War, and probably also its accompanying displacement, necessitated the engendering of both aspects: *ara* to wage war and to move and *niki* to protect life and make the return to home and the restoration of peace possible. Extreme kinds of behaviour split the *tama* and the world in two, and have to be reconciled to restore normal circumstances.

The idea of floating *tama* finds perhaps its best expression in the Japanese worship of evil spirits, as one can observe throughout Japanese history. Spirits of persons who suffered premature, unnatural deaths caused by war, exile, grudges or jealousy were unable to depart from the world until they avenged themselves on the living. Such spirits were feared to cause natural calamities, epidemics, war and social disharmony. In ancient texts, such spirits were not called *aratama* but *onryō* (spiteful spirits), '*ryō*' being the Sino-Japanese pronunciation of *tama*, or *goryō* (august spirits), a term used no doubt as a polite, reverential expression in the worship of these spirits. The kinds of evil these spirits inflicted after death interests us less than the fact that a jealous or grudging living person could harm his or her rivals by his or her *onryō* or *aratama*. Such vengeful spirits could also be engendered by living persons, in which case they were called *ikiryō* that is living '*ryō*' or *tama*. They were believed to harm their rivals according to the same religious power as that of the dead *onryō* (also *shiryō* or 'dead *ryō*'). Though a work of fiction, the *Tale of Genji* (*Genji Monogatari*) reveals well the fear in which *ikiryō* were held, especially in the Heian period (794-1185).

In the *Tale*, Lady Rokujō harboured such an intense feeling of jealousy against her rival Yugao that her '*ryō*' left her body, attacked her rival and killed her.[7] In this case also, Rokujō was not conscious of what her jealous *ikiryō* had done to Yugao. Floating *tama* are not necessarily aware of what they are doing away from the body, or where they are going. Yet if we take other sources into account, people may have been able to direct their floating *tama* towards specific targets, or use outside objects as *tama* carriers. This was the case in lovers who yearned so much for their beloved

148

that their *tama* seemed to leave their bodies.

When Izumi Shikibu (ca. 976-?), the celebrated female poet of the Heian period, was abandoned by her husband, she went on a pilgrimage to Kibune shrine (north of Kyoto) in an attempt to overcome her attachment. As she approached the shrine, however, her grief became unbearable and she sang:

> When I am in love,
> The firefly in the marsh
> Looks as if my longing soul
> Were leaping from my body.[8]

Akoraru (to long for) is a verb often used in classical Japanese for the sensation caused by one's *tama* leaving the body and moving towards someone else.[9]

Love songs such as these led Origuchi Shinobu to interpret most love songs in classical Japanese poetry as a kind of *tama-goi*.[10] '*Goi*' comes from '*koi*,' originally meaning challenge in ritual competitions such as *sumo* wrestling. It came to mean 'love' in the context of the competitive match-making of ritual orgies (*utagaki*).

Love in ancient Japan was seen as a meeting of *tama*, most likely of floating *tama*, as suggested in the following *Manyōshū* song:

> If our *tama* meet
> Let us sleep together,
> Though my mother
> May watch over me
> Like the Shishi-field of Yamada.[11]

A prerequisite for sexual intercourse was a meeting of *tama*. I agree with Origuchi Shinobu's interpretations of love as first a challenge and then a meeting of *tama*, a phenomenon we will examine further in our discussion of *tama* rituals.

The notion of *tama* becomes even more complex when considering mental illness, shock, possession and punishment. Mental and physical illnesses were often treated in ancient Japan as possession by a *tama* coming from a living rival (*ikiryō*) a dead rival (*shiryō*) an animal *tama* or an unspecified *tama*. Hence, the calling upon exorcists to identify and exorcize the *tama* responsible for the illness. Such cases are amply documented in Heian and later period literature. Shock was considered a state of intense agitation which may cause the *tama* to leave the body (*tamage* means lit. *tama* effacing), hence the efforts to calm the patient, and thereby his *tama*. On Okinawa, this process was called *mabui*.[12] Spiritual punishment was feared perhaps as much as physical punishment. Exile was one of the most severe punishments in ancient Japan and when exiles died unpardoned their spirits were especially feared. Exile from home robbed the person of his ontic self. It was feared that living away from home would engender a different and dangerous personality. For this reason, ancient Japanese disliked leaving home, even when conducting official business.

In the case of Sugawara no Michizane (845-903), a statesman who was exiled as a result of the intrigues of a rival, his grudging *tama* identified with the thunder deity (Tenjin) and struck the imperial palace with lightning.[13] This legend seems to point to the belief that even evil-doing *tama* are identified with deities as are the benevolent ones that protect life.

We have so far discussed personal *tama*, that *tama* which constitutes the human soul and which shapes human personality and behaviour. Since that personal *tama* seems to be ontically connected with the outside world, it is only natural that *tama* is also a term used in relation to extra-personal objects and beings. There is *tama* in certain trees, rocks, mountains, rivers and lakes. Concerning trees, we find *tama* in *tamakage* (Lycopodium clavatum), *tamakashira* (Quercus dentata), *tamamatsu* (pine), *tamaizusa* (Betula grossa), *tamabukaki* (ligustrum japonicum), etc. We do not know how these words came to be, whether these trees contained *tama*, whether they were used in rituals or whether the word *tama* only appears in them as a beautifying prefix.

We know, however, that *kami* were often identified with trees, as the Sumiyoshi deity is identified with pines, and the sun-goddess at Ise with paulownia cedars. This stems perhaps from the belief that deities descend or dwell upon trees. In a number of Shinto festivals, people make artificial trees for their deities and decorate them elaborately and colourfully. This practice is one sign that trees and deities were often considered one and the same *tama*.

The *tama* of territories, however, can be discussed more definitely than that of trees. Land had a *tama* of its own, sometimes called specifically *kunitama*. The *kunitama* could rise up and be appeased, a symbolic way to refer to popular uprisings, resistance and the restoration of peace in ancient Japan. Also, sacred land was often surrounded by what was called *tamagaki* or sacred fence, a term used not only for the fences enclosing shrines, but also for the entire nation (*tamagaki no uchi no kuni* or 'The country within the *tama*-fence').[14]

Animals also have *tama*. Birds often appear in ancient text as carriers of the dead souls, as in the myth of Yamato Takeru. His dead soul transferred itself into a white bird.[15] Hence perhaps the belief that *tama* can change form, and assume a different shape. Hitodama (lit. 'man soul') is the name of a bird (more commonly called Yamashōbin or a white-breasted kingfisher), so called in Oita prefecture. When someone dies, the bird is believed to weep. Given this kind of relationship between human *tama* and animals, one may be tempted to claim that there is a totemic soul in Japan, a theory often denied by Japanese scholars. Scholars of Japanese religion sometimes come across animals such as crows, foxes, monkeys and deer in particular serving as servants of certain *kami*. These animals may in fact be more than merely servants, and identified ontically with the deities. Dancers disguised as these animals in ritual performances embody the divine powers inherent in these animals, for instance, and the Japanese verb *naru*, now meaning to become, may have derived from a verb denoting such transmission of divine powers in ritual.[16] These are quite likely signs of complete identification of animals with particular deities.

Some of the examples given above have shown that *tama* extends to *kami*, or deity. *Aramitama* or *nikimitama* denoted certain types of behaviour that deities assumed, justifying perhaps similar kinds of behaviour in man. This fact is also apparent in certain names of deities. According to the *Nenjūgyōji Hishō*, a treatise on imperial rituals, we find the *tama* of the emperor referred to as *kami*.[17] These and other examples indicate that *tama* and *kami* could be used interchangeably. An emperor was both a charismatic, powerful *tama*, the embodiment of his ancestors and his land, and a *kami*. The *tama* of dead persons also became *kami*. When worshipped, a *tama* seems to be referred to as *kami*, and we find in *kami* the same lack of differentiation between *kami* as living forces and *kami* of the dead, as in *tama*.

Tama was often identified with ritual offerings or implements. Ritual food offerings were called *tama*, as in *funa-tama*, the food offered to the spirit (*tama*) of the ship; *tama* also was the food offered to man in ritual (*hito-dama*).

Tama is perhaps best understood through ritual. *Tama* is a force which, as we shall see, often appears to be virtually induced, calmed, strengthened and maintained. It does not seem to be a permanent property, which, once gained, will never change again or remain at the same place or in the same person. A number of rituals of pre-modern Japan tried to control *tama's* formidable force. One of the most ancient on record appears as either *tamafuri*, *mitamafuri* or *mitamafuyu* meaning *tama*-shaking. It appears in the *Kyūjiki* (Book 2, Chapter 2). Before the sun-goddess Amaterasu sent her grandson Ninigi to earth, she gave him a set of ten *musubi* (a word meaning binding) jewels with the instruction: 'Whenever you get sick, count the treasures from one to ten and shake them....'[18] These treasures were more than just jewels. They were *tama* (the character used for them is *tama*) in the sense of spiritual forces and *kami*. They were worshipped in the Jingikan, the office of religion instituted by Emperor Temmu in 645.

We learn much from this myth of the *tamafuri* ritual. We learn that the shaking of *tama* was a ritual means to heal and invigorate a deteriorating *tama*. The earliest detailed explanation of this ritual comes from the *Kōnin Jingishiki* (Rituals of the Office of Religion of the Kōnin Era [810-823]). A female official of the Office of Religion shakes a box containing imperial robes called *tamabako* or *tama*-box, while music is played and dances danced.[19] A number of other documents reveal that this ritual was carried out according to tradition until the middle of the nineteenth century.

Tamafuri is also mentioned in a political context. The *Nihon Shoki*, under the entry of the fourth month, second year of Emperor Kimmei, says: '...if the power of the Emperor is restored by *mitamafuyu*, Mimana will surely be restored.'[20] This refers to the invasion of Mimana, a kingdom (?) friendly to Japan on the southern tip of the Korean peninsula, by Silla, one of the Korean kingdoms. It is not clear, however, whether *mitamafuri* is mentioned here as a ritual or metaphorically for the emperor's spiritual and political power.

Yet *tamafuri* was not limited to rituals at the imperial court. It also appears in love songs sung by lovers separated by great distance as, for instance, in the case of travel. The following poem is most likely a travel

151

song by Nakatomi Ason Yakamori, sung during an unspecified journey:

> Although I shake
> My *tama*
> Mornings and evenings
> My breast hurts
> With the force of my love.[21]

This song, along with some other travel songs of the *Manyōshū*, reveals that, each morning before embarking and each evening after arriving, travellers sought spiritual communion with their beloved at home. By performing this ritual they reinvigorated their own *tama* with the *tama* of home, so that they could master the unfamiliar space they were to traverse. Travelling presented an ontic danger to ancient Japanese travellers. Separated from home, they feared that they might lose their ontic integrity, hence the need to maintain a spiritual link with home to reaffirm regularly their reliance on it. The following two songs confirm this interpretation:

> I present offerings
> At each river crossing
> Along the Yamato road
> So that I can meet my wife
> In my dreams.[22]

The traveller seeks his wife to cross dangerous places along the road. The following poem expresses perhaps even more effectively this ritual need of ancient travel:

> At the crossing of the road
> Where *kotodama* is effective,
> I divine the deity's will
> And ask:
> 'Will my wife come and meet me?'[23]

What is meant here is not the physical presence of the traveller's wife, but her *tama* floating toward him.

The *chinkon-sai* or *tamashizume* (called *mitamashizume* when performed at court) ritual is closely connected with *tamafuri*. In the imperial court, this festival was usually held on a tiger day in the eleventh month and its purpose was to prolong the life of the sovereign and placate the above-mentioned eight *musubi*-deities of the imperial clan. It was held in the office of the Imperial Household Ministry (*Kunaishō*). The celebration included the presentation of symbolic offerings of food, dances and music.[24] This festival, too, is explained in the myths of the imperial clan.

According to the *Kojiki* and *Nihon Shoki*, the sun-goddess Amaterasu, the ancestral deity of the emperors, hid in a cave after being enraged by the unruly behaviour of her brother, the storm-god Susanoo. The world became dark and the deities held council as to the measures which should be taken to make the sun reappear. It was decided that a deity in charge of heavenly liturgical matters, Ama no Uzume, should dance in front of

152

the cave in order to lure her out. In her erotic dance, Ama no Uzume disrobed and exposed her genitals, at which the deities all laughed, attracting Amaterasu's attention. When Amaterasu looked out of the cave, another deity showed her her image in a mirror, in which she discovered a different, superior *tama*. This ritual device may have fixed her attention on her *nikitama* in order to bring her out. When she finally emerged, a sacred rope was hung across the cave, preventing her from reentering. Then the sun continued to shine upon the world as before.[25]

This ritual combined several separate devices to placate the sun-deity. The ecstatic dance drew the sun's *tama* into the dancer; the laughter of the heavenly deities was perhaps meant to reinvigorate her *tama* and is used in many cultures' renewal rituals; the presentation of a mirror, perhaps an exorcist device of Chinese origins, was a means to attract the deity to its own *nikitama* reflection. This myth is the oldest record of *mitamashizume* no doubt included in the imperial myths to explain and justify this important imperial ritual. The subsequent *mitamashizume* rituals at court were officiated over by supposed descendants of Ama no Uzume.

The *mitamashizume* ritual at court was held, like the dance of Ama no Uzume, during the winter solstice, when people thought they had to reinvigorate a much-weakened winter sun, inducing it to shine strongly enough to ensure a good future harvest. The emperor's *tama* representing the sun on earth was believed to be in a weakened state and about to leave his body, an event that would result in illness, political weakness and eventually death. To prevent his *tama* from leaving, a ritual was held in the Jingi-kan, first recorded in the *Jōgan Gishiki* (Rituals of the Jōgan era: 859-876). A *naishi* (lady-in-waiting) comes to offer a box (*mikoromobako*) containing the imperial robes. *Yufu* (a string of mulberry fibre) is placed inside the box. Then musicians begin playing and a dancer, a *mikanko*, performs. As the *ukibume* (a kind of hollow platform) is beaten like a drum with a lance, the officiant of the Jingi-kan ties knots in the *yufu* string. This is followed by further dancing.[26] The *Engi Shiki* (Rituals of the Engi era: 901-922) and other subsequent records affirm that this ritual had been periodically carried out until recently.[27] The *Nenjū Gyōji Hishō* (a thirteenth-century text on imperial rituals) includes songs (a kind of *kagura-uta*) sung during the *chinkon-sai*.[28]

The chief officiant counts eight times from one to ten, knotting the *yufu* each time. By tying knots in this symbol of the emperor's life span, the officiant keeps his *tama* from slipping away. The eight times and eight knots refer to the eight *musubi (binding) tama* or deities.

As one can see by these examples, the *mitamashizume* or *chinkon-sai* was a ritual means to fix the emperor's *tama* so that it would not leave his body. The ancient Japanese greatly feared wandering *tama* and made the utmost efforts to affix them. A similar ceremony is still being carried out secretly each year at the Isonokami shrine (Tenri City, Nara prefecture). This ritual may have to do partly with the *Kyūjiki*, a text which gives much more importance to the Mononobe clan whose ancestral deity is enshrined at Isonokami, than the *Kojiki* and *Nihon Shoki*.

Such *tamafuri* and *tamashizume* rituals were often popularly called *iki-*

bon, the *Bon* of living spirits. The Buddhist Urabon festival of late summer, however, a festival primarily concerned with the souls of the dead, has now superseded in importance this ceremony for the souls of the living.

The *tama* of dead persons were also the objects of special attention. In ancient Japan the placation of the dead was entrusted to groups of professional or semi-professional Asobi-be, guilds of placaters as they were called. The word *asobi*, now meaning pleasure or play, meant placation in ancient Japan. This shift in meaning accompanied the growing prominence of artistic, ritual performances at *tama* festivals. As far as we can tell from the available sources, the need to make sure that the *tama* of the dead rested instead of wandering mischievously over the earth was greatest for those dead who while living had been socially and politically prominent. The ancient Japanese feared that the more powerful a person was in life, the greater placation he or she needed in death, especially if that death had been premature or unnatural. The *Ryō no Shuge* defines the role of the Asobi-be clan as follows: 'This is a clan which mediates between the dark and light worlds. The Asobi-be appease impure and impish spirits which cause disease.'[29] This suggests that Asobi-be officiants were called upon to appease not only the dead but especially those who as *onryō* or *goryō* were believed to cause harm to the living. Both men and women officiated in *asobi* rituals. The following song from the *Manyōshū* may have been sung by a male member of the Asobi-be, Kakinomoto no Hitomaro (dates unknown), who is one of the most prominent poets in the *Manyōshū*.

A song sung by Kakinomoto no Hitomaro upon seeing a dead man lying among the rocks at Samine Island in Sanuki province:

> Is it because of its beauty
> That I never tire of seeing Sanuki Province
> Or is it its divine nature
> That makes it so awesome
> A province which
> Together with heaven and earth
> The sun and the moon
> Like the face of a god
> Grows ever more abundant.
> Having embarked at Nakatsu Harbour
> I come rowing
> A good wind blowing from the big sky;
> As I looked out into the open sea
> The waves rose
> As I looked at the shore
> The waves spilled against the beach.
> A fearful sea,
> And the oars bent as the boat rowed
> Over the whale-haunted awesome sea
> Dotted with many islands
> But none as famous as

Samine Island.
And as I built a simple shelter
And looked around
I found you
Lying on the rough beach
Surrounded by the roaring surf,
Pillowed on rocks.
If I knew your home
I would go and tell,
If only I knew your wife
She would come and tend you;
But not knowing the way hither
She must be waiting,
Forever waiting,
Your dear wife.

Envoys, Two Songs:
If your wife were here
She would have picked
And eaten the asters
Blooming on the high plain of Sami
But has not their season already gone?

You are lying
Pillowed on rocks
On the wild beach
Where the waves come roaring in
Poor man.[30]

By singing these songs, Hitomaro sought to placate the *tama* of a man who died an unnatural death, away from home and family.

Human *tama* were not the only source of fear in ancient Japan. Rituals to appease the *tama* of hunted animals and of plants are also recorded. The following song included in the *Manyōshū* was presumably sung by a Hokai-bito, a professional or semi-professional mourner who would accompany a hunting expedition and sing songs appeasing the *tama* of a slain animal:

My beloved
Wanted to leave home
Where, thought he, he had lived long enough
As if he were going to capture and bring back alive
The legendary tiger of China
And then spread its skin on the floor
And use it as a mat.
So you went to Mt Heguri,
Which lies like an eightfold mat,
To hunt for deer antlers
In the fourth and fifth months

To use as medicine.
When, at the foot of two oaks
Standing on this side of the mountain,
You waited for the deer
With your many catalpa bows,
With the turnip-shaped heads
Of many sharp arrows in your hands -
A doe came,
And with a sad voice said:
'I am about to die
To serve my lord
Say that you will use my antlers
To become the handles of your writing brushes,
And my ears
To become your inkwells,
And my eyes
To become your clear mirrors,
And my hooves
To become your bow tips,
And my hair
To become the hair of your brushes,
And my skin
To become the leather covering your boxes,
And my flesh
To become your food,
And my stomach
To become your salt.
Say that from this old body of mine
Seven kinds, no
Eight kinds of flowers will grow.'[31]

The mourner assumes the role of the hunter's wife and the wife the role of the animal, perhaps because, in ancient Japan, wives were supposed to protect their husbands from evil *tama*. That this concern for premature deaths also extended to plants becomes clear in the rituals that appease the falling cherry blossoms. Pink cherry blossoms scatter in the prime of their beauty, as if a person had died in the prime of life. Hence the fear that the spirit of the blossoms may cause spring epidemics. Rituals of this kind are still being held in present-day Japan. The Chinka-sai or Hanashizume of the Imamiya shrine in Kyoto, for example, is performed in April when the blossoms scatter. Three chanters, representing the harmful spirits of the scattering blossom, arrive at the shrine and, as if to suppress their own desire for revenge, chant 'flowers rest in peace!'

Linked to this concern for fallen blossoms is the fear of cutting down evergreen trees, especially pines near a house. Plants have their own *tama*, often identified, as we have seen, with specific deities.

As an impersonal outside force, *tama* played an important role in pre-modern Japan in the use of ritual language. Words and language could engender their own *tama*, when used in an aesthetic and symbolic context.

This was called *kotodama* or word-soul. *Kotodama* is associated primarily with ritual efforts to control a potentially hostile environment, in order to subdue it for human benefit. *Kotodama* appears in most ancient Japanese literature, but especially in *uta* (song) and *katari* (recitation of stories). Much classical Japanese literature must be seen in the light of ritual and ritual language which, with the aid of symbolic associations, quite often had specific ritual aims.

The best way to understand how *kotodama* operates is to consider the use of names, personal names and names of deities and territories. There were usually two names, a *tadanomina* or name for everyday use and a taboo name (*imina*) for ritual purposes. The latter interests us most, since it included *kotodama* powers. These powers are particularly apparent in the revelation of names as documented in ancient texts, where these revelations are described so consistently as to leave little doubt that whoever reveals a taboo personal, territorial or divine name, surrenders them to the inquirer. In the *Nihon Shoki*, written in the Age of Emperor Temmu, for instance, we find the following episode:

> The Emperor [Jimmu] arrived [by boat] at Hayasuhi-no-to. At the same time, a fisherman also arrived in his boat. The Emperor summoned him and asked: 'Who are you?' He replied: 'Your servant is the deity of this land. My name is Uzuhiko.'[32]

After Uzuhiko thus revealed his identity, he was made an official of the Emperor, and the founder of a prominent family serving the emperors. Uzuhiko is therefore also referred to as a deity, most likely the ancestral deity of his clan. Whenever such revelations occurred in ancient Japanese history, they were always followed by peaceful surrender and submission rather than confrontation or battle. These revelations of names thus were essential to ritual diplomacy.

Similar ritual questions and replies are recorded in the *Yamato-hime no Mikoto Seiki*.[33] Princess Yamato (daughter of Emperor Suinin) was looking for a place to enshrine the sun-goddess Amaterasu permanently and travelled from one land to another. Upon arriving at each territory, she was met by a local chieftain and confronted him with the same question: 'What is the name of your land?' The chieftains always revealed its name, and were immediately instated by the Princess as imperial vassals. Such questions and replies must have belonged to an ancient Japanese ritual of surrender.

During the Daijō-e, the Great Kingship Festival, the emperors receive the *tama* (kunitama) of the nation in the songs that local female shamans sing to them, songs which reveal place names and at the same time wish the emperor a long reign. Some of these Daijō-e songs, called *kunifuri-uta* or land-shaking-songs, are included in the *Kokinshū*, the first imperial collection of poetry compiled in 905:

> The Fujiwara river of the Barrier
> of Mino Province
> Will never cease
> To serve you
> For eternity.[34]

A revealed place name, which in this case is also the name of a tutelary deity, simultaneously indicates the willingness of the people living there to serve the emperor. The *kunifuri* ritual literally means shaking the *kunitama* or land-soul into the emperor. Such songs as these were believed to contain the power of the places whose names they reveal. They are *kotodama*.

Name-revelations like these also occurred at a personal level in ancient marriage rituals. The following poem, perhaps the oldest in the *Manyōshū* was sung by the young Emperor Yūryaku (the twenty-first emperor) to a girl he wanted to possess:

> Oh your basket
> With your good basket
> Oh your trowel
> With your good trowel
> You, digging up herbs
> On this hill
> Tell me of your home,
> Tell me of your name
> It is I who rule
> Over this wide land of Yamato
> It is I who reign over all
> Will you not reveal to me both
> Your home, and your name?[35]

The girl's reply is not recorded, but the emperor clearly wanted her to reveal her name as well as her homeland; by doing so she would surrender both herself and her homeland unconditionally to the emperor.

Names therefore had *kotodama* and the revelation of them released their powers, a power to be appropriated by the inquirer, an outsider or conqueror.

Rituals involving *kotodama* can be encountered quite often in *Manyōshū* travel songs. The following example is a farewell song addressed to a prospective traveller:

> *A Poem from the Collection of Poetry*
> *of Kakinomoto no Hitomoro*:
>
> The rice-abounding Land of Reed Plains
> Is a divine land [where things are as the gods will]
> And man need not offer prayers [kotoage]
> Yet, [today] I must offer prayers:
> 'Travel safely and be fortunate!
> So that no evil will hinder you
> So that you will be fortunate
> I will offer prayers over and over
> Like the waves spilling on the rocky shore
> A hundredfold, a thousandfold.'

Envoy:
The Land of Yamato
Is a land protected by
The power of the word [kotodama]:
[Therefore I offer prayers:]
Fare you well![36]

This poem explains its own purpose. The poet tells us that the song has *kotodama* power, power to prepare the way for the traveller, to keep him attached to his home. The song functions both as *kotoage* (prayer) and *kotodama*; *kotoage* is here *kotodama*. Through the power of the word - word in this case meaning the song - the poem prayer is in itself the charm, the talisman that is supposed to secure the traveller's safe return. This is a kind of magical language, words forming a song to achieve ritual ends.

These various examples of *tama's* manifestations and power will enable us to attempt a preliminary definition. *Tama* is an invisible (in Japanese folklore often visible) force which inheres in all things, living or dead, and in their tutelary deities. *Tama* was conferred upon the emperor from deities, ancestors, people, animals, plants and the land itself. Thus *tama's* power fluctuates; it can wane and be revived ritually. *Tama* is also ethically neutral, since it engenders extreme dualities of behaviour. It is good when at rest, appeased when properly enshrined; it is bad if it wanders unattached, free and restless, unable to leave the world if its possessor in life had been wronged.

This definition also needs at least a summary treatment of the need for reinvigoration in regular, elaborate and aesthetically pleasing rituals. All ritual implements, and all ritual means and actions such as language, song, recitation, dance and mimicry, have or engender a *tama* of their own. Japanese texts often fail to differentiate between what is *tama* and what has *tama*; moreover, in ritual, everything from officiants to implements are *tama* and have *tama* in which the onlooker can participate. *Tama* can only be handled, transferred and appeased in ritual. *Tama* is taboo (*imi*) and can therefore only be treated in ritual; otherwise it can bring about ill effects. Harmony, beauty and especially art forms that have one-dimensional or multi-dimensional symbolic association, are ways to deal with *tama* in order to control its power.

This operative definition now lets us compare *tama* with the Polynesian and Micronesian *mana*. The term *mana* has been widely discussed ever since R. H. Codrington published his book *The Religious Beliefs and Practices in Melanesia* in 1891. Scholars discovered in Codrington's description of *mana* a new and more primitive stage in human religion. Based on their many studies of *mana*, a comparison of *mana* and *tama* reveals many similarities, but also differences.

Mana and the *mana*-derived vocabulary from Hawaii to Madagascar indicates that *mana* is a force enabling man to do or to create extraordinary things and actions. It is seen as a kind of special skill and power which explains and justifies special physical and mental powers, and the political and social authority or influence that emanates from it. When people in positions of authority speak, then their words are believed to have *mana*, like the *kotodama* they possess in Japan, as in the *semmyō* (imperial edicts). Oracles, sympathetic magic and spells have *mana* and *tama*.

Like *tama*, *mana* can inhere in animate objects such as people, animals and plants, and also in inanimate objects such as stones, rivers, lakes and mountains and the sea.

There are, however, limits in identifying *tama* with *mana*. Most scholars, from R. H. Codrington to Mircea Eliade,[37] understand *mana* to be an impersonal, often unspecified force which, under certain circumstances, can be appropriated by man. *Tama*, on the contrary, seems more often to be a personal entity although it can, again, under certain conditions, leave the body and unite with extra-personal *tama* forces in nature and people. Even when we consider the transmigration of personal *tama*, *tama* and *mana* seem different. During the Chinkon-sai, for instance, the emperor's *tama* identifies with that of the sun, the reinvigoration ritual affecting both; the sun *tama* seems more specific than the often unrecognizable source of *mana* forces.

F. R. Lehman, assumes that *mana* is 'outstanding effectiveness in action.'[38] We can apply this interpretation of *mana* to *tama* only in a very limited fashion. *Tama* is outstanding effectiveness, if by that we mean extraordinary power, only when applied to the *tama* of authority, such as imperial authority, or to Japanese ritual. The *mana* of war heroes which leads to extraordinary action and success would be more difficult to find in Japan, except perhaps in the case of Yamato Takeru or in the worship of dead military leaders such as Toyotomi Hideyoshi (Toyokuni-san) and Tokugawa Ieyasu (Tōshō Daigongen).

Yet local chieftains and emperors have *mana* more by virtue of their special relationship with their powerful ancestral deities than simply by the exercise of power. We find little trace in the South Pacific of the Japanese worship of fallen heroes, yet we might find a similar worship of certain weapons, which in the South Pacific assume a specially powerful *mana* when used in extraordinary heroic action. A case in point might be the Futsunushi sword enshrined at Isonokami shrine and the Mikazuchi of Kasuga shrine (Nara). In addition we find in the *Nihon Shoki* the legend of Ama no Hiboko's sword which by its own power disappeared and flew to the Island of Awaji where it was enshrined.[39] Ama no Hiboko was an ancestral deity of Korean origin.

Tama and *mana* are both quite arbitrary forces; a respected chieftain has *mana*, but if he loses that respect and power people say that he has lost his *mana*. In Japan, however, the need to periodically invigorate the *tama* through ritual is more pronounced than in South Pacific cultures.[40] *Mana* is, like *tama*, ethically neutral, hence the ancient pre-Confucian belief that political authority does not necessarily have to be good and benevolent. Like *tama*, *mana* can sometimes cause actions opposed to the welfare of individuals or the community.

Mana is often described as a kind of luck, a powerful force that sometimes quite arbitrarily can attach itself to one person rather than another. As an aspect of the *nikitama*, the Japanese *sachi-tama* or 'luck-tama' is a more personal rather than an outside force.

160

As we have seen through our discussion so far, *tama* and *mana* cannot be compared when we consider the concrete belief systems attached to them. The most certain point of comparison may lie in the animism out of which both concepts have grown, and on which the notion of a spirited world and floating soul depends. Since both *tama* and *mana* are notions pertaining to the totality of the world view of both the Japanese and South Pacific tribes, further study is required to reach a more conclusive understanding of these concepts.

23

'Sleeves' and 'Tears' in Classical Japanese Poetry and Lyrical Prose

TZVETANA KRISTEVA

Probably most readers of Japanese classical poetry and lyrical prose have been puzzled by the recurrence in them of 'sleeves': 'sleeves retaining the fragrance of the flowers' ('hana nioi-wo utsusu sode'), 'the moon shining on one's sleeves' ('sode-ni utsuru/yadoru/tsuki'), and a lot of 'tear-wet sleeves' ('sode-no namida'), 'dew-wet sleeves' ('tsuyu oku sode'), 'streams or rivers of tears flowing over one's sleeves' ('namida-gawa...'), 'sleeves that are never dry' ('kawaku toki naku') etc. And probably for occidental readers this fact might have seemed even boring - 'Why did the ancient Japanese shed so many tears upon their sleeves?'

This question 'Why...?,' but with a positive connotation, is of crucial importance for critical readers as well, because the conspicuous presence of the metaphors of the 'tear-wet sleeves' type in the figurative language of the classical *waka* and lyrical prose is not so much a sign of the too sentimental nature of the ancient Japanese, as it is an important textual trace that calls for a new supplementary reading.

As regards 'tear-wet sleeves' references from classical Japanese *waka*, as found in *Kokinshu* and *Shinkokinshu*, the approximate calculations show that such metaphors are to be found in about 40 out of nearly 1000 *waka* of *Kokinshu*, and in about 150 out of the nearly 2000 *waka* of *Shinkokinshu*. The relative ratio is also of importance, and I shall come back to it afterwards, but before that I would like to dwell upon the major poetic themes, revealed through these metaphors.

In *Kokinshu* almost all the metaphors are in the poems included in the five 'Love' chapters, and even the several poems from the other chapters, such as 'Spring,' 'Autumn,' 'Parting,' are dedicated to love. The major themes are the following:

Parting with the beloved:

akazu shite	I shall wrap them up
wakaruru sode-no	as a memento of you
shiratama wa	and take them away - these
kimi ga katami to	clear beads that strike my sleeve
tsutsumite zo yuku	as we part, alas, too soon.[1]

/No. 400, anonymous/;

Leaving the beloved after a night spent together:

akenu tote	I set out for home,
kaeru michi-ni wa	'Now that day begins to break,'
kokitarete	and as I journey
ame mo namida mo	raindrops and tears together
furisobochitsutsu	descend to dampen my robes.

/No. 639, Fujiwara Toshiyuki/;

Loneliness of the neglected loving heart:

tsurezure-no	Unable to meet you,
nagame-ni masaru	I am lost in lonely thought,
namidagawa	my sleeves drenched with tears
sode nomi nurete	abundant as the waters
au yoshi mo nashi	of a rain-swollen river.

/No. 617, Fujiwara Toshiyuki/;

the theme of true/untrue love:

orokanaru	Tears that do no more
namida zo sode-ni	than turn into beads on sleeves
tama wa nasu	are formal indeed.
ga wa sekikaezu	Mine flow in a surging stream
tagitsu se nareba	try though I may to halt them.

/No. 557, Ono-no Komachi/;

In *Shinkokinshu* the themes are more varied. The 'lovelorn tears' in the poems of the five 'Love' chapters comprise about one-third of all the metaphors with 'sleeves' and 'tears' in the anthology.

A major theme which has just been hinted at in *Kokinshu*, is the theme of *the secret love hidden/unveiled by the 'tear-wet sleeves'*:

shinobi amari	Bear with my tears
otsuru namida-wo	that fall in spite of me.
sekikaeshi	O Sleeve, and drink them in
osauru sode yo	leaving no telltale trace.[2]
ukina morasu na	

/No. 1122, anonymous/

162

Another important theme in *Shinkokinshu* revealed through the metaphors of the 'tears flowing over one's sleeves' is *the theme of bygone days*:

yo mo sugara   All night long
tsuki koso sode-ni   my tear-wet sleeves
yadorikere   reflected the bright moon
mukashi-no aki-wo   I, thinking of the bygone autumns.
omoiizureba

/No. 1531, Saigyo/

Closely connected with the theme of memories from bygone days is *the theme of old age and death*:

ito kaku ya   Never were my sleeves
sode wa shioreshi   thus wet with tears when young
nobe-ni idete   on seeing the autumn flowers
mukashi mo aki-no   out in the field.
hana wa mishi

/No. 341, Fujiwara Toshinari/

mishi hito wa   Many of my friends are gone.
yo-ni mo nagisa-no   Each time I write their names,
moshiogusa   like dripping seaweed on the shore
kakioku tabi-ni   falling tears wet my sleeves.
sode zo shioruru

/No. 843, Hokkyo Gyohen/

To conclude with this brief review of the major poetic themes, expressed through the 'tear-wet sleeves' metaphors, I would like to add that in *Shinkokinshu* there are a number of poems in which these metaphors represent the passion for *the beauty of nature throughout the four seasons*:

ume-no hana   The tears upon my sleeves,
nioi-wo utsusu   smelling of plum flowers,
sode-no ue-ni   reflect the moonlight
noki moru tsuki-no   leaking from the eaves.
kage zo arasou

/No. 44, Fujiwara Teika/

oshimu to mo   I shall not miss the autumn
namida-ni tsuki mo   for then the moon shines on my sleeves
kokoro kara   ever wet with tears incited
narenuru sode-ni   by the pathos of the thing.
aki-wo uramite

/No. 1762, Daughter of Fujiwara Toshinari/

Now, from the standpoint of classical criticism these metaphors have been viewed as manifestations of the so-called 'poetical etiquette' of the time, or, in other words, as 'poetic cliches,' exemplifying the structural and typological characteristics of medieval literature within its hierarchization of representation. Such an approach is correct and seems to be still operative, especially in the field of comparative or typological studies. But although it has produced interesting findings, its results are not definitive. The very presence of the word *trace* (ato) - a basic Derridean term,[3] in some of the poems containing these metaphors, is an irresistible temptation to endeavour further supplementary reading trying to transgress, to break through the oppositions literal/figurative, present/ absent, inside/outside and altering the context to mobilize further possibilities for/of the meaning, implied by these metaphors.

Reading justifies itself when it goes beyond the scope of mere textual speculations and succeeds in the discovery of the meaning, or of the chain of meanings implied by a given text. For that reason reading should be perceived as an 'attempt to understand writing by determining the referential and rhetorical modes of a text, translating the figurative into the literal.'[4] Such an approach is of crucial importance for the reading of metaphors, being the most typical manifestations of the figurative language, which are often misread and misunderstood exactly because of the failure to differentiate between their figurative and literal meaning, or, in other words, 'to translate the figurative into the literal.'

Every metaphor generates new meanings through the process of signification of a given object. Thus the 'never dry sleeves' represent tears. The reasons that make poets say their tears are flowing like a 'stream' or a 'river' upon their sleeves, are love, loneliness, sorrow over old age, etc., i.e. concrete manifestations of emotions, which have been mentioned above as major poetic themes, or, in other words, they are representations of passion in general. And although the expression 'never dry sleeves' is exaggerated or not true with regard to the referential object, it is true with regard to passion, or the idea that passion presents to us. Thus we have a complex structure of the process of signification: the idea of 'never dry sleeves' is at once the metaphoric sign of the object (tears), because it is false with regard to it; the metaphoric sign of the concrete emotions (love, loneliness, sadness, sorrow, etc.), because it represents them indirectly; and the literal sign of the representer of passion, i.e. it represents passion literally through the representation of a false representer.[5]

Thus, the complaint, mentioned in the beginning, of 'too many tears upon the sleeves of the ancient Japanese' turns out to be a result of misreading - attaching a literal meaning to a metaphoric sign (tears), and vice-versa.

And now, let us try to broaden the context in quest for new referential models of the text, and for new meanings generated by the 'tear-wet sleeves' type of metaphors.[6] In order to do this it seems to be necessary to move for an instant from the written text to the text that wrote it, i.e. to the cultural background of Heian Japan.

I shall not go into details, because a thorough analysis of that period of unsurpassed aestheticism is both beyond the task of this paper, and beyond the abilities of a single researcher. The very fact that it is open to an endless chain of rereading demonstrates indisputably its unfading aesthetic impact, which is a constant challenge for scholars all over the world.

My main interest will be focused, first, on the roots of the creative imagination and poetic afflatus of that period, i.e. on the 'origin' of writing, and, second, on the specific characteristic points of the graphic writing itself.

As is well-known, the Heian society, which considered art and literature to be of high social prestige, did not make the distinction between 'higher' and 'lower' genres, characteristic of Medieval European literature. Moreover, it valued highly precisely the type of writing which in Europe was attributed to the 'lower' genres, i.e. writing as implementation of spontaneous personal feelings. The literature of Heian Japan is emotional through and through, and in a number of written texts it itself has defined passion as its major driving force. Suffice it to mention the much quoted discussion on the art of *monogatari* in the famous 'Hotaru' chapter of *Genji monogatari*, or the Introductions to *Kokinshu* and *Shinkokinshu*, in which the 'songs of Yamato' (yamato-no uta) are said to be 'born out from the human hearts' (hito-no kokoro-wo tane to shite...), which is again a metaphor signifying *passion*.

As for the characteristic points of the graphic writing in that period, it is well-known that *waka* and the lyrical prose inspired by it, were written in *kana*, and besides, they were written with brush and ink. Another important point is that according to the newly-formed principles of Japanese calligraphy, aestheticized graphic writing comprised indiscrete continuous vertical lines, thus resembling flows of ink on the paper. The fact that up to the late Middle Ages the Japanese preferred to write their personal works of art by hand, although they are said to have known xylographic printing not later than the eighth century, shows among other things that the beauty of calligraphic writing was part and parcel of the aesthetic perception of the work of art. Or, one can say, that only the lines of the brush, viewed as vibrations of the human heart, were capable of expressing the 'songs of Yamato,' born out from the human heart.

Now, if we assume that graphic writing was an integral component of works of art in Heian Japan, we can expect it to be infiltrated into the texture of the works as well.[7] And if we assume that passion was the major driving force and poetic theme of literature, it is only natural to search for the traces of this infiltration in the metaphors signifying passion, one of them being the 'tear-wet sleeves' type.

In order to prove this presumption I shall reread one of the *Shinkokinshu* poems (No. 807, written by Princess Kishi), using the comments to it.[8]

inishie-no	These traces left
naki-ni nagaruru	by his writing brush long, long ago
mizuguki wa	now make my sleeves
ato koso sode-no	all wet with tears.
ura-ni yorikeri	

Unfortunately, the English translation fails to suggest all the referential modes of the poem, but probably no translation whatsoever can manage it.

Inishie is an old word for *mukashi* - 'the past,' and *inishie-no* means 'from the past,' 'coming from the past'; *naki-ni nagaruru* means literally 'flowing (in/from the past) after one's death,' and is associated with *naki-ni nakaruru* - 'weeping over and over again' (from *naku* - 'weep'); *mizuguki* is an old word for 'brush,' and *nagaruru mizuguki* stands for the traces of the brush strokes, which have been transmitted as a memento from the past, whereas the *mizu* from *mizuguki* is associated with tears; *ato* ('trace') is a key-word, combining both meanings of the 'traces of the brush strokes' and the 'traces of tears,' thus fixing the deep interrelation between them; *sode-no ura-ni yorikeri* ('remain hidden in the sleeves') - the last words of the poem, called to existence according to the poetic rules of *engo* (*nagaruru, mizu, ura*, and *yori* are *engo* words), once more justify this interrelation, i.e. 'traces of tears and traces of the brush remain together hidden in the sleeves.'

As it could be seen, the text itself suggests the possibility of a new process of signification of the 'tear-wet sleeves' type of metaphors. In this supplementary signification the idea of 'tears flowing over one's sleeves' is a metaphoric sign of the brush strokes, or the flow of ink (object); a metaphoric sign of the designations of the brush strokes, i.e. the major poetic themes (love, loneliness, sadness, sorrow, etc.), which in turn are the representers of writing itself. Thus it could be said that in this supplementary signification the metaphors of 'tears flowing over one's sleeves' literally represent the idea of writing itself, or, in other words, through these metaphors the process of writing refers to itself and defines itself.

Basing oneself on this supplementary reading one could give a new answer to the question 'Why did the ancient Japanese shed so many tears upon their sleeves?.' The tears upon their sleeves are a sign of their passion for writing, of their desire in language.

If we now reread closely the above-cited poems using this newly generated meaning, we can discover new dimensions in them and enjoy an increasing pleasure of reading. This might also bring us closer to the understanding of all those 'lovelorn' and 'reminiscent' tears as 'precious keepsake' (*katami*), or to the understanding of the complaint of such prolific poets as Ariwara Narihira and Ono-no Komachi that their sleeves are 'too narrow' to stem their tears 'running in a seething current.'

It could also be argued that the broadening of the 'river of tears,' running from *Kokinshu* to *Shinkokinshu*, mentioned in the beginning in figures (40 poems in *Kokinshu*, containing the 'tear-wet sleeves' type of metaphors, to 150 in *Shinkokinshu*), is a mark of the development of literary consciousness of the times, which was infiltrated unconsciously into the texture of the poetical works.

* * *

In the title of my paper I promised to look for 'tear-wet sleeves' both in *waka* and in the lyrical prose, inspired by it. However, so far I have discussed only the poems. Frankly speaking, I first got the idea for this paper not from *waka*, but from one of my favourite works of the Japanese classical lyrical prose - the lyrical diary *Towazu-gatari*, written by Lady Nijo, which I had the pleasure of translating into Bulgarian a few years ago. The Bulgarian readers seemed to like it very much, and it even became a best-seller. The only thing that puzzled them were the tears on the sleeves of the ancient Japanese. So this is how I started thinking about the possible reasons for them.

And although in *Towazu-gatari* there are instances of 'tear-wet sleeves' in the prose parts, too, their main area is poetry, and this fact made me turn my attention to *waka*. Thus my paper attempts a strategy of a supplementary reading of the metaphors of the 'tear-wet sleeves' type in *waka*, which I hope to become applicable to the reading of the lyrical prose, incited by it, as well. In fact I have tried to use it in *Towazu-gatari*, and the effect has turned out to be really encouraging.

To conclude, I would like to express my hope that my supplementary reading has been inadequate enough to suggest possibilities for further supplementary readings aimed at eliciting an even greater pleasure from the text, for, in Derrida's felicitous remark, 'Thinking is what we already know we have not yet begun.'[9]

24

From Insularity to Internationalism: Kabuki in the Twenty-first Century

LEONARD PRONKO

At the end of the nineteenth century Kabuki attempted to renew itself under the impact of changing conditions brought about by the Meiji Restoration. The efforts came from within the Kabuki world, headed by major figures of the day, Danjuro IX and Kikugoro V. Ashamed of its overt use of eroticism, the grotesque and exaggerated stylization, the Kabuki world tried to enhance its prestige by imitating the aristocratic and refined tone of the Noh theatre on the one hand, and the realism and historicism of the newly discovered Western theatre on the other. This two-forked voyage towards an ill-conceived renewal led Kabuki to a double denial of its own essence. Eschewing its own rich past, it leapt over several centuries of popular success, in order to find inspiration in a dramatic (or ceremonial) form that is in many ways at odds with Kabuki. At the same time it rejected those qualities it considered childlike and attempted to create a more mature art reflecting a realistic, serious point of view.

Kabuki's history is full of changes and adaptations, drawing now on this dramatic form, now on that trendy music, today including this fad, tomorrow that; for it is a popular drama that depended on the support of its audiences, and not on government subsidies. But in its long history, until Meiji, despite a strong trend towards realism, or even naturalism in some phases of its presentation, Kabuki never fully embraced the kind of realism we find in the West at the end of the nineteenth century. And for a very good reason: Western realism is a denial of Kabuki's very essence. A total form of theatre that developed organically (rather than from the intellectual concepts that lie at the root of total theatre in the West), Kabuki, like all major forms of Asian theatre, is an amalgam of acting, music (or singing) and dance. The very characters of the name tell us so: Ka=song, bu=dance, ki=technique. Any renewal that involves the disappearance of song and dance is a denial of Kabuki and a turning of that rich, old form into a new path which, while it may have an interest of its own, is no longer the path of Kabuki.

Kabuki, as the twentieth century draws to a close, is still not at home in its own skin, and continues to dally with the refinements of Noh and the realism and psychologism of Western theatre. But the future lies elsewhere: once again, after a cataclysm as great as that of the Meiji Restoration, adventurous souls within the Kabuki world, and elsewhere as well, are turning to the West and to Japan's past for inspiration. But with a difference. The Western theatre of the 1980s is very different from that of a century ago, and although Kabuki cannot see a mirror image of itself in the West, it can see forces at work that reflect Asian influences or at least currents that are clearly non-realistic. Turning again to Japan's past, at least some actors in the Kabuki world are drawing inspiration from Kabuki's own traditions, and seeking, like Ichikawa Ennosuke, to revive the spirit of Bunka-Bunsei Kabuki, an era that some would describe as vulgar and decadent, but whose vitality, as far as Kabuki is concerned, none can deny.

Conservative forces within the Kabuki world are, of course, critical of anything that changes the *status quo*, forgetting that the tradition of Kabuki is a 'tradition of change.' As is so often the case, the radicals are more firmly rooted in tradition than the conservatives who betray tradition by remaining faithful to a form that has taken on the overly-refined flavour of Noh or the 'butter-smell' of psychological realism. The changes that began to be felt about twenty years ago arise from a number of sources and are reflected in numerous ways. This paper explores those changes, beginning with the Kabuki world itself, then passing to the related but now separate world of Kabuki Dance (Nihonbuyo), then to the stimulating uses of Kabuki (however transformed) by outstanding directors in the non-kabuki world in Japan, and finally to experiments with Kabuki in the West.

The Kabuki world in the twentieth century has been arch-conservative, organized along hierarchical medieval lines, with power and choice emanating from the top. Youth and adventurous imagination must normally give way to the wisdom and fixed ways of old age. The attitudes which gave rise to *shinkabuki* a hundred years ago still dominate, and the usual concept of neo-kabuki is simply a newly written play performed by kabuki actors, whether it be highly stylized, completely naturalistic, accompanied by music, dance, poses, stylized speech as in classic kabuki, or reduced to the realistic movement and uninspired conversation of much modern Western drama. Among the *shinkabuki* created during the last hundred years two kinds dominate: historical plays approached in a realistic, psychological manner; and dance plays based upon the choreography of the past. The latter, because they employ the stylization of dance, are often successful, and continue to embody the flavour and characteristics of Kabuki. The former exercise an appeal to modern audiences because they are written in a comprehensible language, but in most cases that is their only virtue, and they represent in no way the total theatricality that has characterized Kabuki since its heyday in the late seventeenth century.

The insularity of the Kabuki world itself lies in its belief that only the veterans of kabuki are privileged to understand that ancient art and only they should be allowed to tamper with it - usually following the precepts of Meiji Kabuki noted above. It lies furthermore in their belief that only those who are born into the Kabuki world, or adopted into it at a relatively young age, are capable of mastering the intricacies of the art. Signs that such beliefs are beginning to give way in the modern world, and that new more methodical ways of learning Kabuki are developing are to be found in the Kabuki Training Programme opened at the National Theatre of Japan, Tokyo, in 1970. Every three years since then a new group of ten young men, usually between the ages of fifteen and 20 or so, have entered the two-year training programme, and followed it by a year of apprenticeship to an established actor.

Even here, however, the heavy control of the Kabuki world is apparent: when the programme began in 1970, Westerners who could prove themselves serious students were accepted in the programme. It was soon discovered, however, that Westerners wished to study Kabuki in order to use the techniques in their own countries. The Kabuki actors, apparently feeling that this was improper, forced the National Theatre to stop accepting foreigners. The programme is now closed to them, except as occasional observers. For a time foreigners were accepted but only if they signed a contract promising that they would not do Kabuki in their own country when they returned home. The paradoxical situation of a theatre programme willing to train people only if they will *not* perform is indicative of the insularity of actors who often perform Shakespeare in a Western manner, but reject the idea that Kabuki should belong to the international artistic community.

Students in the National Theatre training programme are told that they must give their entire concentration to their studies, since they must learn in two years what a Kabuki actor normally (by a kind of osmosis) learns in ten or fifteen years. Systematic approaches to actors' training have been developed, and the young men at the end of two or three years are, in

169

many cases, astonishingly adept at techniques which, before their studies began, they had no knowledge of whatsoever. Needless to say, the grip of the great Kabuki families is still firm, and the National Theatre depends upon their cooperation for its programme, so it must obey the dictates of the Kabuki princes, and never be so experimental that it would offend the hierarchies. It also goes without saying that the young actors graduated from the programme have virtually no hope of ever winning glory in Kabuki, for that is reserved to the scions of the major Kabuki families.

There has been one exception: a young actor taken into the troupe of Ichikawa Ennosuke III. This is not entirely surprising, for if any exceptions to the rigidity of Kabuki in the twentieth century are to be found, they will be found in the circle of this astonishing virtuoso actor of incredible imagination and energy. Almost alone he has begun to make inroads into the conservatism of Kabuki and to establish a beachhead that marks a return to the glories of the early nineteenth century. At forty-eight, Ennosuke is at the top of the Kabuki ladder, and because he is the grandson of the revered Eno, he is allowed a liberty denied lower-ranking actors. But it is the combination of this liberty with Ennosuke's personal gifts, his inventiveness, creativity and intellect along with brilliant technical accomplishments, that allows him to create and perform the most popular productions in Kabuki today.

His family traditions prepared him no doubt for this role, for his grandfather, having seen the Russian ballet, conceived the brilliant *Kurozuka*, which remains today one of the present Ennosuke's key pieces. Based upon a Noh play, *Adachigahara*, this piece sweeps us into the twentieth century with its use of two-dimensional scenery and the fascinating transposition of ballet's toe-dancing in a dazzling moonlight scene as the old witch of Adachigahara dances on the balls of her feet (unheard of in Kabuki dance until then) to celebrate her hoped-for redemption under the symbolic Buddhist moon. Despite such reminders of the West, and elements which clearly derive from the Noh, *Kurozuka* is full of the flavour of true Kabuki, with its blending of dance, song and stylized speech, its grand and colourful costumes and make-up, and the astonishing energy of Ennosuke as he transforms from old lady to demon.

Old classics like *Yoshitsune Sembonzakura* become, in Ennosuke's choreography, more Kabuki than Kabuki itself, one might say. Enhancing the classical *kata* (patterns) with the rapid changes (*hayagawari*) for which he is famous, Ennosuke plays two or more roles, introduces acrobatic tricks including his popular flying through the air at the end of the play. The Kabuki-za in Tokyo is the scene of a triumphant Ennosuke Kabuki every July, as the tireless actor plays from five to twenty roles in one play, appearing from eleven or twelve in the morning until after ten in the evening, in role after role. Many of the plays he performs are his own adaptations of classics that have fallen from the repertoire, or arrangements of several old plays with new flamboyant theatrical moments introduced for the stars.

In 1986 Ennosuke presented a new Kabuki play based upon ancient Japanese history, and made history himself with it. He has already performed it throughout Japan to great acclaim - and criticism, too, of course, from the more conservative. *Yamato Takeru* has been called 'super kabuki' by its admirers. It embodies the extravagance, colour and rapid pace that Ennosuke thinks necessary to capture the attention of a broad Kabuki public today., 'I am simply producing the excitement of Kabuki in 1986 that actors created in its golden age,'[1] he declares.

Such a return to golden age Kabuki is at the same time a renewal through modern technology and arts, for Ennosuke, taking advantage of what is popular and appealing, had his sets and costumes designed by famous designers and couturiers foreign to the Kabuki world, and his lighting designed to take advantage of twentieth-century advances, rather than following the full unvarying white light that is normally used in Kabuki today. He *does* sometimes follow the dictates of the past, but in *Yamato Takeru* and in a recent production of *Sembonzakura* he used contemporary lighting, 'to see if and how the traditional make-up and costumes of classical Kabuki can be used in new contexts with modern theatrical lighting techniques.'[2] Like classical Kabuki, he was taking advantage of whatever offered itself to increase the pleasure of the Kabuki experience.

Unlike the disciples of Meiji era Kabuki, Ennosuke rejects the turn to Western realism and the aestheticism of Noh. 'You try to make Kabuki realistic,' he said in an interview, 'all it gets is boring. You cut down on the variety in Kabuki, it loses its point. It's a popular theatre, it's not a single-style art like Noh; and if you try to make it into one, it gets stale.'[3]

In Ennosuke we find the outstanding example within the Kabuki world today of a major actor creating a new Kabuki that is faithful to the aesthetic of the form at the same time that it advances into the twentieth century. Emphasizing popular elements, the colourful, grotesque and energetic, Ennosuke, who is a supreme master of technique, does not avoid the subtleties and finesse of the most classic modes, but he is able to infuse them with a strength, conviction and credibility that carry them straight to the hearts of his audiences. Aware of the tastes of contemporary spectators (as were the creative spirits of Kabuki in its heyday), he understands that a person travelling at the speed of the Bullet Train finds it difficult to slow down simply because he is at the theatre. He knows that many young people are not brought up as connoisseurs of Kabuki, and must be met at least part way if they are to become lovers of this rich classic/romantic form.

Nor does Ennosuke restrict his efforts to Japan. Like many Kabuki stars since the Second World War, he has travelled to Europe, the United States and Asia, where he has exercised an extraordinary impact, not only through performance, but by his demonstrations and classes, and his direction of a Kabuki version of Rimski-Korsakov's opera, *Le Coq d'Or* in Paris several years ago. He continues to perform *Le Coq d'Or* in Japan, but as a Kabuki piece.

If Ennosuke is virtually alone in his efforts to renew Kabuki from the inside, there are multiple efforts from without. Most closely related to Kabuki itself are those presentations based on the techniques of classic Kabuki dance, but drawing on other forms as well, modern dance, ballet, folk dance and so forth. These are most often produced by teachers and choreographers from the vast world of Japanese Dance, Nihonbuyo. Until

171

the late nineteenth century, the teachers and choreographers of Nihonbuyo were simply a part of the Kabuki world who served the theatre, taught their own non-actor students, but never performed in public. It was only as a result of conflicts with the Kabuki hierarchies that the choreographers began to perform, and today the world of Japanese Dance has grown quite apart from the Kabuki world. Indeed, dancers often complain that the actors do not know how to dance, and the actors complain that the dancers do not have any feeling or flavour, but only replicate correct *kata*.

As the dance world grew away from Kabuki in the early twentieth century, realizing that its strengths lay in lyricism and beauty of movement rather than in drama and character portrayal, it began to create more abstract kinds of dance, divorcing the movement from the words to which it is invariably tied in Kabuki. By the end of the Second World War the New Dance (*shinbuyo*) that had evolved began to move even further from Kabuki as it accepted foreign kinds of movement, and even adopted non-Japanese themes. Thus was the Creative Dance, *sosakubuyo*, movement born. Many of the finest teachers of classic Kabuki dance, who even choreograph on occasion for the Kabuki stage, are active in the Creative Dance world. It is not unusual to see impressive and imaginative performances of solo dances or of complex dramatic dances based on the stories of Salome, Faust or other Western traditions.

The rise of *shinbuyo* and *sosakubuyo* are illustrations of the fruitfulness of a break away from the hierarchic control of the Kabuki world. Without the conflicts which resulted in the division of *buyo* from Kabuki, we might never have discovered the glories of Creative Dance.

In 1987 one of the most exciting performances of Sosakubuyo was created by Hanayagi Yoshijiro, who had earlier assisted Maurice Béjart in his creation of *The Kabuki*, a piece which blended ballet, modern dance and Kabuki dance to retell for a modern audience the story of one of Japan's favourite classic tales, *Chushingura*. Yoshijiro, no doubt impressed by the impact of Béjart's genius, decided that he would undertake a similar work, but going in the opposite direction. With a group of superbly trained dancers, he produced his version of *Carmen*. Unlikely as the prospect of Carmen in kimono may strike us, Yoshijiro had the imagination to find unexpected parallels between Nihonbuyo and flamenco that made his *Carmen* seem not only natural but so obvious that one wondered why it had not been done before. Using the long trailing kimono as they are often worn by Kabuki women, he suggested the long skirts of flamenco dancers. The high twelfth-century style wigs just suggested a point from which a mantilla might hang. Utilizing hand clapping and stamping, both characteristic of Spanish and Japanese dance, Yoshijiro formed a believable, passionate form that answered to the needs of the story and emotion without denying the traditions of Japanese dance. Following the inspiration of Shinbuyo, and unlike most Kabuki dance which features solo, or at most duo dancing, Yoshijiro choreographed exciting group dances suggesting the busy life of the city, and offering a comment on the main story through punctuated movement and group characters that seemed to stand for passion or fate.

Bizet's music formed an instrumental suite, punctuated here and there by several of Carmen's arias actually sung, and twice by a fiery flamenco guitar played by a lone figure in black who rose on an elevator upstage. When Don José and Carmen finally give in to their passion, Bizet gave way to Ravel, and they danced a torrid 'Bolero,' perhaps a reminder of Béjart's influence, but very different from his table-top performance. Costumes were rich, gorgeous, the lines invariably Japanese, but containing reminiscences of Spain. Escamillo, for example, wore a huge cape and just visible beneath it at one side was something that might have been the gold embroidered vest of a *traje de luces*.

Yoshijiro and other inspired choreographers are carrying at least the Bu part of Kabuki into the twentieth century and forming a bridge to modern audiences in Japan and across the seas. Accessible to Westerners who have no understanding of Japanese dance, pieces like *Carmen* offer a familiar story, well-loved music and parallels with recognizable Western dance forms that make Nihonbuyo at once lively and meaningful. It is to be hoped that *Carmen* and pieces like it will tour internationally and help dispel the insularity that characterizes much Japanese art.

Further removed from Kabuki than Nihonbuyo is the modern theatre of Japan. Reacting against Kabuki in the early twentieth century, it went out of its way to avoid being kabuki-like in any way. It is only in the last fifteen or twenty years that the *shingeki* world, or that of the underground (experimental) theatre has begun to rediscover the richness that lies in classical forms revitalized and reworked for modern ends. Among contemporary directors, two stand out for their work deriving from Kabuki (and other forms as well, for none of them are purists): Suzuki Tadashi and Ninagawa Yukio. Both have received international acclaim for their intensely inventive work. Both have revitalized Western classics by infusing them with the power of Japan's classic forms of Noh and Kabuki transposed or reinvented.

Although he admires Noh and Kabuki actors for their mastery of a discipline which allows them to exhibit a great freshness even in old age, Suzuki does not believe that these old forms can be used just as they are in the contemporary theatre. Instead, viewing them as 'in some ways more contemporary than our newest theatrical ventures,' he would draw on what he calls 'the splendid concepts and emotions at the very heart' of Kabuki and Noh. In the movements and gestures, in the energy of the forms, he has sought inspiration for his own very special techniques which he has been experimenting with since the 1960s. Working with 'stars' of the Kabuki and Noh worlds, Suzuki has striven not only to suggest ways of modernizing Noh and Kabuki, but to bring their concepts into today's theatre.

'My ultimate goal,' he says 'is to restore vitality to the theatre in a process similar to that of remodelling an old piece of architecture in order to bring it back to a new and useful life.'[4] Thus far Suzuki's major successes have been with Greek tragedies that he has rewritten to reflect contemporary concerns. Invariably starring the charismatic actress Shiraishi Kayoko, works like *The Trojan Women*, *The Bacchae* and *Clytemnestra* have toured through Europe, the US and Asia. An important part of Suzuki's work is his training programme, and the highly individual

173

system he uses is imparted to an international group during summers in the tiny village of Togamura in the Japan Alps. At other times, Suzuki has taught workshops at the University of Wisconsin, the Juilliard School of Theatre and the University of California in San Diego.

Recently his performances have used both Japanese and English, mixing casts from both countries. Most striking was a version of *King Lear* in which the events of the play were viewed as a dream of the mad king. At least one troupe was made up of American actors and toured the piece in English.

Intense, deeply centered, the actors in Suzuki's pieces reflect the aesthetic of Noh as well as Kabuki. There is a simplicity, a constant paring away in Suzuki's productions where the emphasis is clearly on the actor, often in a kind of possessed state. One is tempted to compare him to Copeau in a number of ways and to describe his approach as Calvinistic in its austerity, discipline, purity, concentration and devotion to an ideal.

The work of Ninagawa Yukio, perhaps because it has been developed within the framework of the commercial theatre, is more spectacular, using large performing areas, high-tech production values and gorgeous costumes, wigs and make-up. Ninagawa, like Suzuki, has drawn on great Western classics for his international tours, although in Japan he does contemporary pieces as well. His *Medea* and *Macbeth* have been seen at the Edinburgh Festival and elsewhere in Europe, while North America has only seen the *Medea*.

Blending the old and the new, Ninagawa uses pneumatic lifts, blazing spotlights and popular contemporary music at the same time that his actors strum old folk-type Japanese stringed instruments, move in Kabuki-like patterns and perform before ancient temples and other structures in Japan, Greece or England. Working outside any given tradition, he is free to use whatever he wishes, embracing a wide-ranging eclecticism. In *Macbeth* he used both men and women, but in *Medea* the entire cast was male, thus adding another traditional element to a performance that in many ways, despite its solid Japanese derivation, must have been by far the most faithful production any Greek tragedy has received in the past 2,400 years.

Medea is representative of Ninagawa's theatricalist style, with its swirling Chorus, vocal pyrotechnics, sudden movements, rushing up and down the multiple steps of a Buddhist temple before which the play is performed in Japan. The strength of a male Medea stresses the unmotherly elements in the character, and yet Hira Mikijiro's characterization struck at least one critic as more convincing and moving than any number of women he had seen in the role. In the *Manchester Guardian* (7 September 1986) Michael Billington confessed, 'It is hard to explain how a man can come closer to maternal passion than most actresses.'

While *Macbeth* reminded Billington how exciting and beautiful Shakespeare could be, *Medea* proved to him that 'the Kabuki mixture of drama, dance and song' offered a key to Greek tragedy. Here at the end of the twentieth century, two ancient traditions are reinvigorating each other. Moving away from classical Kabuki in his use of a Western play, Western baroque music, contemporary Japanese popular music, outdoor staging, etc., Ninagawa has renewed the Kabuki traditions by bringing them into contact with modern and Western elements. While the choreography is not strictly Kabuki, it is based firmly on Kabuki stylization. Indeed, the choreographer of *Medea* was the imaginative young Hanayagi Kinnosuke, known as an exponent of Nihonbuyo, but also as a creative choreographer in the more recent Sosakubuyo style. Blending modern dance, folk elements and Kabuki dance, he has realized an earthy, moving choreography that harmonizes with the total style of *Medea* while underscoring its themes.

It is to be noted that major Kabuki actors have also undertaken classic Western roles ever since Japan discovered Shakespeare. But unlike the Kabuki-like *Medeas, Macbeths* and *Clytemnestras* of the brilliant directors we have just glanced at, Western classics as performed by true Kabuki actors tend to exhibit a faithfulness to Western tradition - which is to say, to no tradition whatsoever. The actors appear to consider it a point of honour to prove that in Western plays they are capable of forgetting their Kabuki training and performing entirely in a non-Kabuki manner. The future of Japanese theatre, however, and even the future of a living Kabuki (as contrasted to the museum-like Kabuki of the past hundred years) lies in this vital blend of modern and traditional, Japanese and foreign, classic and popular - precisely as Kabuki evolved and stayed alive in its golden age. Rather than keeping Kabuki compartmentalized and distinct from all other theatre - although this may well be necessary to maintain the purity of its great classics - renewal lies no doubt in the direction of cross-fertilization, as it has in every great age of theatre we have known in the West since the Greeks.

If the Kabuki world itself has been conservative in this regard, and the most inspired experiments have come from the outside, it should not be surprising to find that a number of inventive approaches to Kabuki have developed in the West. Of late, we can point to the international successes of artists like Ariane Mnouchkine and Maurice Béjart. But before they astonished and delighted us with their genius and imagination, and even at the same time that adventurers like Suzuki were beginning their inspired work in the early 60s, scholars, teachers and directors were carrying on experiments that were breaking new ground in a more restricted terrain, but delighting and astonishing small groups of audiences in cities in the United States.

Three universities in the United States have a tradition of annual or biennial kabuki performances: the University of Hawaii, where productions go back as far as the 1920s; the University of Illinois at Champaign-Urbana and Pomona College in Claremont, California. Using varying approaches, each of these schools has attempted to create performances of Kabuki as authentic as could be found anywhere outside Japan. But in addition to their replicas of Japanese performances, they have carried on a number of experiments that foreshadowed those of Ninagawa and Mnouchkine.

James Brandon at Hawaii has created plays on Japanese history or Japanese legend, like *The Cross and the Sword* (the early Christians in Japan) and *Earless Hoichi* (the legend of the Heike), in which he has blended Western techniques of acting with various oriental techniques, including those of Noh and Kabuki.

Shozo Sato at the University of Illinois created a Kabuki *Macbeth*, which was subsequently mounted by a small theatre in Chicago with such success that it was awarded a Chicago Drama Critics Prize. His next Chicago production, a Kabuki *Medea*, received a similar prize. Since those productions, Sato has undertaken Kabuki versions of *Othello* and *Faustus* as well.

Sato's productions are invariably visually stunning, drawing on his own keen artistic instincts and training and displaying a full panoply of the visual excitement possible in Kabuki. Colourful costumes and make-up, dramatic poses, frequent *hikinuki* changes of costume, flamboyant fight scenes and highly choreographed moments are featured in plays which, while following the plot of the original, are usually rewritten to take advantage of Kabuki techniques and the Japanese settings and costumes. The original Shakespeare text, for example, is eschewed in favour of a less poetic text which lends itself more readily to Kabuki vocalizations, repetitions and patterns.

In our own productions of Shakespeare's contemporaries at Pomona College we have attempted to cope with the difficulty of performing an Elizabethan or Jacobean text as it was written, while infusing it with the Kabuki spirit both visually and vocally. The problem is to find Western parallels for the typically Japanese movements that are the foundation of Kabuki patterns, or to justify the introduction of *mie, roppo, tachimawari* and other obviously exotic movements in a context where they seem foreign.

In Marlowe's *Jew of Malta* (1965) Elizabethan staging and Renaissance costumes were used, but the latter were exaggerated, padded, with bold patterns and great bulk. The courtesan, Bellamira, took advantage of the high wooden shoes that were worn by Renaissance courtesans, and which approximate the high black-lacquered geta of the Kabuki *oiran*. The comic bully, Pilia-Borza, was played in outlandish *aragoto* style. Symbolic colours, like those of Kabuki, helped distinguish characters: Barabas the Jew, for example, wore the traditional red wig of the medieval vice character. And when he went crying out for his lost money, he exited dramatically through the midst of the audience on the hanamichi. For audiences unaccustomed to actors performing energetically in intimate proximity, the impact was immense.[5]

Some years later, in 1980, Tourneur's *Revenger's Tragedy* was presented with what the *Los Angeles Times*' reviewer called 'a broad and haunting treatment with Kabuki overtones that emphasize the grandeur of the form and majesty of the writing without neglecting its satirical undercurrent.' Sylvie Drake's chief complaint was that we had not gone far enough in following Kabuki exaggeration. While this may be difficult with poetic Renaissance texts, it becomes entirely possible when one writes one's own text.

In 1977 Pomona College Theatre produced a Kabuki Western, blending the theatricality and heroics of East and West. The story was modelled on three favourite acts from Kabuki classics, *Yoshitsune, Sembonzakura* and *Tsuchigumo*, but they were transposed from the heroic era of early Japan to America's nineteenth century in order to depict the tragic struggle between the Indian and the US government forces who were taking over their land. Battles between the Heike and the Genji became those between Indians and whites; a travel-dance scene (*michiyuki*) showing a princess and her servant in a forest of cherry blossoms, became the flight of the Indian hero with his white sweetheart into the desert filled with blossoming cactus flowers. The fierce evil spider demon of Kabuki and Noh became the loving but still fierce Spider Woman of Indian myth, who finally destroys the evil white man and surrounds him with her gossamer webs before disappearing into a trap deep within her cave.

Again the *Los Angeles Times*' reviewer was impressed, and praised the production for its 'creative adaptation of an oriental mode to an occidental theme,' and declared that 'the understanding of Kabuki as a form and of its immediacy and its enormous possibilities has never been better demonstrated.'

Subsequently we presented our own Kabuki version of the Arthurian legends, *Lancelot Bewitched*, and in December, 1987, the legend of Prometheus, *Fireplay*. The possibilities of Kabuki in English (or French or Italian or any other language, for that matter) are virtually unlimited. Kabuki's themes, and the situations depicted, are often universal. The theatricality of the Kabuki mode is strikingly appropriate for many of the legendary, historical or folkloric themes of the West. It also offers us a means of retheatricalizing a theatre which has lost its classical traditions and has suffered too long from the tedium of realism and naturalism. The greater-than-life characters and situations of the Renaissance drama or of Greek tragedy seem a natural terrain for Kabuki, and suggest a way of finding again an appropriate style.

Apparently Ariane Mnouchkine had some such intuition when she approached her Shakespeare productions. The one most akin to Kabuki - and the most successful according to a number of observers - was *Richard II*. Those spectators who know Kabuki well realized immediately that Mnouchkine was not attempting a copy of Kabuki. What she so brilliantly succeeded in doing was to unify Kabuki, Noh and Chinese Opera techniques with Western forms like *commedia dell'arte* and circus. Rehearsing over a period of many months that most troupes do not have at their disposal, she was able to teach various techniques to her actors, and let them work with them until they had transposed them and made them their own. Indeed, Mnouchkine herself is not trained in Kabuki. Instead, following intuition and her own creative ideas, she arrived at a style that was neither Oriental nor Western, but an organic form that served perfectly her actors' needs, enhancing the theatricality inherent in *Richard II* and releasing the actors to explore it.

The proliferation of such professional experiments fusing East and West is significant. In the past few years alone there have been three or four Kabuki versions of *Macbeth* in the United States, including a prize-winning performance in Chicago, a *Shogun Macbeth* originating in Dallas and subsequently performed in NewYork, and a touring production originating at the National Theatre in Washington, DC. The educational theatre became aware of untapped riches many years ago, but today the professional theatre is beginning to mine this ore.

As the twentieth century draws to a close, Japanese artists can look to the West and see not only a tired realism, but a healthy presentational theatre as well, including performances that are based on Kabuki. The result of this will be a new awareness on the part of the Japanese Kabuki world itself, encouraging it, or perhaps even forcing it, to renew itself by following its own tradition of change, rather than continuing to turn in upon its museum-like image. Looking to the Japanese Dance world, or to the efforts of its own Ennosuke, following the vigorous lead of Suzuki and Ninagawa, or even seeking inspiration in the extravagant theatricality of Mnouchkine or the sensuous spirituality of Béjart, perhaps Kabuki, freed of its inferiority complex, seeing itself recognized everywhere not as a dead tradition of the past, but as a living theatre of the future - perhaps then Kabuki will be reborn gloriously, and will take its first truly international steps into the twenty-first century.

25

The Shingeki Movement Until 1930: its Experience in Western Approach

GIOIA OTTAVIANI

One of the main characteristics of the Shingeki is the great quantity of Western references that it chose when conducting its own experiments. In observing this theatrical movement in its first twenty-years of experimentation, we find ourselves, therefore, taking account of the presence, or better, the image of Western theatre, reflected in the productions, in the repertoire and in the interpretations of the actors.

This image imposes itself as an element which gave direction to the research of the Shingeki movement, and, in front of it, the Western historian finds himself in a particular kind of cultural involvement. What I intend to suggest is an example of the problems and the reflections which the Western historian must face if he wants to overcome the problem of the apparent 'dependence' of the Shingeki on the Western experience.

It was Iwata Toyoo, in his book *Shingeki to watakushi*,[1] who offered one of the principal keys to the reading of the Shingeki: 'I felt that what I had seen in Paris was not so much the modernism of the theatre, as the theatricalization of the modern spirit.'

In fact the problem was this, not only to create a modern theatre but to confront the modern world with the theatre, and in particular, modern Japan. Between the end of the last century and the beginning of the twentieth century, Japan had several times risked being involved in simple modernism. The work of Tsubouchi Shōyō and still more, that of Osanai

178

Kaoru, gave rise to the wish to avoid that risk. An event took place which reveals how the concept of a new theatre was put into effect, not as a simple formal attempt, but as an effort to translate the signs of the 'modern spirit' into theatrical terms.

I am referring to the inauguration of the Jiyū Gekijō at the Yurakuza on 27 November 1909, with the production of Ibsen's *John Gabriel Borkman*. Many accounts have reached us from contemporary publications or from the pages of some of the major representatives of the literature of the period. Masamune Hakuchō, Shimazaki Tōson, Yoshi Isamu, Nagata Ideo and also Tanizaki Jun'inchirō and Mori Ogai have spoken about it. Shimazaki Tōson recounts:

> 'While I was present at the performance together with Messrs Kamahara, Tayama and Tokuta, all of a sudden the door of the box flew open and the excited figure of Mr Yanagida appeared, who, with his heart in his mouth and all in one breath, exclaimed: "Well, my goodness, I happen to be at a *passionate*[2] moment in time!" Then he stopped to reaffirm: "Never before had the moment been so right for uncontrollable enthusiasm as now".'[3]

Yoshi Isamu, in some verses composed about that occasion, speaks even of 'intoxication,' 'adventure' and 'dream'[4].

Obviously the reactions were varied. For example, Masamune Hakuchō left the theatre before the end of the performance. Others like him reacted to the lack of formality in the production, but, for many others, their emotional reactions were even stronger in seeing a theatrical language which was not perhaps artistically complete, but which responded to the expectations and the questions which at the moment were being addressed to the theatre.

The sensation of that evening seems to be linked not so much to the artistic success of a new theatrical product, as to its capacity to exemplify new expressive directions with which to bring to light some aspects of a new and modern cultural condition.

Sugai Yukio expressed something similar when he wrote:

> 'One could say that, more than renewal, one should talk of rebirth. The requirement of reforming the specific canons of art was not born in relation or reaction to a reality in constant progress, or to a rigid involution, but was the result of an absolute need to transmit or reaffirm new conditions and new civil and human dimension, through an artistic form which extended its limits and rendered its values more human....'[5]

But what makes the sense of that initiative most evident to us is the sentence pronounced by Osanai Kaoru before the performance and reported by Tanizaki Jun'ichirō in the *Seishun Monogatari*: 'The opening of the Jiyū Gekijō is nothing other than the expression of our desire to live.'[6]

The real motives of an existential character were mixed up with the intellectual animation and enthusiasm towards the example of the new theatre.

These pieces of evidence seem to suggest a particular direction for our observation work. Our attention is directed away from the single productive intentions of the various stylistic choices manifested by the movement, to the incentives and the motivations from which they were born. This causes us to examine more fully the Shingeki movement in order to look for the way in which the audience and the animators interpreted that particular theatrical experience, and what they asked of the theatre, and in particular the Western theatre.

In acceptance of these trends I find myself supported by how much is suggested by the editors of a book dedicated to the Western theatre of the twentieth century, when they gave us this methodological indication: 'For the science of the theatre of the twentieth century it seems necessary not only to be empirical, but to give an account of the research and the questions, respecting the anxiety of the: "Why the theatre?"'.[7]

Perhaps, however, it is not right to support our hypotheses on the Japanese experience with methodological criteria of interpretation which are born in Western historiography applied to Western theatre. It remains only to analyse more fully some aspects of the Shingeki of those years.

Western historians, for the most part interested in the progression of the new Japanese plays, and also in their literary identity, rightly understood the character of uncertainty and incompleteness in the life of the performance in the first part of the century. Other studies like those of Brian Powell[8] and Horie Webber[9] (preceded by the translation of the *Shingeki Undō* by Komiya Toyotaka)[10] look instead at the experience of the first Shingeki in a perspective of reconstruction of the most significant trends and events. Or, like Thomas Rimer,[11] bring to light the work of a playwright, Kishida Kunio, and the group of relationships which bind him to the life of the theatre.

This type of study points to a renewed Western interest in the history of the Japanese theatre of this period, and guides us to a necessary reevaluation of the specific cultural nature of those experiences. The major reservations which the Shingeki aroused, also among contemporaries, revolve around its apparent 'dependence' on the Western model. And it is in relation to this that our embarrassment arises, because while we observe the Shingeki, we find ourselves observing the way that we have been observed, and we are obliged to produce a narcissistic study in order to ask ourselves what has been observed about us.

The thing that is most evident is that the world of Japanese theatre at the beginning of the century found itself involved in the widening of the scope of theatrical expression, which pervaded the Western world and led to the search for completely new roads compared with those that tradition had defined in the course of eighteenth and nineteenth centuries. In the case of Japan this took a more radical direction because most of the new ideas made references to the West and resulted in being more incisive compared to the traditional theatrical behaviour and opinions.

With regard to this problem, the Jiyū Gekijō movement is conclusive in so far as it represents a border line, precisely for the Western references it chose. The attention of the protagonists of the movement was turned directly to the new Western theatre, that is to say, to those experiences just finished, or still in action, which introduced profound changes in the Western idea of theatre. The allusion is no longer to the French Classicism or to opera, as had happened at the beginning of the Meiji period, but to the initiatives of Free Theatre, Little Theatre and Art Theatre. From the time of the Jiyū Gekijō the references are always more precise: Stanislavskij, Copeau, Mejerchold, Reinhardt, or the principal poetics like Naturalism, Symbolism or Expressionism.

Faced with this type of choice, it is not the comparison on the plane of results that interests us, so much as the analogies and the correlations created between the Japanese and the Western theatres, which represent the premise of the whole complex of selections used by the Shingeki. The basic choice which is behind those selections refers to the role which the directors and teachers of the West attributed to the theatre.

The concept which the Shingeki movement shares with the West is that of a theatre lived as an active experience of the culture in a process of change - at least according to Sugai Yukio whom we have already mentioned. A constructive role which in the East, as in the West, put the new experiences in contrast to contemporary theatrical forms which were running the risk of modernism, or barely taking root in contemporary life, and were, above all, rejected on account of their clear commercial objective.

So it is from these basic choices that the Western example finds itself being concretely structured into the work of the Shingeki. First of all, as regards the repertoire, it is a fact that for the Bungei Kyōkai Western texts accounted for eighty per cent; for the Jiyū Gekijō about sixty per cent and for the Tsukiji shogekijō about eighty per cent, in an increasing number of performances.

Another determining working hypothesis concerns the theatre management. The Jiyū Gekijō was in fact supported by an association of which the actors, the producer and the audience were part, which guaranteed great freedom with regard to the commercial requirements. Let us remember that it had been the selfsame Ichikawa Sadanji who had observed this kind of management in the English and French theatre. The third determining element concerns the importance of naturalistic inspiration which led to the sober style, to thematic essentialism, to an interest in psychological development and to the importance of the basis of dramaturgic composition.

In observing how we have been observed, we thus find ourselves making a necessary methodological distinction between, on the one hand, the acceptance of the new hypotheses on the role of the theatre that the new Western theatres proposed, and, on the other hand, all those examples through which the effort to theatricalize the 'modern spirit' of the new Japanese society had passed.

What involves us more, however, is not the success of a product regarding for example, the application of naturalist or expressionistic poetics, but, in some way, the questions which support the numerous choices. In this context we can remember that later, in 1937, the painter Hasegawa Saburō wrote in the magazine *Atelier*, in the article 'To place the avant-garde painting':

> 'We have no right to hide the aspiration which leads us towards
> Western culture. It is necessary to take this aspiration to its furthest
> point. What counts is the depth of this aspiration. Even at the risk
> of beginning with a "I have the same dreams as Salvador Dali".'[12]

In reality, in the Shingeki we do not see the self-awareness or complete formation of this or that theatrical poetic, but we see someone who wants to dream the same dreams as Ibsen, Craig, Stanislavskij and so on. Someone who, as we have seen, attributes the foundation of a theatrical movement, such as the Shingeki, to the need to want to live.

We cannot, in my opinion, limit the repertoire and all the other Western examples presented by the Shingeki in the cliché of the 'exprimere,' in the sense of translating everything literally; rather we must interpret them as an expression of the most complex desire of 'vertere,' in the sense shown by Cicero concerning translations from the Greek: 'It seemed to me necessary that one offers to the reader not the number but the weight of these words.'

A desire and an undertaking without doubt very complex for the obvious ambiguities they put on to the anthropological as much as the theatrical plane, as Kishida Kunio has revealed in this example:

> 'To take an obvious example, suppose a woman is discussing her
> unfortunate personal situation. A Western woman would certainly
> never smile: a Japanese is likely to. In presenting a translated play,
> how should this be handled? A smile becomes an adaptation, no longer
> a translation.'[13]

The Shingeki sought in the new theatre of the West the hypothesis of a new theatrical culture, a new 'weight' of the theatre in regard to a changing society. That which can be interpreted as dependence, modernism or imitation, reveals itself, instead, as one of the territories it was necessary to cross to confront the hypothesis of a theatre for modern Japan, with new means: a route perhaps necessary but certainly not definitive. It is implied not only in the sentence of Osanai Kaoru at the inauguration of Jiyū Gekijō, but also in what he said on the occasion of the opening of Tsukiji Shōgekijō in 1924: his insistence on the value of that initiative, not for the present, but for the future.[14]

Osanai maintained the necessity of the cultural opening out to the outside world, but attributed to his initiatives a character above all formative, and the audience which turned to it was by no means mainly students. If the questions put to the theatre were found to correspond to those of the West, the examples which were applied to the scene were instruments for the future of the Japanese theatre. This seems to me to be the Shingeki's great strength of that period: the fact that it did not attempt to define, but only to search.

We can now appreciate that our point of departure although apparently narcissistic, can be an integral part of the critical path which leads us to some specific aspects of the experience we want to investigate. Asking ourselves how and what was chosen from the Western theatre, is a study which has the advantage of overthrowing the Eurocentric temptation and leading us to the specific nature of the culture expressed by the Shingeki.

Not only are the conditions of a general character which lead us to this course. The same can happen regarding more particular aspects of the life of the Shingeki. Let us consider, for example, the relationship between the Shingeki and the Kabuki. The Kabuki appeared in theatrical experimentation during those years, like a sort of conscience difficult to deceive and with which inevitably to take account, as much as to render it necessary to pose the question 'What does Kabuki mean for us?', as did Osanai Kaoru in 1912.[15]

In fact, the Jiyū Gekijō, which also chose the allusions of 'Liberty' which had emerged in France, England and Germany, draws its experimentation from the Kabuki, working with its actors and the technical memory which these possessed. In the Tsukiji Shōgekijō, in the Twenties, the actors were now the professionals of the new theatre, but the questions put by the Kabuki had remained an object of doubt and reflection. At the end of the Twenties, one finds that the Western masters recognized in the Kabuki the terms of the 'theatricality' with which they wanted to re-establish their own theatre, and in the Kabuki theatre they looked for what was lacking in the West: an autonomy of scenic language, a tradition, a school. The recovery of Kabuki within the new Japanese theatre found an ulterior motive and a further confirmation in the vision that the West has given of it. It is what happened to Hijikata Yoshi, the founder, along with Osanai Kaoru, of the Tsukiji Shōgekijō. Hijikata Yoshi wrote:

> 'In reforming old plays we are taking elements away that the old plays possessed. Ichikawa Sadanji's tour to Russia answered many questions as to what we can learn from a classic play.'[16]

All this is only a premise, but I hope that it can point out the knot that Western studies must be able to untangle, given their unavoidable involvement. Seeing the effects of exchanges between East and West, the compatibilities and the meetings which took place in the theatre during the first part of the century, we feel sufficiently free if we adopt instruments which still profess to be Eurocentric, but of which we are aware of the risks and the limits. The important thing is that as a result of our analysis, our perspective should be stimulating and not reducing. The positive aspect that one can draw about the Shingeki, it seems to me, is the necessity to set great store by the questions and the diversity of the replies stimulated by the West, more than by the solutions which in those years it was very difficult to give.

PART II
LINGUISTICS

26

Rethinking Translation: The Role of Word Systems in the Translatability of Texts into Japanese

JEANNE JACOB

INTRODUCTION

A major but underlying issue in understanding Japan is linguistic, in particular, the problem of translation of texts. The problem of translatability in Japanese texts is usually dealt with on a micro-textual level, i.e., specific lexical items, non-equivalence in cultural or grammatical elements (Miner 1961, Seidensticker 1963, Cho 1973).[1] This paper views a text as an integral whole (Aphek and Tobin 1983) and as a system for communication in the Saussurean sense (Saussure 1959). It is the contention of this paper that textual translation must involve more than 'accurate and adequate representations' of the original text (Miner 1961) or fluent equivalences of individual lexical items.

This paper examines two texts - a novel in English and its translation into Japanese - using a macro-textual method of analysis based on the concept of 'word systems' (Aphek 1979). This method was initially used by Aphek and Tobin (1981) in analyzing Hebrew texts and their translatability into English. The concept of word system, based on Buber's Leitwörter (leading words in the Bible), was formulated by Aphek (1979) and is defined as 'a matrix of words with a common denominator which may be semantic, phonological, etymological, folk-etymological, or associative' (Aphek and Tobin 1981:57).

This analysis views a text as a language system that is exploited in a specific way by its author to convey a specific message or messages. A text is regarded as a system of word systems that interrelate in various ways to express certain messages. A writer expresses his message or messages in multiple variations, in various contexts, throughout the text.

This analysis considers the relationship between two texts, the original text in English, and its translation into Japanese. The texts are Virginia Woolf's *A Room of One's Own* [*Room*] and its translation into Japanese, *Watakushi Dake no Heya* [*Heya*], by Nishikawa Masatoshi and Ando Ichiro. The English text was chosen because it is short, its style distinct and its word systems fairly straightforward (but this last reason was only to be discovered later).

The aim of the analysis is to search for word systems in *Room* and determine their relationship to other word systems in the text, as well as their relationship to the entirety of the text: and to see whether these word systems have been transferred in the Japanese text *Heya*. It must be stressed that this analysis is not meant to criticize this particular translation or translation in general.

METHODOLOGY

Data collection involves extracting words, phrases, sentences and paragraphs that contribute to the textual message(s). (At this stage, it is not possible to predict which form the data may take, and thus the data collector must necessarily be open to various forms.) What constitutes a valid datum is dependent on two factors: the context in which the datum is found, and a basis for binary opposition, either within the same context or some other context elsewhere in the text. The context must be such that it replicates the overall textual message. These data are the components of groups called 'word systems' which are given labels for classification.

The actual methodology does not proceed in strict linear order. The postulated textual message is checked against the growing body of data to see whether it is still a valid message.

Word systems continually suggest themselves as data collection and collation proceed. Phonological, semantic, conceptual, etymological or associative relations of data with other data are continuously triggered during the process, necessitating reclassification of previous data entries and a search for data that may have been previously ignored before the current association had been established. This recursive process of data gathering, classification and reclassification results in a keener 'word system sense,' because those word systems that have been discovered serve as directional guideposts to as yet undiscovered systems.

The final stage is classifying the data by context, and statistically determining the distribution of the word systems. The contexts are considered as replicates of the greater textual whole, and as such contain variations of the invariant message of the text. The co-occurrence and also non-occurrence of word systems in specific contexts should serve to support the final postulated message.

It is not claimed that these word systems are consciously created as such by the writer. 'Word system' is simply used here as an analytic device.

As mentioned previously, word systems function *throughout* a text, and such artistic micro-textual devices as metaphor, theme, puns, alliteration and allusion can only be considered within the analytic framework of word systems if these devices, or variants thereof, occur repeatedly throughout the text.

A ROOM OF ONE'S OWN

Virginia Woolf's *A Room of One's Own* is a talk to a group of women. The subject that has been given to the speaker is 'Women and Fiction.' Instead of taking this subject's 'simple' meaning, the speaker decides to take its 'deeper' significance, that is, women and what they are like; women

188

and the fiction that they write; or women and the fiction that is written about them, or all three mixed together. The speaker, though considering this perspective more interesting, decides that it is problematic and instead offers her opinion on what she calls a 'minor point' - a woman must have money and a room of her own if she is to write fiction. The speaker then relates how she came about this opinion.

Through a fictitious character who seeks the truth about women and fiction, Virginia Woolf touches on the history of women, contrasting their situation with men, namely, how women need to be independent, financially as well as mentally. Woolf goes on to say that writing is one way in which women can earn their own money, and with privacy (a room of one's own) and financial independence (money), they should eventually be able to create art. Woolf concludes by telling the all-female audience to write and to be true to themselves.

Room begins with a heavy bias towards women but ends with the balanced realization that men and women must cooperate. It is interesting that within the text, various male writers are praised for the quality of their work, while female writers, with the exception of one or two, are criticized for their creations. *Room* concludes that there are 'male' and 'female' sides of the mind, and that only by unifying both sides can art be achieved. Unity of the mind, Woolf writes, can only be achieved by living in reality.

CONCEPTUAL WORD SYSTEM

The above is the basis for the overall conceptual word system in *Room* which I shall label YIN/YANG, in which are grouped all of the bipolar oppositions found in the text (see Tables 1a and 1b). The label YIN/YANG has been chosen because the data in the text, starting with the primary units 'male,' 'female,' were found to be in the same relationship of opposition as in the traditional Oriental framework of dual classification, Yin and Yang. By giving this label, it is not implied that Woolf was aware of this Oriental system, nor do I intend to utilize its mystic philosophy in this analysis. It is simply a convenient label to use.

TABLE 1a

A Representative Sample from the YIN/YANG Word System, Context 'Duality'

(Traditional Categories)		Passage from *Room* with Components
Yin	Yang	of YIN/YANG Word System
female	**male**	Instinct rather than reason came to my help; he was a **Beadle**; I was a *woman*. This was the turf; there was the path. Only the **Fellows and Scholars** were allowed here; the gravel is the place for me.(8)
darkness	LIGHT*	All was *dim*, yet intense too, as if the scarf which the *dusk* had flung over the garden were torn asunder by star or sword - the **flash** of some terrible reality leaping, as its way is, out of the heart of spring.(28)

189

It is all half LIGHTS and *shadows* like those serpentine caves where one goes with a CANDLE peering up and down, not knowing where one is stepping.... For I wanted to see how Mary Carmichael set to work to catch those unrecorded gestures, those unsaid or half-said words, which form themselves, no more palpably than the *shadows* of moths on the ceiling, when women are alone, *unlit* by the capricious and coloured LIGHT of the other sex.(146)

left   **right**   To the **right** and *left* bushes of some sort, golden and crimson, GLOWED with the colour, even it seemed BURNT with the HEAT, of FIRE.(6)

autumn SPRING   I dare not forfeit your respect and imperil the fair name of fiction by changing the season and describing LILACS hanging over garden walls, CROCUSES, **tulips** and other flowers of SPRING. ...it was still *autumn*.... But for all that there was something odd at work... it was nothing of course but fancy - that the LILAC was shaking its flowers over garden wall ... and the dust of the POLLEN was in the air.(25-26)

emotion REASON   They had been written in the *red* LIGHT of *emotion* and not in the *white* **light** of TRUTH. (55)

red   **white**   Meanwhile the wineglasses had **flushed** yellow and **flushed** *crimson*; had been emptied; had been filled.(17)

night   **day**   What was the **truth** about these houses, for example, *dim* and **festive** now with their *red* windows in the *dusk*, but raw and *red* and squalid... at nine-o'clock in the **morning**?(25)

(food)

beef   **sole**   ...lunch began with **soles**, sunk in a deep dish, over which...[was] spread a counterpane of the **whitest** cream, save that it was branded here and there with brown spots like the spots on the flanks of a doe. After that came the **partridges** ... many and various, ...with all their retinue of sauces and salads, the sharp and the sweet...(16) [eaten at a men's college]

potatoes **partridge**   Dinner was being served... Far from being SPRING it was in fact an *evening* in October... Here was the soup. It was a plain gravy soup. There was nothing to stir the fancy in that... Next came *beef* with its attendant greens and *potatoes* - a homely trinity...(28) [eaten at a women's college]

Note: *WORDS IN UPPER CASE DENOTE REPEATED COMPONENT IN ANOTHER PASSAGE.

TABLE 1b

Representative Sample of YIN/YANG Word System, Context 'Unity' and Japanese translation from *Heya*

1. INTEGRITY*, in the case of the novelist, is the conviction that he gives one that this is the TRUTH.(125)
SEIJITSU to iu koto wa, shosetsuka ga dokusha ni, kore wa SHINJITSU da to nattoku saseru chikara o sasu no de aru.(104)
2. One holds every phrase, every scene to the LIGHT... for NATURE seems... oddly, to have provided us with an inner LIGHT by which to judge of the novelist's INTEGRITY or DISINTEGRITY.(125)
Watakushitachi wa, yonde iru sai ni, dono kotoba mo, dono jokei mo, hitotsu bitotsu, HIKARI ni atete miru - ...SHIZEN wa, kiwamete fushigi na koto ni, shosetsuka no SEIJITSU o handan suru uchinaru HIKARI o, watakushitachi ni sonaete kurete iru no de aru.(105)

3. ...she wrote as a WOMAN, but as a WOMAN who has forgotten that she is a WOMAN, so that her pages are full of that curious sexual quality which comes only when sex is unconscious of itself.(161)

...kanojo wa, JOSEI to shite, soremo jibun ga JOSEI de aru koto o wasureta JOSEI to shite kaita no da. Sore yue, kanojo no shobutsu no ko ni wa, 'sei' ga sore jishin o ishiki shite inai toki ni nomi arawareru, ano kimyo na 'sei' no tokushitsu de ippai ni natte iru no de atta.(135)

4. What is meant by 'REALITY?' It would seem to be something very erratic, very undependable - now to be found in a dusty road, now in a scrap of newspaper in the street, now in a daffodil in the SUN.(191)

GENJITSU to wa, ittai, do iu imi de aro ka? ...aru toki ni wa, hokorippoi michi no ue ni ari, aru toki ni wa, michi no shimbun no kirenashi, aru toki ni wa, HIKARI o abiru kiizuisen ni aru, to iu guai de aru.(159)

5. ...it is fatal to be a man or woman pure and simple; one must be WOMAN-MANLY or MAN-WOMANLY.(181)

...dare ni shitemo, mono o kaku mono ga, jibun no zokusuru sei no koto o atama ni oku no wa, tomeiteki de aru.... Hito wa, JOSEIteki ni OTOKOrashii ka, DANSEIteki ni ONNArashii ka, sono izure ka denakereba naranai.(150)

6. So that when I ask you to earn money AND have a ROOM of your own, I am asking you to live in the presence of REALITY, an invigorating life... whether one can impart it or not.(192)

...okane o moke, jibun hitori no heya o motsu yo ni, to watakushi ga iu no wa, anatagata ga GENJITSU ni sesshite, kakki ni michita SEIKATSU to omowareru ga, sore o jibun ga hoka ni watasu koto ga dekiru dekinai wa betsu to shite, soshita SEIKATSU o yatte yuku yo ni osusume shite iru no de aru.(160)

Note: *UPPER CASE DENOTES COMPONENTS OF YIN/YANG SYSTEM.

The word system YIN/YANG is governed by the contexts which shall be termed 'duality' and 'unity.' The context 'duality' denotes a situation in which there is prejudice and discrimination against either sex. The context 'unity' denotes a situation in which harmony and cooperation between the sexes is expressed.

SYNTACTIC WORD SYSTEM

In contrast to the conceptual word system YIN/YANG, there is a syntactic word system, which I shall label LINK, with two components, 'but', 'and'. LINK co-occurs with YIN/YANG throughout the text: whenever the harmony and unity of the sexes is expressed, the LINK component 'and' occurs more frequently in sentence-initial position than LINK component 'but'; whenever the opposite is expressed, LINK component 'but' occurs more frequently than LINK component 'and' in sentence-initial position.

Table 2 presents a statistical distribution of word system LINK. The frequency of usage of component 'but' is greater (29/189 quotes) in relation to the frequency of usage of component 'and' (16/189 quotes) in Column 1, which corresponds to the writer's presentation of discrimination and prejudice against women. In Column 2, corresponding to the presentation of a growing realization that men and women must cooperate, the frequency of usage of 'but' and 'and' increase but their positions are now reversed: 'and' (41/165 quotes) is dominant over 'but' (31/165 quotes). In Column 3, corresponding to the period of the writer's realization that the mind must unite its 'male and female sides' for artistic creation, 'and' (14/62) continues to occur more frequently than 'but' (10/62).

TABLE 2

Non-Random Distribution of LINK with Other Systems

Word or Word System	1 (pp3-112) n = 189 quotes	2 (pp112-176) n = 165 quotes	3 (pp117-199) n = 62 quotes
BUT	29	31	10
AND	16	41	14
YYu*	4	36	14
YYd**	19	14	2
BUT, AND	2	17	4
BUT YYd	5	2	0
BUT, YYu	1	3	0
AND, YYd	2	5	0
AND, YYu	1	7	0

* YIN/YANG, context 'unity'
** YIN/YANG, context 'duality'

The frequency of occurrence of YIN/YANG shows a similar pattern. The decrease in the frequency of occurrence of components of the YIN/YANG system *in the context 'duality'* (Col. 1 = 19; Col. 2 = 14; Col. 3 = 2) echoes the decrease of occurrence of LINK component 'but.' The increase of occurrence of components of the YIN/YANG system *in the context 'unity'* (Col. 1 = 4; Col. 2 = 36; Col. 3 = 14) echoes the increase of occurrence of LINK component 'and.' It should not be surprising that 'but,' a syntactic element denoting contrast, should tend to occur more frequently at sentence-initial position in the context 'duality,' i.e wherein one sex has been presented in a more favourable light than the other. Nor should it be a similar surprise that 'and,' a syntactic element denoting unity, should tend to occur more frequently at sentence-initial position in the context 'unity,' i.e. wherein the cooperation of the sexes is presented.

The co-occurrence of LINK and YIN/YANG also illustrates the same tendency. 'But' co-occurs with YIN/YANG in the context 'duality' (Col. 1 = 5/189) more frequently than does 'and' (Col. 1 - 2/189). Column 1, as mentioned above, represents the parts of the text that give the history of women's oppression, and present men in a negative light. However in Col. 2, which in contrast represents those parts of the text wherein the writer comes to terms with the inevitability of cooperation between men and women, 'and' co-occurs with YIN/YANG in the context 'unity' (Col. 2, 7/165) more frequently than does 'but' (Col. 2, 3/165).

The non-co-occurrence of LINK and YIN/YANG in Col. 3 ('and' with YY, context 'duality' = 0; 'and' with YY, context 'unity' = 0; 'but' with YY, context 'duality' = 0; 'but' with YY, context 'unity' = 0) also serves to point out a significant fact: that the juxtaposition of 'and' or 'but' with components of the YIN/YANG system in both contexts, 'duality' and 'unity,' is no longer as significant to that particular part of the text as is the greater occurrence of 'and' (14/62) and components of the YIN/YANG system, in the context 'unity' (14/62). It is also worth noting that 'but' occurs only 10 times vs. 14 times for 'and' in Col. 3, and that components of the YIN/YANG system in the context 'duality' occur only 2 times.

In view of the figures obtained above, it seems reasonable to assume that the frequency of occurrence of 'but' and 'and,' as well as their co-occurrence with components of the YIN/YANG system, is non-random. The distribution of 'but' and 'and' throughout the text mirror the distribution of components of the YIN/YANG system in the contexts 'duality' and 'unity,' respectively. This paper therefore contends that Woolf's use of 'but' and 'and' in sentence-initial position throughout the text is a non-random macro-textual stylistic syntactic device that underlies and reinforces the concepts expressed in the lexical system, i.e., the YIN/YANG system, of the text.

WATAKUSHI DAKE NO HEYA

Let us take the Japanese translation *Watakushi Dake no Heya* (*Heya*) and see whether it has taken into account the macro-textual non-random use of the syntactic system LINK. Only the component 'but' will be dealt with in this analysis. The following were found in *Heya* as equivalents given for 'but': 'tokoro de,' 'tokoro ga,' 'shikashi,' 'shikashinagara,' 'keredomo,' 'dakedo,' 'ga,' 'daga.' All, except for 'dakedo' occurred at sentence-initial position. 'Shikashi,' 'shikashinagara,' 'keredomo,' 'ga,' and 'daga' also occurred in sentence-medial position; only 'ga' appeared in sentence-final position as well. While the repeated occurrence of 'but' and 'and' in sentence-initial position and in co-location with the conceptual lexical system YIN/YANG in *Room* was evidently non-random, the use of eight equivalents in *Heya* clearly suggests that the macro-textual function of these two (admittedly small and usually overlooked) words has been ignored.

It is significant that the very first sentence [see a) below] of *Room* begins with 'but.' And, to balance this, the last sentence [see b) below] as well begins with 'but' (numerals after quotes refer to page numbers):

> a) But, you may say, we asked you to speak about women and fiction - what has that got to do with a room of one's own? 3
> b) But I maintain that she [Shakespeare's sister] would come if we worked for her, and that so to work, even in poverty and obscurity, is worth while. 199

The equivalents of 'but' in the sentences above are 'tokoro de' and 'keredomo' in *Heya*:

193

a) *Tokoro de,* anata gata wa ko ossharu kamo shirenai, kochira wa fujin to shosetsu to iu koto ni tsuite, hanashite moraitai to tanonda no ni - sore ga, jibun hitori no heya to do iu kankei ga aru no daro ka, to. 7

b) *Keredomo,* watakushi tachi ga kanojo no tame ni chikara o tsukuseba, kitto, kanojo wa arawareru de aro shi, mata, tatoi hinkon to fugu ni aru to mo, sono yo ni chikara o tsukusu koto wa, kai aru shigoto ni soi nai, to watakushi wa iitai no de aru. 166

While it can perhaps be argued that for the sake of variety, the translators gave various equivalents to what they might have considered as a monotonous usage of 'but' in the original text, there is evidence that Woolf was consciously using the same lexical item throughout the text. She writes:

> But...I had said 'but' too often. One cannot go on saying 'but.' One must finish the sentence somehow. I rebuked myself. Shall I finish it, 'But - I am bored!' But why was I bored? 174

The same passage is rendered in *Heya* as:

> Keredomo...watakushi wa, amari ni 'keredomo' to iu kotoba o tsukai sugiru yo da, itsu made mo 'keredomo,' 'keredomo' dake de wa sumasarenai, nan to ka shite, hitotsu no bun o kanzen ni shinakereba narani de wa nai ka, to watakushi wa, iibun o semeru no de atta, soko de, hitotsu no bun ni shite miyo, 'keredomo - watashi wa unzari suru no da!' Keredomo, watakushi ga unzari shita no wa naze daro? 145

While it is not surprising that at this point in *Room,* the writer should be aware of an abuse of 'but,' the same cannot be said of 'keredomo' in *Heya.* The total number of occurrences of 'keredomo' in *Heya* is only 26. The most frequently used equivalent of 'but' in the Japanese translation is 'ga' (116 occurrences). Moreover, while the Japanese translation has eight variants (i.e., ga, daga, shikashi, shikashinagara, keredomo, dakedo, tokoro de, tokoro ga), 'but' in *Room* had only one other synonymous word in contrast - 'however' - and its frequency of occurrence was minimal (5 times). It is also to be noted that the Japanese variants are not interchangeable; 'shikashinagara' cannot always be substituted for 'ga.' And, in terms of register, 'dakedo' clearly cannot be used where the form 'shikashinagara' would be suitable, and vice versa.

CONCLUSION

Some linguists and translators may perhaps consider the lexical items 'but' and 'and' as insignificant and unworthy of analysis. In the case of Virginia Woolf's *A Room of One's Own,* however, the non-random distribution of a syntactic word system whose components are 'but' and 'and,' and the co-occurrence of this syntactic system with a conceptual lexical system were found to support the notions of duality and unity expressed by the author in the text. On a micro-textual basis, the eight different equivalents given for one component of this syntactic word system ('but') may seem suitable or even reasonably accurate representations of the original. But on a macro-textual basis, the overall effect of the repeated use of 'but' in contrast with the similar repeated use of 'and' in the original text has been lost in the Japanese translation.

194

The instance of a small syntactic system operating throughout the entirety of a text in support of the textual message delivered by a large conceptual lexical system may or may not have been intentionally created by Virginia Woolf. The issue of Woolf's intention is irrelevant. What is relevant is that the two word systems discovered in the text present a facet of the text that would have been hidden otherwise.

It is the contention of this paper that the use of textual analysis based on the concept of word systems may prove to be an aid in the translation of texts.

27

The Changing Language in a Changing Society

KUMIKO TAKAHARA

Rapid industrial and economic growth during the last thirty years has brought the Japanese radical socio-cultural changes that affect their patterns of life and mode of thinking. Never before have they been so heavily exposed to foreign cultures through travel, international business, publications, mass-media, direct contact with foreigners and so on. Nor have they made mental and behavioural adjustment to new cultural experiences and values to such a great extent. The language is also undergoing innovations to allow the speaker to develop a new mode of communication to deal with and talk about his/her new world.

This paper will examine some of the current linguistic changes in morpho-lexical, semantic and syntactic areas of Japanese, and their pragmatic effect on communication. The paper will also investigate the question of whether these linguistic changes can be explained on the basis of the general principles of language changes, and determine if these changes have any impact on the general structural principles of Japanese. The main data sources for the present study are a number of widely circulated journals, business leaflets and brochures, TV commercials and advertisements and selected written texts which are likely to represent the most frequently used, and the most casual variety of Japanese which is spoken or at least understood by the majority of people.

1. MORPHO-LEXICAL LEVEL

A set of new and derived words are classified based on their formations into (1) pure loans, (2) external and internal loan-based compounds, (3) internal loan-based compounds, (4) loan-based derivatives and (5) new creations. Furthermore, a list of random samples from the frequently occurring foreign words are categorized into semantic classes to identify the areas of foreign cultural influence in Japanese everyday life and speech.

(1) PURE FOREIGN LOANS

(1).1 *Consumer goods and fashion*

ubideo dekki	'video deck'	antiiku	'antique'
benhaa sandaru	'Ben Hur sandal'	butiiku	'boutique'
burendo	'brand'	besto karaa	'best colour'
doraiyaa	'dryer'	fasshon	'fashion
		koodineetaa	coordinator'
fresshu pakku	'fresh pack'	fasshon jaanaristo	'fashion journalist'
fasto fuddo	'fast food'	instanto	'instant food'
guddo dezain	'good design'	jiinzu	'jeans'
manshon	'condominium'	meekaa	'maker'
siito beruto	'seat belt'	siifuudo restoran	'seafood
			restaurant'
supaisii	'spicy'	ranjerii	'lingerie'
teeku hoomu	'take-out food'	teisuto	'taste'
tii shatu	'T-shirts'	torendo	'trend'
treiningu	'training/sports clothes'		

(1).2 *Mass media, entertainments and sports*

aidoru	'idle'	erekutoronikkusu	'electronics'
chuunaa	'tuner'	aerobikkusu	'aerobics'
fikushon	'fiction'	gattu poozu	'gatsy pose'
gesto	'guest'	hitto	'hit'
heddo hon	'headphone'	haadoboirudo	'hard-boiled
		tatchi	touch'
kabaa stoorii	'cover story'	komaasharu	'commercials'
kyarakutaa	'character'	katarusis	'catharsis'
kuraimakkusu	'climax'	masukomi	'mass
			communication'
oonaa	'owner'	oodio	'audio equipment'
puro supootu	'professional	rasuto	'last scene'
	sports'		
pitto	'pit'	ruukii	'rookie'
repootaa	'reporter'	riquesto kooru	'request call'
raibu spotto	'live spot'	reesu	'race'
rodji	'lodge'	roman	'romance'
sinsesaizaa	'synthesizer'	sadisutikku	'sadistic'
sasupensu	'suspense'	suponsaa	'sponsor'
siriasu dorama'	serious drama'	terebi	'television'

(1).3 *Business, office and equipment*

afutaa saabisu	'after service'	deeta beesu	'data base'
greedo appu	'grade-up'	guruupu intabyu	'group interview'

hai reberu	'high-level'	haitekku	'high technology'
insaidaa	'insider'	interijento biru	'intelligent building'
kyariaa	'career'	kyasshingu saabisu	'cashing service'
noohaw	'know-how'	ofukon	'office computer'
ooeru	'office lady'	pureshaa	'pressure'
paahoomansu	'performance'	puranaa	'planner'
pawaa	'power'	raifu waaku	'lifework'
sheaa	'shares'	sofuto	'software'
tenshon	'tension'	waapuro	'word processor'

(1).4 *Socio-cultural entities and concepts*

borantiaa	'volunteer'	charitii	'charity'
chuutaa	'tutor'	doraibu in	'drive inn'
gyaru	'girls'	mazakon	'mother complex'
midoru kurasu	'middle-class'	mini skuuru	'mini-school'
mai hoomu	'my home'	oiru shokku	'oil shock'
pakku tuaa	'package tour'	roon	'loan'
ruutu	'root'	sinboru	'symbol'
saabisu taimu	'service time'	tii taimu	'tea time'
yangu	'young people'	yangu gyaru	'young girls'
wan patan	'one pattern'		

Various social phenomena can be linguistically reconstructed, using these loan words. For example, a typical urban life of middle-class Japanese can be profiled based on just these foreign loans alone. The loan word, *midoru kurasu* 'middle-class' to start with, is related to one of the fundamental changes in Japan's social structure. The indigenous term for the middle-class, *chuusan-kaikyuu* inherently symbolizes a social status which is neither upper-class nor lower-class and which has never commanded much of social prestige. During the last few decades Japanese society has evolved as truly a middle-class, or no-class society. The majority of contemporary Japanese who are part of Japan's immense economical machinery are well paid and enjoy a relatively affluent life. This non-traditional social experience requires an appropriate label. A stigma-free foreign word, *midoru kurasu* 'middle-class' is therefore adopted to identify their newly acquired social status of power and prosperity.

Now average middle-class Japanese in cities live in small condominiums which are euphemized as 'mansions' by the real estate agent, and are referred to as 'my home' by the residents. Those are the people who are alienated from the traditional large family system without a family home to return to or emotional ties with the parental family. Their life is confined in a small nuclear family which does not constitute a home in the traditional sense, but it is nonetheless an only place for 'privacy' and an escape from the competitive world outside. In such a household, the father may often be employed by a 'high tech' industry, working long hours with his mind always set on his 'career' goal. He keeps business records on his 'office computer,' attends a 'television' conference in an 'intelligent building,' and has a hurried, discount lunch during 'service time.' He might relieve his 'tension' from the pressures at work in the traditional way at a Japanese bar or *nomiya* or at a western style 'bar,' but his 'one pattern' life goes on and on. Occasionally he might take his family out for a Sunday drive, treat them to a meal at a 'drive inn,' and come home exhausted from fighting heavy holiday traffic. The father may prefer spending his holiday at home watching 'pro-sports' and night games on T.V.

In a middle-class household the mother may also work 'part-time' to supplement the income to meet the desire for 'high level' life, famous 'brand' 'goods' from 'boutiques,' 'personal computers' and games, or for a 'package tour' to race through eight foreign countries in ten days, and so on. The mother who has been emancipated from the kitchen and childcare may often come home with 'fresh packed' 'instant' food or 'take-out' 'fast food' to feed her family. The children who have no open space to enjoy the outdoor fun spend a great deal of time watching T.V. 'commercials' which are designed to capture 'young people' as potential consumers and put on the air attractive 'commercial songs'. T.V. dramas and 'suspense' movies with 'hard boiled' type heroes are often targeted at young viewers. The father being rarely at home, the mother often takes over the traditional father's role of disciplining their children, and domineering motherly authority often causes a prevalent social disease of 'mother complex'. Thus, by putting these foreign loans together we can draw a fairly accurate picture of the innovative life-style of ordinary Japanese people.

The massive use of foreign loan words allows the Japanese people to make verbal distinctions between new experiences and events for which they have no words or phrases in their native conventional vocabulary. The native words which have served social needs for centuries are not quite adequate to represent the concepts which emerge from the gap between the old and new ways of life. Nor have the Japanese sufficient time to develop a new vocabulary to meet the speed and amount of socio-cultural changes. Thus, at least for the present, Japanese resolve the linguistic deficiency by actively borrowing and integrating foreign words in their daily speech.

(2) EXTERNAL AND INTERNAL LOAN-BASED COMPOUNDS

In addition to the direct borrowing of foreign loan words, noun compound formation from the mixed base of foreign and native words is also a common device for expanding the lexicon. Interestingly, in the hybrid compound nouns, a native or native-like word is usually a second component which occurs in a more stable syntactic position. Since Japanese has only prenominal modifiers, the first word in a compound is functionally still a modifier to the core element in the second position. This structural characteristic may reflect the Japanese speaker's inherent preference for a native base in newly derived compounds for the clue of their meaning. In fact the foreign component in the compound nouns is observed to mainly attribute new characteristics to an already existing entity but not creating a new entity. The selected samples below are presented in the same semantic categories as before:

(2).1 *Consumer goods and fashion*

aidea-shoohin	'idea goods'
burando-sikoo	'taste for famous brand'
gifuto-yoohin	'gift items'
gifuto-ken	'gift coupon'
guddo-dezain-shoo	'good design prize'
hausu shokuhin	'reserve food'
ojoosama-look	'young elegant miss look'

(2).2 *Mass media, entertainment and sports*

akushon eiga	'action movie'
baiorensu-ha	'fans of violent acts'
baiorensu-shoosetu	'violent novels'
hitto-kyoku	'popular song'
koin-ya	'coin shop'
raibu-taiken	'live experience'

(2).3 *Business, office and equipment*

eigyoo-man	'management personnel'
haiteku-kinoo	'high technological abilities'
honyaku-sofuto	'automatic translation programme'
jinzai-katuyoo sentaa	'human resources centre'
ninki-sofuto	'popular software'
soogoo-entaapuraizu	'cooperative enterprise'
sinsoo-oopun	'post-remodelling opening'
terebi-kaigisitu	'television conference room'

(2).4 *Socio-cultural entities and concept*

gekisin-boom	'boom for extra spicy curry and rice'
kaku-sherutaa	'nuclear shelter'
rirakkusu-kuukan	'space for relaxation'
sutoresu-kaishoo	'solution for stress'
uchuu-roketto	'space rocket'

(3) INTERNAL LOAN-BASED COMPOUNDS

Compound word formations with native morphemes are also quite productive. In contrast to the foreign loan-based compounds, only a small number of words in this class are derived by simple compounding processes, while the majority involve syntactic transformations and a complex structure consisting of a sentential modifier and a noun complement:

(3).1 *Simple compounds*

burik-ko	'girls with innocent look'	chibik-ko	'kids'
genki-jirusi	'health symbol'	imo-jirushi	'potatoes'
kawaik-ko	'cute girls'	kyuukyoku-kun	'social misfit'
kaidan-ji	'stair climber'	sin-jinrui	'neo homosapiens'

datu-sara	'an escapee from a salaried man's life'
geemu daisuki ningen	'game fanatics'
kinniku mukimuki	'awesomely muscular'
kodawaru hito	'people with exclusive taste'
noodo batugun	'extra sensitive'
taberu koto daisuki ningen	'enthusiastic eater'
taberu hito	'people who eat'
tukuru hito	'people who cook'
runrun kibun	'great feeling'

The foreign loans are used predominantly for labelling non-traditional material objects, and newly evolving roles, status and functions of people in a changing social structure. The internal loans on the other hand, seem to reclassify the traditional entities and experiences in light of new socio-cultural values. Take, for example, *chibik-ko* 'kids.' In an age when children are treated as individuals and represent a considerable consumer market, a class of kids are gaining identity as *chibik-ko* in contrast to the generic classification of young individuals as *kodomo* 'children.' Likewise, *burik-ko* 'girls who try to look innocent' and *kawai-ko* 'girls who try to look cute' seem to represent a class of young women who defy the current role model of being female, as being progressive, independent and strong. These new expressions are thus distinguished from the neutral term, *musume* 'young women' which has inherent connotations of young womanhood such as innocence, youthful beauty, inexperience, and so on. In the present age of the youth culture of health and sophistication, healthy looks are glorified as *genki-jirusi* 'symbol of health,' which supersedes the conventional term, *genki* 'healthy.' Those who are not concerned with youth fashions and life-styles are downgraded as *imo-jirushi* 'potatoes.'

Even in adult culture sophistication ranks high as is exemplified in the new compound, *kodawaru hito* 'people with sophisticated taste' which means literally 'fussy people.' The expression, *kodawaru* 'to be fussy' did not have a favourable connotation in the past, but has been reinterpreted and upgraded enough to find its way into exclusive advertising language. More extraordinary are the phrases like *taberu koto daisuki ningen* 'enthusiastic eaters' and *taberu hito* 'eaters.' Literally, these expressions refer to any individuals who like eating or who just eat, but people who are engaged in our fundamental daily activity are stigmatized and classified as slightly odd in an age of dieting for a slim and trim figure. A similar example is *kaidan-ji* 'people who use stairs.' In contemporary life of speed and efficiency, an archaic habit of walking up the stairs for fitness or out of necessity is parodied as *kaidan-ji* 'stair-climbing kid' possibly based on an analogy with two homonyms, *kaidanji* 'odd guy,' and *kaidanji* 'nice, masculine person.'

A rapidly changing society tends to produce individuals who do not fit in any conventional patterns. *Sin-jinrui* 'neo homo sapiens' represents those who are utterly apathetic, aimless and who lack ability of verbal communication. In addition, their ultimate prototype is then labelled as *kyuukyoku-kun* 'Mr ultimate.' The equally unconventional individuals who

200

have, however, a more positive orientation to life are given a classification, *datu-sara* literally, 'an escapee from salaryman's life,' i.e. one who gets dismayed with a salaryman's life and finds a way of self-supporting. In a society of establishment and regimentation any free spirit who gives up the security of salaried employment in order to set out on his own into the uncertain future is worthy of a special name. Incidentally, although *datu-sara* contains the foreign loan constituent, 'salaried man,' the term has been adopted in the language for more than a hundred years, and is practically a native morpheme.

(4) EXTERNAL-INTERNAL LOAN-BASED DERIVATIVES

The new concepts and experiences may be efficiently linguisticalized by borrowed words and phrases, but they tend to be iconic and afford little flexibility in use. Adjectives, verbs and adverbs, on the other hand, can combine with other lexemes, expressing new entities in innumerable ways. The next step after direct borrowings, therefore, is deriving new syntactic classes of words out of the external and internal loans and compounds. These linguistic activities are nothing new to Japanese who have a long history of linguistic borrowing and have developed a set of morphological rules for integrating them in their own linguistic system. The suffixes, *-na, -no* and *-teki* are the endings for the foreign base adjectives, and *-ni* and *-de* for the adverbs, in contrast to the inflectional endings which mark the native adjectives and adverbs. The verbs with a foreign stem are commonly distinguished from the native verbs by a pro-verb, *suru* 'to do something,' and *naru* 'to be something.' Some examples are given in the following:

(4).1 *Adjectives*

biggu-na	'big'	fansii-na	'fanciful'
haado-na	'hard'	hotto-na	'hot'
haisensu-na	'high sense'	haafu-no	'half-breed'
kompakuto-na	'compact'	kurassiku-na	'classic'
kuuru-na	'cool	mero-na	'mellow'
misuteriasu-na	'mysterious'	meruhentikku-na	'fairy-tale like'
nyuutoraru-na	'neutral'	nau-na	'modern'
pyuaa-na	'pure'	puro-teki	'professional'
paasonaru-na	'personal'	rafu-na	'rough'
raibu-no	'live'	riberaru-na	'liberal'
sekusii-na	'sexy'	simpuru-na	'simple'
suriringu-na	'thrilling'	stairisshu-na	'stylish'

Distributionally, the suffix, *-na* occurs redundantly with foreign adjectives, *-no*, with a nominal base, and *-teki* with a reduced adjectival base such as *puro-teki* which is formed from 'professional.'

(4).2 *Adverbs*

paato de	'on part time'	riaru taimu de	'in real-time'
sinpuru ni	'simply'		

(4).3 Verbs

eskareeto-suru	'to escalate'	hotto ni naru	'to be sensational'
kajuaru-ka suru	'to become casual'	katto-suru	'to cut'
kopii-suru	'to copy'	konbi ni suru	'to make a combination'
nomineeto-suru	'to nominate'	naabusu ni naru	'to become nervous'
ofurimitto-suru	'to off limit'	oopun-suru	'to open'
*ranku-zukeru	'to rank'	riido-suru	'to lead'
shaapu ni naru	'to become sharp'	stanbai-suru	'to standby'
*kaidanji-suru	'to climb staircase'	*otoosan-suru	'to play a father'
*ojoosama-suru	'to act like a young lady'		

The asterisked verbs seem to be exceptions to the general rules in that the verb, 'to rank,' for example, does not occur with the pro-verb -*suru*. It may be explained that since Japanese has a native verb, *iti-zukeru* 'to rank' which is equivalent in meaning, and furthermore it is a compound of a noun stem, *iti* 'rank' and a verb *tukeru* 'to attach,' the nominal stem is replaced by a novel foreign stem of 'rank.' *Kaidanji-suru* 'to climb stairs,' *otoosan-suru* 'to play a father,' and *ojoosan-suru* 'to act like a young lady' have all Japanese noun or noun compound (see (4)3. Verbs) stems. These stems are either recently created or reinterpreted in meaning, and are not yet permanently accepted in the lexical system of Japanese. They may eventually become part of Japanese or may go out of use. This unstable condition makes them similar to the foreign words, and in fact they are morphologically categorized as foreign at least for the present. The reason why they are so treated will be discussed in the next section on the semantic changes.

(5) New Creations

boketto	'absent-minded'	tuppari	'to be obstinate'
dasai	'unsophisticated'	sekoi	'cunning'

In addition to these frequently used words, there are a number of onomatopoeia which describe muscular strength, *mukimuki*, chaos, *hachamecha*, happiness, *runrun* and etc. There is a noticeable tendency to use them as substitutes for regular verbs to give the listener a vaguely impressionistic effect rather than clearly executed verbal affect.

We have already seen in (3) that the individuals who have broken away from the traditional pattern and value of life in Japanese society are singled out and labelled. Their characteristics are further modified and defined by the new adjectives or noun modifiers which are listed here. *Boket-to* 'absent-minded' applies, for example, to *sinjinrui* 'neo homo sapiens,' and *tuppari* 'obstinate' goes with the life-style of *datu-sara* 'escapee from salary man's career.' *Sekoi* 'cunning' and *dasai* 'unsophisticated' describe those who do not quite match the ideal model of contemporary society wherein they are sophisticated, relaxed, conversant with and receptive to modern technology and convenience.

An attempt to infer the life-style and thinking of Japanese people based on these words alone may be trivial and may lead us to a generalized or biased representation of them. It is certain, however, that the Japanese language is undergoing the lexical innovations in such ways as have been described in this section. The new entities and concepts which are named and concretized as new experiences by means of foreign loans and internal borrowings must indicate some changes in the behavioural patterns of the speakers, and as we examine the linguistic changes on semantic and syntactic levels further, it will turn out to be the case. The words which occur in daily communication cannot be independent of the speaker's world view and attitude of life.

2. SEMANTIC LEVEL

Even direct foreign loans are bound to undergo some meaning changes when they are adapted to a new cultural environment. The original meanings are reinterpreted in particular semantic situations through the processes of broadening, narrowing, upgrading and downgrading of the sense of the words as well as reinterpreting the associated sense of the words.

The meaning of the word, 'middle-class' is one example of generalization which comes to refer to the majority of Japanese. In contrast 'my home' is narrowed to mean the common housing of a city family, 'brand' is elevated to exclusive and famous brand names and 'potatoes' are downgraded to symbolize lowly, peasant-type images.

Likewise, the word 'mansion' in Japanese today refers to any small dwelling in a communal residence such as town-houses, condominiums and individually-owned apartment houses. In this use of the word 'mansion', its primary meaning of 'a large, stately house' is broadened to incorporate any communal housing for the urban, middle-class. In addition, the vaguely associated sense of the word 'mansion' such as splendour, exclusiveness or upper-class gives the Japanese borrowing of 'mansion,' a desirable, euphemistic effect. 'Palace' could have served the same semantic upgrading of the communal housing, but a possible semantic conflict between a 'palace,' being the official residence of a royal person and a 'condominium,' being the non-official residence of a non-royal person may have constrained the borrowing of the word 'palace' by the real estate agents.

More complex processes seem to be involved in the semantic changes of native words in general. Take one of the most common expressions in Japanese, *otoosan* 'father', for example. The word 'father' in Japanese used to entail a male parent who has an inherent authority to command the respect and obedience of his family. His authority was based on the responsibility to look after and protect his family. The traditional behavioural patterns of a male parent have changed. A father, for example, who is busy at work coping with daily pressures for more productivity and the improvement of his company has little time for the family nor does he wish to be bothered by family matters, leaving parental authority to his wife. The diminishing role of the male parent who was once central to Japanese life prompts semantic reinterpretation of the meaning of 'father.' In old days a father may not have just wielded his authority, and may have entertained his family with Sunday outings, movies, dinners and so on, but these were peripheral attributes of being a father. In sharp

203

contrast, today the only times when a father restrengthens his ties with the family is by treating them to some kind of entertainment. Thus an associated semantic feature of a father, 'one who occasionally keeps good company with his family,' is reinterpreted as the primary component of the meaning of *otoosan* 'father.' So unconventional and exotic is the concept of *otoosan*, the word itself is classified as a foreign loan, and its verb form, *otoosan-suru* 'to play a father' which is incidentally derived with the foreign verbal morpheme *-suru* symbolizes the playing of a temporary father role by a male parent just as he plays golf, *gorufu-suru*, or other leisure pursuits.

Another instance of an expression which undergoes similar semantic shift is *ojoosama* 'young lady' whose primary connotation of 'a secluded and well-bred daughter of a socially respectable family' has become obsolete at the present time when most young women work regardless of their social background. Subsequently, an innovative meaning of the word has evolved which refers to any woman whose behavioural patterns somewhat satisfy the sufficient conditions of the word, *ojoosama* such as 'conservatively dressed, well-mannered, non self-assertive, or polite in speech' and so on. An individual's novel experience to appear like a young lady, which obviously still has social value, by putting on modestly designed clothes or by changing her speech patterns acquires verbal distinction through internal borrowing. The semantic changes in the meaning were so radical that the word, *ojoosama* has split into homonyms, and the one with innovative interpretation is now categorized as a foreign morpheme. The subsequent formation of the derived verb, *ojoosama-suru* 'to play the role of a young lady' further generalizes the innovative meaning of *ojoosama*.

A young woman who is opposite in characteristics to *ojoosama* 'young lady' is designated as *gyaru* 'girl.' For nearly two hundred years, the word 'girl' has been in the Japanese lexicon. Although the word has never acquired the generic meaning of 'young women' which is still expressed by the native term, *musume*, it has been popularized in such common expressions as *ereveetaa gaaru* 'elevator attendant,' *gaaru sukauto* 'girl scout,' and etc. The re-importation of the word, 'girl,' is associated not only with the new semantic sense but with an unusual phonological property as well. The first syllable of Japanese transliteration, *gaa*-ru is palatalized. The newly adopted *gyaru* has not replaced nor alternated with the native word for young females, *musume*. Instead, *gyaru* 'girl' means easy-going, unreserved and in short, a breed of untraditional young women. A subtle mockery of such young women as a new social phenomenon emerges as the effect of palatalization. Historically, palatalized syllables in Japanese were foreign derived, and apart from loan words, their occurrences are still restricted in onomatopoetic or nursery words such as in *syaa-syaa* 'unabashfully,' *kyoro-kyoro* 'without composure,' *gyaa-gyaa* or *kyaa-kyaa* 'noisily,' *nyan-nyan* 'a kittie,' etc. Incidentally, a word *onyanko* 'promiscuous young women' has already been created based on a nursery word for a cat. Thus in consideration of sound symbolism of palatalization to indicate the speaker's socio-cultural stigma, we may conjecture that the word, *gyaru* 'girl' which was originally derived from a foreign loan is narrowed in sense and is semantically incompatible with the native, neutral term, *musume* which symbolizes young women in general.

Non-traditional individuals and their roles in society arouse curiosity, uneasiness, suspicion or slight contempt within the majority of Japanese. Their attitude is to make fun of these individuals rather than taking them seriously at least linguistically. They use the humorous labels, *sinjinrui* 'neo homo sapiens,' and *kyuukyoku-kun* 'an ultimate one' for a generation of young social misfits and their prototypes. On the other hand, the neutral expressions for youth, *seinen* or *wakamono* continue to be used for the young people who conform to traditional, social norms. Foreign loans such as *yangu* 'young people' and *gyaru* 'girl' are also used to refer to non-conformist young people, but all of these labels imply that their unprincipled opposition to the social convention is not taken seriously.

In the area of contemporary adult life, successful businessmen, bureaucrats and other professionals are also parodized as *eriito*, 'elite' by a foreign loan, and those who are striving for higher status and success, by the internal loans, *mooretu ningen* 'ultra man' or *mooretu shain* 'ultra company man.' This phenomenon may reflect the traditional work ethic in which compromise and harmony in working relationships and avoiding intense competition used to be valued. In the traditional, permanent employment system, even the incompetent may not be dismissed easily, and can survive on the periphery of their company till the day of retirement. An internal loan, *madogiwa-zoku* 'men by the windows,' aptly describes the employees who are cut off from the central management and operations, enduring the life of 'shame.' Even a compound *gaman no ko* 'a kid of patience and perseverance' has been created to describe people of this type who live by the dying virtue of patience like an obedient child.

Interestingly, all the adjectives derived from foreign loans such as *bigguna* 'big,' *sutairisshu-na* 'stylish,' *riberaru-na* 'liberal,' *kuuru-na* 'cool,' etc. have favourable connotations, and play the semantic function of upgrading the entities they modify. For example, only the sense of 'being casual or relaxed' of the meaning of *rafu-na* 'rough' finds its way into Japanese to upgrade its complement as in *rafu-na fukusoo* 'casual clothes,' and *rafu-na stairu* 'casual style of clothing.' These adjectives mostly occur in the language of advertisement which promotes new products, both foreign and domestic, to the consumers. The novelty and myth of the foreign words associated with the advertised goods directs consumer's interest to the goods themselves, often to the extent of purchasing them. Naturally, the foreign loans which are used for commercial purpose should have a positive pragmatic effect on the hearers.

The two semantic changes of upgrading and downgrading in the external and internal borrowings have been observed. The nature of these contrastive changes is explained through systematic analysis of the contexts of their uses. The borrowed expressions are mostly related to entities and concepts which are new to Japanese society. When these entities are commercial goods and products, upgrading of the meaning of borrowed words occurs, whereas unfavourable connotation downgrades the meaning of loan expressions which name unconventional socio-cultural experiences.

In comparison with the lexical level, syntactic changes are much slower in progress and the effect less obvious. The three syntactic changes which are discussed in this section had been in progress for some time, but they came to surface only recently as innovative syntax which is widely adopted by Japanese speakers, in the language of mass-media and of popular publications.

(3).1 *Potential Verb Conjugations*
One of the areas which is rapidly affected is the potential verb category. Historically, potential verbs used to be derived by the addition of an auxiliary *-uru* or *-eru* 'can' to a verb stem.

aru	'to be'	ari*eru*	'can be'
miru	'to see'	mi*eru*	'can see'
tasukeru	'to help'	tasuke*uru*	'can help'

Later, a passive auxiliary, *-areru* was introduced into the potential verb paradigms to distinguish homonymous verbs by separate conjugations. Homonymy occurs frequently among the *-ru* ending verbs,

kiru	'to cut'	neru	'to knead'
kiru	'to wear'	neru	'to sleep'
kaeru	'to return'	iru	'to roast'
kaeru	'to change'	iru	'to shoot an arrow'

Subsequently, one of the homonymous pairs was assigned the true potential auxiliary, *-eru*, and the other, with the passive auxiliary, *-areru*. Incidentally, the passive auxiliary *-areru* is originally a compound consisting of an existential verb, *aru* and the potential auxiliary, *eru*. Thus,

kir-*eru*	'can cut'	ner-*eru*	'can knead'
kir-*areru*	'can wear'	ner-*areru*	'can sleep'
kaer-*eru*	'can return'	ir-*eru*	'can roast'
kaer-*areru*	'can change'	ir-*areru*	'can shoot an arrow'

The occurrences of the two auxiliaries, *-eru* 'can' or *-areru* 'can' with the *-ru* ending verbs are based on their classifications as the consonant stem verb or the vowel stem verb. Thus, the consonant stem *-ru* ending verbs continued to occur with the potential auxiliary, *-eru* 'can.'

kaku	'to write'	kak-*eru*	'can write'
yomu	'to read'	yom-*eru*	'can read'
kiru	'to cut'	kir-*eru*	'can cut'
iru	'to roast'	ir-*eru*	'can roast'

While on the other hand, the *-ru* ending verbs which conjugate as the vowel stem verbs started to occur with the potential auxiliary, *-areru*. Complications developed, however, as the auxiliary, *-areru* also started to contribute passive voice and polite style to the host verbs. Thus the potential form of vowel stem *-ru* ending verbs has become so overloaded functionally as to result in multiple ambiguity in the utterances unless sufficient contexts are given. Observe,

sore wa *kirare*masu ka 'can you wear it?'
'can it be worn?'
'would you wear it?'

Furthermore, homonymous conjugations of the potential verbs were not totally eliminated, since pairs like *yoru* 'to twist' and *yoru* 'to move aside' are both classified as consonant stem verbs, and pairs like *kakeru* 'to hang up' and (*denwa o*) *kakeru* 'make (telephone call),' are arbitrarily classified as vowel stem verbs.

yoru	'to twist'	yor-*eru*	'can twist'
yoru	'to move aside'	yor-*eru*	'to move aside'
kakeru	'to hang up'	kaker-*areru*	'can hang up'
kakeru	'to make (phone call)'	kaker-*areru*	'to make (phone call)'

The current innovation has started by universally applying the true potential auxiliary, -*eru* to all verbs. This new conjugational rule will eventually eliminate from the auxiliary, -*areru* 'potential, passive, honorific' its potential marking function. This will simplify the potential verb conjugations as illustrated in the following.

Base Verb		Conservative potential	Innovative potential	
kiru	'to wear'	kir-*areru*	kir-*eru*	'can wear'
miru	'to see'	mir-*areru*	mir-*eru*	'can see'
taberu	'to eat'	taber-*areru*	taber-*eru*	'can eat'
kaeru	'to change'	kaer-*areru*	kaer-*eru*	'can change'
okiru	'to get up'	okir-*areru*	okir-*eru*	'can get up'
kariru	'to borrow'	karir-*areru*	karir-*eru*	'can borrow'

The potential verb regularization not only avoids assignment of -*ru* ending verbs into different, conjugation classes, but has the important pragmatic effect of unambiguous interpretation of the potential function of a given verb. In reality, however, the innovative potential forms are still restricted to the most frequently occurring verbs such as *kireru* 'can wear,' *mireru* 'can see,' *tabereru* 'can eat,' *nereru* 'can sleep,' *okireru* 'can get up,' etc. Furthermore, the new potential expressions are used mainly by younger speakers in their teens and twenties for predominantly casual style discourse. The syntactic conservatism of Japanese speakers is in sharp contrast to their receptiveness to foreign loans on the lexical level.

(3).2 *Relational* ga *and Ergative Verb Agreement*

The direct object case marker *o* is relatively stable with the transitive verbs in Japanese. Probably the only exception occurs with the ergative verbs such as, *suki da* 'to like,' *kirai da* 'dislike,' *joozu da* 'be skilled in,' *heta da* 'be clumsy at,' *hosii* 'want to have,' *dekiru* 'be able to do,' *wakaru* 'to understand,' *ikitai* 'want to go,' etc. The direct object of these verbs takes the nominative case relational, *ga*. Lately, the regular object relational, *o* has been in competition with the ergative object relational, *ga*, as in the following:

Conservative *ga*	Innovative *o*	
sore *ga* mitai	sore *o* mitai	'I want to see it'
sore *ga* hosii	sore *o* hosii	'I want it'
sore *ga* ki ni iru	sore *o* ki ni	'It is pleasing to me'

Replacement of the ergative object marker *ga* by *o* is, as a matter of fact, predictable by virtue of the fact that ergativity is not an extensive phenomenon in Japanese, and the reinterpretation of ergative verbs as regular transitive verbs has little effect on the syntactic system of Japanese. This change, however, is still severely constrained structurally. On one hand, the direct object relational *o* alternates freely with the conservative *ga* when the ergative verbs are in an embedded structure. When the ergative verbs are in the main sentence, on the other hand, the occurrence of the regular object relational *o* is more restricted. Compare, for example, the following cases of ergative verb and object relational agreement in the matrix and embedded sentence structures.

Main Sentence	Embedded sentence
kore *ga* wakaru	kore *ga* wakareba ii
?kore *o* wakaru	kore *o* wakareba ii
'I understand this'	'I wish that I understand this'
kore *ga* dekiru	kore *ga* dekiru hito
?kore *o* dekiru	kore *o* dekiru hito
'I can do this'	'a person who can do this'
hana *ga* suki da	hana *ga* suki rasii
?hana *o* suki da	hana *o* suki rasii
'I like flowers'	'they seem to like flowers'

In the main structure of a sentence the innovative agreement between the ergative verb and regular object relational *o* is noticeable as a violation of the regular agreement rules, therefore the innovation is possibly taking place in the less crucial syntactic positions in the embedded clauses of a sentence.

(3).3 *Sentence Relationals*

In an SOV language like Japanese, sentence final position is rigidly fixed for a verb phrase, and the only sentencial expansion allowed is the addition of sentence relationals for marking various illocutionary forces. A declarative sentence, for example, becomes interrogative with the addition of sentence relationals, *ka* or *ne*.

ikimasu	'I will go'	ikimasu *ka*	'will you go?'
ikimasu	'I will go'	ikimasu *ne*	'you will go, won't you?'

An assertion becomes an exclamation with *nee*.

kirei desu 'it is pretty'   kirei desu *nee* 'how pretty it is!'

Request becomes persistence with *yo*, promise becomes uncertainty with *kedo*, and so on.

208

mite kudasai 'Please look' mite kudasai *yo* 'please be sure to look'
kimasu 'I'll come' kimasu *kedo* 'I'll try to come but...'

Recently, the use of another relational, *wake* 'the reason for this consequence is...' has become predominant. The relational *wake* originally developed as a connective between the consequent and cause clauses, identifying a causal event which brought about a particular state of affairs. For example,

koko ni kita *wake* wa kikoo ga ii kara desu
'the *reason* why I came here is because the climate is nice'

The consequent and causal clauses can be reversed in their order to place the connective *wake* at a sentence final position as a result. Thus,

kikoo ga ii kara koko ni kita *wake* desu.
'because the climate is nice, I came here for that *reason*'

or

kikoo ga ii no ga koko ni kita *wake* desu.
'that the climate is nice is the *reason* why I came here'

At the next stage, these *wa*-marked clauses of sentence final position start to occur by themselves, independent of a causal clause only if the causal event can be retrieved from previous contexts. For example,

kikoo ga ii tokoro ni kitakatta n desu. sorede koko ni kita *wake* desu.
'I wanted to move to somewhere with a nice climate. So I came here'

or

kikoo ga ii tokoro wa ii desu ne. sore ga koko ni kita *wake* desu.
'The place with a nice climate is desirable, isn't it. That is
the *reason* why I came here.'

This practice has become gradually degenerate to finally allow *wake*-marked clauses without causal clause nor any clues for a cause in the immediate context. Thus we have,

kita *wake* desu   'we came here, because...'
soo omou *wake*   'I believe so, because...'

The sentence relational *wake* in these instances has lost its syntactic role of a connective, but it has acquired such compensatory pragmatic effect that the speaker may appear to have a reason for his course of action or state of affairs even when he has none. Observe the following:

(a) soo omoimasu   'I think so'
(b) soo omou *wake* desu   'I think so because (of some unknown reason)'

The speaker of sentence (a) explicitly commits himself to his belief, while in sentence (b) the speaker is vaguely hinting at some possible ground for his belief. The hearer of (b), therefore, may be misled to think that the speaker has indeed a reason for his belief when the use of *wake* in fact

209

implies the opposite. At present, this evasive sense of *wake* is exploited for concealing the speaker's lack of self-assurance in everyday speech as well as in writing. Interestingly, *kamo* 'may be,' a sentence relational which has also gained much popularity, is another relational of uncertainty. *Kamo* has been derived through the simplification of a full idiom such as,

(a) dekakeru *kamo sirenai* 'I don't know whether I will go out or not'
(b) dekakeru *kamo* 'I may go out, but not sure'

Both of these relationals, *wake* and *kamo* indicate the speaker's uncertainty, but *wake* does so implicitly and *kamo*, explicitly.

It is tempting to speculate if there is any correlation between the frequent uses of the relational *wake* by Japanese speakers and their current socio-cultural background. People in a fast-changing society are in many ways uncertain how to deal with new cultural experiences, new social norms and values, and new patterns of life. In addition, with the development of mass media and mass communications which affect every aspect of Japanese life, the linguistic and communicative skills of the Japanese people are fast declining. The characteristic of the speech patterns which we have just examined was the speaker's lack of precision in articulating his thinking. Inaccuracy of speech is often generated by the speaker's inability to assess reality and justify his own course of action. The sentence relational *wake* may have evolved as a communicative device for concealing the speaker's uncertainty of how to reason the course of events under these circumstances.

4. SUMMARY

Current linguistic changes in Japanese were examined on the lexical, semantic and syntactic levels. A set of new and derived words and phrases were investigated as to their formation. There are a large number of foreign loans mainly from English, and many derivative and compound phrases which were created based on both externally and internally borrowed words. Any perceivable meaning shift in them through the process of borrowing was examined, and two general tendencies in semantic changes were identified. In the area of syntax, innovative potential verb formation, regularization of agreement between the ergative verb and the object case relational, and emergence of sentence relational *wake*, were discussed with reference to their pragmatic effect. All these changes may appear to have serious linguistic consequence, but on the contrary, they are conservative enough not to affect the basic structural principles of Japanese. New words are created without radical departure from the general morphological formation. They are added to the Japanese vocabulary without disturbing its lexical systems.

Semantic changes in the meaning of new and old words occur as a result of reinterpreting their secondary or associated meaning as primary, rather than in the total replacement of their inherent meanings. Likewise, in the new syntax, innovation occurs in the verbal paradigms which are already functionally overloaded and ready for a linguistic remedy. Changes in the object case and verb agreement do not occur sporadically, but in accordance with the structural principles and the law of linguistic regularization. Occurrences of innovative sentence relationals are fixed in the final position of a sentence which is open for expansion anyway as a rule of an agglutinative language like Japanese. In conclusion, these linguistic changes have little effect on Japanese as a linguistic system, but they have an important effect on the verbal, communicative behaviour of Japanese speakers. The on-going linguistic changes are for this reason more of sociolinguistic rather than linguistic concern.

28

How to Carry Something on Your Head in Japanese

GÖTZ WIENOLD

I

The title of this paper might also read: 'On the difference between carrying something on your head in English and in Japanese.' Although I talk mainly about expressions of movement in the Japanese language, my interest in this specific topic was stimulated by the different ways of expressing notions of carrying something in English and in Japanese. These differences are shared by other languages. German behaves in much the same way as English does and Korean in much the same way as Japanese does. So we can expect to come across some deep typological and/or historical (genetic or areal) differences between these languages during investigation.

An English sentence like:

(1a) 'I carried the box on my head' may be translated naturally into Japanese using the sentence:
(1b) (watashi-wa) hako-o atama-ni nosete hakonda.

In this translation English *carry on* is rendered by the verb *hakobu* plus a second verb *noseru* 'to put s.th. on s.th.' plus the *ni*-case. Thus *atama-ni nosete hakobu* corresponds to *carry on* (one's) *head*. Now this is not an idiosyncratic characteristic of the Japanese verb *hakobu*, as can easily be seen from the fact that there are quite a few other cases of English expressions consisting of a verb plus a preposition and having as a natural translation into Japanese a sequence of two verbs. In each case the first Japanese verb will be in the *te*-form and govern the noun-phrase which corresponds to the English noun-phrase which is the object noun-phrase or is governed by a preposition (or a verbal particle):

(2) kare-wa himo-o tsutatte orita
    'He descended by a rope'

(3) kanojō-wa kawa-ni sotte aruita
    'She walked along the river'

(4) okāsan-wa kodomo-o dōbutsuen-ni tsurete itta
    'Mother took the children to the zoo'

(5) hon-o motte kimashita
    '(I) brought the book with me'

(6) Haruko-wa uma-ni notte hashitte ita
    'Haruko was riding a horse'

(7) yotto-ni notte mizumi-o watatta
    '(I/he/she/they...) sailed across the lake'[1]

(8) o-kane-o kinko-ni irete kagi-o kaketa
    '(He/she) locked the money into the safe'[2]

(9) koronde te-o utta
    '(He/she) fell on (his/her) hand'

(10) kao-o shita-ni shite taoreta
     '(He/she) fell on (his/her) face'

(11) kuruma-o oshite michi-o aruita (or: [in written language] itta)
     '(He/she) pushed the cart along the way'
     (in case of this taking place on the way)

(12) kuruma-o michi-ni sotte oshita
     '(He/she) pushed the cart along the way'
     (in case of this taking place on or next to the way)

(13) denki-wa dotai-o hete kikai-ni nagareru
     'The electric current flows through the conductor into the machine'

(14) semai michi-o hedatete mukai-no ie-no nikai-kara ichinichijū
     gachingachin mokkin-o tsukuru oto-ga suru
     'From the second floor of the house on the other side all day the
     sounds of making xylophones come across a small street'

(15) nanika-o mochi-agete (or: dareka-o dakiagete) kakine-no soto-ni dasu
     (or: kakine-no naka-ni ireru)
     'to lift s.th. (or s.o.) across a fence'

(16) nagare-ni sakaratte oyogu
     'to swim against the current'
     (Example 16 from Tamamushi 1979)

A first point to be noted is: in many cases actually two movements take
place. In the case of carrying something, the object being carried is moving
and the person doing the carrying is moving. In the case of riding on
something the person riding (the horse/the train and so on) is moving,
and the vehicle or animal by way of which the person moves, is moving.
In the case of taking someone to some place the person who takes someone
else is moving just as the person who is being taken along. Again this
applies to the cart pushed along a way. And in each of these cases one of

212

the movements is subordinated to the other, like the movement of the rider to the movement of the horse, or the movement of the box to the movement of the carrier. Less obviously this could be said about the examples of following a river or a rope in performing a movement, although languages present objects of considerable dimensions like rivers or roads along which people move sometimes as quasi-moving objects - e.g. *The road descended the mountain slope* - and at least about a river of course it can be said that the water is in movement. In the examples relating to falling down, of course, jointly with the person falling also the part of the body on which he falls is moving as any other part of the body, but it seems strange to maintain that in these cases two movements take place as well. If someone smiles while greeting someone we might again say, there are two somehow separable actions taking place, and we note the Japanese construction:

(17) bishō-o ukabete aisatsu-shita
     '(He/she) greeted (s.o.) with a smile'

But then we also note sentences like

(18) ryōmen-o arau mono-ni awasete tsukaiwakeru koto-ga dekimasu
     'According to what one is cleaning one can use both sides distinctively'
     (from the directions how to use a scotch-brite sponge)

Thus, at a first glance, it may have some appeal to say: What is actually expressed here is a movement taking place in coordination with or in dependence on a second movement and the Japanese language quite naturally expresses these two movements by employing two verbs and the coordination of the two movements by the 'Verb-*te* + Verb'-construction. But, as we have seen, the examples go well beyond such cases. Actually, verbs like *sou* or *tsutau* have one of their main uses in such constructions:

(19) hachi-no heri-ni sotte o-sashi-ni natte kudasai
     'Plant (the plants) along the rim of the flower-pot'
     (from an explanation given in a TV programme)

(20) dorobō-ga yane-o tsutatte nigeta
     'The thief ran away over the roofs'

(21) honō-ga hari-o tsutatte hi-ga hirogaru
     'The flames follow the beam and (thus) the fire spreads'

(22) hae-ga biryō-o tsutatte hitai-ni agatta
     'The fly went up to the forehead along the ridge of the nose'

Of course, it is an important aspect of the use of the 'Verb-*te* plus Verb'-construction of Japanese to express two separate actions which in some way are coordinated (by taking place simultaneously or in sequence, the one being related causally or circumstantially to the other) as comes out in example (21) with two different subjects (*honō* 'flame' and *hi* 'fire'). Still, we will look for a more general explanation by discussing some typological aspects of verbs of motion in Japanese and in English.

213

As in two previous papers on Japanese verbs of motion (Wienold 1987 and in prep.), I take reference to a typology developed by Leonard Talmy (Talmy 1985). Talmy's analysis distinguishes:
- the *figure* which moves or is localized,
- the fact of *movement* or *localization*
- the *ground* with regard to which motion or localization is indicated
- the *path* which a movement takes
- the *manner* of movement or of being localized
- the indication of a cause of the movement or localization.

Of course, finer distinctions can be made; e.g. Talmy devotes a specific section of his paper to varieties of causation (wilful, unwilful, the possible sources of causation etc.).

According to Talmy's analysis of movement verbs of motion differ as to the categories lexicalized, e.g. *swim, walk, fly, stroll* contain an indication of the manner of movement; *rise, descend, penetrate* contain an indication of the path which the movement takes. Verbs like *swim, walk, fly* also contain an indication of a kind of locality - the movement takes place in water, on ground, in the air - but in spite of this they do not specify a path which the movement takes in water, on earth or in the air; the path would be indicated only if additional elements were expressed like *swim across, fly down, walk into*.

Now, according to Talmy, languages differ as to which elements of the analysis are typically lexicalized in monomorphematic verbs of motion. English, like most Indo-European languages, has many motion verbs which specify the manner of movement: *walk, hang, slide, roll, bounce, jump, stumble, glide, swing, soar, limp, rush, amble, clomp, goosestep, hike, jog, lope, march, meander, plod, prance, promenade, ramble, romp, rove, scamper, sprint, stagger, stalk, stomp, stray, stride, stroll, strut, traipse, tramp, trot, wander* (cf. Talmy 1985, 62f.; Nilsen/Nilsen 1975, 79f.). But English also has quite a few motion verbs which specify the path. Yet, except for *rise/raise*, the English verbs of motion which contain in the morpheme which expresses the motion also an indication of the path which the movement takes are verbs borrowed from Romance languages.[3] Also, most of these verbs do not belong to the most commonly used English verbs of motion. The Romance languages differ from their neighbouring Indo-European languages in being languages that preferably have verbs of motion specifying a path. Schwarze 1985 shows that Italian actually is a language with a large amount of motion verbs specifying the path and, equally, a large amount of motion verbs specifying the manner of the verb. Azugewi, an American Indian language studied by Talmy is a language which preferably specifies the figure which is moving.

Japanese belongs to the languages which typically contain the path of the motion lexicalized in a monomorphematic verb of motion. This fact was also noted by Miyajima Tatsuo in a comparative study of motion verbs in Japanese and in several European languages (Miyajima 1984). Miyajima, in using categories of classification like *yōsu* 'manner' and *hōkō* 'direction' - of course also noted the wealth of verbs in English and German expressing the manner of the movement. Korean again is a language which typically lexicalizes the path of a movement in a verb of motion.

A brief, but by no means complete list of Japanese verbs of motion containing the path of the movement runs like this: *agaru, noboru, sagaru, kudaru, oriru, hairu, deru, tōru, heru, sugiru, yoru, tsuku, hanareru, mawaru, meguru koeru* (and *kosu*), *wataru, kuguru, mukau, zureru, saru*. Japanese, as is well known, has a rich array of morphological causative expressions. Besides the regular causative formation with *-(s)ase-* there are many 'irregular' formations. The motion verbs listed each have a corresponding causative of this second sort:[4] *ageru, nobosu* (and *noboseru*), *sageru, kudasu, orosu, ireru, dasu, tōsu, sugosu, yoseru, tsukeru, hanasu, mawasu, megurasu, koesasu, watasu, kugurasu, mukeru, zurasu* (cf. also Sakuma 1983, 114ff.).

Let us return to the Japanese sentences expressing a movement by using two verbs in the 'Verb *-te* plus Verb'- construction. In all examples of this nature - that means excluding sentences (17) and (18) - in every case the expression using the *-te*-form is an expression of motion specifying a path, and in all these cases - except for one, that is example (10) - this expression consists of just a verb of motion, causative or non-causative: *noseru* 'to make something move on top of s.th.,' *noru* 'to move on top of s.th.,' *tsutau* 'to move along the surface of s.th.,' *sou* 'to move along s.th. without touching it,' *tsureru* 'to make s.o. move along with oneself,' *motsu* 'to move s.th. along with oneself,' *ireru* 'to make s.th. move into s.th.,' *korobu* 'to fall on s.th. on which one is positioned before the fall (usually standing or sitting),' *heru* 'to move through s.th.,' *hedateru* 'to move to a place separated from s.th.,' *osu* 'to push.'[5] Except for the last one, all of these verbs of motion are verbs which contain an indication of the path of the movement in the base morpheme.[6] So I consider this fact typical of the construction as far as it used to express movement. Of course, there are quite a few other uses of such constructions, including aspectual ones like *-te iru, -te aru, -te shimau* or *-te oku*.

We noticed in the beginning that Japanese uses two verbs in the 'Verb *-te* plus Verb'-construction instead of just one verb plus preposition or particle in English. We have seen now that in cases expressing movement the second verb in Japanese is a verb of motion. We have also noted that English and Japanese belong to typologically different groups of languages with respect to patterns of lexicalization in verbs of motion. Now we will try to show that the use of the 'Verb- *te* plus Verb'-construction is related to that typological difference. This means that we have to go beyond looking just at the lexical items themselves and consider the syntactic constructions in which they are used.

Japanese has three ways of expressing a local relation:
1) case particles
2) nouns expressing a spatial relationship
3) verbs of motion, containing the lexicalization of a path, that is verbs like the ones we have been concerned with.[7]

The use of case particles can be seen in expressions like: *tōkyō-ni modoru* 'to return to Tokyo (without being a resident there),' *tsukue-de kaku* 'to write at (or on) the table,' *minato-kara hanareru* 'to move away from the port.' The use of nouns expressing a spatial relationship can be seen in constructions like *tsukue-no shita-o katazukeru* 'to clean up under the table,' *eki-no mae-de matte iru* 'to wait in front of the station,' *mori-no naka-o aruku* 'to walk in (or through) the forest.' The use of the third way of expressing a spatial relationship, that is a verb of motion, has been amply illustrated above. (The use of this construction in translations of some uses of German prepositions is also mentioned in Tamamushi 1979).

Among the Japanese expressions of a specific spatial relationship the second group - nouns like *mae, shita, ue* - seem the obvious counterpart of English prepositions. We have *ue* corresponding to *on* and *over, above; shita* corresponding to *under, mae* corresponding to *in front of, ushiro* corresponding to *behind, soba* corresponding to *by, next to, close to, yoko* corresponding to *beside, to the side of, mawari* corresponding to *around.*[8]

In the examples given, however, only the first and the third way of expressing a spatial relationship can be used. We may either say *atama-de hakobu* or *atama-ni nosete hakobu*, but we cannot say **atama-no ue-de hakobu*. We may say *densha-de iku* or *densha-ni notte iku*, but we cannot say **densha-no ue-de iku*. We have to be more precise, though, to understand the role of the third group of expressions for a spatial relationship, that is the verbs of motion containing the path. The case particle *-de* in *atama-de hakobu* or *densha-de iku* does not actually express a spatial relationship in these uses. In examples like *kodomo-wa niwa-de asonde iru* 'the children play in the garden,' *de* expresses the location of an activity; however, in examples like *atama-de hakobu* or *densha-de iku, de* expresses the means of an activity (on the uses of *de* cf. Rickmeyer 1985, 298f.; Teramura 1982, 182f.). In the ungrammatical expressions **atama-no ue-de hakobu* or **densha-no ue-de iku, de* might be said to come close to expressing a location (next to *ue*), but then we just may not say this. So verbs like *noru, noseru, tsutau, sou* and so on are one important correspondent to expressing something like a spatial relationship as an English preposition does.

I have argued in two earlier papers on different grounds, that in some important respects verbs of motion expressing a path are the real Japanese (or Korean) counterpart of prepositions in languages like English or German. The arguments given there are:

1) Quite a few prepositions of English or German do not have a counterpart among Japanese nouns expressing a spatial relationship: *through, along, across, past, against, over* (when referring to a movement, not when referring to a locality). Those, however, do have counterparts in verbs of motion containing a path: *tōru, heru, sou, tsutau, wataru, sugiru, koeru* and *kosu* (plus their respective causatives). *mawaru* and *meguru* can be added to this list as *mawari* clearly is a nominalization of *mawaru*.

2) English or German prepositions can be used as particles of verbs which themselves do not express a motion or do not express the path a motion takes. In this case, the Japanese nouns expressing spatial relationships can hardly be used at all. What are used - and very elaborately and richly used - are verbs of motion, expressing a path: *to fly up to - tobiageru, to move about - ugokimawaru, to copy out of - kakidasu* (for a comparison of German and Japanese in this respect see Iwasaki/Nitta/Sengoku 1984).

216

3) English (and German) prepositions can be used as particles in conjunction with verbs to express other functions besides a spatial relationship, one of these functions being to express an aspect: *to die out, to eat up, to carry through* (or German: *aussterben, aufessen, durchfechten*). Again the Japanese nouns expressing local relationships cannot be used for that, yet verbs of motion containing the path may: *tobidasu* may mean 'to fly or run away from' but also 'to begin to fly,' *kakidasu* may be used to express 'to copy out of something' but also 'to start writing,' *yomiageru* can mean 'to read aloud,' but also 'to finish reading' and so on.

So our present discussion adds a fourth argument. In some 'Verb *-te* plus Verb'-constructions Japanese verbs of motion (particularly verbs containing a meaning element referring to the path of the motion) play the role which corresponds to English prepositions.

IV

There is one further important point in which English prepositions and Japanese verbs of motion containing a path are alike. The Japanese nominal counterparts of English prepositions behave like other nouns in that they can take only adnominal adjuncts combined with the relational particle *-no: tsukue-no ue, mori-no naka, eki-no mae* etc.[9] The relational nouns are related to the verb by a case particle:

(25) tsukue-no ue-o katazuketa
    'I cleaned the top of the table'

(26) mori-no naka-kara mieta
    '(I) saw (that) from inside the forest'

That means such nouns take a place within the frame of nominal positions open for a given verb or for a use of a given verb. In this respect (25) is just like:

(25a) tsukue-o katazuketa
    'I cleaned the table'

and

(26) just like:
(26a) mori-kara mieta
    '(I) saw (that) from the forest'

Relational nouns specify a spatial relation:[10] *tsukue-no ue-de kaku* more precisely states the location of the action of writing as 'on the table' rather than referring to a whole area which extends from 'at' or 'by' to 'on.' *hako-no ue-de turanpu-o yaru* in the same way states more precisely the location of the action of playing cards, and so on. But *ue, shita, mae* do not open a new case position for a verb, they use one. Verbs like *noseru, noru, sou, tsutau* and so on have their own case frames and so instead of just saying:

217

(27) yane-kara orita
    '(he) descended from the roof'

we may say:

(28) yane-kara nawa-o tsutatte orita
    '(He) descended from the roof by a rope'

Again instead of saying:

(29) ie-kara hako-o hakonda
    '(I) carried a box from the house'

we may say:

(30) ie-kara hako-o atama-ni nosete hakonda
    '(I) carried a box from the house on (my) head'

instead of:

(31) michi-o yukkuri aruita
    '(She) slowly walked on the road'

(32) kawa-ni sotte michi-o yukkuri aruita
    '(She) walked slowly along the river on the road'

And in some cases there the only way open actually is the use of a second verb, *uma-de hashitta* for 'rode (on) a horse' seems strange; if we do not just want to say *hashitta* 'hurried, ran,' that is if we want to specify that the action *hashiru* takes place by riding a horse we have to employ *noru*: *uma-ni notte hashitta*.[11]

The specific uses of 'Verb -*te* plus Verb'-constructions we have been discussing, in this view, then are like the 'Verb -*te* plus Verb'-constructions which express 'to do something for the benefit of somebody:' -*te kureru*, -*te kudasaru*, -*te yaru*, -*te ageru*, -*te sashiageru* 'for the benefit of somebody' is expressed in each case by the second verb. In these uses, however, in Japanese even the noun phrase expressing for the benefit of whom something is being done is lacking.

We then arrive at the conclusion that Japanese verbs of motion expressing spatial relationships open positions for arguments just like English prepositions. One may wonder whether this is not related to the typological background which has been touched on in this paper: English and German being rich in prepositions and uses of prepositions as verbal particles, being rich in verbs of motion expressing manner in the lexical base and being (relatively)[12] poor with respect to verbs of motion expressing the path in the lexical base and having no cases which by themselves express spatial relationships or location. Japanese on the other hand has only a - in comparison with English prepositions - restricted array of relational nouns expressing spatial relations, it does not have many verbs of motion expressing manner,[13] it does on the other hand have a wide range of motion verbs expressing the path of the motion and does have cases which among other things express spatial relationships and locality. The same can be said of Korean and there are some indications that also the languages commonly classified as Altaic share some if not in all of these properties.

Definitely, a proper evaluation of the role of prepositions in languages like English or German are an important topic in this discussion. At this

time, I add only two notes:
1. In the Japanese examples for 'Verb -*te* plus Verb'-constructions used in place of English verb plus preposition or particle there were some which do not employ a verb of motion in this position. This field of examples can be enlarged. Here, I go only into one area of enlargement. A movement through an area in Japanese is ordinarily expressed by *tōru* 'to move through s.th.' or the causative counterpart *tōsu* 'to make s.th. move through s.th.,' respectively. Next to it we can use *heru* and in some instances when the passing by s.th. is actually what is important, *sugiru*.[14] In cases when what is expressed actually is not a movement but something like looking through something, the situation gets more complicated. 'To look through the window' might be translated in some cases by *mado-o tōshite miru*, and again we use path-verb (*tōsu*) in the -*te*-construction. But one may also just say something like *mado-kara soto-o miru* 'to look from the window at the outside' - which is parallel to a very usual rendering of 'to enter through the door:' *doa-kara hairu* that is 'to enter from the door' - or one might say something like (*soto-kara*) *heya-no naka-ni dareka-ga iru ka dō ka miru* 'to look (from outside) whether someone is in the room.' Finally, there are expressions like *madogoshi-ni miru* or *mieru* with *goshi* derived from *kosu*, one of the movement verbs listed above. (Parallel to sentence (15), similarly, find *kakinegoshi-ni watasu* 'to hand s.th. over across a fence'). 'To look through a hole (or a break in the wall)' finds its most natural translation in *ana-o* (*wareme-o*) *nozoku*. If, however, a specific object is added we get a 'Verb -*te* plus Verb'construction, this time not with a verb of motion: *nozoku ana* (*wareme*)-*o nozoite hito-o miru* 'to look at a person through a hole (or a break)' or *ana-o nozoite hito-ga iru ka dō ka miru* 'to see through a hole whether someone is there.' But also *ana*(*wareme*) -*kara hito-o nozoku* (or *nozokimiru*) are possible; finally also *ana-de hito-o nozoku* 'to look at a person by (the instrument of) a hole.'

That is, we definitely need a more thorough analysis of many cases of expressions to be able to state more precisely the realm of usage of each.
2. Christoph Schwarze (University of Konstanz) in a discussion pointed out to me that English and German prepositions - besides spatial interpretations (cf. on this point also Döpke/Schwarze 1981; Schwarze in pr.) - have manner-interpretations.[15] *To lie on one's back/auf dem Rücken liegen* and similar uses, rather than expressing the location at which someone is lying, express the manner in which he is lying. *Die Katze fällt auf die Füsse, the cat falls on its feet*, rather than expressing the location to which the falling of the cat takes place, expresses the manner of falling. In such cases of manner-interpretations the Japanese renderings definitely do not allow for *ue*. *He is lying on his back* would normally be rendered by (*kare-ga*) *aomuke-ni natte iru* '(He) has become in a looking up-turned (position),'[16] but might also be translated as *senaka-o shita-ni shite nete iru* '(He) makes his back (his) underside and is lying.' *He stands on his head/Er steht auf dem Kopf* has as a natural translation into Japanese (*kare-ga*) *sakadachi-o shite iru* '(He) is doing a reverse-stand.' For *The cat falls on (its) feet* I got translations like *neko-ga ashi-de jimen-ni tsuku* 'The cat gets to the surface with its feet' or *neko-ga chakuchi shita* 'The cat made a ground-arrival' (employing the Sino-Japanese compound *chakuchi*) or again *neko-ga ashi-o*

shita-ni shite ochita 'The cat fell in making (its) feet (its) underside.' Whatever translations we choose in these cases we do not get a translation using the relational noun *ue*. The relational noun *shita* is employed in some of them. Some employ verbs of motion like *tsuku* (*chaku* of *chakuchi* is the Sino-Japanese counterpart of this use of *tsuku*), some employ 'Verb *-te* plus Verb'-constructions.

In all these cases we do get outside of an area that is characterized by the combination of case particle plus verb of motion in Japanese. This may actually suggest that we have moved into areas of Japanese grammar of diverse structural properties, each to be looked at in its own right. That is if we compare languages like Japanese and English and look at the use of English prepositions outside their spatial interpretation we probably are in a field which has to be structured quite differently from the one I employed in discussing expressions of movement and space. I only opened up a small window on this field. But we may take this as an additional indication of quite strong, probably typological differences between Japanese and English which lie behind verbs of motion, prepositions, relational nouns and cases.

29

On the Necessity of Contrastive Analysis of Japanese and Minor Languages of Europe

TOSHIAKI TAKESHITA

1. INTERPRETATION OF THE EXPRESSION 'LINGUISTICS OF THE JAPANESE LANGUAGE'

Our section is labelled linguistics. Since the symposium is dedicated to Japan, linguistics in this case is intended obviously as linguistics of the Japanese language. Today this expression in English has two corresponding terms in Japanese: *kokugogaku* and *nihongogaku*. Thirty or forty years ago very few would have hesitated to identify the expression with *kokugogaku*, but now along with it we have also *nihongogaku*. Their object of study is the same Japanese language. Then why is it that two disciplines, so easily confused, exist at all? And what are the differences between the two? It is not my purpose to discuss here these points in detail, and yet I think it better to explain briefly my interpretation of the linguistics of the Japanese language in this paper.

Kokugogaku is, so to speak, the traditional Japanese linguistics, the discipline offered in the departments of Japanese language and literature in Japanese universities. It has its organic system as a science, and the researchers occupied with it are called *kokugogakusha* (literally, scholars of the Japanese language). According to my understanding, the term *nihongogaku*, which is not yet listed in dictionaries, is the sum of various new types of research. Contributions come from different fields: from certain areas of *kokugogaku* itself, from linguistics of various schools, from the teaching of Japanese as a foreign language, from the teaching of foreign languages to the Japanese people and finally from research on the Japanese language by foreigners. Thus its contents seem to be of mixed nature at least for the present. Today those researchers who have something to do with it are called *nihongo-semmonka* (literally, specialists of the Japanese language) independently of their main fields of activity. Thus a specialist of the Japanese language can be, for instance, a linguist of the transformational-generative school, a teacher of Japanese as a foreign language, or a teacher who teaches, for example, Chinese to the Japanese people. However the opposite is not always true, nor do I think that the teachers who teach Japanese to the Japanese students are specialists of the Japanese language.

I think that the differences distinguishing the two disciplines can be summarized in the following three points: 1) While *kokugogaku* considers only the Japanese language, works done within *nihongogaku*, in spite of their miscellaneous nature, have a common attitude of viewing Japanese as one of the languages of the world. To put it in other words, when we say *nihongogaku*, we have in mind its counterparts, that is, foreign languages. We might also say that *nihongogaku* examines Japanese as a foreign language. 2) Within *nihongogaku*, since diachronic research presents many difficulties, the object of analysis is limited to contemporary Japanese, and finally 3) *nihongogaku* presupposes language universals.

'Linguistics of the Japanese language,' in its broad sense, must include both *kokugogaku* and *nihongogaku*, but here I interpret it in the sense of *nihongogaku* defined roughly as above.

I am a Japanese language teacher and what draws my special interest in *nihongogaku* is its contrastive point of view that leads us quite naturally to contrastive studies. By saying this I mean that my interest is not in talking about the Japanese language itself, but in giving the student the ability to perform in Japanese. On this occasion, with this concern in mind I intend to call attention to the necessity of beginning contrastive analyses of Japanese and so-called minor languages of Europe.

2. CONTRASTIVE STUDIES AND TEACHING MATERIALS

Before coming more closely to the point, let me provide a couple of quotations and observations with regard to teaching materials.

1) The following is from an article of a professor of French at Waseda University, Tokyo: 'For the teaching of French we have a method developed at the CREDIF under the auspices of the French Government. [...] But the materials prepared at this centre are not good for the Japanese students. [...] The reason for it lies, in short, in the absence of consideration of the differences of French and Japanese with the consequence of ignoring almost all the pitfalls for the Japanese students' (Itō 1978, 2-3).

2) Among the materials available for teaching Italian to foreigners we have this one: *La Lingua Italiana Insegnata agli Stranieri* (Italian taught to foreigners) by A. Roncari & C. Brighenti. Though it is a well-known text-book, we can make the same observations on it as on those of the CREDIF: for the Japanese there are considerable points that are missing or not dealt with at all. Some of them are extremely serious.

If the interference of the mother tongue is unavoidable for language learning, we must say that all text-books prepared for the use of people of different mother tongues are inevitably imperfect for any given people. It is unreasonable to say that Japanese language text-books for universal use can be the exception.

With regard to Japanese language instruction, along with materials for universal use, those with English as a medium are widely used. This second type of text-book usually contains a contrastive viewpoint with English. Compared to British and American students, Italian ones, for example,

222

are disadvantaged. To see what it is like to use in Italy text-books for the use of English-speaking people, I would like to quote some points of description on the Italian articles, given specifically with Somalian students in mind (the original is in Italian):

3) 'In Italian the articles are always before nouns. The articles are only before nouns. They are not before other words. The nouns are words that have the article before them. [...] In Italian it is always necessary to indicate clearly whether one wants to talk about a precise and determinate person or thing, or about an indeterminate person or thing. For this reason we put the definite article or the indefinite article before nouns' (Amato 1979-1980: 91). I believe that this description is necessary and at the same time sufficient for Somalians. However, a Japanese would say: 'Here is repeatedly written a self-evident matter for us, but not the information I really want and need.'

Materials for the use of A are not good for B. It is the same with Japanese language text-books with English as a medium.

4) One more example: Among many points of difficulty Japanese language learners must overcome, there is the question of whether to use the particle *wa* or not. On this problem, in my opinion, there is a certain remarkably consistent parallelism between Japanese and Italian, and we can find it only after closely examining both languages. This parallelism can help us in teaching activities to the Italians, but maybe only to the Italians. Unfortunately, but quite naturally the materials both for universal use and with English as a medium are prepared without taking it into account profitably.

The imperfectness of teaching materials can be corrected and integrated to a certain degree by us as teachers, if we are trained and experienced with a good knowledge of the mother tongues of learners. It appears, however, that in many European countries these requirements can hardly be satisfied. I think that one possible way to solve this problem is to prepare materials which incorporate the results of contrastive analyses and that one condition indispensable for their realization is to begin research in that direction.[1]

3. PRESENT SITUATIONS OF CONTRASTIVE STUDIES IN JAPAN

At present, Japanese language teaching circles in Japan are very busy, pressed by the necessity to prepare a large number of well-trained teachers and specialists. In those private schools that offer training courses in conformity with the model curriculum of the Ministry of Education, contrastive linguistics is one of the compulsory subjects and, to my knowledge, in universities that confer a degree in the teaching of Japanese as a foreign language it is among the basic disciplines as well.

Now let us examine what is taking place at research level. Here contrastive studies are more and more active. The first results were given through analysis between Japanese and English conducted by linguists or linguists of English. Generally speaking, however, these studies seem not to be connected directly with Japanese language teaching, whereas a series of researches carried on by the National Language Research Institute

(Kokuritsu Kokugo Kenkyūjo) intend to contribute precisely to the improvement of Japanese language instruction to foreigners. It would seem that special emphasis is given to the contrast with Asian languages.[2] The third group of studies consists of dissertations submitted by foreign researchers to their graduate schools in Japan. Their works are characterized by practicality that permits the utilization of the results of analyses directly for teaching activities. As far as I can discern through journals of the Society for the Teaching of Japanese as a Foreign Language, Asian researchers far exceed those of the West in number. There is one point worthy of special mention: their same analyses could be hardly conducted, if not completely impossible, by Japanese specialists, because perhaps except for Chinese, the languages contrasted are minor ones; exotic languages to the Japanese. The fourth and last category concerns teamwork through international cooperation. It has come to my knowledge that there exists such cooperation between Japan and the People's Republic of China, France and West Germany.[3] Among the members of the group there seem to be specialists of Japanese language teaching. I understand, therefore, that Japanese language instruction to Chinese, French and German-speaking people is part of the studies of each group.

From a quantitative point of view, English comes first, no doubt far above any others. Then comes a group formed by German, French and Asian languages such as Chinese, Korean, Indonesian and Thai. We have good reason to believe that in the near future analyses with languages of East and South-East Asia will show an explosive increase. As for Spanish and Russian we have only sporadic works and when it comes to the minor European languages, so far as I know, there is no contrastive study in Japan (except perhaps for some works conducted by European researchers at graduate schools in Japan).

Analyses cover various fields of sounds, grammar, semantics and recently also verbal behaviour, but there exists no common approach yet with the result that every researcher, so it seems, has a personal method and viewpoint different from those of others.

4. NECESSITY OF BASIC CONTRASTIVE STUDIES WITH MINOR LANGUAGES OF EUROPE

Language is above all a means or an instrument of communication. The transmission of information and knowledge is included in communication. The essential task of foreign language teaching lies in getting the learners to acquire this *practical* means and ability as efficiently as possible. In spite of this, however, Japanese language teaching carried out within the framework of European Japanology has been expected to fulfill its role within the scope of explaining, simply, the ethos. There may be some exceptions, but on the whole the result is that between language and literature, the balance has been consistently weighted towards literature - the study of which is possible to some extent through the use of materials in English, French or German as has often been and still is the case. Such a tradition within European Japanology has resulted in almost no room being made either for basic research on the language itself, or for the improvement of the methodological and technical side of teaching which is a very important consideration at lower level courses. As proof of this European tradition of Japanology, it is sufficient to point out that among the joint studies already referred to, those of Japan-France and Japan-Germany do not seem to have been born from within the Japanology of the respective countries. In the case of Japan-Germany in particular, it is clear from the literature[4] concerned that the initiative was taken outside the world of German Japanology.

I am pleased to report that in Italy, for the first time in this symposium, linguistics stands on equal footing with other areas, and I am quite sure that in the future the linguistics of the Japanese language will be cultivated and taught as one of the essential areas of study. However, as far as its teaching is concerned, much more preparation remains to be done. At present, we have very little to teach on the linguistics of the Japanese language, based on contrastive analysis of Japanese and Italian.

We have said that in Japan contrastive studies are on the increase. However, many years will pass before Japanese is contrasted with, say, Italian, Dutch, Danish, Greek and so on. If we are to raise the level of Japanese language studies and Japanese studies in general, we must initiate basic contrastive studies here in Italy and other European countries as well.

I feel that because Japanese is completely different from Indo-European languages, it is one of the best languages for them to be contrasted with. If it is set free from the tradition of Japanology in Europe, it will also favour the study of European languages and the progress of linguistics in general. We welcome this approach to the Japanese language on the part of students and scholars of linguistics, but especially by those whose mother tongues are minor European languages. The results of their analysis will be beneficial not only to their own purposes, but also to European Japanology itself.

30

Japanese Relative Clause Strategies

STEFAN K. KAISER

1. INTRODUCTION

In traditional Japanese scholarship, the notion of 'relative clause' was non-existent. This is perhaps not surprising when we compare Japanese relative clauses with the sort of structure that used to come under that name in the Western philological tradition, where basic relative clause structure was seen to be characterised by the presence of a relative pronoun.[1]

As far as I am aware, the first to recognise the existence of relative clauses in Japanese was the Portuguese Jesuit missionary Joao Rodriguez in his *Arte da lingoa de Iapam composta pello*, published in Nagasaki between 1604 and 1608; not surprisingly, he forms his description around the non-existence of relative pronouns in the language (1604:87):

> A lingoa Iapoa carece do relatiuo, *Qui, Quae, Quod*: pello que he multo necessario saber o modo como se fazem as orações relatiuas por todos os casos, & como se explicam em noßa lingoa.
> (The Japanese language lacks the relative pronouns *Qui, Quae, Quod*: therefore it is imperative to know how relative clauses are formed for all cases, and how these are expressed in our language.)
> O Relatiuo, qualquer caso que seja se entende no modo de falar, & se enclue na oraçam sem se exprimir: conuem a saber, pera fazer oraçam relatiua, o Antecedente. i. a cousa relatada se pospoem immediamente ao verbo, do qual se rege o Relatiuo que se entende. Vt, *Vonoreni xicarazaru monouo tomoto surucoto nacare*. i. Não tomes por companheiro a pesoa, que não ser melhor que tu. *Monouo*, he o Antecedente: *Xicazaru*, he o verbo de que se rege o relatiuo *Que*, o qual se entende, & he Nominatiouo do verbo ser melhor.
> (Regardless of which case is employed, the relative pronoun is understood by the way things are put, and is included in the clause without being expressed. In order to form a relative clause, it is useful to know that the antecedent, i.e. that which is being relativized, is placed immediately after the verb by which the understood relative pronoun is governed. For example, *Onore ni sikarazaru mono o tomo to suru koto nakare* 'Do not take as a companion a person who isn't better than you.' *Mono o* is the antecedent: *sikarazaru*, the verb by which the relative pronoun *Que*, which is understood and is the subject of the verb *ser melhor*, is governed).

Rodriguez subsequently proceeds to discuss relativization of subjects, genitives, indirect and direct objects, but before doing so he makes the following observation in Appendix 1 (:*ibid*):

> As particulas, *Va, Vo, Voba*, pospostas aos verbos muitas vezes se poem em lugar das cousas, & tambem do Antecedente, ou sam Antecedente quando se poem em lugar dos Pronomes, Este, Isto, Aquillo, &c. Vt, *Cayŏni mŏxitaruua*. Aquelle que, &c.
> *Ya? corenaru cotjiquino coxi caquetaruua masaxŭ sotobanite soro*. i. Aquillo em que esta aßentado.
> *Sono tocoroni amatano quiŏ attauo torareta*.
> (The particles *wa, o, oba* placed after verbs often take the place of things, and likewise of the antecedent; without the antecedent they take the place of the pronouns *Este* ('this,' masc. pronoun), *Isto* ('this/ that,' neuter pronoun), *Aquillo* ('that,' neuter pronoun) &c. e.g. *kayoo ni mositaru wa. Aquelle que* ('that one who'), &c.
> *Ya? Kore naru kojiki no kosi kaketaru wa masasyuu sotoba nite soro*. 'that on which he is sitting'...).

From our twentieth-century vantage point, we may say that not only is the above the first discussion of Japanese prenominal relative clauses, but also constitutes the first description of a further relative-clause strategy in the language.

Research during the last two decades or so has considerably advanced our cross-linguistic knowledge about relative clauses, not only in relation to the word-order typology of the languages exhibiting them, but also in terms of the types, or strategies, of their formation.

Unfortunately, types of relative clauses and the terminology applied to characterize them in the literature are far from being uniform, but if we adopt C. Lehmann's (1984:49) hierarchical binary representation of relative-clause types, we can distinguish five major strategies:

(1)

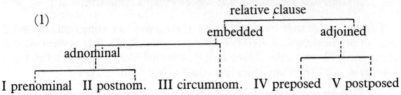

I prenominal II postnom. III circumnom. IV preposed V postposed

A brief explanation of terms is in order;[2] a relative clause is *embedded* if it is an immediate constituent of a nominal which in turn functions as a noun phrase in the matrix clause; otherwise it is *adjoined*. An embedded relative clause is *adnominal* if it functions as a co-constituent of its head, whereas it is *circumnominal* if the head is absent and the relative clause contains its semantic head, while the relative clause occupies the gap (the noun phrase that is relativized) that features in other types of embedded relatives. A relative clause is *prenominal* if it precedes its head, and *postnominal* if it follows it. An adjoined relative clause is *preposed* if it precedes the main clause, and *postposed* if it follows it.

Below are some examples to illustrate the difference between strategies I and III in Japanese (II is commonly found in European languages and therefore hardly needs to be exemplified here):

(2) Watasi   wa   [tumetai] biiru   ga   ii
    I   TOP cold   beer   SUB   good
    'I'd like cold beer'

(3) Watasi wa [biiru no tumetai]   no   ga   ii
                     GEN   PRO
    'I'd like beer which is cold'

(2) may not look like a relative clause but rather like an adjectival clause, although there are of course examples which can only be rendered into English as relative clauses, such as (4):

(4) Watasi wa [kinoo   katta] biiru ga ii
               yesterday bought
    'I'd like the beer which we bought yesterday'

Nonetheless, in (2) the difference between a relative clause and an adjectival clause is less than clear cut (despite the possibility of alternatively translating it as 'I'd like beer which is cold'), and the question arises as to how we should define a relative clause. (5) below is the working-definition used in Andrews (1975:4):

227

(5) 'a subordinate clause that modifies a constituent external
to it by virtue of containing a constituent that is in some sense
semantically equivalent to the modified constituent'

Similar, but more concise, is the working-definition in Lehmann (1984:47):

(6) 'alle untergeordneten Sätze und satzartigen
Konstruktionen..., die ein Nominal modifizieren, welches in
ihnen selbst eine semantische Rolle hat.'
('any subordinate clause and sentence-like construct
...modifying a nominal that has a semantic role within it')

Tumetai in (2) may be regarded as a 'sentence-like construct' in that it
can (in predicative function) constitute a sentence. In that respect we can
distinguish (2) from the following (7), where *kinoo no* does not fulfil this
condition, and therefore does not constitute a relative clause:

(7) Kinoo no biiru ga ii
'I'd like yesterday's beer'

Returning to (2) and the distinction (or the lack of it) between adjectival
and relative clauses: in many languages, e.g. English, the two main
functions of the adjective, modification of the noun and predication, are
clearly separated by the use of the copula, which appears only in the latter
function. In some languages, however, the adjective does not require a
copula in predicative function, either; if, moreover, the ways of forming
adjectival clauses and relative clauses are identical, the two functions fall
together and relative clauses are formally indistinguishable from adjectival
noun-modification.[3]

This falling together of functions applies only to adjectives 'proper'[4] in
Japanese; the so-called 'nominal' class of adjectives differs in its noun-
modifying and predicative functions:

(8) Oisisoo   na   biiru ga aru
    Tasty-looking COP-DEP   there-is
    'There is some tasty-looking beer'

(9) Kono biiru wa oisisoo da
    This TOP   COP-FIN
    'This beer looks delicious'

3. MULTIPLE MAJOR STRATEGIES IN ONE LANGUAGE

It is not unusual that a language employs more than one major[5] strategy:
for instance, Tagalog has both I and II,[6] Navajo II and III,[7] and Turkish
I and II/V.[8]

The case of Turkish is often cited as an instance of the influence of
language contact on relative clause structure: besides the indigenous type
1, type V was borrowed from Persian. Apart from considerations of cultural
dominance, it also appears that unlike the native strategy, the borrowed
type can be used - and is stylistically acceptable only in this function - for
extraposition (postposition).[9] It is therefore possible to argue that it
represents type V rather than II.

In the case of Tagalog and Navajo, however, language contact does not seem to have played any part in the existence of multiple strategies, as far as we can tell, at any rate; in accordance with the principle of 'one form one meaning' it is of interest to observe if any differences exist between major strategies in any one language. In Navajo, III is the more common, primary strategy in the language, with I being an alternative, secondary strategy.[10] Exactly why a secondary strategy is needed in the language is unclear, although there are some minor differences between the two strategies with regard to their interpretation, as seen from the following two examples.[11]

(10) [At 'eed yiyiiltsa-(n)ee]   ashkii   yalti'
     girl   3:PERF:3:see-REL   boy   IMP:3:speak
     'The boy who saw the girl is speaking'

(11) [Ashkii at 'eed yiyiiltsa-(n)ee] yalti'
     'The boy who saw the girl is speaking'
     'The girl whom the boy saw is speaking'

The circumnominal relative clause (11) is ambiguous in its interpretation as to which of the two nouns is the semantic head, whereas no such ambiguity exists in the prenominal relative clause (10).

For Tagalog, it has been suggested that prenominal relative clauses are available, 'especially when short,'[12] but are avoided when ambiguity would arise.[13] As prenominal relatives are the secondary strategy in the language, the situation is the reverse of what we observed about Navajo. Mallinson & Blake (1981:296) point out that as the verb-initial language Tagalog allows adjectives to precede as well as follow nouns, there may be some correspondence in languages between the order of adjectives and relative clauses in relation to the head noun. According to Keenan & Comrie (1977:79), the relativizable positions in the two strategies are exactly the same, with only subject being permitted.

4. ARE THERE STRATEGY-SPECIFIC DIFFERENCES IN JAPANESE?

Japanese, as we saw earlier, has two major strategies: of these, I is clearly the primary strategy, while III is marginal, at least in Modern Japanese. The statistical imbalance between the two types is less conspicuous if we go back in history, but there is no question that I is still the primary strategy.

One typical difference betwen the two strategies (which follows from the explanation of terms given above in 2.) is that prenominal Japanese relative clauses normally feature an argument gap; observe the following two examples from Classical Japanese:

(12) [mi- ke   moti   suru] *Wakauka no me no mikoto* (EN:97)
     PREF food handling do
     'Wakauka no me no mikoto, who handles the emperor's food'

(13) [ame no sita   no oo-mi-takara   no   tori-tukureru] *okitu-mi-tosi*
     sky ASS under ASS PREF subjects SUB PREF grow   rice- plants
         (EN:117)
     'the rice-plants which the subjects of the state grow'

229

In (12), the gap is the subject of the constituent verbal (interpretable as coreferential with the head noun [in italics]), whereas it is the object in (13). Occasionally, a pronoun (in bold) is retained optionally in place of the gap as the following example from Modern Japanese shows:

(14) [**sono** ryoosin ga sude ni naku natte ita] kodomo
    its   parents SU already had-died   child
    'a child/children whose parents had already died'

However, pronoun retention is possible only with genitives, and does not occur with, for instance, subject or object gaps.

The circumnominal strategy, on the other hand, does not feature a gap within the relative clause:

(15) [**kiku**   **no** **hana** no uturoeru] o orite (IM :18,2)
    chrysanthemum GEN flower   faded   DO pick+
    'she picked a chrysanthemum which had faded'

(16) [**mi- te** nado no kokoro todomete   kaki-tameru]
    PREF hand etc.   heart   fasten+ write+fix
    tune yori   mo midokoro arite   (GM:311,13)
    always more than MOD merit   there-is+
    'his hand(writing), which he wrote with special care commanded even more attention than usually'

In the above (15) and (16), the semantic head (in bold) is manifested as subject in the first example, and as object in the second; apart from subject and direct object, a variety of non-direct objects can also be relativized, but that also applies to the prenominal strategy; there is, then, no difference between the two strategies as regards relativizability.

Are there any characteristics in which the two strategies differ apart from the typical differences mentioned above? In the following sections, I shall examine a few examples that provide us with some clues on this question.

4.1 Restrictiveness and choice of strategy

Circumnominal relative clauses may be divided into a number of subtypes depending on the particle (postposition) attached to Rel NP. These particles include the following:

(17) Case-marking: *no, ga*, O, *o, ni.*
    Modal: *wa, mo, zo, namu, ya.*
    Adverbial: *bakari, nomi, nado* etc.

With one substrategy of circumnominal relative clauses, *no*-relatives, examples that are clearly restrictive in meaning are observed:

(18) [umi no   ko no   kiyoku akaki kokoro o   motite
    birth GEN child   pure+ clean heart DO have+

230

mikado ni tukae-maturamu] o   ba   (SNS:329,2)
court at   serve SUF   DO MOD
'the descendants who serve the imperial court with pure, unspotted hearts'

This type of example receives restrictive interpretation because the semantic head is a larger category or comprehensive/plural entity, of which a part or subset is delimited in the relative clause. This interpretation is occasionally reinforced by the presence of a pluralising suffix such as -*tati* attached to the semantic head, but is generally conditioned by contextual factors. The following example serves to illustrate this point:

(19) ko no kokoro asiki [ko no kokoro arabiru]
     this heart bad boy   heart is-rough
     wa ...sizume-mature   (EN:363)
     MOD 'appease   SUF ... this malicious, rough boy'

As Japanese does not normally make a formal distinction between singular and plural, (19) can be interpreted as:

(19) 'appease ... those among the malicious boys who are rough'

However, the context clearly indicates that a singular entity is referred to, namely *Homusubi no kami*, the God of Fire. For this reason (19) can only be interpreted as a nonrestrictive relative clause in the sense indicated in the earlier translation: the context preceding (19) has in fact a sentence quoting the goddess Izanami as saying:

(20) kokoro asiki ko o   umite-okite konu   (EN:361)
     heart bad boy DO bear+leave+came
     'I have given birth and left behind a malicious boy'

The noun phrase *kokoro asiki ko* recurs almost immediately in a further sentence uttered by the goddess, of which (19) forms the initial part. Something which has already been introduced into the text previously is therefore taken up anaphorically, and is expanded on further in the relative clause. It seems clear that in this instance the non-anaphoric section, i.e. the relative clause that follows the semantic head, carries a greater degree of importance or emphasis than the prenominal relative clause preceding it.

The following example also contains a restrictive clause:

(21) menotogo   no   daitoku, sore kara ozi   no   azari,
     nurse-son   GEN priest then from uncle GEN s.priest
     [sono desi no mutumasiki] nado, [moto yori siritaru] oi-boosi nado...
     his disciples intimate   etc.   origin from know old-priests etc.
                                              (GM:1936,10)

231

'the nurse's son, who was a priest, then his uncle the senior priest, the (more) intimate ones of his disciples, and old priests he had known since earlier times....'

Here we have a juxtaposition of noun phrases referring to persons, of which two are expanded by modifying sections; the last one, *moto yori siritaru oi-boosi*, is a prenominal relative clause, whereas the one preceding it is circumnominal. It seems doubtful whether the circumnominal clause could have been expressed as a prenominal one in this instance: *sono mutumasiki desi* ('his intimate disciples') does not seem to convey the restrictive sense[14] of the circumnominal relative clause required here. The choice between strategies in this case seems therefore conditioned by the need to form a restrictive clause (although the restrictive meaning relies on the context only).

Incidentally, there are examples where it is not possible to express a circumnominal clause prenominally while preserving the meaning:

(22) [take   no arituru] o mi-tukete   (KM V:97,6)
toadstool   existed DO find+
'he found a toadstool, which happened to be there'

(23) *[arituru] take o mi-tukete
'he found the toadstool that was mentioned earlier'

In prenominal usage, *arituru* normally has the idiomatic sense of 'the aforesaid,' and for this reason (23) is not possible in the sense of (22).

4.2 The order of modifying sections relevant to the semantic head

Simplex prenominal relative clauses in Japanese can be augmented (like any other noun-modifying construct) by adding further modifying sections, thus forming a complex structure:

(24) [[roo ari]   [okasiki]] hitobito ari   to   kikite
experienced interesting ct.ladies exist COMP hear+
                                        (YM:534,2)
'he heard that there were court ladies that were experienced and interesting'

(25) [[koe omosiroku]   [yosi aru]] mono wa   haberi ya
voice attractive   refined   person MOD exist   Q
                                        (YM:547,2)
'are there persons of attractive voice and refinement?'

(26) [[kagirinaku omoite] [kodomo nado aru]]   me
boundlessly love+   children etc   exist wife
ni wa tiri   bakari mo saru kesiki   mo   misezarikeri
IO MOD a-bit not-even such sign   MOD didn't-show
                                        (YM:602,8)
'to his wife, whom he loved boundlessly and with whom he had children, he didn't show the slightest sign of this'

Here, the second modifying section is, as is usually the case in a relative clause in classical Japanese, in the dependent form; however, the first one is in the suspensive form (of a verb in (24), and an adjective in (25), with the conjunction *-te* ('and') attached to the verb in (26)). This structure may be called a coordinated relative clause, as the two modifying sections combine to form a single noun phrase.

There are also cases where the two (or more) modifying elements are all in the abnominal form:

(27) [Ki no   kuni   no   tisato   no   hama ni arikeru]
     GEN prov. GEN 1000-mile GEN beach at existed

     [ito omosiroki]   isi   tatematureriki   (IM:196,10)
     very attractive   stone   presented

     'they presented him with a very attractive stone, which was from the Thousand-mile beach in Ki province'

(28) sore wa [Hie ni sumu] [In   no   tenzyoo
     that MOD   on live   ex-emp GEN palace-access
     mo suru] hoosi   ni   namu arikeru   (YM:516,2)
     MOD do monk   COP MOD COP

     'that was a monk who lived on Mt Hiei, who also was granted access to the ex-emperor's palace'

Here, we have two NPs of the same type modifying one head - this is generally referred to as 'stacking.'

Stacking is observed in many languages and for the majority of relative-clause types;[15] stacked RCs are therefore also found with circumnominal relative clauses:

(29) ima wa   mukasi [[soo no arikeru] ga [yamugotonaki
     now MOD long-ago monk   existed   eminent
     soo   no   moto ni   miyazukae sikeru]]   arikeri (KM V:207,6)
     monk GEN place at   serving   did   existed

     'long ago, there was a monk, who lived (then), who served under an eminent monk'

In theory, there is of course no such thing as a longest sentence, and the number of modifying sections pertaining to one noun is therefore limitless; in practice, however, no more than four modifying sections are observed in stacked examples in my data, and that is a figure that includes combinations of prenominal and circumnominal sections. If we consider the question how these are distributed around the semantic head, then, for instance, in the following example, the semantic head (*warawa*) is preceded by a prenominal relative clause (*tosi 16.7-sai bakari aru*), and followed by *katati birei-naru, tsukizukisi-ge-naru* and *siroki koromo o sidokena-ge-ni nakayuitaru*:

(30) [[[tosi zyuuroku, siti-sai   bakari aru   warawa *no* katati
        age 16,   7 years   about have child   face
birei-naru] *ga* [tukizukisi-ge-naru] *ga* [siroki koromo o
beautiful   decent-looking   white garment DO
sidokena-ge-ni nakayuitaru]]] O yuki-gusitari.
slovenly   tucked-up   caught-up-with

(KMIII:567,10)

'he caught up with a child of about 16 or 17 years of age, who had beautiful features, who was decent-looking, who had a white garment slovenly tucked up'

As we saw above in examples like (26) and (27), prenominal relative clauses can stack in various ways, too; if elements are stacked to the right of the head of a prenominal RC as well, one gets examples such as (30). A variation on (30) is the following (31), where the semantic head is preceded by two prenominal sections and followed by one circumnominal relative clause:

(31) Saisyoodono wa   sukosi   iro   hukaki ōn-naosi ni
                  MOD somewhat colour   dark   PREF with
[tyōzizome *no*   kogaruru made simeru] [siroki] aya *no*
clove-dyed GEN get-burnt till   dyed   white damask
[natukasiki] o   ki-tamaeru, kotosaramekite en-ni miyu
intimate   DO wearing   stylish+   attr. look

'the Saisyōodono's (Yugiri) wearing a *naosi* of somewhat dark colour, and with it a(n overgarment of) white damask that was clove-dyed to such an extent that it had a burnt appearance, looked stylish and attractive'

As it is rare to have stacked circumnominal examples with an unmodified semantic head,[16] and likewise unusual for simplex circumnominal relative clauses to have an unmodified semantic head, it would appear that if a single noun is 'crowded' with modifying sections, they tend to get distributed around it in the way seen above in (30) and (31). Naturally, we can expect that this distribution does not take place at random, so it is useful to watch for signs indicating which of such modifying sections has the greatest relevancy to the semantic head. There are some examples that provide us with some information on this question; I proceed to discuss these in the following.

4.31 In a story in the *Konzyaku Monogatarisyuu*, a powerful saint/wizard has bottled up all the raingods after he once slipped in the wet, and as a result India is facing a severe drought. In order to lure him out of the wilderness and remedy the situation, the king's wily minister advocates the dispatch of a contingent of beautiful women with siren-like singing voices. The order of modifying sections in the relevant sentences is as follows:

234

(32) yamugotonaki syoonin nari   to iedomo, [[*iro ni medezu*]

                                            M1

    eminent   saint is COMP even-if sex at dislike+

    [*koe ni hukeranu*]]   **mono**   wa   arazi   (KMI:349,12)

    M2

    voice   in indulge-not person EMP there-is unlikely-to-be

    'even though he may be an eminent saint, there is nobody
    who dislikes sex'

(33) [*tanzyoobirei-naramu*] **nyonin** no [*koe bi-naramu*]   o

    M1   M2

    beautiful are   women   voice beautiful DO

    mesi-atumete

    call+gather+   (*ibid.*:349,13)

    'he gathered women of classic beauty who had beautiful
    voices'

(34) [[*tanzyoobirei-ni-site*] [*koe bi-naru*]]   **onna**   o   erabite

    M1   M2

    beautiful+   voice beautiful women DO choose+

                               (*ibid.*349,16)

    'he chose women who were of classic beauty and had
    beautiful voices'

The order of the two modifying elements pertaining to the semantic head (M1 and M2, in italics) is the same in all three examples; in (32) and (34), the head noun (in bold) is preceded by two modifying sections (the second one in the dependent form, and the first one in the suspensive form, modifying the second one). The combination modifies the head noun.

It has been pointed out[17] that in the order of adjectives pertaining to a head noun those that *characterize* the head (i.e. indicate its inherent properties or intension) are positioned in greater proximity to it than those which *specify* it (i.e. determine the reference or extension of the head), and this difference can be extended to modifying sections in a more general way.[18] In (31), for instance, *siroki* characterizes *aya*; *tyoozizome no kogaruru made simeru*, which specifies *aya*, is ordered in front of the colour adjective *siroki*.

In the above group of examples, however, both modifying sections seem exactly parallel, without such semantic differences, and yet M2 is positioned at times before, at times after the semantic head.

When comparing *no*-relatives against prenominal relative clauses, we may say that *no* makes for a higher degree of markedness. This greater markedness can be seen to induce a contrastive[19] interpretation, and it is this sort of difference that can be seen to obtain between (33) and (32)/(34). That M2 in (32)/(34) is the relatively more emphasized section is of course also obvious from the fact that M1 is subordinated to it by means of a suspensive form, i.e. only M2 directly modifies the semantic head. In Thai,[20] which uses postnominal relative clauses with the choice of a minor strategy generally available as to use with or without relative pronoun, the greater markedness of the former makes for interpretation of 'speaker's judgement/opinion,' i.e. contrastive usage, whereas the latter conveys 'the general public's evaluation,' i.e. characterization.

4.32 Secondly, observe the following example:

> (35) mukasi onna-harakara hutari arikeri. Hitori   wa   iyasiki
>   of old woman sisters two existed one   EMP lowly
> [otoko no   mazusiki] O hitori wa   ate-naru otoko motarikeri[21]
>   man   poor   one EMP noble   man had
>   (IM:41,1)
> 'of old, there were two sisters. One had a husband of low standing, who was poor, the other a husband of noble rank'

A feature about this example that is useful for our purposes is the parallel structure of the sentence containing the circumnominal relative clause:

> (35') hitori wa [iyasiki]   [otoko no mazusiki]
>   motarikeri
>   hitori wa [ate-naru] [otoko   ]

The two parallel noun phrases (both objects of the verb *motarikeru*, marked by zero object-marker) are zero-conjoined by means of juxtaposition. In both noun phrases the parallel noun *otoko* is modified by an adjective of an antonymous nature. In the first instance, however, *otoko* is also followed by a circumnominal relative clause formed by *no*, whereas in the second, *otoko* (which denotes a person different from the *otoko* in the first noun phrase) stands on its own.

In terms of semantic content, there is little difference between *iyasiki* and *mazusiki*, and in view of the parallel nature of the sentence it may be said that the prenominal (and comparatively unmarked modifier) *iyasiki* is used contrastively, as can also be inferred from the fact that in the story which follows after (35), *iyasiki* and *ate-naru* are used for anaphoric reference to the husbands or their wives:

> (36) *iyasiki otoko motaru* siwasu   no   tugomori ni ue   no
>   lowly man has   December GEN   last-day on top GEN
>   kinu   o   araite tezukara   harikeri (*ibid*.: 2)
>   garment DO   wash+ with-own-hands starched
> 'the one with the lowly husband washed (his) top garment on the last day of December, and starched it herself'

> (37) kore o   kano *ate-naru otoko* kikite   (*ibid*: 6)
>   this DO that noble   man hear+
> 'the noble husband heard this'

The second modifier, *mazusiki*, is not mentioned again, but the effect of the whole story depends on the fact that the first couple are *poor*.

236

Mazusiki, therefore, does not represent an incidental addition, as one might infer from the English rendering tentatively given under (35) above, but a contrastive/emphatic one which concords with its greater markedness. Thus, it seems more appropriate to render the circumnominal relative clause by marking it prosodically, or perhaps as 'who was *moreover* poor;' this is in keeping with the cross-linguistic principle observed by Lehmann (1984:201) that contrastively used modifying elements tend to be positioned last among modifying elements pertaining to the same head.

4.33 Thirdly and finally, observe the following groups of examples:

(38) saru ori   simo [siroki] **tori** no [hasi to   asi to   akaki]
                      M1   M2
that time EMP white   bird   beak and feet and red
O [sigi no   ōkisa naru] O mizu   no ue ni asobi-tutu io   o   kū
   M3
snipe GEN size   is   water GEN on play-play   fish DO eat
                                                    (IM:9,30)
'just then a white bird, whose beak and feet were red,
and which was of the size of a snipe, was playing on the
water eating fish'

With regard to the order of modifying sections in relation to the semantic head *tori* it is interesting to see how the same story, which is built around a famous poem, is phrased in other texts.

One such text is the KKS, where it is found in the *kotobagaki* for No. 411 (the same poem that is contained in the section of the IM containing (35)) in the following form:

(39) saru ori ni [siroki] **tori** no [hasi to asi to **akaki**] O **kawa** no
              M1   M2

hotori ni asobikeri   **river** GEN
side   at played   (KKS:411)
'just then a white bird, whose beak and feet were red,
was playing by the river'

This is not a stacked but a simplex circumnominal relative clause which does not contain the information given in M3 (*sigi no ookisa naru*) in (38). This comparative paucity of information is, incidentally, quite in keeping with the more concise nature of the *Kokinsyuu kotobagaki* when compared to the more elaborate text surrounding the poems of the *Ise Monogatari*.

Ten of the about 70 MSS of the *Kokinsyuu* give the relevant section of this example in an even more concise form:

(39') [siroki] tori no [hasi akaki] O ...
'a white bird, which had red feet'

The same story (complete with poem) is also related in the *Konzyaku Monogatarisyuu* in the following form:

(40) sikaru aida mizu no ue ni [sigi no ookisa aru] [siroki] tori no
      that   time   have

237

[hasi to asi to wa akaki] O asobi-tutu uo o kuu (KMII:331,6)
      MOD   fish
'at that time, on the water a white bird having the size of
a snipe, whose beak and feet were red, was playing on the
water eating fish'

This is again a simplex circumnominal relative clause, but unlike the 'condensed' version of the *Kokinsyuu*, this example contains exactly the same amount of information as (38), the difference being only the position of the modifying sections in relation to the semantic head (*tori*). It is, however, only *sigi no ookisa aru* which is positioned differently, as both *siroki* and *hasi* (*to asi to wa*) *akaki* are ordered in exactly the same way in all four examples given above, and their relation may be understood in the same way as in the examples seen earlier ((33)/(35)). The issue here, then, is the implications of the different positions of *sigi no ookisa(n)aru*.

In both (38) and (40), *sigi no ookisa(n)aru* occupies the position furthest away from the semantic head; unlike in (33), there is no subordination of prenominal modifiers in (40), but in (40), in the normal (unmarked) case, the second prenominal modifier can be assumed to carry the greater emphasis, i.e. *sigi no ookisa aru* is less prominent. Now, that same section is mentioned last in (38) - does that mean that it is emphasized in this case?

I think not, in (38), M3 is not connected to M2 by means of *ga*[22] (see examples (29) (30)), but by means of zero particle. This may be seen to indicate that M3 constitutes an after thought-like parenthesis. Loetscher (1973) has shown that intrasentential nonrestrictive relative clauses consistently contain low-ranked information; in Japanese, the possibility of including a parenthetical nonrestrictive relative clause in a relative-clause sequence apparently was available only in the case of strategy III.

31

A Contemporary View of the Japanese Verbal System

PATRIK LE NESTOUR

SUMMARY

I   A traditional presentation of the verbal system consists of ichi-dan/go-dan (or yo-dan) verbs, and some foreign grammarians even call them

238

weak/strong verbs, in an excessively Western way. It will be proved that ichi-dan does not in fact exist. But rather than give the verb category the adequate zero-dan (or mu-dan) nomenclature, why not simply reach a consensus by naming the two categories: regular verbs/semi-regular verbs...?

II   Going a morphological step further, i.e. after the Ø/a-i-u-e-o basis (dan) conjugation, there has not been, up till now, any consensus in admitting suffixes, auxiliaries and/or longer idiomatic forms in the diverse grammatical categories.

The agglutinant characteristic of the Japanese verbal system provides a model for the notion of 'extension,' allowing the interrelation between 'notional extension' and 'morphological extension.' In fact, hundreds of such extensions exist. Such a double feature analysis may even be ... extended to other languages.

III   Such categorizations lead not only to general rules concerning verb extensions but to the general scheme of language as well. This theoretical correspondence has to be kept in mind until some new metalinguistics, i.e. some more accurate science, allows language categories to be analysed without the help of (approximate) metalinguistic words.

DISCUSSION

1. Morphological categorization at post-stem level

Relevant features.

1. Regular conjugation/verbs

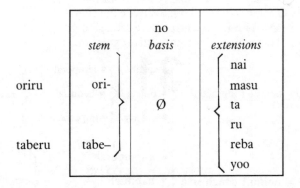

vocalic -i/-e- stem;
clear-cut syllabic isolation from extension;
hence, '*kana*lytic' or alphabetic description.

2. Semi-regular conjugation/verbs

stem		basis	extensions	
kau	ka–			katta
oku	ok–			oïta
oyogu	oyog–	a	–nai	oyoïda
hanasu	hanas–	i	–masu	hanasita
		★	–ta	
tatu	tat–	u	–	tatta
sinu	sin–	e	–ba	sinda
tobu	tob–	o	–o	tonda
nomu	nom–			nonda
toru	tor–			totta

vocalic or consonantic stem;
vocalic stem makes latent -w- appear with -a- basis conjugation;
5 basic conjugations;
9 phonological differentiations with -t- extensions:
-ta/-tara/-tari/-te; hence, alphabetic description, kunrei-shiki.

3. Irregular conjugation/verbs, more or less linked to regular and/or semi-regular verbs

II *Morpho-functional/notional categorization at extension level*

A. Minimal morphological extension. Syntactic differentiation.
1. (rad.)+Ø = tabe,   : suspensive extension
   (rad.)+Ø = tabe-   : compositive extension
2. nom+i+Ø = nomi,   : suspensive extension
   nom+i Ø = nomi-   : compositive extension

nom+u+Ø = nomu~: adjunctive
- agent
- object
- locative
- temporal
- habitual
- imperfective
extensions

nom+u+Ø = nomu.: conclusive
- a-temporal
- habitual
- imperfective
extensions

nom+u+Ø = nomu?: intentional inquiry extension.

B. Complex morphological extension.

240

1. tabe
2. nomi

takunakatta : perfective negative volitive extension.

C. Maximal morphological extension.
'Aki no hekai ga kanjirareru<u>yooninattekimashi</u>ta.'
perfective, socio-distant, referentially resultive to the speaker,
transformative, self-active extension (or extensions).

D. Any morphological extension. Post-stem.
Exhaustive listing problems.
Clusters: 'Tabetakunakunatteshimaimashitakana.'
        'Tabeyooka.'

E. Marker/notion correspondence
1. One marker/one notion extension correspondence
   'Mita.' : '-ta'/perfective extension
2. One marker/ n notions extension correspondence
   'nomu' : '-u'/3x3(x3) extensions (see II, A)
3. n markers/one notion extension correspondence
   'Ikanakerebaikenai.' : '-nakerebaikenai'/obligation extension.

F. *N*ational or idiomatic grammatical view-point.
1. Idiomatic constraints.
   'I've got to get used to it.' 'Naretekita.'
2. Option of grammatical core/extensions.
   'Have you finished *insulting* me?!'

III General definitions
A. Extension

If at least one language features a special marker (morphological extension,
or 'morphex') for one notion (notional extension, or 'notex'), such a notion
belongs to 'the general list of extensions,' or 'glex,' and *may* find some
idiomatic (i.e. morphological) correspondence in any other language. Such
a definition extends to grammatical categories concerning not only verbs
but other lexical items as well.

B. General Language Scheme

Generative system	Equivalent configuration class	(operative marker combining)	UTTERANCES including (verb) extensions
Lexis Relation cluster	Paraphrastic family Modulate abstract occurrence class		

The following explanatory remarks are meant both for readers who are not fully conversant with Japanese, and for those who wish to pursue argument further.

The presentation of the three verbal categories in Japanese varies substantially from one higher education body to another.

Taking into account the European participants in the linguistics section of the 'Rethinking Japan' symposium alone, the following differences are to be observed, that can be divided into six types of nomenclature (numbered 1 to 6).

The third category, however, groups together the 'irregular' verbs, those that do not fit into the first two, and the divergence of classification could only concern certain verbs that have very few irregular forms, such as 'kureru' (imperative: 'kure!' and not *kureyo).

Type of presentation	Verbs 'kau' 'oku' etc.	Verbs 'oriru' 'taberu'	University (among others)	Argumentation
●1	yodan (4 bases)	ichidan (1 basis)	Lyon III Paris-INALCO	●'yodan' applies to classical language and literature, not to contemporary Japanese; and...
●2	godan (5 bases)	ichidan (1 basis)	Venezia Paris VII	●'ichidan' does not fit linguistic criteria, as no 'basis' appears in the conjugation.
●3	strong	weak	Paris-ENA	●metalinguistic terms borrowed from the Germanic verb systems, with no grounds for weakness/strength
●4	others	IRU/ERU verbs	London SOAS	●impossibility of opposing 'kiru' (wear) to 'kiru' (cut), or 'kaeru' (change) to 'kaeru' (go home)
●5	consonantic	vocalic	Konstanz	●inadequate as the differentiation is purely diachronic; the stem of 'kau' (buy) is vocalic in contemporary Japanese
●6	group 1	group II	Lille III	●(any observations will be welcome)

Following the practice of many Japanese teachers, initiated by Suzuki Shigeyuki in 1972, and the advice of a French colleague, Nadine Lucas (CNRS - CRLAO), we will give the group (I and II) categorization priority over our distinction between 'semi-regular' and 'regular' verbs.

I. 1. and 2. Regular/semi-regular verbs: selection of extensions

This selection depends entirely on the table of semi-regular verbs, in which each extension corresponds to one of the five 'bases.' But such a selection is not limitative, since dozens of other extensions are available using the same bases. With regular verbs, to feature these five extensions - to which may be added the '-ta,' '-tara,' '-tari,' '-te' extensions, which are (phonologically) problematic enough - is simply to copy the reference extensions corresponding to the five bases of the semi-regular verbs, for which it is possible to obtain the following translation equivalents:

Extensions	Examples (the choice of 'he' does not exclude the other persons)	Japanese
• (imperfective) negative	'He is not coming down'	'Orinai'
• (imperfective) (socio-)distant (vis-à-vis addressee)	'He is coming down' (future meaning)	'Orimasu'
• perfective	'He has come down'	'Orita'
• suppositive	'If he comes down (...)'	'Oritara (...)'
• alternative	'Sometimes he comes down (...)'	'Oritari (...)'
• injunctive 2nd person (rather non-distant)	'Come down, will you!'	'Orite!'
• imperfective non-distant	'He's coming down' (future meaning)	'Oriru'
• suppositive (rather distant)	'Should he come down (...)'	'Orireba (...)'
• injunctive 1st person (non-distant)	'Let's go down!'	'Oriyoo!'

I. 1. and 2. The problem of transcription and analysis

Since their stem ends with a vowel, regular verbs conjugate and fit together with the various extensions at the junction of two Japanese syllables, which are by principle open syllables, therefore (consonant+) vowel, (C)V. This structure is clearly shown when kana are used, corresponding to the open syllables: 'o-ri-ru,' 'o-ri-na-i,' etc.

The stem of semi-regular verbs, on the other hand, splits into five bases, which *kana*litic writing does not reveal; although it is possible to discern the stem 'ka-' in 'ka-u' (buy), in kana we find 'o-ku' (put down) whereas the stem is 'ok-,' to which the basis '-u' has been added = 'ok-u.'

So it is only in alphabetic transcription that we can oppose 'kiru' (put (clothes) on), which can be analysed 'ki-ru,' regular, and 'kiru' (cut), which can be analysed 'kir-u,' semi-regular.

Furthermore, however useful alphabetic transcription may be for such an analysis, it does not account for the constant recurrence of the final consonant of the stem if the Hepburn transcription is used, based on the correspondence sound/grapheme in English:
'hanasu' / 'hanasanai' / 'hanashimasu' / 'hanashite' (speak)
'tatsu' / 'tatanai' / 'tachimasu' / 'tatte' (stand up).

On the contrary, the phonological transcription - known as 'kunrei-shiki' - more faithful to the structure of Japanese, retains sa/si/su/se/so to transcribe [sa], [ci], [su], [se], [so], and ta/ti/tu/te/to to transcribe [ta], [tci], [tsu], [te], [to], phonologically providing a more economic presentation of the ingredients of the Japanese verbs:
'hanasu' / 'hanasanai' / 'hanasimasu' / 'hanasite'
'tatu' / 'tatanai' / 'tatimasu' / 'tatte.'

I. 1. and 2. The notion of 'stem'

According to the historical position held, the notion of stem and/or root will vary, to answer more or less pragmatical purposes. In Japanese, particularly, the problem can only be resolved by confronting synchronic and diachronic perspectives.

The factitive notional extension - 'notex' - of the verb 'taberu' (eat) is borne by the morphological extension - 'morphex' - '-saseru,' affixed to the stem (in the simple case of a regular verb, without 'basis'): 'tabesaseru' (make/let...eat). This pattern, however, is not applicable to 'oriru' (come/go down): *orisaseru. 'Another' verb pre-exists: 'orosu,' which offers a morphex '-su' the '-s'of which is doubly present in the morphex '-saseru,' both corresponding to the factitive notex.

Although 'oriru' (come/go down) and 'orosu' (make/let...come/go down) have indeed the same root, they do not have the same stem in conjugation:

'ori-ru' / 'ori-nai' / 'ori-masu' / 'ori-te' (regular conjugation), 'oros-u' / 'oros-a-nai' / 'oros-i-masu' / 'oros-i-te' (semi-regular conjugation).

If languages such as English and French etc. were to be examined from a similar point of view, synchrony and diachrony could also be confronted, the latter alone accounting for mechanisms in the grammar of the present day.

SYNCHRONIC STEM	DIACHRONIC STEM
[eksplik]-	
(in)*explic*able	(in)ex*plic*able
*explic*ation	ex*plic*ation
*expliqu*er	ex*pliqu*er
[eksplis]-	
*explic*ite	ex*plic*ite

244

expliciter	*expliciter*
	(dé)*plier*
	(dé)*pliable*
regular verb *oriru* (come down)	*oriru*
semi-regular verb *orosu* (make/let...	*orosu*
come down)	

II. A.1. Further extensions

A zero morphological extension - 'morphex Ø' -, delimited that is by the stem alone of a Japanese regular verb, can, according to the context, hence the syntax, correspond to different notional extensions - 'notexes.' Such is the case of 'tabe,' from the verb 'taberu' (eat):
●'tabe,' suspensive, indicating that the sentence is not finished:
'O-tsumami o tabe, biiru o nondeimashita.'
'I was eating tit-bits, and drinking beer.'

Without going so far as to investigate the conditions in which each of the extensions put forward here is used, it is to be noted that this suspensive bears the mark - the morphex - neither of the perfective, '-ta,' nor of the socio-distant, 'mas-.' In other words there is neither tense agreement nor socio-linguistic register (comparable to 'vous' in French). The choice of this particular suspensive rather than another, '-te,' does however mark a written register, together with either a 'distant' or a 'non-distant' register.

- 'tabe-,' compositive, used for noun-forming, nominalizing:
  'tabekata' (way of eating)
  'tabemono' (thing to eat, food - cf feed)
  'tabenagara' (while eating)

From an epistemological point of view, it can be pointed out that as the words suspensive and compositive concern sentence structure and not the aims of the utterance - moods - or other elements of predication - aspects - they hardly belong to the field of 'notion.' That is something that could apply to a good many (meta)linguistic words that do not clearly define 'functions' or 'intentions' in the grammar of Western - or international? - languages, such as 'infinitive' - which may correspond to a nominalization - or 'present' - which may correspond to any of a number of things, as we shall see.

II. A.2. Further, often implicit extensions

The suspensive and the compositive notexes of a semi-regular verb are borne by the morphex '-i ' affixed to the stem:
'Biiru o nomi, o-tsumami o tabeteimashita.'
'I was drinking beer, and eating tit-bits.'
'nomikata' (way of drinking)

'nomimono' (thing to drink, drink)
'nominagara' (while drinking).
In the same way, it is the morphex '-u' affixed to the stem of semi-regular verbs that bears various and varied notexes:

- •• 'nomu ' = noun adjunct, in a more global, less detailed category than the various relative propositions in Western languages:
- • agentive:
  'sake o nomu hito' = 'the people who are drinking sake.'

- • objective:
  'Itsumo nomu sake wa (…)' = 'The sake she always drinks, (…)'
- • locative:
  'Itsumo nomu tokoro da' = 'It's the place where I always drink.'

It may be noted that, according to context, other notions are also implicit:

- • temporal: the three examples are associated with a moment of time that is more or less precise, or even with the a-temporal, as habitual, but always imperfective:
  'Juusu o nomu toki wa (…)' has either the future meaning of 'When I drink fruit juice, (…)' or the habitual: 'When(ever) I drink fruit juice, (…).'
- •• 'nomu.': sentence conclusive, not only covers one or more of the three notexes: 'a-temporal', 'habitual', 'imperfective', but, at the end of a sentence, can also mark the socio-non-distant register. The exception concerns the same morphex '-u' borne by that other morphex '-masu', verbal notex of distance, and by 'desu', linking verb in the same 'distant' register. But by an interesting phenomenon of time-wear, in both these exceptional forms the '-u' is not generally pronounced; so that what is heard is '-mas' and '-des'. This is the written form in which they will appear in our examples form now on.
  To conclude on the conclusive non-distant '-u', let us note that it is the 'zero distant', the absence of '-mas-', that characterizes it.
- •• 'nomu?': interrogative; and conclusive, as in the 'nomu' above. Needless to say, the interrogative extension combines with the a-temporal/habitual/imperfective notexes.

As a morpheme, the interrogative rising intonation presents certain characteristics: it belongs to the non-distant register, rather like the French 'tu ' among others; except of course, when it is applied to the socio-distant markers '-masu' and '-desu.' These markers can indeed be fully pronounced, adding an affected, attentive note to the socio-distant register:
'Itsu made imasu?': 'How long will she be staying?'
'Nan desu?': 'What is it about?'
On the other hand, if the register is just distant - close to 'vous' in French, etc. - the '-u' will be reduced by the obligatory presence of the interrogative morphex '-ka':

'Itsu made imas'ka?': 'How long's she here for?'
'Nan deska?': 'What's it all about?'

Socio-distance means that one implies 'vous' to one's addressee, even though the utterance may concern no 'vous' nor even the addressee himself.

II. B.1. and 2. Notional/morphological

'Tabetakunakatta': 'I didn't feel like eating (any)'
'Nomitakunakatta': 'I didn't feel like drinking (any)'
Notionally we have here the *perfective* '-ta'-; which has here become '-atta' for adjectival reasons - preceded by the *negative*, '-nai' - here in the compositive form '-nak-' since '-nai' bends to an adjectival conjugation - the negative '-nai' being itself preceded by the *volitive* '-tai' - here in the compositive form '-taku' (whereas in '-nakatta' the adjectival compositive '-u' is eliminated by the first '-a-' in '-atta').
Morphologically, the elements that are dissectable (more or less diachronically), are seen to be more numerous than the notions consciously conveyed.

II. C. Maximalism

'Aki no kehai ga kanjirareruyooninattekimashita': 'There's a touch of Autumn in the air' - or literally, to coin a phrase: *As regards hints of Autumn, it has come of it that they are making themselves felt.* (The asterisks mark a literal translation that does not sound natural). This sentence, which is not particularly literary or stereotyped, can be seen on a postcard sent by an average Japanese speaker, reporting on the state of the season. It is not, therefore, a sentence made up by some linguist trying to stretch...things too far.

Once again, Japanese is using extensions that many languages - Western and others - feel no need to use. Conversely, the notions - and extensions?! - of personal pronoun, article, gender, number, etc., are completely missing from this sentence and from a large majority of Japanese utterances.

Here we find, working back from the end: the *perfective*, '-ta', preceded by the *distant*, '-masu', here in its compositive form, '-mashi', preceded by the verb and auxiliary 'come', 'kuru', here in its compositive form, 'ki-', and representing the notex *referring the action in time to the speaker*, preceded by the verb and auxiliary 'become', 'naru', here in its successive form, '-natte', used when two verbs follow one another in the text and in the logical course of action, and this 'becoming' combines with 'seemingly', 'sort of', 'yooni', to express the *transformative* notex, which is preceded by the *self-active* notex-auxiliary, '-rareru', in its a-temporal - or imperfective - form; the self-active - 'jihatsu' - is one of the notexes of the diathesis of those verbs seen as agent-less, expressed in French by the conjunction of the pronominal and factitive morphexes: 'se font sentir', where an English paraphrase could use the factitive and passive morphexes: *(Autumn) is making itself felt*. Or both languages could simply use the active 'on sent', 'one feels', or with a pinch of the potential: 'on peut sentir', 'one can feel'. In fact, English usually prefers to pretend to implicate

247

the addressee, involving him with the help of an impersonal 'you'. This procedure, which is common in several languages, is impossible in others, such as Swedish...and Japanese.

Finally, the stem 'kanji-', compositive form of 'kanjiru', the active verb 'feel', behaves as a regular verb, as does the auxiliary '-rareru-', while 'naru' is semi-regular, as is '-masu', except for a few details which make it irregular, while 'kuru' is an irregular verb, a kind of hybrid of regular/semi-regular...

As far as the verb is concerned we are out of the wood. What comes before means 'hints (a touch) of Autumn.'

If the notexes used by Japanese in this predication - only some of which, appearing as morphexes, are italicized in the analysis above, and again below - are compared with those used by languages such as French or English, the following table can be drawn up:

notex	morphex		
	Japanese	French	English
'perfective'	. . .–ta	est arrivé ('est' + past part.)	has come ('has' + past part.)
'distant'	–mashi–	Ø	Ø
'referring the action in time to the speaker'	–te-ki–	est + arrivé (passé composé + 'arrivé)	has + come (perfect + 'come')
'transformative'	–yooninat–	Ø	Ø
'self-active'	–rareru–	Ø	Ø
referring to 'in-determinate/ indefinite agents' leading in some languages to an	–rareru–	on	you
'active' verb etc	Ø	sent	feel

It is to be noted that most of the morphexes, which are not explained in this table, are in fact traces of diachronic constraints, and the speaker is not consciously aware of this or that notion. The same applies to the order of morphexes, which may differ not only from one language to another, but also within one language, as is illustrated by the sequential variations of the combination verb (V) - object (O):

V-O 'J'ai rencontré Marie.' O-V 'Je l'ai rencontrée.' V-O 'I met Mary.'/'I met her.' O-V 'Mari ni atta.'/'Kanojo ni atta.' (O)-V 'Atta.'

Even though the present study is centred on the extension of the verb, it is necessary to take into account predication as a whole, and to realize that the nucleus of the predication is difficult to identify. In the predication considered here, is it the Autumn, its arrival (in the shape of epiphenomena), or the sensation felt, or yet again, the 'you' that feels it? If everything that does not belong to the common denominators is eliminated, this 'you' cannot occupy the central, nuclear position. Nevertheless, the theme taken in the Japanese is 'the impressions hinting at Autumn', 'aki no kehai', about which it is said: ⋆It has come of it, kind sir, that they are making themselves felt.⋆ ('King sir' or 'kind lady' being a means of introducing the 'socio-distant.'

Western languages often tend to weigh the indeterminate agent and the active verb against the object and what happened to it. The arm of the scales then takes the shape of a conjunction, 'que,' 'that,' 'dass,' 'che,' affording logico-syntactic play that Western languages orientate as main versus completive, and not as theme versus predicate or theme versus rheme.

Such choices may be considered as vernacular constraints, not totally free, however, from diachronical constraints.

Above all it is necessary to turn to the previous, socio-cognitive stage, which consists in deciding whether or not to speak of the season as an opening to a letter.

In the case of the sentence we have here, any attempt to translate or paraphrase is doomed in advance if the context is taken properly into consideration, that is if the way of starting a letter in a society other than Japanese is considered, rather than the way of expressing the arrival of Autumn in such and such a language other than Japanese. The season would then probably lose its importance.

These considerations lead us so far that we reach a socio-cultural stage which is situated within the elements on the left of the table in the third part of this study, of which you are reminded here:

General Language Scheme

Generative system	Equivalent configuration class	(operative marker combining)	
→————————————————————————→			UTTERANCES including (verb) extensions
Lexis	Paraphrastic family Modulate		
Relation cluster	abstract occurrence class		

Let us return, however, to verbal extensions to examine another example of maximalism.

II. C. Addendum to maximalism

The previous example presented five notexes - notional-extensions - for some twelve morphexes - morpho-extensions.

Here is an example containing ten notexes (underlined), on one verbal stem, acting as semantic nucleus, for some sixteen morphexes.

'Go-chuuron no shina wa, mōo tsukurihajime- sase<u>te</u>itada<u>ite</u>oru-yoo<u>de</u>shi<u>ta</u>wa<u>yo</u>ne.' (Example taken from *Nihongo kyōiku jiten* (Japanese Teaching Dictionary) by Ogawa Yoshio et al., Taishūkan, Tōkyō, 1982, p. 174).

'It would seem that the article you ordered is already being made, wouldn't it?!' That is, word for word, with exclamation marks to account for untranslatable exclamatives, that are however expounded and explained further on: *(...) it seems that you have indeed let us begin to make it, was it not so, Madame?!!*

The last morphex, '-ne', like a question tag, *requesting confirmation* is preceded by *exclamative* '-yo', to which '-wa' is assigned, the *feminine exclamative*, the speaker therefore being a woman, a salesgirl; then we find the *perfective*, '-ta', preceded by the *socio-distant* 'des-', here in its compositive form 'deshi-', preceded by the *apparent* 'yoo' (usually followed, as here, by the linking verb 'des' or 'da'), preceded by a sort of progressive form, the *continuous*, '-teiru', here in its *deferential and non-exteriorising* form, '-teoru', which means the action refers to the person who is speaking in the deferential register. The action in question is *required by the speaker*, as is indicated by the auxiliary '-teitadaku', here in its compositive form (slightly irregular) '-teitadai-', preceded by 'sase-', compositive of 'saseru', *factitive* of 'do', 'suru': this factitive conveys the notions of 'allow... to do', and 'make... do' (cf 'Let us do it.' *'Let's do it.').

Western languages, not knowing how, or being able to 'clutter themselves up' with such a triple articulation - * (I) get (you) to have (me) make)* - prefer to do away with most of the relational considerations, - deferential, as becomes a Japanese salesgirl addressing a client - and put the object (the article in question) with the action (the making): 'It is already being made.' To reach the nodal verb, 'make', 'tsukuru', here in the compositive form, 'tsukuri-', there remains the *inchoative*, the auxiliary '-hajimeru', 'begin to', here in its compositive form '-hajime-'.

Alongside the problem of enunciative and notional choices such as the need or not for personal pronouns or relational verbs orientated to mark register, the distance set between speaker and addressee, analysis dictates options concerning notional and morphological nomenclature: the extension '-saseteitadaku' is composed of the *factitive* '-sase-' (linked to the following auxiliary by the successive '-te'), and the *deferential obtention*, '-itadaku' but the whole expresses a *non-exterior action, in the deferential register*. This is what is found in the stock phrase: 'Miseteitadakimashita.' 'I (much) admired (your exhibition),' used to compliment an artist. A rough literal translation might be: *I obtained that you give me to look.*

II.D. Problems of exhaustive listing

In another cluster of extensions, some extensions that have already been considered may be recognized, combined with others. 'Tabe<u>taku</u>naku<u>natte</u>shimai<u>mashi</u>taka<u>na</u>': 'He may have lost his appetite completely.'

The final particle '-na' is the *exclamative* extension, expressing regret.

The final particle '-ka' is the *interrogative* extension. Just as it is not possible to ask oneself a question about an intention concerning *self-knowledge*, - *Do I feel like...?* (see LE NESTOUR, 1978, 'Détermination de la personne en japonais contemporain,' in *Cahiers de Linguistique Asie Orientale*, No. 3, CRLAO Paris)-, this extension particle '-ka' constitutes a perfect shifter to orientate the action towards an exterior referent - 2nd or 3rd persons - that the context helps to determine. This enables Japanese - at least half of the time - to get along without those other shifters that are personal pronouns and personal verbal inflexion.

In the utterance under consideration the (final) extension - particle '-ka' is alone to play this part, whereas the two previous examples are more complex in this respect, since the extension '-teitadaku' ('obtain') acts as a shifter to P1 (1st person) - *me I obtain that*, or *us we obtain that* -, and the extension '-(sa)seru' (factitive) acts as a shifter to P2 (2nd person) - 'you let (me)(see/make/etc.).' The complexity arises from the combination of the two, since together they refer to 'P1 (holding P2 in high esteem).' This combination is all the more complex as event predication and intricate socio-enunciative predication are interwoven. It should be noted that traditional linguists, grammars, glossaries and dictionaries give greater importance to the event, marked by the verb, disregarding or scorning socio-enunciative elements, the markers of which, if they are inflexions, are not even to be found in dictionaries.

It can be pointed out that the 'personal pronouns' in Japanese, which do not figure in the examples considered here, are usually treated as nouns ('meishi') in Japanese grammars and dictionaries, and not as one of the utterance moods. The presence of a Japanese 'personal pronoun' followed by 'wa' (particle 'marking the syntagmatic relationship' - mrs - of the 'theme' group with the rest of the utterance, which constitutes the 'rheme,' comment, the predicate) does indeed afford it a degree of importance that can only be translated in French, English, etc., by the 'emphatic personal pronouns': 'moi,' 'toi,' 'lui,' in French, stressed pronouns in English, etc. As for 'yo,' 'tu,' 'él' in Spanish, - and other similar phenomena in other Romance languages -, they play a so-called emphatic part, which is in fact 'exclusive', just like 'wa': '*me*' (not him, not you), etc.

After these remarks touching on the socio-enunciative, let us return to extensions. No further personal shifters occur in the utterance. If we continue to work backwards towards the nodal stem, we find, after '-na' and 'ka', the *perfective* '-ta', preceded by the *distant* '-mas-', in its compositive form, '-mashi-', preceded by the '*quite*', '*completely*', '-teshimau', in its compositive form, '-teshimai-', in which the successive '-te' can be seen, followed by the auxiliary verb '-shimau', 'finish (off)', 'perfect'. Stepping further back, the *invalidating* '-nakunaru' is found again, in its successive form '-nakunatte-', made up of the negative '-nai' in its adjectival compositive form, '-naku-', followed by the transformative '-naru', 'become'. Finally the nodal stem 'tabe-' is reached, compositive of 'taberu', 'eat', passing through the *volitive* '-tai', in its compositive form '-taku-'.

And so 'Tabe<u>takunakunatteshimaimashitakana</u>' comprises seven notio-extensions - seven notexes, underlined in the analysis above -, but many others have had to be mentioned in order to account for the fifteen or sixteen markers that can be diachronically distinguished.

The problem of an exhaustive list cannot be dissociated from a complete inventory of all conceivable extensions, in Japanese or in any other language already studied or remaining to be studied.

A much shorter example like:

'Tabeyooka.'

'Shall we eat?' or 'Are we going to eat?'

can once more pose the problem of exhaustivity in two ways.

To begin with, in regard to the traditional description of the marker '-yoo', described above (in Remarks, I, 1 and 2. Regular/semi-regular verbs. Selection of extensions) in terms of *1st person injunctive*, taking as example the verb 'oriru', 'go down', which yields 'Oriyoo', 'Let's go down!', it should be remembered that this inflexion-extension '-yoo' marks a person (P1), a fairly exceptional phenomenon in Japanese, where personal inflexion is reputedly lacking.

So traditional grammar, in accordance with tradition (?), still classifies '-yoo' in the category of *eventuality*, (suiryō), a mood which has no doubt a longer past than that of *1st person injunctive*. If it persists in a good many utterances, such as '-deshoo', 'it is doubtless' (to the obvious exclusion of any injunctive), it can by no means be applied to the action verbs 'go down' or 'eat.' And yet, however, - and this is the second problem set by exhaustivity - these notexes, *1st person injunctive interrogative* - that can be syncretized in *1st person incitative*, suggestion, proposal, is also rendered in other languages by a modal or mood, *hypothetic subjunctive* such as 'Suppose we ate?!' Which of these three notional nuances should be selected? Dilemma or ambiguity?

II. E. *Marker/notion correspondence*

Only paragraph 3 requires a little explanation here, concerning the morphex (morpho-extension) '-nakerebaikenai' on the one hand and the notex (notio-extension) that it 'translates': the mood of *obligation*. Japanese speakers have obviously no need to be reminded of the periphrase used in Japanese to express *obligation*: impossibility, 'ikenai', 'that can't work', preceded by the negative suppositive, '-nakereba', 'if (it) does not...'

Elsewhere, *obligation* can take on other forms, use other periphrases:
if (it) does not...it will not become,
'-nakerebanaranai'
when (it) does not...it can't work,
'-naitoikenai'
etc.

It is only in translation, however, that these are felt to be periphrases, and the translations sound so peculiar that they are set between asterisks. The phrases, morphexes, simply correspond to the notex of obligation.

The Japanese also by no means feels the morphological redundancy to be strange in:

252

'Ikanakerebaikenai.'
If we don't go it can't work.
'We must go.'
No more than the verb 'go' really sounds redundant, in English, when expressing *intention* in 'going to':
'He's going to go there to-morrow.'
Ashita iku koto ni iku.
No more than the verb 'aller' sounds redundant, in French, in the expression of the (so-called 'immediate') future:
'Elle va y aller dans deux ans.'
Ni nen nochi ni iku koto o iku.
'She'll be going there in two years' time.'

II. F.1. Idiomatic constraints

In the same way, one can but notice the similar 'non-redundancy' of 'get' in the English expression of *obligation* followed by *tranformative*:
'I've got to get used to it.'
Nareru koto o eru kato o eta.
'Naretekonai to ikenai.'

F.2. Option of grammatical core/extensions

Many examples can be taken to raise the problem of the choice of the nucleus, which differs from one language to another. Although it has already been raised in the remarks on C. Maximalism, the observation made can be confirmed by showing that to render the *interruptive* aspect 'finir de...'/'stop...'/'...yameru', is not sufficient to translate the *outraged, exasperated* element in the remark-rebuke-retort:
'Vous avez fini de m'insulter?'
'Stop insulting me, will you?' 'Ii kagen ni shitekudasai.' *Make good measure.* 'Measure (your words)!'
    While the French and English analyse their versions as having a verb in the *imperative*, 'arrête de...', 'stop...', with a *completive*, 'insulter', or a *nominalized*-complement, 'insulting', it might be expected that Japanese, on the contrary, would have a verb, 'insult', followed by a certain number of extensions.
    And yet, because of syntactic constrains, here too, it is the modality-verb - here *(make) measure*, if not 'stop' - that occupies the nuclear position, to the exclusion of the verb 'insult', which remains simply implicit, but which would be neither incongruous nor impossible: only the need for the retort to be brief is...imperative...:
    '(Bujoku suru no wa) ii kagen ni (shitekudasai).'
    (Insulting [me]) good measure (make [please])
On the principle that the situation is sovereign - in the land of situationalism - it is true that other languages, similarly leaving implicit the 'stream of insults,' 'fact of being insulted' elements, opt for short retorts that are highly imperative, in various meanings of the word: 'Ça suffit!'
'Stop it, will you!?', 'Stop it!'

253

III. General definitions

A. Extension

If at least one language features a special marker (morphological extension, or 'morphex') for one notion (notional extension, or 'notex'), such a notion belongs to 'the general list of extensions', or 'glex', and may find some idiomatic (i.e. morphological) correspondence in any other language.

Such a definition extends to grammatical categories concerning not only verbs but other lexical items as well.

B.   General Language Scheme

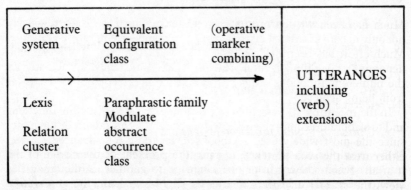

Most of the elements in this table are taken from CULIOLI ANTOINE, 'Valeurs modales et opérations énonciatives,' in *Modèles Linguistiques*, tome I, fascicule 2, 1979, Presses Universitaires de Lille. The right hand section is entirely by the author of the present article.

32

Synchronic and Diachronic Approaches to the *noda* Sentence

YOKO KUBOTA

Much has been written on the *noda* sentence which is used extensively not only in conversational discourse but also in modern literature narrative. Much effort has been made especially since 1970 in search of a common denominator or a fundamental principle which could explain systematically the numerous functions of *noda*, but a generally acceptable theory is far from being achieved.[1]

In the meantime it is essential to make an exhaustive list of its functions and to elaborate a comprehensible way to present it to students of Japanese, since the most widely used textbooks, even those for advanced classes, either treat the *noda* sentence in a totally inadequate way or do not treat it at all. From a practical point of view, i.e. from the learner's point of view, the chapter on *nodesu* written by Alfonso 20 years ago can still be considered the most comprehensible of all, though even this fails to enumerate *noda's* many functions.[2]

The first part of this paper will list as many *noda* applications as possible and present them in a more systematic way to serve an educational purpose. Because of the limitation on space, I'm obliged to limit myself to a summary of my study. In the second part, there will be a brief discussion on how *noda* was used in the past, dating back to the Edo period, as well as on the process of its popularization, of which knowledge is indispensable in the search for *noda's* basic function.

1.	*Dakara* P *Sorede* Q *noda.* *Shitagatte*	Ex. *Kobo wa byōin da. Dakara* *shizukani suru* <u>*noda*</u>
2.	*nodakara* P *noda. Dakara* Q *noda. Sorede*	Ex. *Koko wa byōin na* <u>*noda*</u> *Dakara shizukani shinasai.*
3.	*nodakara* P *noda. Dakara* Q *noda.* *noda. Sorede*	Ex. *Koko wa byōin na* <u>*noda*</u> *kara* *shizukani suru* <u>*noda*</u>.

Let us now look at the patterns in which *noda* expressions appear. First of all, the *noda* assertive often appears in Patterns 1 to 3. By using *noda* the speaker indicates how a proposition is related to another or more propositions. Most frequently the relationship made evident by *noda* is that of 'cause and effect,' or 'premise and consequence.' As shown in the patterns, *noda* can follow either P (cause or premise) or Q (effect or consequence).

4.	*Kekkyoku* P₁, P₂ ... Pₙ. *Yōsuruni* Q *noda* *Tsumari* *Jitsuwa*	Ex. . . . *Kōshite, dare nimo hontōno riyū ga wakaranai mama, shichinen tachi minpō dai sanjūjō ni yotte kekkyoku shibō no nintei o ukeru koto ni natta node aru.* (*Suna no onna*)

4.

P₁, P₂ ... Pₙ. *Kekkyoku* / *Yōsuruni* Q *noda* / *Tsumari* / *Jitsuwa*

Ex. . . . *Kōshite, dare nimo hontōno riyū ga wakaranai mama, shichinen tachi minpō dai sanjūjō ni yotte kekkyoku shibō no nintei o ukeru koto ni natta <u>node</u> aru.* (*Suna no onna*)

5.

P₁, P₂ ... Pₙ. *Kekkyoku* / *Yōsuruni* Q₁, Q₂ ...Qₙ *noda.* / *Tsumari* / *Jitsuwa*

Patterns 4 and 5 show the contexts in which a premise or a series of facts (P₁, P₂, ...Pₙ) is paraphrased, summarized and explained in Q, or a new interpretation (Q) is added to the premise (P). These are frequently used in writing.

6.

Q.   P *noda*   'Q. It's because P.'

Pattern 6 is used when a reason is added after Q is uttered as in: *Kinō watashi wa ie ni imasen deshita. Kyoto e itta <u>nodesu</u>.* This *noda* can be replaced by *karada* except in the following cases:
1) if Q is a request, imperative, desire or feelings
Ex. *Komatta na Nijuppun ijō kakaru to tokkyū ni norenaku naru <u>nda</u>.*

2) if Q represents an additional information related to what is previously said.
Ex. *Kore wa Ginia no kitte desu. Tomodachi ni moratta <u>ndesu</u>.*
In addition, Q and P can be uttered by two different persons in a dialogue as in Pattern 7.

7.

A: Q *ne.*
B: P *noda.*

Ex. A: *Y-san wa yoku hatarakimasune.*
B: *Ee, ano hito wa totemo majimena <u>ndesu</u>.*

Noda is obligatory when one affirms or negates a reason as seen in Patterns 8 and 9. Pattern 8 affirms the reason (P) for a fact or situation (Q), whereas Pattern 9 negates it. Notice that Pattern 9 does not negate the predicate Q. Patterns 8 and 9 can also be explained as follows: that *noda* affirms and *nodewanai* negates P in a PQ combination set up by the speaker or by the listener.

8.	P *kara* Q. *noda.* *tame ni*

Ex. *Shinji rarete iru kara hashiru <u>noda.</u>*

9.	P *kara* Q *nodewanai.* *tame ni*

Ex. *Asobu tame ni nihon e kita <u>nodewa nai.</u>*

10.	*nodesuga* P *nodesukedo* Q. *nodakedo*

Ex. *Atsui <u>ndesu</u> ga, mado o aketemo yoroshii deshō ka?*

Pattern 10, instead, demonstrates a *noda* with polite value used in the expression *nodesuga*. Some textbooks say that *noda* attenuates the tone, but this is misleading, because it induces students to make sentences like *Sensei, aisu kuriimu ga tabetai <u>ndesu</u> ka?* which most probably offends the teacher. Therefore, it must be clearly taught to the students that only this form of *noda*, unlike many others, can attenuate the tone or can be polite.

The *noda* sentence at the beginning of a discourse as in Pattern 11 serves as an introductory information to help the listener understand the story that the speaker is going to tell. Pattern 10 can also be interpreted as one form of Pattern 11.

11.	P *noda.* $Q_1, Q_2 \ldots Q_n.$ *nodakedo*

Ex. *Kondo, tonari no heya ni ryūgakusei ga hikkoshite kita <u>ndesu</u> yo. Nihongo ga hanasenai no ka to omottara, totemo jōzu deshita.*

Now let's look at *noda* in questions. WH-questions asking why, how or in what way almost always contain *noda*, but other WH-questions and Yes-no questions have both versions with or without *noda*. Generally speaking, the version without *noda* is a simple information seeking question, whereas the *noda* version has various conditions and connotations.

12.	*Naze* *Dōshite* + *nodesu ka?* *Dōyatte*	
13.	*Doko* *Itu* + *nodesu ka?* *Nani* *(masu ka?)* *Dare*	
14.	Yes-no questions	*nodesu ka?* *masu ka?*

Firstly *noda* is obligatory when the question is based on what the speaker has observed or is observing

Ex. A: (observing that B is going somewhere) *Doko e iku ndesu ka?*

                                   *iki masuka?

    B: *Chotto eki made.*

Secondly, *noda* often implies surprise, doubt or reproach.

Ex. A: (seeing that B looks sick) *Dō shita ndesu ka?*

                    (Cf. *Dō shimashita aka?*)

    B: *Onaka ga itai ndesu.*

Thirdly, in WH-questions, the *noda* version is used when the speaker assumes that the listener knows the answer which he simply asks the listener to tell.[3] Fourthly, in Yes-no questions, the *noda* version asks for a confirmation of an assumption made by the speaker. Therefore, appropriate answers are *Sō desu* or *Chigai masu.*

Ex. A: *Kinō eiga e itta ndatte?*

    B. *Un, sō da yo.*

Lastly, the use of *noda* is obligatory when one wants to ask, not whether the predicate is true or not, but whether his assumption made on where, when, why, etc. about the predicate is correct as in Pattern 15. And the negative answer to such a question is represented by Pattern 16.

15.	A: P_1 Q *nodesu ka?* B: *Hai, sō desu.* (P_1 about Q is correct). *Iie,* P_2 Q *nodesu.*

Ex. A: *Byōin e ashita iku ndesu ka?*

    B: *Ashita iku nja arimasen.*

    Asatte iku ndesu.

    (Here, what is negated is when, and not the predicate).

16.	P_1 Q *nodewanai.* P_2Q *noda*	'It's not P_1 but P_2 that Q.'

Ex: *Sō iu riyū de kaite yaru nodewanai.*
'It is not for that reason that I write him.'
Cf. *Sō iu riyū de kaite yaranai.*
'For that reason, I don't write him.'

Noda's functions like confirmation and emphasis are reinforced by certain final particles as seen in Patterns 17 and 18. With these expressions the speaker wants either to confirm what the listener is saying or to emphasize what he himself is saying. Pattern 18 is also used as imperative, as observed by Alfonso, usually by parents speaking to their children, for example, *Jidōsha ni ki o tsukeru ndesu yo.*

17.		*noda na.*	'You mean...?'
	What the listener is saying +	*noda ne.*	'You are saying..., right?'
		nodarō?	
18.		*noda.*	'Listen, I'm saying...'
	What the speaker is saying +	*noda yo.*	'..., you know.'
		noda na.	

Now if we pass on to the form *nodarō*, it can be classified in the following patterns.

19.	*P kara,* *Q nodarō.*	P: premise based on a fact or on observable evidence
	P Dakara	Q: - conjecture on reason
20.	*Q nodarō.* P.	deduction
21.	A: P *ne.*	
	B: Q *nodarō.*	

Ex. - *Ii nioi ga shitekuru kara keeki wa mō dekita nodarō.*
- *Keeki wa mō dekita nodarō. Ii nioi ga shitekuru.*

Pattern 19 is used when the speaker makes a conjecture on a cause/reason or a deduction based on a fact. P and Q can be inverted as in Pattern 20 or can be uttered by two different persons in a dialogue as in Pattern 21. Moreover, the premise can be verbally latent as in Pattern 22. In this case, circumstances or what the speaker is observing constitutes the premise on which he makes a conjecture.

| 22. | (observable evidence) Q *nodarō.* | Q: - conjecture on reason - deduction based on observable evidence. |

Ex. (seeing C coming in a sweat) *Kare wa hashitte kita nodarō.*

259

| 23. | [P *kara* Q]   *nodarō.* | P: fact |
| | [P *Sorede* Q] | Q: fact |

Ex. *Kare wa okusan ga byōki da kara konai <u>nodarō</u>.*
'He doesn't come probably because his wife is sick.'
Kore wa kinu da kara takai <u>nodarō</u>.
'This is expensive, probably because it's made of silk.'

Pattern 23 looks similar to Pattern 19, but is different in meaning. It's used when both P and Q are facts and the speaker assumes that the reason why Q is P.

These numerous functions of the *noda* sentence can be systematized in the following scheme, in which P represents not only a proposition, but also a group of propositions, an adverbial phrase or a noun phrase put in a certain relationship with Q which can be a proposition or simply a predicate. Moreover, the *no* has the function of relating propositions and delimiting the area on which various sentence ending forms following the *no* can extend their own functions. As we have observed in many paragraphs, without the nominalizer *no*, these sentence ending forms can act only on the immediately preceding predicate (Q), in other words *no* is indispensable if one wants to affirm, negate or make an assumption on other elements of the sentence (P).

			sentence ending forms
[P Q]	*no*	*da*	assertion
		da yo ⎫	confirmation
$[P_1, P_2... Q_1, Q_2...]$		*da ne* ⎬	emphasis, etc
		da na ⎭	
etc.		*darō*	conjecture
		desu ka?	asking for confirmation
		dewanai	negation

Now, as I mentioned in the Introduction, among the previously proposed theories on *noda's* basic function, none has ever been demonstrated comprehensive enough to be considered generally acceptable. As some scholars observe, it could be because the modern usage of *noda* is not stabilized yet. Or it could have been abused or misused in the past. This is why it is significant to trace back the history of *noda's* development in the hope that a diachronic approach would help us to understand actual variegated usages. The following is what emerged from a preliminary survey.

Early examples of *noda* or *nodesu* must be looked for in the spoken language, i.e. a literature which represents the spoken language of the period. This is simply because the *no* which nominalizes verbs and adjectives appeared after the appearance of *da* and *desu* which are colloquial versions of *niteari* in the case of *da*, and *nitesōrō* or *degozaimasul/dearimasu* in the case of *desu*. Both *da* (or *ja* which was mainly used by aged respectable men) and *desu* were originally attached only to a noun to specify or identify the subject, and constituted assertive sentences. In classical language, which dominated as official written language up till the end of WWII, this specifying and assertive function was assumed by *nari*.

Early examples of *da* and *desu* cannot be found in literary works with certain pretensions to being culturally refined, since in such cases the long-established classical language was to be used. Instead, they can be found mainly in *gesaku*.

The history of *da* and *desu* is an intriguing yet fascinating subject, even if much is still unknown, but here, discussion will be concentrated on early examples of *noda* and *nodesu*.

Materials consulted:

around the Kan'ei era	(*kanazōshi*)	*Kinō wa Kyō no Monogatari*
		Seisuishō (1623)
around Genroku era	(*hanashibon*)	*Shika no makifude* (1686)
	(*ukiyozōshi*)	*Keisei Kintanki* (1711)
around Tenmei era	(*hanashibon*)	*Kanokomochi* (1772)
		Kikijōzu*(1773),
		Tai no misozu*(1779)
	(*sharebon*)	*Yūshi Hōgen* (1770)
		Tsūgen Sōmagaki* (1787)
	(*kibyōshi*)	*Edo-umare Uwaki no Kabayaki**
		(1785)
around Bunka and	(*kokkeibon*)	*Ukiyoburo** (1809)
Bunsei eras	(*ninjōbon*)	*Shunshoku Umegoyomi** (1832)

*works in which examples of the *noda* sentence have been found.

Among the materials consulted, examples of *noda* and other related forms were found only in *hanashibon*, *kibyōshi*, *kokkeibon* and *ninjōbon*, more specifically in dialogues among common inhabitants of Edo from the Tenmei era on. Other related forms of *noda* are: *nosa*, *noka*, *nokae*, *nodesu*, *nodearimasu* and *nodegozaimasu*.

The following is the summary of the preliminary study on the early use of *noda* and other related forms based on the above-mentioned materials and some previous studies.

1) *Da* is considered to be typical of the spoken language of the oriental regions, and its first written examples, though very scarce, can be found in works like *Zōhyō Monogatari* and *Saiō Tōhyakuin* of the early Edo period.[4] On the other hand, examples of *da*'s prior forms, *ja* and *ya*, can be found in writings of the Muromachi period on mainly in *kyōgen*, *kanazōshi* and *shōmono* (commentary works on Chinese classics) which reflect the spoken language of *kamigata* region.

2) *Da* was originally attached to a noun and its use was extended to verbs and adjectives by means of an additional particle *no* which nominalizes

them. According to Yuzawa Kōkichirō, when *da* was attached to a verb or an adjective, *no* was normally inserted in between, and that *da* assumed an assertive function.

He adds that there are cases in which *no* does not accompany *da*, for example, *shiranē da* or *aruku da*, but that this constitutes a rude speech.[5]

3) Concerning the origin of *desu*, several theories exist. The scholars are, however, instead almost unanimous in saying that the modern *desu* with polite value originates in the prostitutes' jargon of Edo, and that its use diffused among men and women of other social classes only towards the end of the Edo period.

Note that there is another *desu* which appears in *kyōgen*, and continued appearing till the middle of the Edo period, but since this was used exclusively by males with an arrogant tone, it is distinguished from the polite *desu*.

As for *desu* attached to verbs and adjectives, there existed two versions, with or without *no*, but the version with *no* was considered to be normal. Later in the Meiji era, the version without *no* constituted a jargon for young male intellectuals, *shosei*, and in *mandan*.[6]

4) Examples of *noda* in the late Edo period (posterior to the Tenmei era) can be classified as follows according to their usages:
a. Questions: WH: *Itsu jibun kara warui nodae. (Shunshoku Umegoyomi)*
   Dōshite shitte kita noda. (")
   Yes-no: *Omahan wa wazuratte isassharu nokae.* (")
b. Rhetorical questions expressing reproach:

   Kore dō suru noda. Ore o dare da to omou. (Shinagawa Nori)
   Koresa nani o fuzakeru noda. (Myōchikurinbanashi Shichihenjin)
   Dō shiyagaru noda. (Tōkaidōchu Hizakurige).

c. Introductory remark
   Sono musuko ga...ii yome ga aru ndaana. Sore wo nandemo fukaku kakushite... (Musume Setsuyō)
d. Explains why or how of one's action
   Kyō no asa-mairi niwa nan demo tazuneyō to omotte...dete kita nde arimasaana. (Shunshoku Umegoyomi) Matte orimashita yo, hisashiburide ouwasa ga kikitai ndesu yo. (Sandai Banashi)
e. [P *kara* Q] *noda* which affirms the reason P
   Jimee da sō da kara...dete iru nodarō. (Tsūgen Sōmagaki)
f. Asking for confirmation in the sense 'You mean...?'
   Mata noru noka. (Tōkaidō Hizakurige)
   Mō omee keeru noka. (Shunshoku Umegoyomi)
   Wachiki o oijime naharu ndesuka. (Shunshoku Edomurasaki)
g. Imperative
   Korya Kin-bō ya...anmari sewa o yakasezuni otonashiku shite iru noda yo. (Musume Setsuyō)
h. Assertive
   Kitsune o ketsune to iu yori ii nosa. (Ukiyoburo)
   Are wa nan no ka gan o kakeru nosa. (Tsūgen Sōmagaki)

Tada, ma ga warui to mōshita ndesu wa ne. (Shunshoku Edomurasaki)

5) These examples show clearly that most of the actual usages of *noda* were already present in the late Edo period, when *da* and *desu* were gaining popularity.[7] It must be remembered that it developed in the spoken language, thus always addressed to an interlocutor.

6) On the other hand, in the materials, there were quite a few cases in which the speakers of the Edo period do not use *noda* but the present-day speakers would use it:

Kono aida watashi ga ne...hashitte mairimashita ga.... (Today one would say: *mairimashita ndesu* ga) (*Ukiyoburo*)

Dōzo go-fukuzō naku osshatte kudasai mase. Sore ga watashi no tame ni narimasu. (Today: *narimasu node* or *naru nodesu*). (*Ukiyoburo*)

Dōshite kita. (Today: *kita nda.*) (*Shunshoku Umegoyomi*)

Kesa wa Myōken-sama e mairi ni kita tsumori de uchi wa demashita yo (Today: *deta ndesu* ga ne) (*Shunshoku Umegoyomi*)

Sa, sore dakara mo koko o keeritaku arimasen yo. (Today: *nai ndesu* yo) (*Shunshoku Umegoyomi*)

Chito matanse. Inma daiji no okyaku ga aru. (Today: *aru nda.*) *Tōkaidō Hizakurige*)

The use of *noda* from the Meiji era on was largely influenced by the complicated process towards *genbun itchi* (the search for a new writing style based on the colloquial language). Some important facts relevant to the *noda* sentence are as follows:

1) The use of *desu* was rapidly generalized in the Tokyo area among men and women of various social classes, which constituted a positive element for its later standardization. However, given its provenance from the gay quarters, *kuruwa*, there was an initial resistance to its use in writing. Two facts contributed to its further diffusion:

a) the style in *desu* was employed by Yamada Bimyō from 21st year of Meiji in his literary works (ex. *Kochō*) not only in dialogues but also in the narration.

b) The style in *desu* was adopted by elementary school Japanese textbooks starting from 1903.

2) As for *desu* attached to verbs and adjectives, while the use of *desu* without *no* was considered to be a jargon or somewhat dialectal, the use of *nodesu* gained more and more popularity.

3) Yoshida Kanehiko points out some literary works in which the use of *noda* is prominent, if not abused (ex. *Diving* by Funabashi Seiichi, *Shin'ya no Shuen* by Shiina Rinzō) and observes that among *debut* works of post-war writers, the tendency is rather diffuse.[8]

4) The origin of *nodearu* is attributed to the style adopted by early translators of Western languages and then by politicians in assembly speeches. It has been consistently used by various writers, including Ozaki Kōyō, Natsume Sōseki and Mori Ōgai, and in most cases, these writers used *nodearu* even in cases where it was not necessary, in other words they abused *nodearu*.

In conclusion, by the late Edo period, *noda* and other related forms were widely used in the colloquial language, and most of its actual usages were already present. Its popularity was reinforced by the adoption of the writing style in *da*, *desu* and *dearu*, promoted by Meiji writers, and diffused throughout the country by newspapers and elementary school textbooks. In addition, in this period, it began to be used in the narration as well as in dialogues, and as a consequence, it was extended to public speeches and editorials. Moreover, writers must have found in *noda* an efficient tool in comments and expositions to define complicated ideas precisely, as *noda* is indispensable to negate an adverbial phrase in order to present another, differently from simply negating a predicate.

The adoption of *noda* in writing probably contributed to the reinforcement of its certain usages which appear more typically in writing than in dialogues, for ex. *noda* relating various sentences and propositions in a paragraph, or *noda* which explains circumstances and motives of actions. *Nodatta*, which was analyzed by Mikami Akira, is also used typically in writing.[9]

Lastly a comment must be added concerning the role of this diachronic study in the search for a basic function of actual usages of *noda* and other related forms. Many studies have been done on phrases which end in the form *noda*, with *da* that has its own assertive value, differently from other sentence ending forms equally attached to the *no*. Moreover, *noda's* basic function has been widely perceived as explanation by many scholars starting with Alfonso and Kuno Susumu. Tanomura Tadaharu who has recently presented the most complete survey on *noda* studies to date, attributes the origin of this theory to Kindaichi Haruhiko who had studied the form *nodearu* in Mori Ōgai's literary works.[10] If this is true, Tanomura's doubt on the validity of the explanation theory is legitimate, because as is clear from the diachronic study, *nodal nodearu* assertive was not necessarily the most basic form amongst all the forms of the *noda* sentence. Besides, there is a risk that, concentrating only on the form *noda*, which today also appears frequently in writing, one tends to neglect other original forms and usages, i.e. exclusively in dialogue, hence subject to emphasis and various emotional overtones. Thus, it is natural that proposals based on the form *noda* have never been successful in explaining other forms of the *noda* sentence.

33

Intersection of Tense and Aspect in the Dynamic Predicate in Japanese

REIKO SHIMAMORI

Tense is a grammatical category which localizes an utterance in time by projecting it onto one of the temporal points. Various ways of categorizing tenses are possible. The Japanese language adopts that which opposes past to non-past.

Aspect is another grammatical category which expresses, in one word, the representation of the duration of a process. Various kinds of representations of aspect are possible. We will select only the perfective/ imperfective opposition as being an aspectual opposition which is expressed by V/V-*te iru* (V-*ta*/V-*te ita*), for this opposition is the only systematic and significant one in the Japanese language.

Thus, tense and aspect are two fundamentally different categories. However, the perfective, as an aspectual notion, is very often confused with the past, as a notion of tense. This is why *ta* is understood to be either a temporal sign or an aspectual one by linguists, which leads to quite interesting controversies.

Matsushita Daizaburō calls *ta* the 'auxiliary of the perfective.' Kindaichi Haruhiko states that *ta* indicates the past with a static predicate and the perfective with a dynamic predicate, both belonging to the temporal category. According to Suzuki Shigeyuki, *ta* can have two values: the past and the perfective, but the latter is only a variant of the former. Finally, Teramura Hideo states that *ta* can express the past (temporal notion) or the perfective (aspectual notion) depending on the context.

Let us compare these two sentences:

1-a. Kyonen wa sakura ga *saita*.
   'Last year, the cherry tree was in flower.'
1-b. Sakura ga kirei-ni *saita* nā.
   'The cherry tree blossom is beautiful.'

For Matsushita and Kindaichi, *saita* in examples 1-a and 1-b has the same value: the perfective. This does not explain why example 1-a refers to a past state, while example 1-b expresses a present state. For Suzuki and Teramura, *saita* in example 1-a has a past value and 1-b a perfective value. However, the value of the perfective (aspectual notion) cannot be a variant of the value of the past (temporal notion), and why should the same verbal form take on a temporal or an aspectual value in different contexts?

On the other hand, how can we explain the difference in meaning between sentences 1-b and 1-c?

265

1-c.   Sakura ga kirei-ni *saite iru* nā.
       'The cherry tree blossom is beautiful.'

All these examples illustrate the problems of tense and aspect notions. We propose in this study to examine in depth the intersection of these two notions, and not to definitively solve the problems, but to clarify them.

First of all, we will talk briefly about the different values assigned to the verbal form V-*ta* and to the state form V-*te iru*. Then we will examine closely some examples which are subject to different interpretations, and by analyzing them, we will try to solve the problem of the intersection of tense and aspect.

The main object of this study is to clarify the tense and aspect system in Japanese, in order to foresee and explain certain kinds of mistakes made by foreigners who are learning this language.

I. VALUES OF TENSE AND ASPECT

I-1. Values of tense (past/non-past)

The tense system in Japanese is grammatically based on a past/non-past dichotomy, which is morphologically expressed by the opposition V-*ta*/V.

The temporal category links the moment of the process concerned to the moment of the enunciation (or to the moment of the main clause for a relative time). It is, therefore, a relative value linked to a point of reference.

Moreover, tense will express the moment which the speaker has in mind. The past indicates that the speaker has focussed on a bygone moment; the non-past, on and after the instant of the enunciation.

I-2. Values of aspect (perfective/imperfective)

Aspect too concerns time. However, unlike tense, aspect is not related to another point of reference. It expresses the speaker's view of the course of the process. In Japanese, only the opposition perfective/imperfective can be considered as aspectual, other values (ex. inchoative, progressive, iterative, resultative...) being 'semantic extensions.'

By 'imperfective' we understand the durative aspect: the action is presented linearly, and its middle phase is emphasized. This value is, in Japanese, mostly expressed by a state form V-*te iru* (or V-*te ita*). By 'perfective' we understand a non-durative aspect: the action is presented as a whole, like a point. The simple form (the past and non-past form) of the verb usually has this value.

II. TEMPORAL AND ASPECTUAL VALUES OF THE PAST FORM V-*TA*

The values of the past form V-*ta* are still the subject of controversy. Various interpretations of *ta* have been distorted (in our opinion) by the hypothesis that tense and aspect are on the same level, the one eliminating the other automatically. This is because our predecessors have presupposed that one form should represent a single value. Tense and aspect are, in fact, two notions located at different levels, because aspect can combine freely with tense, and one verbal form can normally express these two values at the same time.

Let us examine the following sentences:

2-a. Kesa, shimbun wo yomimashi*ta* ka.
      'Did you read the newspaper this morning?'
2-b. Iie, yomimasen-deshi*ta*.
      'No, I did not.'
3-a. Kesa no shimbun wo mō yomimashi*ta* ka.
      'Have you already read this morning's newspaper?'
3-b. Iie, mada yon*de imasen.*/mada yomi*masen*.
      'No, I have not read it yet.'

Ta in examples 2-a and 2-b expresses the 'past' from a temporal point of view (because the speaker places himself at a completed moment: *kesa* 'this morning'), and the 'perfective' from an aspectual point of view (for the action is presented as a whole without showing the medial phase).

Similarly, *ta* in example 3-a indicates the 'present' and 'perfective.'

One might be puzzled by the 'present' value given to the 'past' form V-*ta*. However, if we consider the origin of *ta*, it will be easier to accept this idea which may seem somewhat original today. This morpheme now called the 'past auxiliary' comes from *tari* which is a mixture of *te* and *ari*. The presence of the state verb *ari* in this auxiliary plays a decisive role in its meaning: *tari* expressed the 'present' state resulting from a past action. The speaker places himself at the moment of enunciation, and not at the moment of completion of the action. The second value of *ta*, present/ perfective, comes from the value of *tari*. *Ta* in this sense does not describe an action completed at a given moment in the past, but its present result. This is why we assign the value of 'present' to the past form.

To facilitate understanding, we will schematize these two values of *ta* in the following table:

Table 1

Aspect \ Tense	Past	Non-past (Present)
Perfective	yon-*da*(1)	yon-*da*(2)

N='Now'   S: The speaker's point of view

In this table, the action in the two cases is presented as a point. The past form *yonda* 'to have read' then has the aspectual value 'perfective.'

Concerning the temporal value, the speaker can place himself at the moment of the process, which in this case is a completed moment. The action is considered to be totally detached from the present. This is the case for *yonda*(1) which has a past value. In this acceptation, *ta* will be used in a narrative description, a story, a historical text...; it describes a past fact in an objective way.

For *yonda*(2), the speaker places himself at the moment of the enunciation. He describes the action as being in contact with the present, as its consequences are being envisaged at the present moment. The present state is emphasized, the completion of the action being secondary. *Yonda*(2) has a present value. *Ta* in this use expresses the recognition of a new fact and a particular feeling of the speaker: e.g. surprise, joy,.... It describes a fact from a clearly subjective point of view.

III. ASPECTUAL VALUES OF STATE FORM V-*TE IRU*

Iru is principally a state verb. When employed as an aspectual complemental verb, it retains its static features. When it is placed after a verb of action, *iru* changes the predicate's status from dynamic to static. Consequently, the *te iru* form expresses a state of the subject in its continuing aspect, and not the action itself. This is why we call this form the 'state form.' The state form, because of its durative aspect (linear action), is opposed to the simple form which depicts an action as a point.

The fundamental value of the state form is its continuity. This can be the continuity of the action if the verb (or the circumstances) insists on the action process. In this case, the state form receives the 'imperfective' value. Continuity can also be the state resulting from a past action, if the verb emphasizes the subject's change of state. We then attribute the value of 'perfective' to the state form.

We shall summarize here various aspectual values of the state form, illustrated by examples:

1. IMPERFECTIVE VALUES (LINEAR PROCESS)

1-1. *Progressive value: action on the move*

PAST PROGRESSIVE

4. Fujin wa kao de koso *waratte ita* ga, jitsu wa sakki kara zenshin de *naite ita* no de aru. (Akutagawa Ryūnosuke '*Hankechi*' 'In fact the woman, while showing a smiling face, was crying her eyes out.'

PRESENT PROGRESSIVE

5. Hayaku ikō. Niisan mo *matte iru*. (Natsume Sōseki '*Sanshirō*') 'Let us hurry; your brother is waiting for us.'

FUTURE PROGRESSIVE

6. Jūsan. nichi ni Tokuzawa-goya de *matte orimasu* wa. (Inoue Yasushi '*Hyōheki*') 'I will be waiting for you at the Tokuzawa hut, on the 13th of this month.'

1-2. *Iterative value: action repeated by the same single or collective subject*

ACTION REPEATED BY THE SAME SUBJECT

7. Watakushi wa sono hito wo **tsune ni** sensei to *yonde ita*. (Natsume Sōseki '*Kokoro*') 'I would always call him teacher.'
8. Kono goro wa **maiban** neru mae ni sake wo *nonde iru*. 'Recently, I have been drinking every evening before I go to bed.'

9. ...ōrai ni wa mada **shikkiri-naku** hito ya kuruma ga *tōtte imashita*. (Akutagawa Ryūnosuke *'Toshishun'*) 'In the street, people and vehicles were still ceaselessly moving.'

10. **Zuibun** hito ga *shinde'ru* ja nai ka. (Kawabata Yasunari *'Yama no oto'*) 'Don't you find that many people are dying?'

2. PERFECTIVE VALUES (POINT ACTION)

2-1. *Resultative value: present state resulting from a past action*

11. Sora, Yoshikawa mo asuko e *kite iru* darō. (Natsume Sōseki *'Meian'*) 'You see, Yoshikawa too is there.'

12. Pan ga mō *yakete'masu* yo. (Yokomitsu Riichi *'Ryoshū'*) 'The bread is already toasted.'

13. Shigai wa...aomuke ni *taorete orimashita*. (Akutagawa Ryūnosuke *'Yabu no naka'*) 'The corpse was lying on its back.'

2-2. *Retrospective value: past action, seen from the present*

14. Ano shigai no otoko ni wa tashika-ni sakujitsu *atte orimasu*. (Akutagawa Ryūnosuke *'Yabu no naka'*) 'I can assure you that yesterday I saw the man who has been found dead.'

15. Yuki arite chijimi ari, yuki wa chijimi no oya to ifu beshi to, mukashi no hito mo hon ni *kaite iru*. (Kawabata Yasunari *'Yukiguni'*) 'It is thanks to snow that there is crepe. We should say that snow is the mother of crepe - that is what the Ancients have written.'

Table 2

Tense / Aspect	Past	Non-past (Present)
Imperfective	tabe*te ita* S N	(ima) tabe*te iru* N=S
Perfective	(sakki) tabe*ta* S N	(mō) tabe*ta* (mō) tabe*te iru* N=S ---- (sakki) tabe*te iru*

The arrow indicates the flow of time. N: 'Now' (the moment of the enunciation)
S: The point where the speaker places himself on the temporal axis.

IV-1. *Superposition of temporal and aspectual values*

Tense and aspect are, as we mentioned before, two different notions, but in practice these two values fuse into one single verbal form. When studying a verbal form (at least, one of the dynamic verbs which express a motion), it is necessary to observe it from two angles: the temporal angle (past/non-past) and the aspectual one (perfective/imperfective).

Table 2 above is a simplified table of the combination of tense and aspect values expressed by each form of dynamic verbs. The table reveals two oppositions of a different nature. Firstly, from a temporal point of view, *tabete ita* 'was/were eating' and (*sakki*) *tabeta* 'ate' are classified in the 'past' (the speaker considers the completed moment), compared to (*ima*) *tabete iru* 'to be eating' and (*mō*) *tabeta* 'to have already eaten,' (*mō*) *tabete iru* 'to have already eaten' (- 'to be in the state of one who has already eaten'), (*sakki*) *tabete iru* 'to have eaten,' which are classified in the 'present' (the speaker places himself at the moment of the enunciation).

Secondly, from an aspectual point of view, *tabete ita* and (*ima*) *tabete iru* present the action as a line, by insisting on the middle phase. They both have the 'imperfective' value. On the other hand, (*sakki*) *tabeta*, (*mō*) *tabeta*, (*mō*) *tabete iru* and (*sakki*) *tabete iru* represent a global action from beginning to end, like a point. Here it is the 'perfective' value.

Note that in this table, each verbal form appears under both the temporal and the aspectual headings. This table will be very useful to us in order to explain for instance the differences in meaning of the same form which is shown in each square of the table (e.g. *tabeta*, which appears in the squares of the 'past/perfective' and the 'present/perfective').

In the following paragraph, we will try, with this table, to clear up the problem of interpreting the verbal forms which are subject to inconsistent explanations. We will restrict ourselves to the questions concerning the past/perfective and present/perfective values.

IV-2. *Problems of interpretation of the past/perfective and the present/ perfective*

IV-2.1. *Ta* (past/perfective) vs *ta* (present/perfective)

The interpretation problem often arises when we try to explain the differences in meaning between the two following sentences:

16-a. Isha wa sakuyū kimashi*ta*. ('*Sanshirō*') 'The doctor came last night.'
16-b. Yatte ki*ta* ne. ('*Sanshirō*') '(What a surprise!) You're here!'

We usually say that *ta* in example 16-a indicates the past, because it locates the utterance at the moment before the present instant (indicated by the word *sakuyū* 'last night'), and that *ta* in sentence 16-b expresses the perfective, because we are concerned with the completion of an action at the moment of the enunciation.

However, if the 'perfective' was defined as 'an action which was

270

completed before the moment of the enunciation,' the distinction between past and perfective would be unclear. It would be preferable, in order to avoid serious confusion, not to introduce the moment of enunciation in the definition of aspect.

As we mentioned before, tense concerns localization on the temporal axis (in relation to the speaker), whereas aspect concerns duration.

This being so, let us go back to our preceding examples. In both examples, *ta* has a 'perfective' value, because we apprehend an action from beginning to end and present it globally without including the idea of continuity. What distinguishes *ta* in example 16-a from *ta* in example 16-b is the speaker's point of view. In example, 16-a, the speaker places himself at the moment of the utterance (*sakuyū* 'last night') which is a definite moment in the past. In this context, *ta* has the past value which can more precisely be called 'definite past.' The verbal predicate can be modified by a word designating a given moment in the past.

Other examples of past/perfective:

17. Haha ga shinde kara roku nemme no shōgatsu ni, oyaji mo sotchū de nakunat*ta*. (Natsume Sōseki '*Botchan*') 'My father died of an apoplexy in January of the sixth year after my mother's death.'
18. Watakushi wa tsuki no sue ni Tōkyō e kaet*ta*. (Natsume Sōseki '*Kokoro*') 'I came back to Tōkyō at the end of the month.'

Ta in example 16-b, on the other hand, describes a state of action perceived at the very moment of the enunciation. The speaker naturally focuses on the present moment. As a result, the temporal value of *ta* is here the 'present.' The verbal predicate can never be modified by a word indicating the past clearly. It can, however, be accompanied by a temporal modifier referring to the present time, such as *ima* 'now', *tōtō* 'at last,' *mō* 'already,' etc...

Other examples of present/perfective:

19. Aa, kutabire*ta*. (Shimazaki Tōson '*Haru*') 'Oh, I am tired!'
20. Taisō kirei-ni o-nari ni narimashi*ta* nē. (Enchi Fumiko '*Onnazaka*') 'She has become really beautiful.'
21. Ima kaerimashi*ta* yo. ('*Hyōheki*') 'Now I am back.'

IV-2.2. *Ta* (present/perfective) vs *te iru* (present/perfective)

When we want to express a present state resulting from a past action, we have a choice between two forms: V-*ta* and V-*te iru*, which both have the present/perfective value. Let us compare, for example, these sentences:

22-a. Momiji no furuki no miki ni, sumire no hana ga hiraita no wo Chieko wa mitsuketa. 'Aa, kotoshi mo sai*ta*' to Chieko wa haru no yasashisa ni deatta. (Kawabata Yasunari '*Koto*') 'Chieko noticed the violets in bloom on the trunk of an old maple tree. "Oh, they have bloomed this year again." Chieko felt the softness of springtime.'

22-b. Densha ga Kita-Kamakura no tani wo tōru to 'Yoku ume ga sai*te'masu* wa' to Kikuko wa mezurashi-sō ni nagameta. ('*Yama no oto*) '"The plum tree blossoms are out," said Kikoku gazing at them anew,

271

while the train was crossing the valley of Kita-Kamakura.'

In these two cases, the speaker discovers the flowers in bloom at the moment of the enunciation. She views the action (here, 'to open out') as a finished one and describes its result which is still valid at the moment of the enunciation.

In example 22-a, the speaker insists on the action or changing of state she noticed at the very moment of the enunciation. It is a dynamic sentence. There is no notion of duration. In this context, *ta* is equivalent to the expression *ni keri* in the classical language; in other words, it expresses both the completion of the action (value of *ni* variant of *nu* in classical language) and the present feeling of the speaker (surprise, joy, etc.) born after a discovery (value of *keri*).

In this example, the speaker places himself at the moment of the enunciation. Therefore, ta has the value of the 'present.' However, its use is quite complex for it to be called simply the 'present.'

First of all, ta does not express a simple recognition of a present state, like static predicate does, but the recognition of the subject's change of state. The speaker describes a subject's state of comparing it to its former state. In other words, he considers a state from a diachronic angle. The following example explains this difference between the 'non-past' form of an adjective (A-i) and the 'past' form of a verb (V-ta).

23. Ōkii hana da nē. Jitsu-ni rippa-da. to (Shingo wa) itta. Onna no ko wa sukoshi hanikamu yōni hohoenda. 'Hana wo hitotsu dake ni shita n'desu' 'Hitotsu dake ni ne. Sorede konna-ni ōkiku natta n'da ne...' ('Yama no oto') '"This is a beautiful flower (=sunflower)! Really gorgeous!" he said. The girl smiled, a little shy. "We have made sure there would be only one flower. - Only one, I see. This is why it has become so beautiful".'

In this example, Ōkii hana 'big flower' describes the very state, as we see it. After the girl's explanation, Shingo (he) answered: Ōkiku natta 'has grown' 'has become gorgeous,' by referring to the extraordinary growth of this flower. By using the past form of the verb naru 'to become,' he mentally follows the progressive growth of this flower whose final phase is located at the moment of the enunciation.

Secondly, when the verb expresses a gradual change and the exact moment of the completion of the action cannot be clearly perceived, its past form can never be modified by a word referring to 'now.' For example, we cannot say, as in English: *Ima hana ga saita '*The flowers have opened out just now,' nor *ima ōkiku natta. '*You have grown just now.' In such a case, the present moment is somewhat considered to have already fallen into the past, precisely because the verb stresses a change in the subject's state.

Unlike the past form, the state form in example 22-b insists on the present state, and not on the action which directly caused it. It is a static sentence. The action is considered in its completed state, as a starting point, and the resulting state is presented as a line which links this point to the moment of speech ('now'). This *te iru* value comes from *tari* in classical language which is itself a contracted form of *te ari*. The presence

272

of the verb *iru* (or *ari*) emphasizes the notion of continuity, so that the verbal predicate can receive a modifier which indicates the duration.

24. 'Nagai koto *saite'ru*?' 'Ee' 'Ikunichi kurai *saite'ru* no?' ('*Yama no oto*') 'Has it been in flower for a long time?' 'Yes' 'How long?'

By using the state form, the speaker expresses more particularly the middle phase of the state, yet remains aware of its beginning. From this point of view, the state form contrasts with the past form which stresses the final phase.

IV-2.3. *Ta* (past/perfective) vs *te iru* (retrospective)

Ta with the value of past/perfective locates the account at a completed moment, without considering the connection this fact can have with the present moment. It expresses definite past, modifiable with a word referring to the past.

Sometimes we may represent a completed action at a determined period of the past, seen from the present moment. The verb takes the *te iru* form with its 'retrospective' value. The utterance can be accompanied by some temporal word which refers to the past.

What are the differences then between *ta*, past/perfective mark, and *te iru*, retrospective mark? Let us compare the following sentences:

25-a. Musume wa ni.nen mae ni kekkon shi*ta*. 'My daughter got married two years ago.'
25-b. Musume wa ni.nen mae ni kekkon shi*te iru*. 'My daughter got married two years ago.' ('It's two years since my daughter has got married').

In example 25-a, the speaker places himself at the moment of the utterance 'two years ago.' It is an objective report of a past fact, detached from the present. The style of the utterance is narrative and descriptive.

In example 25-b, on the other hand, the speaker places himself at the present moment. He describes a past action in a retrospective way. In other words, the speaker tries to link a past fact to the moment of the enunciation, either because this fact would explain a present state, or because he is examining anew the value of a past action. *Te iru* in this acceptation acquires an explanatory function. Therefore, sentence 25-b can precede one of the following sentences:

25-b(1) Dakara ima watakushi wa rōsai to futari de kurashite iru. 'Consequently, I now live alone with my aged wife.'
25-b(2) Kono kekkon wa watakushi-tachi ni fūfu to iu mono no arikata wo aratamete kangaesaseru keiki to natta no da.
'This wedding gave us the opportunity to think once more about the couple as it should be.'

IV-2.4. *Te iru* (resultative) vs *te iru* (retrospective)

Let us compare the following examples:

26-a. Kono inu wa *shinde iru*.
'This dog is dead.'

26-b. Mō kono toshi de wa shitashikatta hito wa ōku *shinde iru*. ('*Yama no oto*')
'At this age, many of my friends have already died.'
26-c. Natsume Sōseki wa Taishō go.nen ni ikaiyō no tame ni *shinde iru*.
'Natsume Sōseki died of a gastric ulcer in the fifth year of the Taishō era.'

Example 26-a would be uttered when in the presence of a dog's corpse. This sentence implies in general that the speaker has not seen the dog's death and he only sees the motionless dog. The speaker links this present state to the action (here 'to die') which obviously happened in an undetermined moment of the past. This is not then a direct expression of the immediate observation, as is the case in the state form with progressive value.

As this expression describes a state whose beginning cannot be situated at an exact moment in time, it cannot usually be modified by an adverbial phrase which specifies a starting point, such as N *kara*. Therefore we cannot say:

26-a' *? Kono inu wa san jikan mae kara *shinde iru*.
'This dog has been dead for three hours.'

Sentence 26-a appears to emphasize a present state, without considering the former action. This use of *te iru* is reserved for resultative verbs underlining a change in the subject's state.

In example 26-b also, *te iru* has a resultative value, while approaching *te iru* with a retrospective value as well. Here, the speaker does not of course find himself face to face with his friends' corpses; he thinks back over the list of his friends who are no longer alive. By placing himself in the present (indicated by the adverb: *mō* 'already'), the speaker goes back in time to note the present result of a past action: 'many of my friends are already dead.' The sentence can be modified only by the words referring to the present moment, with a completed touch, such as *mō* 'already,' *ima* (*de*) *wa* 'nowadays,' etc. Example 26-b underlines the completion of the action more than sentence 26-a does. Resultative verbs as well as non-resultative verbs (ex. *kaku* 'to write,' *nomu* 'to drink,' etc.) can take this value in their state form.

27. Are dakara idai-na kurayami da. Nandemo *yonde iru*. ('*Sanshirō*') 'This is why he is nicknamed "great darkness." He has read everything (and knows everything).'

Unlike examples 26-a and 26-b which express 'indefinite present/perfective' (the exact moment of the process completion not being specified), sentence 26-c indicates 'definite present/perfective.' The utterance usually receives an adverbial time phrase referring to the past. We insist on the completed action, which is represented as a point. Here, the notion of duration, characteristic of the state form V-*te iru*, is missing, so that the predicate can never be accompanied by a nominal phrase governed by *kara*. This can be explained by the fact that *kara* indicates a starting point, with implicit continuity until another point presented as a point of arrival. The following sentence then is ungrammatical:

26-c' *Natsume Sōseki wa T̲a̲i̲s̲h̲ō̲ g̲o̲.̲ n̲e̲n̲ k̲a̲r̲a̲ *shinde iru.*
'Natsume Sōseki has been (in the state of being) dead since the fifth year of the Taishō era.'

It is worth stating here that *te iru* can also be used as an adjective. In this case, the result of the action cannot be directly perceived, but remains within the subject (of the sentence) as an experience. The quality acquired thus is used to distinguish that person from others who do not possess it.

Let us examine the following cases:

28-a. Kare wa Tōdai wo *sotsugyo shite iru.* 'He is a graduate of Tōkyō University.'
28-b. Kare wa kyonen Tōdai wo *sotsugyō shite iru.* 'He graduated from Tōkyō University last year.'

Example 28-b has a retrospective value: it describes a past action from the point of view of the present moment.

Example 28-a, on the other hand, has a resultative value: it insists on the present state. The fact that this person is a graduate of Tōkyō University gives him a quality that others do not possess. We can say that example 28-a expresses a subject's state which is observed from a synchronic or a static point of view. This kind of sentence, which is close to an adjectival sentence, cannot be expanded with any temporal phrase that specifies either the present moment, such as *ima* 'now,' or a starting point, like N-*kara.* Thus we cannot say:

28-a' *Kare wa i̲m̲a̲ Tōdai wo *sotsugyō shite iru.* 'He is now a graduate of Tōkyō University.'
28-b' *Kare wa k̲y̲o̲n̲e̲n̲ k̲a̲r̲a̲ Tōdai wo *sotsugyō shite iru.* 'He has been a graduate of Tōkyō University since last year.'

IV-3. Intersection of tense and aspect

We saw, at the beginning of our study, that the distinction between tense and aspect is not always clear, especially where the past and the perfective are concerned. There are different ways of interpreting the *ta* value in the following sentence:

29. Sakura ga kirei-ni sai*ta* nā.
'The cherry blossoms have opened out beautifully.'

Some linguists say it is the 'past,' others, that *ta* in this context expresses the 'perfective.' If the past (temporal notion) is confused with the perfective (aspectual notion), it is because we define both of them in relation to the moment of the enunciation: the past as 'a tense locating the utterance in a moment before the present instant,' and the perfective as 'an action considered in its completion in relation to the speaker.'

We have proposed in this paper another definition of tense and aspect, namely: tense is a value in relation with the reference moment, whereas aspect is a representation of duration; the perfective marks a 'point action,' and the imperfective indicates 'a linear process.'

275

Moreover, we have suggested above that tense and aspect blend into each other in a verbal form. We can conclude then that here there is superposition of two values, namely: past/perfective, present/perfective, etc., and not an alternative, that is, either past or perfective.

We have not yet examined an important fact which is also at the intersection of tense and aspect. It is what some linguists call 'perfective in a subordinate clause.' For example:

30. Nihon e *itta* toki ni jisho wo katte koyō.
'I will buy a dictionary when I go to Japan.'

Here, *ta* seems to us to be connected to relative time rather than aspect. The problem of real time and relative time on the one hand, and relative time and aspect on the other hand, are the subject of another work which we would like to carry out.

The categories of tense and aspect intersect in different ways. In this study, we have tried in particular to demonstrate that the problem is not to choose which is the more appropriate label to attach to such and such a verbal form, but what matters here is a multi-dimensional approach towards the analysis of a form in a given language, because it is a formal expression of various linguistic needs.

CONCLUSION

This paper has considered multi-dimensional interpretations of a verbal form. Unlike preceding studies which consider tense and aspect as two notions opposed to each other on the same level, we considered that these notions are situated at different levels. We are convinced this will throw new light on the problems of tense and aspect, and in particular on the interpenetrating phenomenon of these two notions.

34

On Predicate Nominals in Japanese

LONE TAKEUCHI

This paper surveys adjective and noun predicate (copula) forms of Classical Japanese and Modern Japanese dialects in the light of recent accounts of these phenomena in other languages. Tentatively, it is proposed that the varied adjective morphology in Japanese reflects residual predicate nominal forms originating in bipartite structures of old focus or subject particle + existential verb.

1. It is an often noted fact that the adjective morphology divides the

Japanese dialects into three areas, roughly characterized by DA(/I), KA and SA[1] in their finite forms:

1.a GENKI-SA   TAKA-SA   in some Ryūkyū dialects[2]
   'is fine'   'is high'
 .b GENKI-KA   TAKA-KA   in some Kyūshū dialects[3]
 .c GENKI-DA   TAKA-I   in all other (=central) dialects[4]

It is also generally acknowledged that Japanese adjective conjugations present accretions to a nominal root[5] and that they are historically more recent than verb conjugations. In fact, the central dialects have two distinct adjective formations, of which the productive one (DA) coincides with noun predicate forms; the I-formation, while encompassing the core vocabulary, has to all practical purposes, been unproductive for centuries. The two other dialect groups have distinct adjective and noun predicate forms. The noun predicate forms of the KA dialects are, to my knowledge, similar to those of the central area, whereas the SA dialects use a focus particle DU to form a marked affirmative noun predicate, although as in most other dialects the predicate noun can be left unmarked.

1.1 I shall refer to the three groups as NI, KA and SA dialects. The central NI dialects comprise Honshū with the possible exception of northernmost Tōhoku, Shikoku and two belts along the east and west coasts of Kyūshū.

The KA dialects cover a belt stretching north-south through the central part of Kyūshū from Nagasaki and Kumamoto to Kagoshima, extending to Amami Ōshima dialects, and a pocket of the Miyako shotō dialects (except Tarama dialect). The remaining Ryūkyū dialects have SA adjectives.

1.2 It has gone unnoticed, however, that each of these three adjectival morphemes enters an almost identical morpho-semantic configuration which, I think, gives us valuable clues to predicate nominal formation in Japanese. Thus, in each of the three above-mentioned dialect areas, (near) homonymy exists between the particular finite adjective forms just mentioned, and one or more case markers, commonly labelled instrumental and/or locative, thereby suggesting the ultimate relatedness of these forms:

2.a SA : SAAI   in the SA dialects[6]
 .b KA : KARA   in the KA dialects[7]
 .c DA : DE (NITE)   in the NI dialects[8]

Further, actional goal constructions are formed by means of conjunctors which can plausibly be considered cognate with KA, SA and DA in approximately corresponding dialect areas:

3.a MI SA IKU[9]   'goes to see'
 .b MI KA IKU[10]   id.
 .c MI NI IKU   id.

Besides, KA dialects have several other conjunctors with velar consonantism, often glossed by obvious NI cognates in NI dialects.[11]

1.3 The configurational similarity is striking, and certainly sufficient to confirm the forms of each of the three morphological sets as cognate. Undoubtedly they represent parallel (recurrent?) formations which must be well entrenched by properties of Japanese grammatical structure.[12]

Thus, the fact that the KA and SA adjectival affixes seem to relate to one or more case markers in the same way as the nominal predicate DA of the central NI dialects relates to DE, suggests that KA and SA, too, originally were used to form predicates of adjectives and nouns alike. I shall assume that the direction of development is more likely to have been from a general nominal to a more specific adjective predicate function, on the basis of the historical evidence that DA (NI) developed a general nominal predicate function, superseding the specific adjective formations in the process.

2. The syntactic and semantic terminology needs a brief mentioning. Following Nichols,[13] I distinguish between three kinds of syntactic relationships within a clause: controlled, governed and circumstantial. Predicate nominals are a type of *controlled* relations, defined as relations where 'an actant or a modifier is semantically crucially dependent on another nominal in the same clause, the controller.'[14] Examples from Modern Japanese are:

4. Tanaka-san wa **isha da**.
    'T is a physician.'

5. Tanaka-san wa **isha ni** natta.
    'T became a physician.'

6. Tenki ga **waruku** natta.
    'The weather got worse.'

7. Shushō wa Tanaka-san o **daijin ni** ninmei shita.
    'The prime minister appointed T a minister.'

8. Shushō wa Tanaka-san o sensei to yobu.
    'The prime minister addresses T as "sensei".'

(4)-(6) are instances of subject-control: the subject **Tanaka-san wa** is said to control **isha da** and **isha ni** in (4)-(5); **tenki ga** controls **waruku** in (6). (7)-(8) exemplify object control: the object **Tanaka-san o** controls **daijin ni** in (7) and **sensei to** in (8).

Control is a semantic dependency. The controlled noun-phrase often does not surface as a predicate, but appropriate paraphrases are usually at hand,[15] such as (9.b)-(9.c) paraphrasing (9.a):

9.a N o **okashiku** omotta   'I thought N strange'
 b N o **okashii** to omotta   'I thought that N was strange'
 c N **ga** okashii to omotta   'I thought that N was strange'/
                'I thought: N is strange'

In each case, the two nominals of (4)-(8) form part of the valence of the predicate. That is, they belong to the configuration of actants or complements for which a given verb (**da, natta, ninmei shita, yobu** in

(4)-(8)) must be specified. Such indispensable actants are said to be *governed*.

Governed actants are distinguished from dispensable, *circumstantial* ones, such as **sono shunkan kara** in (10):

10. Sono shunkan kara tenki ga waruku natta
   'From that moment the weather got worse'

Controlled relations can be governed as in (4)-(8), or be circumstantial as in (11)-(12):

11. Tanaka-san wa Tōshiba de **gishi to shite** hataraite iru
   'Tanaka-san works with Toshiba as an engineer'

12. **Gishi no** Tanaka-san wa Tōshiba de hataraite iru
   'T., an engineer, works with Toshiba'

3. The Kinki dialects of the central area (attested from the eighth century onwards) provide us with perhaps the only instance where we can actually observe a major change in a predicate nominal construction. What I have in mind is the **te**-accretion: finite form **ni ar-i/nar-i** > **nite ar-i; ni** > **nite** non-finite, which occurred in Classical Japanese (CJ) of the Heian Period.

3.1 The particle **ni** in Old Japanese and (early?) CJ characteristically entered not only controlled, governed relations, but also circumstantial relations. (13) is an example of **ni** marking place of action:[16]

13. **Sono safa ni** kakitubata ito omosiroku sakitari (Ise Monogatari 9) '**In that marsh**, irises, beautiful, were blooming'

3.1.2 As a conjunctor, the innovative element **te** sequenced the events of the two clauses it conjoined. The mode of sequencing is disputed, but probably the action of the **te** clause referred one actional limit (beginning or end) as relevant to the event in the upper clause. Also CJ **te** was subject to conditions of coreferentiality of subjects.[17]

3.1.3 Te-accretion in CJ, therefore, highlighted the indeterminacy as to whether N **nite** constituted a clause to itself, or functioned as a phrasal adjunct. Its ultimate, post-CJ effect was to implement a clear-cut morphological distinction between governed, non-controlled relations expressed by **ni**, and circumstantial ones expressed by **nite** > **de**. To the extent that **de** allows for clausal readings, the indeterminacy is still maintained.

3.2 There are indications that the te-accretion was originally functional. The te-accreted form was almost certainly used if a state was regarded as qualified or delimited, e.g. 'is now' implying a previous change; 'is still' comparing two moments for which the predication holds with the presupposition that it will discontinue later, etc.[18] For example:

14. aru kuni no zizou no kwannin no **me nite namu aru** to kikite,...
   (Ise Monogatari 60)
   (the man)... hearing that **she (his former wife) was now the wife** of the official who was to accommodate him in the province,....

279

Depending on the semantic properties of the noun, N **nite** can be translated 'is now/is still with N' or 'has come = is now/is still at N.' For instance:

15. Sibasi fa **Rokkaku no ya nite arisi** ga, fuduki zifuyonniti no yoru, Kafazaki no yado fe uturofisi ni mo ...(Towazugatari, book 1)
    'For a while, father **remained at the Rokkaku house**, but on the night of the 14th day of the 7th month, he moved to the Kawazaki house, yet...

By contrast, **nari-i** did not limit the duration of the state, as for instance in (16):

16. ..., sono yo no fito, **wonna naredo**, kasikou ya ariken, ...(Hamamatu Chūnagon Monogatari, book 3).
    '...perhaps because people in that country (China) are clever, **even if they are women**...

3.2.1 It may also be significant that the **te**-accretion in noun predicates exactly models, morpho-syntactically as well as semantically, the slightly earlier verbal predicate formation of the CJ perfects:

V-**eri** < *V-i **ar-i**   non delimited perfect
V-**ite ar-i** - V-**itar-i**   delimited perfect[19]

3.2.2 Only the old morphological class of I-adjectives was apparently resistant to **te**-accretion. It is difficult to imagine any morphological or syntactic reasons why **adjective stem + kute ar-i** should be so rare in CJ (viz. **-ku arimasen** in the modern language). Perhaps it is a lexical reflex of a more general semantic condition that adjectives, which are low in referentiality, tend to qualify rather than identify, and therefore, less likely to select **te**-accretion[20] which (inter alia?) could specify temporal duration.

The precise conditions governing **te**-accretion in CJ nominal predicates are still to be formulated, and several different parameters, such as tense and mood, are likely to be at work. It is obviously of great significance to get a more precise idea of this distinction, since it might suggest, among other things, an explanation for the rise of the specific adjective morphology: adjectives retain old nominal predicate forms, because the conditions by which innovative forms are implemented, apply less well to adjectives.

3.3 Post-classical (post-Kamakura period) changes include a return to the circumstantial adnominal form **no**, e.g. **koko na hito** (in Kyōgen plays) to **koko no hito** in the modern language upon the demise of the **nari**-forms.[21] Secondly, **te** has developed in the modern language to allow simultaneity of the events or states it conjoins and more generally, switch-reference,[22] as in (17) below:

17. Tarō wa **isha de**, Jirō wa haisha da
    'Tarō is a physican, Jirō a dentist'

3.4 The effects of **te**-accretion in CJ can be summarized as follows: It perpetuated the bipartite structure: **N N particle existential verb** setting the copula construction off anew with evident compound sentence (clausal) characteristics. In the short term, it gave rise to a semantic distinction, (inter alia) delimited or identifying predicate nominal, as opposed to the unlimited or qualifying **nari**-forms. This distinction was probably also available to some governed (perhaps mainly existential locative) arguments (cf. (15) above). However, later, as the older predicate forms were superseded by the **te**-accreted ones, **te**-accretion was used distinctively only with actants, in such a way that non-governed circumstantial functions were marked by **te**-accreted **de**, governed functions by **ni**. More specifically, the distinction was between actional locative and existential/goal locative; and between instrumental and passive agent.

4. Significantly, the innovative copula formation (**te**-accretion) in CJ shares syntactic and semantic characteristics with similar phenomena from other languages, e.g. in Yuman (Munro 1977), where copula formation likewise involves clausal status inside a compound sentence with restricted or blocked switch-reference, as well as the notion of the delimited character of the state.

Frajzyngier (1986) mentions the importance of (pragmatic) focus in the formation of copula. It has been claimed by Harries-Delisle (1978) that focus (contrastive emphasis in her terminology) invariably tends to imply an equation. Whatever the ultimate explanation for that is, it agrees with the observation that languages use focusing devices, whether specific focus markers or subject markers, to form copula constructions, and that the formative element often originates in the category of shifters: Yuman copula reportedly originates in a NP + subject marker + existential verb construction; Mandarin copula in an anaphoric resumption by a demonstrative pronoun (Li & Thompson 1977). The deictic element anaphorically resumes what precedes it by nesting it onto an existential predicate (pronominal resumption) in the upper clause, as **that** in (18):

18. 'To be or not to be **that** is the question.'

Presumably, the nominal of the predicate more often than not is the one to be defined, and if necessary,[23] focused. Hence, a general focus device is likely to develop into a marker of the predicate nominal function.[24] According to Frajzyngier 1986, the formation of this function and the loss of focus and deictic functions happen in interaction with the rise of new deictics and/or focus markers.

4.1 There appear to be at least two pieces of morphological evidence in Japanese which are in accord with the just-mentioned scenario for copula formation and therefore point to anaphoric-deictic markers (demonstrative pronouns) or focus markers as the ultimate source for KA, SA and NI predicate nominal forms.

One is the morpho-semantic configuration, consistently found across dialects, of the copula; markers of circumstantial actants, notably locatives;

and the existence of residual constructions involving motion in space, such as the actional goal constructions exemplified in (3) (cf. **1.** above). An additional related piece of evidence is furnished by the locative-temporal use of SA in Old Japanese in a closed set of what I would interpret as compound clauses with identical subject: the verb of the first clause in each case is a motion verb conjoined by **sa**, e.g. **kaferu-sa V** or **kafesa V** 'V-es on the way back,' **yuku-sa V** 'V-es going along' and **ku-sa V** 'V-es coming.'

Secondly, under the assumption that new demonstratives and focus/subject markers developed, as older ones were established in copula function, the distribution of demonstratives and/or focus particles should be expected to reflect this and to differ among the KA, SA and NI dialect areas, which in fact, it does: of several sets of demonstrative pronouns found in Japanese and Ryūkyū dialects: proximal **ko** and distal **so,ʔu/(w)ona**, **ka** and **a**,[25] the SA dialects generally have **ʔu-** corresponding to **so-** in KA and NI dialects; NI and KA dialects use **a-** to the exclusion of **ka-**, which is found in many SA-dialects. Furthermore in NI dialects, the subject-focus marker **ga** is used predominantly or at least more extensively than **no/nu**, whereas **no/nu** dominates in KA and SA dialects.[26]

4.2 It is beyond the scope of this paper to address the complexities of Old Japanese, let alone details of how the modern dialects relate to it and to each other historically. The following remarks are merely meant as general observations on the categories of case marking, focus and copula as they occur in (a sample of) modern dialects.

Japanese of the Nara and the early Heian Periods had a complex system of focus marking and elaborate pronominal systems. In fact, all the form categories which have been suggested as relevant in copula formation: (demonstrative) pronouns/spatial marker; focus/subject particle; circumstantial case marker; and copula form, seem to be represented at this stage of the language in all the three cognate sets:

	KA	SA	NI
demonstrative pronoun	kaku, kare, kore	sa, sore	nare (2.p.p.)[27]
focus/subject particle	ka/ga, koso	zo, si	namu
circumstantial case	kara	site	nite[28]
copula form	ku (>kari), ki	sa, si	ni (>nari)

CJ therefore, comprises all the three systems found in present-day dialects.

4.2.1 There exist conspicuous systematic differences in focus and subject encoding between the dialects. In the central dialects and presumably in parts of the KA dialect area as well, subject and focus are both marked by **ga** (and **no**) with cleft-sentences as an alternative device. In the SA area and in parts of KA dialect area, subject and focus are encoded separately: the subject is marked by **no/nu** (with a rather restricted occurrence of **ga**),[29] focus by **du**,[30] and focused subjects by the combination of the two, **nu du** or **ga du**.[31] According to the available surveys, zero predicates appear to occur more freely in the SA dialect area.

CJ stands apart from the modern dialects, sharing the split focus-subject devices with the SA dialects, and the trend for overt copula expression with the NI dialects. The three nominal predicate systems can be summed up as follows:[32]

	NI dialects	CJ		SA (and KA) dialects	
neutral	N wa N da	N	N nari	N nu/ga	N
focused predicate	N wa N da zo	N no/ga	N ni zo	N nu/ga	N du aru
focused subject	N ga N da	N zo	N naru	N nu/ga du N	

4.2.2 The historical development in the central NI dialects with its decline of SA cognate predicate nominal forms and change from focus-subject to topic-subject encoding, and the present-day distribution of SA dialects in peripheral geographical areas, both seem to point to the SA dialects with focus marking as representing an older system.[33]

Moreover the following facts about the morphological structures of the dialects can perhaps be taken to indicate different origins of the nominal predicate construction in the SA dialects, on the one hand, and in the KA and NI dialects, on the other. As shown above, the adjective paradigm in all dialects always has cognate circumstantial case markers, but not necessarily cognate governed ones. The relative centrality of the three morphological groups SA, KA and NI is, in fact, the same across dialects: SA elements have almost exclusively circumstantial functions,[34] and while there are KA dialects without SA derived case markers,[35] the reverse - a SA dialect without KA derived case markers - does not seem to occur.[36] Arguably, NI elements (**ni** rather than **nite** derivatives), would seem to have more governed and governed-controlled functions than any of the other two[37] in most, if not all dialects. However, if, as it seems, there is a case for assuming the possessive-subject marker **ga** to be cognate with the KA predicate nominal,[38] the predicate nominal forms in both KA and NI dialect groups are plausibly derived from forms with governed functions (**no/nu/ni** and **ga/ka**, respectively).

In sum, there is some evidence for alternative copula formation in Japanese: based on focus markers in SA dialects, and on subject (or governed actant) markers in the other dialects.[39] The question, however, remains whether or which characteristics of the overall grammatical system favour one over the other.

Notes

PART 1: LITERATURE & VISUAL ARTS

Chapter 2 YOKO McCLAIN *Rethinking Soseki's Mon*
1. Matsuoka Yuzuru, *Natsume Soseki*, (Kawade Shobo, 1953), 299.
2. Natsume Soseki, *Soseki zenshu*, ed. Komiya Toyotaka (34 Vols.; Iwanami Shoten, 1953), V. 18, *Bungakuron*, 286-87.
3. Beongheon, Yu, *Natsume Soseki* (New York: Twayne Publishers, Inc., 1969), 180.
4. Komiya Toyotaka, *Soseki no geijutsu* (Iwanami Shoten, 1942), 178.
5. Soseki Natsume, *Mon*, tr. Francis Mathy (Rutland Vermont and Tōkyō: Charles E. Tuttle, Inc., 1972), 153.
6. *Ibid.*, 135.
7. *Ibid.*, 136.
8. *Ibid.*
9. *Ibid.*, 135.
10. Natsume Soseki, *Soseki zenshu*, V. 29 (Iwanami Shoten, 1953), 115.
11. Edwin McClellan, *The Two Japanese Novelists: Soseki and Toson* (Chicago and London: The University of Chicago Press, 1969), 42.
12. *Soseki zenshu*, V. 25. *Danpan*, 104.
13. *Soseki zenshu*, V. 29, *Shokanshu*, 114-15.
14. Oguri Fuyo, 'Yora to kotonoareru Soseki', *Bungei* (June 1954), 140.

Chapter 3 LIVIA MONNET *The Melancholy Flagellant or the Responsibility of Literature: Takahashi Kazumi and his Project for a Revolution*
1. Donald R. Kelley has recently pointed to 'the extraordinary proliferation of alleged crises in this century.' See 'Horizons of Intellectual History: Retrospect, Circumspect, Prospect,' *Journal of History of Ideas* (January-March 1987): 143-169. Some examples of studies dealing with the 'contemporary crisis' in history, philosophy and literary criticism: Howard Felperin, *Beyond Deconstruction* (Oxford: Oxford University Press, 1985); Harold Bloom, *The Anxiety of Influence: A Theory of Poetry* (New York: Oxford University Press, 1973); Randolf Starn, 'Historians and "Crisis",' *Past and Present* 52 (1971): 3-22; Gene Wise, 'The Contemporary Crisis in Contemporary Intellectual History Studies,' *Clio* 5 (1975): 55-71. On the Japanese side see, for instance, Ōe Kenzaburō, *Shōsetsu no hōhō* (Tōkyō: Iwanami Shoten, 1978): Ōe Kenzaburō, 'Sengo bungaku kara konnichi no kyūkyō made,' *Sekai* (March 1986): 238-248, translated in excerpts as 'Postwar Japanese literature and the Contemporary Impasse' in *The Japan Foundation Newsletter* 2, No. 3 (October 1986): 1-6; Noma Hiroshi; *Atarashii jidai no bungaku* (Tōkyō: Iwanami Shoten, 1982).
2. See Dominick LaCapra and Stephen Kaplan (eds.), *Modern European Intellectual History, Reappraisals and New Perspectives* (Ithaca: Cornell University Press, 1982).
3. Donald R. Kelley, 'Horizons of Intellectual History,' p. 143.
4. Though structuralism and post-structuralism have been accorded sufficient space in literary and philosophical journals (recent examples are the special issues: 'Nihongo no retorikku,' *Kokubungaku kaishaku to kyōzai no kenkyū* 31 (January 1986) and 'Fiction,' *Gendaishi techō* 29, No. 5 (May 1986) deconstructionist readings of say, Natsume Sōseki, Akutagawa Ryūnosuke, Mishima Yukio or Nakagami Kenji are yet to come.
5. Dominick LaCapra, *Rethinking Intellectual History* (Ithaca: Cornell University Press, 1983).

6. 'Postwar Japanese Literature and the Contemporary Impasse,' p. 3. Ōe defines 'active posture' as the writers' capacity to create 'models...that might activate the total humanity of their (the writers') contemporaries, guiding them through the power of the imagination to an organic experience of the future, or to the humanity of the future.' Such models are expected to 'exert a moral influence upon society.'

7. The dynasties which successively made Nanjing (Nanking) their capital: Wu (222-280), Eastern Jin (317-420), Song (420-479), Qi (479-502), Liang (502-577) and Chen (557-589).

8. Critic and literary theorist of the Liang Dynasty. His main work is the treatise *Wenxin Diaolong* (The Literary Mind and the Carving of Dragons).

9. Famous poet of the Southern Dynasties' Song Dynasty (420-479). His best-known poem is *Wujun yong* (Ode to the Five Kings).

10. Renowned poet, contemporary of Yan Yanzhi, author of lyrical landscape poems. The only extant collection of his works is the Ming Dynasty *Xie Kangyue-ji* (Xie Kangyue was another name used by Xie Lingyun).

11. Poet and critic of the Western Jin Dynasty. His treatise *Wenfu* is one of the most important works of classical Chinese literary criticism.

12. See Ishimoto Tarō, 'Takahashi Kazumi nenpu,' in Ogawa Kazusuke (ed.), *Takahashi Kazumi Kenkyū* (Tōkyō: Kyōiku Shuppan sentā, 1976), p. 245. A detailed account of Takahashi's political activities during his student days may be found in Komatsu Sakyō (ed.), *Takahashi Kazumi no seishun to sono jidai* (Tōkyō: Kōsōsha, 1978).

13. 'Takahashi Kazumi nenpu,' p. 250. See also Kawanishi Masaaki 'Takahashi Kazumi no chi,' *Kokubungaku: Kaishaku to Kyōzai no kenkyū* (July 1980).

14. The most comprehensive bibliography to date is in Kawanishi Masaaki's 'Sankōbunken ichiran,' *Fukashi no unmei, arui wa Takahashi Kazumi ni tsuite no danpentekina kōsatsu* (Tōkyō: Kōdansha, 1974) and its sequel, also compiled by Kawanishi, in *Takahashi Kazumi zenshū*, 20 vols, (Tōkyō: Kawade shobō shinsha, 1977-1980), 20. *Sakka-ron*, of course, are legion, but many of them, especially those published in the wake of Takahashi's tragic, premature death are so blatantly sentimental, inept or purely speculative as to have little critical value. A typical example of such absurd *sakka-ron* is Akiyama Shun, *Takahashi Kazumi-ron*, in Haniya Yutaka (ed.), *Takahashi Kazumi-ron* (Tōkyō: Kawade Shobō shinsha, 1972), pp. 7-33.

15. Besides writing articles in support of the movement opposing the revision of the Japan-US security treaty and the radical student movement, Takahashi took part in mass rallies and public debates, travelled to China at the height of the Great Cultural Revolution, etc. See Ishimoto Taro, 'Takahashi Kazumi nenpu.' Also Takahashi Takako, *Takahashi Kazumi no omoide* (Tōkyō: Kawade shobō shinsha, 1977).

16. I have coined this expression from Takahashi's well-known novel, *Yūutsu naru tōha*. (The original English subtitle of the novel, removed from the version published in 1965, was 'Gloom Party') and the title of an essay by Isoda Kōichi, 'Takahashi Kazumi-ron: Jibatsusha no seikon,' in Isoda Kōichi, *Shōwa sakkaron shūsei* (Tōkyō: Shinchōsha, 1985), pp. 648-659.

17. See Haniya Yutaka, 'Kunōkyō no shiso,' in *Takahashi Kazumi-ron*, p. 275.

18. See Takahashi Kazumi, 'Yūutsu o kataru sedai,' in *Ankoku e no shuppatsu* (Tōkyō: Tokuma shoten, 1971). The thinker is a recurrent motif in Takahashi's writings. The serious reflective posture seems to have typified for him the attitude of the historically conscious intellectual.

19. See Takahashi Takako, *Takahashi Kazumi no omoide*.

20. *Ibid.*

21. See Kobayashi Ryū 'Tasogare no hashi: Kyūsai naki chishikijin no unmei,' in *Takahashi Kazumi kenkyū*, p. 167.

22. Haniya Yutaka, 'Kunōkyō no shiso,' p. 278.

23. Noma Hiroshi, 'Atarashii futatsu no hametsu monogatari,' in Haniya Yutaka (ed.), *Takahashi Kazumi-ron*, pp. 259-274.

24. Taira Yoshimasa, 'Shiroku nuritaru haka,' in *Takahashi Kazumi-ron*, p. 210.

25. *Hi no utsuwa*, in *Takahashi Kazumi zenshū*, (Kawade shobō shinsha, 1977-1980), 2, pp. 431-432.

26. Though occasionally capable of showing regret or of having a bad conscience, as when he makes love to his incurably sick wife (chapter 31) or when he reminisces about his colleagues who were persecuted for their convictions before and during the Pacific War, Masaki remains essentially evil throughout the book.

27. See 'Postwar Japanese Literature and the Contemporary Impasse,' pp. 4-5.
28. See chap. 22 and 23.
29. See 'Shisha no shiya ni aru mono,' 'Uchigeba no ronri' and 'Waga kaitai' in *Waga kaitai* (Tōkyō: Kawade shobō shinsha, 1971).
30. Nakayama Kazuko, 'Takahashi Kazumi-ron,' in Ogawa Kazusuke (ed.), *Takahashi Kazumi kenkyū*, p. 51.
31. See especially, 'Sengo bungaku shiron,' first published in *Bungei* (July 1963); the talk with Noma Hiroshi, 'Gendai bungaku no kiten,' *Bungei* (April 1966); and the interview 'Watakushi no bungaku o kataru,' *Mita bungaku* (October 1968).
32. Julia Kristeva, *Soleil noir: Dépression et mélancolie* (Paris: Gallimard, 1987), p. 72.
33. For Bakhtin's conceptions of the dialogical imagination, of the 'polyphonic' and 'carnivalesque' literature, see *The Dialogic Imagination*, ed. M. Holquist, trans. C. Emerson, M. Holquist (Austin: Univ. of Texas Press, 1981); Mikhail Bakhtin, *Rabelais and his World*, trans. H. Iswolsky (Cambridge: Cambridge Univ. Press, 1968) and Tzvetan Todorov, *Mikhail Bakhtin and the Dialogical Principle*, trans. W. Godzich (Minneapolis: Univ. of Minnesota Press, 1984).
34. 'Postwar Japanese Literature and the Contemporary Impasse,' p. 4.
35. See Hans-Georg Gadamer, *Wahrheit und Methode: Grundzüge einer philosophischen Hermeneutik*, (Tübingen, 1965). English translation: *Truth and Method*, trans. Q. Barden and J. Cumming (New York: Harper and Row, 1975).
36. Donald R. Kelley, 'Horizons of Intellectual History,' p.156.
37. For an exultant discussion of Takahashi's 'manliness' see Sugiura Minpei, 'Nihon bungakushi no naka no Takahashi Kazumi,' in Haniya Yutaka (ed.), *Takahashi Kazumi-ron*, pp. 83-94, and Kōchi Satoshi, 'Datenshitachi no kyōen,' in *Takahashi Kazumi o dō toraeru ka* (Tōkyō: Haga shoten, 1972), pp. 7-94. Kōchi even hails 'the revival of metaphysical literature' (*kobungaku no fukkatsu*) supposedly announced by Takahashi. See 'Datenshitachi no kyōen,' p. 68. I should note, however, that recent critical evaluations of Takahashi are more cautious on this subject.
38. See Roland Barthes, *Le plaisir du texte* (Paris: Gallimard, 1973), English trans. *The Pleasure of the Text*, trans. Richard Miller (New York: Hill & Wang, 1975).
39. Vols. 7 and 8 in the most recent edition of Takahashi's complete works (Kawade shobō shinsha, 1977-1980). *Jashūmon* has a total of 900 pages.
40. By unconscious fear I mean a recurrent motif or undercurrent of thought in Takahashi's works which was never formulated as a coherent thesis. In essays such as 'Ansatsu no tetsugaku' (1967), 'Shitsumei no kaisō: Chūkan kaikyū-ron' (1963) and 'Koritsu muen no shisō' (1963), however, Takahashi came very near formulating such a thesis.
41. Takahashi Kazumi, 'Bungaku no sekinin,' in *Essei shū 2: Bungaku hen, Takahashi Kazumi sakuhinshū* 10 Vols. (Tōkyō: Kawade shobō shinsha 1969-1971), Vol. 8.
42. A. D. Nuttall, 'Solvents and Fixatives: Critical Theory in Transition,' *The Modern Language Review* 82 (April 1987): 275.
43. Kōchi Satoshi, 'Bungaku hihyō no kōhai,' in *Takahashi Kazumi o dō toraeru ka*, p. 377.
44. See note 18. Takahashi presented his views on the responsibility of the intelligentsia most cogently in talks he gave in 1969-1970, at the height of the student disturbances. These lectures were collected in *Shōgai ni wataru ashura toshite* (1970) and *Ankoku e no shuppatsu* (1971).
45. Interest in Takahashi has sharply declined since the mid-1970s. One hardly ever hears or sees anything about him in the media. A spate of articles and essays appeared in 1981, the year marking the 10th anniversary of his death, but, with the exception of a few articles and one or two books, hardly anything concerning him seems to have been written since. See 'Takahashi Kazumi shigo jūnen,' *Kyōen* (July 1981), Kunimatsu Akira, 'Yūutsu naru tōha,' *Kokubungaku kaishaku to kanshō* 50, No. 9 (August 1985).
46. A recent study of Takahashi's essays on classical Chinese literature is: Ōgami Masami, 'Chūgoku bungaku kenkyū kara mita Takahashi Kazumi,' *Kōkō tsūshin tōsho kokugo* 251 (May 1985).
47. See the lectures in *Shōgai ni wataru ashura toshite*.
48. Donald R. Kelley, 'Horizons of Intellectual History,' p. 145.
49. Takahashi discussed the 'suicide spirit' underlying Japanese culture in his novelette 'Sange' (1963) and in essays such as 'Sengo minshu-shugi no rikkyaku ten' (1965) and 'Ansatsu no tetsugaku' (1967).

50. See, for instance, Ogawa Kazusuke, 'Takahashi Kazumi to sono jidai,' in *Takahashi Kazumi kenkyū*, pp. 17-39.

51. See Harold Bloom, *A Map of Misreading* (New York: Oxford Univ. Press, 1975).

52. See Jacques Derrida, *Of Grammatology*, trans. Gayatri Chakravorty Spivak (Baltimore: John Hopkins Univ. Press, 1976) and 'Structure, Sign and Play in the Discourse of the Human Sciences,' in *The Structuralist Controversy: the Languages of Criticism and the Sciences of Man*, ed. Richard Macksey and Eugenio Donato (Baltimore: John Hopkins Univ. Press, 1972).

53. See 'Bungaku no sekinin.'

54. Susan Sontag, *On Photography*, quoted after Joe Weixlmann, 'Reading for the Plot,' *Contemporary Literature* 27 (Spring 1986): 64.

55. Frank Lentricchia, *Criticism and Social Change* (Chicago: Univ. of Chicago Press, 1984), p. 105.

56. Karl R. Popper, *A Pocket Popper*, ed. by David Miller (Oxford: Oxford Univ. Press, 1983), p. 8.

Chapter 4 YOICHI NAGASHIMA *Abe Kōbō's 'Ark Sakura'*

1. Among others, Yoichi Nagashima's paper 'Abe Kōbō's Real Box Man' in 'Analecta Hafniensia' (Scandinavian Institute of Asian Studies Occasional Papers No. 3). Copenhagen 1987, pp 105-111.

2. *Ark Sakura*, translated by Juliet Winters Carpenter, Alfred Knopf, New York 1988.

3. All quotations from the novel in this paper are taken from the Japanese original *Hakobune Sakura-maru*, and translated by me.

4. Cf. Kaien, Jan. 1985, 'Shinkan handoku,' pp. 204-212: Kaga Otohiko 'Kokka o meguru dotabata kigeki,' in Gunzō, 1985, No. 2, pp. 266-7: *Mainichi Shinbun*, 17 Dec. 1984 'Ganchiku no fukai gūi.'

5. Cf. *Kyoto Shinbun*, 16 Nov. 1984 'Hakobune Sakura-maru no Abe Kōbō shi' and Yūrin, 10 Dec. 1984 'Abe Kōbō to Hakobune Sakura-maru': or *Tokyo Times* 3 Dec. 1984 'Zetsubōteki ninshiki koete' and *Kōbē Shinbun*, 6 Dec. 1984, 'Sabaibaru no chakusō no naka ni kyomu to romanchishizumu.'

6. Reviews which proclaim that the novel is a masterpiece: Kanno Akimasa 'Bungei jihyō (jō),' in *Tōkyō Shinbun*, 27 Nov. 1984: Isoda Kōichi 'Kaku-jidai ni shinsenna ninshiki,' in *Sankei Shinbun*, 12 Dec. 1984; Donald Keene 'Yūmoa no ura no kanashimi,' in Shinchō, 1985. No. 1, pp. 308-9. Reviews which proclaim that the novel is a fiasco: Shinoda Hajime 'Bungei jihyō,' in *Mainichi Shinbun* (yukan), 27 and 28 Nov. 1984: *Shūkan Asahi*, 30 Nov. 1984, 'Shūkan toshokan'; Kaien, Jan. 1985, 'Shinkan handoku,' pp. 204-212.

7. Cf. Abe Kōbō/Tsukushi Tetsuya 'Kaku-jidai no Hakobune,' in Nami, 1984, No. 11, pp. 8-13; *Tokyo Times*, 3 Dec. 1984, 'Zetsubōteki ninshiki koete'; *Mainichi Shinbun* (yūkan), 18 and 19 Dec. 1984, 'Hakobune Sakura-maru o kaita Abe Kōbō shi ni kiku'; Abe Kōbō/ Kuritsubo Yoshiki 'Gohasan no sekai, hametsu to saisei,' in Subaru, 1985, No. 6, pp. 46-59, also in Abe Kōbō 'Shiniisogu kujira-tachi,' Tōkyō 1986, pp. 115-137.

8. In this context, he should be considered a philosopher rather than a novelist; a thinker, or a think-box who deals with universal problems of our age, ranging from the question of survival in our nuclear age and its political undertone, to environmental problems.

9. His reeling off of 'things,' see 'Hakobune Sakura-maru,' p. 9 and p. 135.

10. In general, his novels are quite different from the nineteenth-century-style orthodox mimesis-novel with clearcut plot and characters.

11. In my opinion Donald Keene is exaggerating a bit, when he says that one cannot read a page without laughing at least once. See Shincho, 1985, No. 1.

12. In fact, we can hear the author's voice in every speech in the novel, whoever delivers it.

13. Cf. 'The monistic description' of Iwano Hōmei (1873-1920). See Yoichi Nagashima 'Iwano Hōmeis litteraturteori,' in Danish with English summary, Copenhagen 1982, p. 329.

14. On 'narrated monologue,' see Dorrit Cohn 'Narrated Monologue: Definition of a Fictive Style,' in Comparative Literature, Vol. 8, No. 2, 1966, pp. 97-112. Dorrit Cohn characterizes 'narrated monologue' in the following way: 'By allowing the same tense to describe the individual's view of reality and that reality itself, inner and outer world become one, eliminating explicit distance between the narrator and his creature. Two linguistic levels,

inner speech with its idiosyncracy and author's report with its quasi-objectivity, become fused into one, so that the same seems to pass through narrating and figural consciousness.' (p. 99).

15. 'Ayu no tomozuri' (p. 35), 'Neko ni katsuobushi' (p. 36), 'Takara no mochigusare' (p. 37), 'Anzuru yori wa umu ga yasushi' (p. 37), 'Omoya o akewatasu' (p. 45), 'Kyodai wa tanin no hajimari' (p. 60) and so on, throughout the novel.

16. Cf. adana (拐 名), doko (何 処), shigusa (仕 草), kōjite (講 じ),

17. Abe Kōbō/Tsutsumi Seiji 'Sōsaku ni okeru wāpuro,' in Nami, 1983, No. 7, pp. 8-13.

18. Hiraoka Tokuyoshi 'Yume-ningen no shūmatsuzu,' in Bungakukai, 1985, No. 2, pp. 224-228; Okuno Takeo 'Bungei jihyō,' in Sankei Shinbun (yūkan), 22 Dec. 1984.

Chapter 5 CHIA-NING CHANG *The Socialization of Literature: the Idea and Prototypes of the Mid-Meiji Social Novel*

1. 'A Conversation with E. L. Doctorow,' *U.S. News and World Report*, 16 December 1985, 74.

2. See Itō Sei's poignant analysis of the character of modern Japanese literary intellectuals in 'Sanbun geijutsu no seikaku' in his monumental work *Shōsetsu no hōhō*, Vol. 13, *Itō Sei zenshū* (Tōkyō: Kawade shobō, 1956), 84-102 and particularly 84-86.

3. See Nagai Kafū, 'Ruzan no rakudo' in *Kōcha no ato*, Vol. 13 *Kafū zenshū* (Tōkyō: Iwanami shoten, 1963), 49. In his characteristically sarcastic tone, Kafū in particular pointed to the example of Edo culture which had succeeded in creating the 'all-beloved' *Bushidō* while banishing all expressions of artistic creativity, with only the exceptions of painting and architecture, from the proper activity of 'decent' society.

4. See Kobayashi Hideo, 'Watakushi shōsetsu ron,' Vol. 3, *Kobayashi Hideo zenshū* (Tōkyō: Shinchōsha, 1968), 119-45. Unlike the Japanese 'watakushi,' Kobayashi noted that in their common attempt to restore the humanity of the self after the onslaughts of nineteenth century French naturalism, such writers as Gide and Proust attempted to reconstruct an 'I' that had by then been sufficiently 'socialized' ('shakaika shita'). See 121-22. Kobayashi's comments on Kume Masao's remark can be found on 120-21.

5. In Vol. 7, *Nakamura Mitsuo zenshū* (Tōkyō: Chikuma shobō, 1972), 526-617.

6. In Vol. 2, *Hirano Ken zenshū* (Tōkyō: Shinchōsha, 1975), 138-355. See in particular the section entitled 'Shishōsetsu no niritsu haihan,' 143-63.

7. In Vol. 6, *Katō Shūichi chosakushū* (Tōkyō: Heibonsha, 1978), 21-42.

8. See Arima Tatsuo, *The Failure of Freedom: A Portrait of Modern Japanese Intellectuals*. (Cambridge, Harvard University Press, 1969), 70-98. His discussion on Katai's dictum of *heimin byōsha* is on 77. Shimamura Hōgetsu's idea of *zettai mushinen* is discussed along with other similar naturalist catch-phrases on 94.

9. See the two chapters 'Hōki to chōwa' and 'Jiga no sayō' in Itō Sei, *Shōsetsu no hōhō*, 52-71.

10. See 'Kindai riarizumu no tenkai' in Nakamura's *Fūzoku shōsetsu ron*, 560-70, and particularly 566-69. For the relationship between *shishōsetsu* and *fūzoku shōsetsu*, see 588-615. See also Kawakami Tetsutarō's commentary ('kaisetsu') in the Shinchō bunko edition of *Fūzoku shōsetsu ron* (Tōkyō: Shinchōsha, 1974), 131-36.

11. See for example 'Nihon no baai' in *Shōsetsu no hōhō*, 51, and Itō's essay 'Tōbō dorei to kamen shinshi,' Vol. 10, *Itō Sei zenshū*.

12. 'Gendai Nihon bungaku no jōkyō: Seikatsu no geijutsuka to geijutsu no seikatsuka' in *Kindai Nihon no bungakuteki dentō*, Vol. 6, *Katō Shūichi chosakushū*, 21-40. See especially 21-25.

13. For a discussion of the social background to the rise of the mid-Meiji social novel in the aftermath of the Sino-Japanese War, see Chia-ning Chang, 'Theoretical Speculations and Literary Representations: Writers and Critics of Social Literature in the Meiji Inter-War Years,' (Ph.D. Dissertation, Stanford University, 1985), 59-61.

14. See Ōkōchi Kazuo, 'Nihon no shakaishugi: sono keifu to tokuchō,' *Shakaishugi*, Vol. 15, *Gendai Nihon shisō taikei* (Tōkyō: Chikuma shobō, 1972), 14-15.

15. See his 'Shōsetsukai no zento,' quoted in Satō Masaru, 'Shakai shōsetsu,' in *Kindai bungakushi: Meiji no bungaku*, Vol. 1, eds. Kōno Toshirō, Takemori Tenyū and Miyoshi Yukio et al. (Tōkyō: Yūhikaku, 1972), 150.

16. See Itō Sei, Hisamatsu Sen'ichi, Kawabata Yasunari et al. (eds.) *Shinchō Nihon bungaku shōjiten* (Tōkyō: Shinchōsha, 1968), 1203, 1075-76.

17. For a detailed study of reportage literature related to the livelihood of the lower classes in Japan at that time, see Tachibana Yūichi, *Meiji no kasō kiroku bungaku* (Tōkyō: Sōjusha, 1981).

18. Satō Masaru, 'Shakai shōsetsu,' 151. See also Odagiri Susumu, *Nihon kindai bungaku no tenkai: kindai kara gendai e* (Tōkyō: Yomiuri shimbunsha, 1974), 18-21.

19. *Kindai bungaku hyōron taikei*, Vol. 2 (hereafter cited as *KBHT*) ed. Inagaki Tatsurō and Satō Masaru (Tōkyō: Kadokawa shoten, 1972), 36.

20. Quoted from Roan's 'Futabatei yodan' (August 1915) collected in the section called 'Futabatei Shimei no isshō' in his *Meiji no sakka*, (Tōkyō: Chikuma shobō, 1941), 211-12. This reminiscence has often been quoted in various critical essays discussing Roan's experience in reading *Crime and Punishment* and his acquisition of a real sense of appreciation of the serious purpose of literature.

21. See *ibid*.

22. Roka writes: '*Les Miserables* completely captivated Keiji. He got up early...and quickly turned to the novel. He was unwilling to give up his time even at meals. His left hand sent boiled chestnuts mechanically into his mouth...while his eyes devoured the pages with burning passion.' Quoted in Nishida Masaru, *Kindai bungaku no hakkutsu* (Tōkyō: Hōsei daigaku shuppankyoku, 1971), 173.

23. Reiun's own words are: 'At that time, I was absorbed in reading Hugo and I treasured every minute of it even while I was walking on the street. On my way to and from school, I read as I walked, and it was not unusual for me to bump my head against sign boards or run into carts or wagons.' *Taoka Reiun zenshū* (hereafter cited as *TRZ*). Vol. 5, ed. by Nishida Masaru (Tōkyō: Hōsei daigaku shuppankyoku), 1973.

24. The growing disenchantment with the frivolity and superficiality of taste of the contemporary literary world after the Sino-Japanese War quite often took the form of decrying the nation's intellectual scene and cultural conditions. Uchimura Kanzō's notable essay 'Naze daibungaku wa idezaruka' (*Kokumin no tomo*, July 1895) proclaimed that all Japan had at that time was 'cheap literature, rubbish journals, bragging magazines, dry, captious periodicals that read like chewing pebbles.' *KBHT*, 29.

25. Reiun attributed the lack of the tragic element in Japanese literature to the refined and moderate nature of the Japanese personality which was nurtured in the country's temperate climate and exquisite natural surroundings. Accordingly, the Japanese had known little bitterness or suffering in life and had no awareness of tragedy. See his essay 'Nihon bungaku no tansho' (*Seinenbun*, 10 April 1895) in *TRZ*, Vol. 1, 316-17. Reiun also elaborated his views on the relationship between Japan's natural surroundings and its national character as well as its resultant effects on its literary productions in 'Nihon bungaku ni okeru shinkōsai' (*Nipponjin*, 5 July 1895), *TRZ*, Vol. 1, 363-67. It should be noted that this kind of argument heralded a comparable line of reasoning in works like Watsuji Tetsurō's now classic *Fūdo: Ningengakuteki kōsatsu* in 1935.

26. Roan's trenchant attacks on the still-prevailing *gesaku* mentality of his contemporary writers can be seen in an array of his critical essays written after 1889 and into the 1890s. See, for example, his 'Shōsetsu wa yūgi moji ni arazu' (*Jogaku zasshi*, December 1889), 'Aeba Kōson shi' (*Kokumin no tomo*, February-May 1891), *Bungaku ippan* (March 1892) and of course his most famous work of criticism *Bungakusha to naru hō* (April 1894) written under the disguised and intentionally clownish name of Sanmojiya Kimpei.

27. Miyazaki Koshoshi, 'Ken'yūsha to sono sakka' (*Kokumin no tomo*, January 1896), quoted in Ikari Akira, *Ken'yūsha no bungaku* (Tōkyō: Hanawa shobō, 1961), 56.

28. See Kimata Osamu, Hasegawa Izumi and Hisamatsu Sen'ichi et al. eds. *Gendai Nihon bungaku daijiten* (Tōkyō: Meiji shoin, 1965) 530-31.

29. Despite its brevity, this announcement precipitated what was to become a lively literary controversy over the meaning, content and scope of the social novel for the next few years. For the announcement, see *KBHT*, 57-8.

30. The views of the *Mainichi* columnist were cited by an unsigned writer in an untitled essay in the February 1897 issue of the *Waseda bungaku*. The essay, usually referred to by today's critics as 'Iwayuru shakai shōsetsu,' the name of the heading of its first section, is collected in *KBHT*, 63-68. The views of the *Mainichi* writer are cited on 63-64. However, neither the date of its publication nor the title, if it had one, was cited.

31. The views of the *Gekkan* writer were also cited in 'Iwayuru shakai shōsetsu,' 64-65. Again, the name of the author, the date of publication and the title of his essay were not cited.

32. See 'Iwayuru shakai shōsetsu' cited in n. 30. For his characterization of the ways how critics had come to use the term *shakai shōsetsu*, see 66-68.
33. See Shimamura Hōgetsu, 'Shakai shōsetsu ron' in *KBHT*, 69-72 and especially 70.
34. See Kaneko's 'Iwayuru shakai shōsetsu' in *KBHT*, 76-80 and especially 78-9.
35. See Irving Howe's thoughtful essay 'The Idea of the Political Novel' in his *Politics and the Novel* (Meridian Books: Cleveland & New York, 1964), 15-24 and especially 15-16. I am indebted to Howe in thinking about the essential nature of the Japanese social novel.
36. Roan's first and perhaps his best-known 'social novel' (which is in fact a short story) was first published in March 1898 in *Shincho gekkan*, a new journal founded by Gotō Chūgai and Shimamura Hōgetsu. The story is collected in Inagaki Tatsurō ed. *Uchida Roan shū*, Vol. 24, *Meiji bungaku zenshū* (Tōkyō: Chikuma shobō, 1978).
37. *Kokuchō*, first serialized in Tokutomo Sohō's *Kokumin shimbun* from January to June 1902, is collected in Vol. 7, *Roka zenshū*, 20 Vols. (Tōkyō: Roka zenshū kankōkai, Shinchōsha, 1928-30).
38. See Nakano Yoshio, Vol. 2, *Roka Tokutomi Kenjirō*, 3 Vols. (Tōkyō: Chikuma shobō, 1972-74), 134.
39. Many of Kagai's earlier poems, published in journals such as *Tōkyō dokuritsu zasshi, Rōdō sekai, Shinshōsetsu* and *Myōjō*, were gathered in *Shakaishugi shishū* published in August 1903, the anthology for which Kagai is best remembered. *Shakaishugi shishū* is now collected in Odagiri Susumu, ed. *Meiji shakaishugi bungaku shū*, 1, Vol. 83, *Meiji bungaku zenshū* (Tōkyō: Chikuma shobō, 1965), 288-309. A telling commentary about the anthology can be found in Okano Takao, '*Shakaishugi shishū* ni tsuite' in Okano, ed. *Shakaishugi shishū* (Tōkyō: Sekai bunko, 1973), 85-112.
40. *Hi no hashira* is now collected in Vol. 2 in Yanagida Izumi, Yamagiwa Keiji and Gokan Toshifumi et al. eds. *Kinoshita Naoe chosakushū*, 15 Vols. (Tōkyō: Meiji bunken, 1968-73). The English translation is provided by Kenneth Strong, *Pillar of Fire: Hi no Hashira by Naoe Kinoshita* (London: George Allen and Unwin, 1972).
41. Quoted in Irving Howe, 21.
42. Quoted in Irving Howe, 24. See also 21-24.

Chapter 7 GIAN CARLO CALZA *Problems of Attribution in Japanese Art: the Case of Hokusai's Paintings*
1. *Ukiyo*, 'floating world,' was originally a Buddhist term indicating the passing, the fatal disappearing of everything in this world. By the mid-Edo period it had come to mean everything in fashion and its art, *ukiyo e*, was the vehicle for conveying images of the most fashionable and much demanded courtesan, for example, or a celebrated actor or a famous beauty spot. All these subjects were mostly conveyed and circulated by means of woodblock prints and their artists were essentially graphic artists whose pictorial output was limited and scarcely considered by academics until fairly recently.
2. How common an opinion this is among qualified art historians has been summarized for all by Richard Lane who in his recent *Hokusai. Life and Work*, New York, Dutton, 1989 (pp. 99; 102; p. 109 note 6), repeatedly refers to the unclear state of Hokusai's paintings scholarship.
3. These terms respectively mean that a) the painting stands a good chance of having come from the artist's hands, but one is not completely sure; b) the painting appears to have been produced by one or more pupils in the Master's atelier or under his supervision, possibly with his hand in it; c) the painting is not by the artist, but by some pupil; d) the painting is a work in the style of the artist, but not by him and probably of a later period.
4. Prints were, and still are, more complex and expensive to be forged and their fakes more easily identified than paintings. There are also countless books on Hokusai's prints that can be used as valuable reference. A big project for a general catalogue of Hokusai's prints is under way at present and, when published, many of the old problems on the subject will be certainly overcome.
5. Especially since after the publication of Jack Hillier's exhaustive: *The Art of Hokusai in Book Illustration*, London, Sotheby-Parke Bernet & University of California Press, 1980.
6. For the myth of the white snake originated in China and successively transplanted in Japan see: Wu Pei-yi, *The White Snake. The Evolution of a Myth in China*, unpublished Ph.D. dissertation, New York, Columbia University, 1969.

7. See, for instance, the painting of a 'Nobleman Offering a Tray to a Snake' and its preparatory drawing in a London collection; Sawers, Robert G., *Hokusai. Prints, Paintings, Drawings and Illustrated Books*, London, Hugh Moss, 1972, pl. 92.

8. See pl. 1. The painting bears an inscription on the lower right with a signature: '*yowai hachijūrokusai* Manji *hitsu*,' it is accompanied by a date '*Kōka futatsu tsuchinoto mi nen / shōgatsu ganjitsu*' (New Year's Day, second year of Kōka, year of the snake, younger brother of the earth) and an *intaglio* KATSUSHIKA seal. It is reproduced in: Hokusai Kan, *Nikuhitsu Katsushika Hokusai*, Ōbuse, Nagano *ken*, 1983, p. 41. The study of this type of seal and its reading have been published in Hokusai Kenkyūjō (ed.), *Ehon saishikitsū*, Tōkyō, 1980, p. 64. Other less convincing readings and interpretations like FUJIWARA FUMOTO NO SAKI and TENGU have been supplied by scholars.

9. See pl. 2. I use this opportunity to thank the staff in the Department of Japanese Antiquities in the British Museum and particularly Mr Lawrence Smith and Mr Timothy Clark for their help and stimulating advice.

10. See pl. 3. I use this opportunity to thank the staff of the Freer Gallery of Art and especially Ms Ann Yonemura, Assistant Curator of Japanese Art, who spared me so much of her time.

11. The inscription and signature read: *Hachijūhachi* Manji Kōka *yotsu hi no to hitsuji nen shigatsu hatsuka tsuchinoto mi no hi fude o orosu* (The eighty-eight-year-old Manji on the day of the younger brother of the earth, serpent, the 20th day of 4th year of Kōka, younger brother of fire, laid the brush down [after finishing his painting]). The seal is a red *intaglio* HYAKU.

12. Fenollosa, Ernest, *Hokusai*, Tōkyō, Bunshichi Kobayashi, 1901, no 166.

13. See pl. 5. Illustrated in: Hokusai Kan, *Nikuhitsu Katsushika Hokusai*, Ōbuse, Nagano *ken*, 1983, p. 21.

14. Extremely elongated fingers are present in Hokusai's production, but only at a much earlier stage, during the 'Sori' and first years of 'Hokusai' periods. However, in those instances the hands retain a grace and charm which is certainly not the case with this painting.

15. See pl. 8. Metropolitan Museum of Art, New York, East Asian Department. I take the opportunity to thank Dr Barbara Brennan Ford, Associate curator of Japanese Art, and Mrs Yasuko Betchaku, once assistant curator of Japanese Art, for their assistance and invaluable help.

16. As it might be expected, there are even less satisfactory studies on Hokusai's pupils than of the Master himself, which makes the problem of attributing their works almost as difficult, hence my tentative attribution.

17. At least since Fenollosa's exhibition of 1900.

18. The poem is actually signed by Sōgai as an 'old man of 87,' which should correspond to 1820 as he seems to have died in 1823 at the age of 90. Even though there is still some uncertainty due to the Japanese way of counting age.

19. The painting is illustrated, among others, in: Hillier, Jack Ronald, *Hokusai Drawings*, London, Phaidon Press, 1960, n. 94, where it is attributed to 'Hokusai or Taitō II' and in Nihon Kenzai Shinbun, *Hokusai ten*, Tōkyō, Nihon Kenzai Shinbunsha, 1967, ill. 28 where it is attributed to Hokusai.

20. Metropolitan Museum of Art, New York, accession no 56.121.1-43:37.

21. This doubtful scroll, once in the Nakayama collection, has been widely reproduced and acclaimed as Hokusai's work. See, among others, Narazaki Muneshige, *Hokusai to Hiroshige*, v. 7 of *Kachō to Fūgetsu*, 8 vv., Tōkyō, Kōdansha, 1971, pp. 36-37; Nagata Seiji, *Katsushika Hokusai ten*, Tōkyō, Ohta Kishin Bijutsukan, 1985, pl. 541; Forrer, Matthi e Goncourt, Edmond de, *Hokusai*, Paris, Flammarion, 1988, no 175, p. 164 and in Lane, Richard, *Hokusai. Life and Work*, New York, Dutton, 1989, pp. 108-109, who all seem to ascribe it to Hokusai.

22. The dating reads: *Bunka jū mizunoto tori nen shigatsu nijūgo nichi* (25th day of the 4th month of the tenth year of bunka year of the cock younger brother of water) and the dedication: *Nenrai jiden sōrō kimō dasoku no in oyuzuri mōshiage sōrō. Goshussei itaru beshi sōrō ijō* (I pass over to you the KIMŌ DASOKU seal in my possession for the past years. You should be as diligent as possible).

23. The pupil seems to have been Hokumei according to some relevant scholarship: Narazaki Muneshige, *Hokusai to Hiroshige*, v. 7 of *Kachō to Fūgetsu*, 8 vv., Tōkyō, Kōdansha, 1971, pp. 36-37; Nagata Seiji, *Katsushika Hokusai nenpu*, Tōkyō, Sansaishinsha, 1985, p. 57; Lane,

Richard, *Hokusai. Life and Work*, New York, Dutton, 1989, pp. 108-109.

24. Narazaki Muneshige, *Hokusai to Hiroshige*, v. 7 of *Kachō to Fūgetsu*, 8 vv., Tōkyō, Kōdansha, 1971, pp. 36-37.

25. News of its discovery in the Museum's store-rooms was given by the author of this article at the international conference 'Rethinking Japan' held at the University of Venice in the Autumn of 1987 and was subsequently taken up by the press: *Il Giornale dell'Arte*, anno V, no 50, novembre 1987, p. 2; *Asahi Shinbun*, 17 November 1987, p. 8; *Japan Foundation Newsletter*, v. XV, no 3, November 1987 issue. Formerly in the celebrated Bigelow collection, the screen (catalogued, yet not illustrated, in Ernest Fenollosa, *Hokusai and His School*, Boston, Boston Museum of Fine Arts, printed by Alfred Mudge & Son, 1893, p. 27, no 144, and considered lost since by scholars) came to my attention in summer 1987 while visiting the Museum store-rooms during a research on Hokusai paintings in Western collections. I use this occasion to extend my thanks to the Department's staff for their kind assistance and help and especially to Dr Money Hickman and Ms Ann Morse who first showed the screen to me. For more details and attribution analysis of this screen see my 'Hokusai's Phoenix Screen at the Boston Museum of Fine Arts,' in *La modernizzazione in Asia e in Africa. Problemi di storia e problemi di metodo. Studi offerti a Giorgio Borsa*, Pavia, Università degli Studi, 1989.

26. I wish to express my thanks to Mme Monique Cohen, Conservateur en Chef, Departement des Manuscrits Orientaux, for her kind help during my research there and to Mme Kosugi Keiko for her most valuable assistance.

27. Goncourt, Edmond de, *L'art japonais du XVIIIe siecle. Hokousaï*, Paris, Charpentier, 1896; Revon, Marcel, *Etude sur Hoksai*, Paris, Lecène, Oudin et cie, 1896; Focillon, Henri, *Hokousaï*, Paris, Alcan, 1914.

28. Some such documents are reproduced in Hokusai Kan, *Nikuhitsu Katsushika Hokusai*, Ōbuse, Nagano *ken*, 1983, pp. 70-74.

QUOTED BIBLIOGRAPHY

An. 'Hokusai. Maboroshi no nikuhitsu byōbu Beibijutsukan ni atta. Itaria no kenkyūka hakken' in *Asahi Shinbun*, 17 November 1987.

Calza, Gian Carlo, 'Hokusai's Phoenix Screen at the Boston Museum of Fine Arts,' in *The Japan Foundation Newsletter*, v. XV, no 3, November 1987 issue.

Calza, Gian Carlo, 'Boston. Nei depositi del museo un paravento capolavoro di Hokusai,' in *Il Giornale dell'arte*, anno V, no 50, novembre 1987.

Calza, Gian Carlo, 'Hokusai's Phoenix Screen at the Boston Museum of Fine Arts,' in *La modernizzazione in Asia e in Africa. Problemi di storia e problemi di metodo. Studi offerti a Giorgio Borsa*, Pavia, Università degli Studi, 1989.

Focillon, Henri, *Hokousaï*, Paris, Alcan, 1914.

Fenollosa, Ernest, *Catalogue of the Exhibition of Paintings of Hokusai. Held at the Japan Fine Art Association, Ueno Park, Tokyo, from 13th to 30th January, 1900*, Tōkyō, Bunshichi Kobayashi, 1901.

Fenollosa, Ernest, *Hokusai and His School*, Boston, Boston Museum of Fine Arts, printed by Alfred Mudge & Son, 1893.

Forrer, Matthi and Goncourt, Edmond de, *Hokusai*, Paris, Flammarion, 1988.

Goncourt, Edmond de , *L'art japonais du XVIIIe siècle, Hokousaï*, Paris, Charpentier, 1896.

Hillier, Jack Ronald, *Hokusai Drawings*, London, Phaidon Press, 1966.

Hillier, Jack Ronald, *The Art of Hokusai in Book Illustration*, London, Sotheby-Parke Bernet & University of California Press, 1980.

Hokusai Kan, *Nikuhitsu Katsushika Hokusai*, Ōbuse, Nagano *ken*, 1983.

Hokusai Kenkyūjō (ed.), *Ehon saishikitsū*, Tōkyō, 1980.

Lane, Richard, *Hokusai. Life and Work*, New York, Dutton, 1989.

Nagata Seiji, *Katsushika Hokusai nenpu*, Tōkyō, Sansaishinsha, 1985.

Nagata Seiji, *Katsushika Hokusai ten*, Tōkyō, Ohta Kishin Bijutsukan, 1985.

Narazaki Muneshige, *Hokusai to Hiroshige*, v. 7 of *Kachō to Fūgetsu*, 8 vv., Tōkyō, Kōdansha, 1971.

Narazaki Muneshige (ed.), *Katsushika Hokusai to sono sekai ten*, Hokkaidō Shinbunsha, 1984.
Nihon Keizai Shinbun, *Hokusai ten*, Tōkyō, Nihon Keizai Shinbunsha, 1967.
Revon, Marcel, *Etude sur Hoksaï*, Paris, Lecène, Oudin et cie, 1896.
Sawers, Robert G., *Hokusai. Prints, Paintings, Drawings and Illustrated Books*, London, Hugh Moss, 1972.

Chapter 10 ROBERT LYONS DANLY *Can Japanese Literature be Translated?*

1. Steiner, George, *After Babel* (New York and London: Oxford University Press, 1975), p. 239.
2. *Ibid.*, p. 240.

Chapter 11 P. T. HARRIES *A Sense of Tragedy: Attitudes in Europe and Japan*

I should like to record my gratitude to the School of Oriental and African Studies, University of London and to the British Academy for their generous support with the cost of attending the conference at which the first draft of this paper was presented.

1. Hisamatsu Sen'ichi, et al., eds., *Heian Kamakura shikashū* (Iwanami Shoten, 1964), p. 463, and Phillip Tudor Harries, *The Poetic Memoirs of Lady Daibu* (Stanford University Press, 1980), p. 189.
2. Attention is drawn to this distinction in Oscar Mandel, *A Definition of Tragedy* (New York University Press, 1961), pp. 5-6.
3. See Mandel, op. cit., ch. 1 (and indeed the whole book) for a typical twentieth-century non-generic approach.
4. Abe Akio, et al., eds., *Genji monogatari* (Shōgakkan, 1974), vol. 4, p. 484.
5. *Ibid.*
6. Richard B. Sewall, *The Vision of Tragedy* (Yale University Press, New Edition, 1980), p. 3. This is but one example of a fairly prevalent view.
7. Mandel, op. cit., p. 20.
8. R. P. Draper, ed., *Tragedy: Developments in Criticism* (Macmillan, 1980), pp. 50-56.
9. Hisamatsu Sen'ichi, *The Vocabulary of Japanese Literary Aesthetics* (Centre for East Asian Cultural Studies, Tōyō Bunko, 1963), p. 16.
10. Quoted in Draper, op. cit., p. 77.
11. Quoted in Clifford Leech, *Tragedy* (Methuen, 1969), p. 4.
12. Jeannette King, *Tragedy in the Victorian Novel* (Cambridge University Press, 1978), p. 46.
13. Leech, op. cit., p. 67.
14. Draper, op. cit., p. 206.
15. From his poem 'Spring and Fall.' A good text is W. H. Gardner, ed., *Gerard Manley Hopkins: Poems and Prose* (Penguin Books, 1953), p. 50.
16. George Steiner, *The Death of Tragedy* (Faber & Faber, 1961), p. 128.
17. King. op. cit., p. 46.
18. *Shinkokinshū*, No. 362: my translation.

Chapter 12 IRMELA HIJIYA-KIRSCHNEREIT *Once More: on Problems of Literary Historiography*
1. Cf. my Kritische Bemerkungen zur japanischen Literaturkritik (Critical Remarks on Japanese Literary Criticism), in: Ostasienwissenschaftliche Beiträge zur Sprache, Literatur, Geschichte, Geistesgeschichte, Wirtschaft, Politik und Geographie, Wiesbaden 1974, pp. 50-64.
2. Cf. my Die nicht existenten Probleme der modernen japanischen Literaturgeschichtsschreibung (The non-existing problems of modern Japanese literary historiography), in: Referate des IV. Deutschen Japanologentags in Tübingen, MOAG LXXIII (Hamburg 1978), pp. 45-53, and: Theoriedefizit und Wertungswut: Die nicht existenten Probleme der modernen japanischen Literaturgeschichtsschreibung (2), in:

Bochumer Jahrbuch zur Ostasienforschung (BJOAF), Vol. 2 (1979), pp. 286-306. A slightly extended Japanese language version of the latter is: Riron ketsujo to kachi handanbyō. Nihon bungakushi ni okeru 'sonzai shite inai' mondai, in: Bungaku 12/1982, pp. 149-161.
3. Annotations on the concept of tradition in modern Japanese literature in: Tradition and Modern Japan, ed. P. G. O'Neill, Tenterden 1981, pp. 206-216 and 301 f.
4. The so-called Miyoshi-Tanizawa ronsō, cf. my Wissenschaft als Kunst. Zur Anatomie einer aktuellen Kontroverse in der japanischen Philologie, in: Bochumer Jahrbuch zur Ostasienforschung (BJOAF), Vol. 4 (1981), pp. 144-165.
5. Cf. Helmut Nobis: Die Bestimmung der konnotativen Funktionen im literarischen Text als Voraussetzung für eine historisch-strukturale Literaturgeschichtsschreibung, in: Probleme der Literaturgeschichtsschreibung, ed. W. Haubrichs (Zeitschrift für Literaturwissenschaft und Linguistik, Beiheft 10), Göttingen 1979, pp. 80-103.
6. 'Dai-san to iu no ga ika naru imi o motsu no ka, ikkō akiraka de nai,' quoted after Watanabe Yoshinori: Daisan no shinjin, sono ta takyokuka genshō, in: Nihon bungaku shinshi, Gendai, ed. Hasegawa Izumi (Kokubungaku kaishaku to kanshō bessatsu) 5/1986, pp. 122-131, here p. 122.
7. Cf. Die nicht existenten Probleme... (1978), pp. 46 ff.
8. In any case, the unfelicitous mixture of gender, generational, and 'content' criteria does not make sense, cf. Tsuge Teruhiko: Kankei gensō no bungaku - Nakagami Kenji, Tsushima Yūko no sekai, in: Kokubungaku kaishaku to kanshō 6/1980, pp. 144-150, here p. 144. Some more examples of sanpa teiritsu are quoted in my Theoriedefizit und Wertungswut (cf. footnote 2), p. 288 f.
9. Yoshida Seiichi in a discussion on Sengo bungaku no mondai: 'Hitotsu no shiryō ga dete, sukkari sakka ni taisuru hyōka ga kawatte kita nante iu koto wa ichiryū sakka no baai nanka wa nai to omoimasu,' cf. Gendai Nihon bungaku kōza, hyōron zuihitsu, Vol. 3, Geppō 12/1963, pp. 9-12, here p. 11. See also my Riron ketsujo... p. 153.

Chapter 13 MIKOLAJ MELANOWICZ *The Problem of Time in Japanese Literature*
1. J. T. Fraser (ed.), *The Voices of Time. A Comparative Survey of Man's Views of Time as Expressed by the Sciences and by the Humanities* (Amherst: The University of Massachusetts, 1981).
2. Mikolaj Melanowicz, *Potega chaosu* (The Power of Chaos), 'Film' Nr. 10.1986.03.09, pp. 3-4, 19.
3. Ivan Morris, *The World of the Shining Prince: Court Life in Japan* (Oxford University Press, 1964).
4. Mikolaj Melanowicz, *Rozwoj teorii powiesci w Japonii'* (Development of the Theory of Novel in Japan). 'Przeglad Humanistyczny,' Nr. 1; 1984, p. 10.
5. Cf. *The Tale of the Heike* (Tōkyō: University of Tokyo Press, 1975), tr. by Hiroshi Kitagawa, Bruce T. Tsuchida as follows: 'The bell of the Gion Temple tolls into every man's heart to warn him that all is vanity and evanescence. The faded flowers of the sala trees by the Buddha's deathbed bear witness to the truth that all who flourish are destined to decay. p. 5.
6. Dōgen, Shōbō genzō zuimonki. Chapter 5.4. In: *Nihon Shisō Taikei* (Tōkyō: Iwanami 1970, 1975).
7. Yamada Takao - see: Nishida Nagao, 'Nakaima no goshaku o megutte,' in: 'Nihon Shisōshi,' Nr. 5, 1977, pp. 3-12.
8. Nishida Nagao, 'Nakaima no goshaku o megutte,' op. cit., p. 4.

SELECTED BIBLIOGRAPHY

1. Nagafuji Yasushi, *Chūsei Nihon to Jikan Ishiki* (Tōkyō: Miraisha, 1984).
2. *Nihon Shisō*, Vol. 4 '*Jikan*' (Tōkyō: Tōkyō Daigaku Shuppankai, 1984).
3. 'Nihon no Bigaku,' Vol. 2 'Renzoku,' (Tōkyō: Perikansha, 'Quarterly The Aesthetics of Japan,' Vol. 1, No. 2 1984).
4. 'Nihon Shisōshi' (Tōkyō: Perikansha, No. 2, 1976, No. 17, 1981).
5. Zdzislaw Augustynek, *Natura czasu* (The Nature of Time) (Warszawa: Panstwowe Wydawnictwo Naukowe, 1975).
6. *The Study of Time*, 4 Vols. (New York and Heidelberg, Springer Verlag, 1972-1981).
7. J. T. Fraser (ed.), *The Voices of Time* (Amherst: The University of Massachusetts Press, 1981).

8. G. N. Schlesinger, *Aspects of Time* (Indianapolis Cambridge: Hackett Publishing Company, 1980).

9. G. J. Whitrow, *The Natural Philosophy of Time* (Oxford: Clarendon Press, 1984).

Chapter 14 KURT W. RADTKE
Chaos or Coherence?

1.   In this paper '*Chenlun*' is used as a reference to the trilogy consisting of three parts - '*Chenlun*', '*Nanqian*' and '*Yinhuise de si*'. In references to page numbers *Chenlun* refers to page numbers of the story *Chenlun*; in the edition I used (Yu Dafu *Chenlun, Nanqian, Yinhuise de si*, Tianxia shudian, n.p., 1947) '*Nanqian*' and '*Yinhuise de si*' have separate page numbers.

2.   Although *Chenlun* is usually classified as a novel '*xiaoshuo*' it seems closer to the short story than a full-scale novel. 'One popular trend in literature was the genre of the short story, with its elements of character development, build-up, climax and denouement.... The short story was his favourite, and he never went beyond this to write a full-scale novel.' Chang, Randall Olivers *Yü Ta-fu (1895-1945): The Alienated Artist in Modern Chinese Literature*, Claremont Graduate School, Ph.D., 1974, p. 13. In contrast with the 'typical' Western short story, however, *Chenlun* is characterized by a large number of retarding elements. Zhang Enhe *Yu Dafu xiaoshuo xinshang*, Nanning, 1986 (2nd ed.), p. 63. Despite the widespread use of the term 'novel' (*xiaoshuo*) quite a few Chinese works belonging to that genre show a distinct reluctance to adhere to common Western definitions of the genre. It is also interesting to note that not only Japanese writers, but also Yu Dafu shows a predilection for the diary and the letter: 'The most suitable *genre* for prose works is the diary and then the letter.' Dolezalová, Anna *Yü Ta-fu: Specific Traits of his Literary Creation*, Bratislava - London - New York, 1971, p. 107.

3.   P. Waddington, 'Introduction,' in Turgenev, I. S. *Rudin*, 1970, p. 30.

4.   Guozhen Zhang, 'Yu Dafu he woguo xiandai shuqing xiaoshuo,' *Zhongguo xiandai wenxue yanjiu congkan* 4 (1981), p. 147.

5.   Lee, L. Ou-fan 'Yü Ta-fu: Driftings of a Loner,' in Leo Lee Ou-fan *The Romantic Generation of Modern Chinese Writers*. Harvard UP, Cambridge, Mass., 1973, p. 117.

6.   Satō Haruo *Denen no yūutsu*, Shinchōsa, 1973 [Shinchō bunko], p. 69.

7.   In the novel *Utsukushii machi* (A Beautiful Town) by Satō Haruo the link with changes in society is much more explicit.

8.   Yu Dafu *Chenlun, Nanqian, Yinhuise de si*, Tianxia shudian, n.p., 1947, pp. 86-87.

9.   See, for instance, *Chenlun*, p. 19-20 (where the protagonist rebels against Christian religious 'superstition' and complains about a stupid American missionary), p. 52; *Nanqian*, esp. pp. 32, 36 where a (in fact, any) religion is described as a means to achieve 'self-respect'. The main protagonist in *Nanqian* appears to be intrigued by Christianity, but his 'philosophical rationality' (*zhexue de lizhixing*) does not permit him to pray (pp. 53-4). See also the numerous references to Christianity on pp. 78ff, which also contains a side swipe at dishonest Chinese converts whose 'faith' is often a means to gain some material advantage.

10.   Michael Egan, 'Yu Dafu and the Transition to Modern Chinese Literature,' *Modern Chinese Literature in the May Fourth Era*, M. Goldman (ed.), Harvard University Press, 1977, p. 315.

11.   Cf., *Denen no yūutsu*, p. 25 which refers to his alienation from *nature*: 'Kare wa mō SOEN sareta: nagai nengetsu no aida, kō iu mono o minakatta koto ya, moshi me ni haitta ni shite mo miyō to mo shinakatta de arō koto ni, kare wa hajimete kizuita. sō ieba, yōen no hi irai - ano koro wa, hoka no kodomo ichibai sonna mono o tanoshimifukette ita ni mo kakawarazu, sono omoide sae mo wasurete ita - ochitsuite, tsuki o aoida koto mo nakereba, tori o mita koto mo nakatta. sonna koto ni kizuita koto ga, kare o myō ni kanashiku, mata yorokobashiku shita.' And further: 'Shizen sono mono kara, shin ni seishin na bi to yorokibi o chokusetsuni tsumitoru koto o shirienakatta koro kara, sorera geijutsu no inshō o tōshite, kare wa kono hana ni nomi wa kō shite fukai ai o sasagete kite ita.' (*Ibid.*, p. 29).

12.   On this topic in modern Japanese literature in general, see also Ishibashi Manabu 'Denen to hendo,' *Shin hihyō kindai Nihon bungaku no kōzō*, 1980 [Kindai Nihon bungaku no fudo, 3], passim.

13.   See for instance *Denen no yūutsu* p. 21 which focuses on images of 'egoistic' behaviour in nature.

14.   Shūji Suzuki, *Chūgoku bungaku to Nihon bungaku* (1978), p. 9.

15. Zhang 'Yu Dafu he woguo xiandai shuqing xiaoshuo,' p.143.

16. For a list of early criticism of Satō's *Denen no yūutsu*, see Kawamura 'Satō Haruo,' passim.

17. Recent political changes have made it easier for Chinese critics to reappraise Yu Dafu's role. There were, however, some earlier noticeable exceptions, where critics like Cheng Fangwu are full of praise of the role and importance of Yu Dafu in modern literary history. (Cheng Fangwu "Chenlun" de pinglun,' p. 103). As far as the literary evaluation of both works is concerned it may suffice to mention that in China, the evaluation of Yu Dafu has invariably suffered from the fact that the open discussion of sex has seemingly forced Chinese critics to associate *Chenlun* with other second-rate 'depraved' novels. (Chang *Yü Ta-fu*, p. 134) A. Dolezalová-Vlckova devoted a special study to Yu Dafu, but she discusses him as a Chinese counterpart of the Japanese 'I-novel,' an approach which seems hardly justifiable. R. O. Chang devotes a whole dissertation to Yu Dafu's work, but he, too, concludes that 'although he was a unique individual who wrote interesting fiction, he is of little significance to modern historians and literary critics.' (Chang *Yü Ta-fu*, p. 134).

18. The term appears in the beginning of *Denen no yūutsu*, p. 6: 'mura wa, jitsu ni chiisa na sanbunshi de atta.'

19. Xu Zidong 'Langmanpai? Ganshangzhuyi? Lingyuzhe? Sixiaoshuo zuojia? - Yu Dafu yu waiguo wenxue,' *Zhongguo bijiao wenxue* 1 (1985), p. 228.

20. Suzuki, *Chūgoku bungaku to Nihon bungaku*, pp. 43ff.

21. See in particular *Denen no yūutsu*, p. 35.

22. Xu Zidong does not agree with A. Dolezalová when she calls Yu Dafu a 'Chinese writer of I-novels.' Xu Zidong, op. cit., 230-1, referring to A. Dolezalová's study *Yü Ta-fu: Specific Traits of his Literary Creation*, Bratislava etc., 1971).

23. Xu Zidong, op. cit., p. 232.

24. Randall Olivers Chang, *Yü Ta-fu (1896-1945): The Alienated Artist in Modern Chinese Literature*, Claremont Graduate School, Ph.D., 1974, p. 17.

25. Chang, *Yü Ta-fu*, p.8.

26. Lee, 'Yü Ta-fu: Driftings of a Loner,' p. 87. We should also remember that there is a confusing array of barely explained quotations and allusions to foreign cultures and literatures in Yu's novels. Perhaps most puzzling of all is the structure of *Nanqian* which shows strong influence of German literature (is this perhaps one of the reasons why this work has been virtually ignored by most foreign and native critics?). In some passages there are clear references to an inferiority complex towards foreign culture (see *Nanqian*, p. 78-9).

27. Of course, *Denen no yūutsu* does not make use of this narrative technique if taken in the strict sense of this technical term. However, the relative lack of reflecting, objective comment by the protagonist on his experiences, and the extremely scant explicit comment by the narrator and author on the weird world of 'natural' phenomena in the protagonist's mind means that we can penetrate to the protagonist's mind only by way of images and imagined phenomena in an indirect, 'broken' way. Images and symbols are not 'closed.' There is no way to find an 'objective' key to the images, whose specific, symbolic meaning must remain somewhat enigmatic and puzzling. To that extent, Satō's technique is a bizarre and fantastic form of the traditional *heimen byōsha* technique. See also May, Ekkehard 'Konstanten der modernen japanischen Erzählprosa und ihr Verhältnis zur literarischen Tradition,' (Bochumer Jahrbuch zur Ostasienforschung 1981), p. 141.

28. Compared to *Denen no yūutsu* Yu Dafu's use of symbols is fairly restrained. For an example, see e.g. chapter 6 of *Nanqian* entitled YAISHANG, *Abgrund* (Precipice) Some images in *Denen no yūutsu* have also become symbols (see Shimada, Kinji "Denen no yūutsu" kō, *Kōza hikaku bungaku* 2 (1973 [Tōdai shuppankai], p. 257.

29. I am not so sure whether we can easily pinpoint a particular narrative technique that would distinguish *Chenlun* as a modern novel. 'Any empathy or feeling for the character comes from a response to the protagonist's personality as revealed by his actions or interior monologues, not narrative comment. This is what marks the story as truly modern - its use of irony.' (Egan 'Yu Dafu,' p. 315). The development towards the climax in *Chenlun* is not properly executed, as was noticed by Cheng Fangwu. Cheng Fangwu '"Chenlun" de pinglun,' in He Yupo comp. *Yu Dafu lun*, Hong Kong, 1972 (reprint of the 1936 Shanghai Daguang shuju edition), pp. 109-10. Zhang also noticed the lack of an action plot, but claims that the story unfolds along the rhythm of the changing moods of the hero; but he, too, hardly refers to the fact that the hero is clearly suffering from progressive *psychiatric* problems.

Zhang, Guozhen'Yu Dafu he woguo xiandai shuqing xiaoshuo,' *Zhongguo xiandai wenxue yanjiu congkan* 4 (1981), pp. 145-146.

30. A. A. Dolin, 'Stilistika romanticheskoj poezii novykh form,' p. 233.

31. C. T. Hsia, quoted in Chang, *Yü Ta-fu*, p. 133.

32. Shimada, '"Denen no yūutsu" kō,' p. 253.

33. I commented on this question in detail in an unpublished paper entitled 'Chinese and Japanese Attitudes Towards Modernization in the 19th Century' presented to the 1976 Conference of the Asian Studies Association of Australia, Melbourne. In Japan Sakuma Shōzan (1811-1864) has been identified with the slogan '*Tōyō dōtoku, seiyō geijutsu*' (Moral Essence from the East, Technical Arts from the West).

34. Cheng Fangwu, '"*Chenlun*" de pinglun,' pp. 108-9.

35. *Denen no yūutsu*, p. 7. Compare also *Nanqian*, pp. 53-4: 'Ta xiang jiao shangdi lai bangzhu ta, danshi tade *ZHEXUE de LIZHIXING* zenme ye buxu ta qidao, bile yanjing, lile 4.5 fenzhong, yaule yiyau tour, tanle yikouqi, ta reng fu zoule huilai.'

36. *Denen no yūutsu*, pp. 21ff.

37. *Denen no yūutsu*, p. 88.

38. *Denen no yūutsu*, p. 35.

39. *Denen no yūutsu*, p. 78: 'kare wa dō iu wake ka tokei no furiko no ugoku no o mitsuzukenagara, rikonbyō ni tsuite no samazama na bungakuteki no kiroku ya, arui wa inu no koto nado o kangaetsutzukete, shinzō no shizumaru jikan o matta.'

40. Suk Choo Chang, 'The Cultural Context of Japanese Psychiatry and Psychotherapy,' *American Journal of Psychotherapy* 19 (1965), pp. 598-600.

41. Satō contrasts this lack of trust in human beings with his dog's unquestioning faithfulness in others. See *Denen no yūutsu*, p. 43.

42. *Denen no yūutsu*, p. 99.

43. *Chenlun*, p. 16.

44. *Ibid.*, p. 17. See also *ibid.*, p. 37.

45. See e.g. *Chenlun*, p. 35.

46. Cf. *Denen no yūutsu*, p. 78.

47. Chang 'The Cultural Context of Japanese Psychiatry,' p. 596. 'Historically, a Japanese word corresponding to "psychosis" appeared in the eighth century, but the first monograph on psychosis within the framework of traditional Chinese medicine was published in 1819. In Japan, a traditional conception of, and attitude towards mental illness existed which was often associated with Buddhism.' (*Ibid.*, p. 595). 'Thus, the year 1902 marked the official beginning of Japanese psychiatry as a branch of modern medicine.... For example, Freud's collected work has been translated in two different versions into Japanese, one in 1926 and another in 1929. (*Ibid.*, p. 597). '...the concepts of ego, unconsciousness and others, as used in psychoanalytic theory, are specifically related to the characteristic assumptions and beliefs of Western society within which the theory arose.' (*Ibid.*, pp. 594-5).

48. Ekkehard May, 'Konstanten der modernen japanischen Erzählprosa und ihr Verhältnis zur literarischen Tradition,' [Bochumer Jahrbuch zur Ostasienforschung 1981], pp. 135-6.

49. Cf. also Ashitani, Nobukazu '[Kunikida Doppo - hikaku bungakuteki kenkyū -] shohyō,' *Hikaku bungaku* (1982) Vol. 35, p. 64. Some critics tend to overestimate the gap between modern writers and their native traditions. Language is a conservative medium, and it would be impossible to discuss Yu Dafu and Satō Haruo without referring to their thorough grounding in their own literary tradition. On Yu Dafu's traditional background, esp. Lee 'Yu Ta-Fu: Driftings of a Loner,' pp. 83-85.

50. D. S. Mirsky, *A History of Russian Literature*, ed. and abridged by Francis Whitfield. London, 1964, p. 430.

51. Shimada '"Denen no yūutsu" kō,' p. 254.

52. Suzuki *Chūgoku bungaku to Nihon bungaku*, p.62.

53. See, for instance, *Chenlun*, pp. 43-44.

54. Traditional Chinese literary attitudes towards 'authenticity' and 'veracity' in literature have their modern heirs in the Chinese and Japanese versions of naturalism; the introduction of personages in Yu Dafu's novels owe stylistically much more to the native Chinese tradition than to naturalist techniques (see, for instance, *Nanqian*, p. 13, and his description of the setting of a certain villa in *Nanqian*, pp. 16-7). In *Yinhuise de si* the traditional trend towards veracity is even stronger (pp. 3-4, 12ff). At the end of the story, Yu added a postscript in English: 'The reader must bear in mind that this is an imaginary tale. After all the author

cannot be responsible for its reality. One word, however, must be mentioned here that he owes much obligation to R. L. Stevenson's "A Lodging for the Night" and the life of Ernest Dowson for the plan of this unambitious story.' See also Lee 'Yü Ta-fu: Driftings of a Loner,' p. 112.

55.   Kurt W. Radtke, 'Concepts in Literary Criticism. Problems in the Comparative Study of Japanese, Chinese and Western Literature,' *Oriens Extremus*, Vol. 28, No. 1 (1981), p. 109 (and footnote 15).

56.   Zhang, 'Yu Dafu he woguo xiandai shuqing xiaoshuo,' p. 157.

57.   Here I do not agree with Xu Zidong who emphasizes the role of foreign influence on Yu Dafu ('Yu Dafu yu waiguo wenxue,' p. 225-6). As I stated above, the function of nature in Yu Dafu is much more easily explained in terms of the traditional distinction between *qing* (sentiment) and *jing* (scene) known from Chinese poetry. In a much more balanced approach Zhang has emphasized a 'general' influence of the lyric novel (*shuqing xiaoshuo*) on Yu Dafu, whether it be the Japanese or the German variety; it is, however, not quite clear whether he is here merely referring to 'purely stylistic' influence (Zhang 'Yu Dafu he woguo xiandai shuqing xiaoshuo,' p. 157). See also Zhang *Yu Dafu xiaoshuo xinshang*, pp. 62-4. Yu Dafu's descriptions of landscapes have at times been praised more than they deserve. One of the more successful combinations of scene and mood is in the description of the precipice in *Nanqian* (pp. 44-5), but the comparison between the growing grain and the mental suffering of the hero in *Chenlun* seems farfetched (*Chenlun*, pp. 31-2),. Even a cursory survey of Yu Dafu's scenic descriptions would show that they virtually all centre in a fairly conventional way on 'large' elements such as mountains, moon, sea and clouds. I am generally more impressed by Yu's landscape descriptions in *Nanqian* and *Yinhuise de si* than in *Chenlun* itself.

58.   Xu Zidong, 'Yu Dafu yu waiguo wenxue,' p. 230. On the concepts '*qing*' and '*jing*', in particular, Zhou Zhenfu, *Shici lihua*, Peking, 1962, esp. pp. 261ff. ['*chentuo*,' *fanchen he peichen*']. On the terms 'subjective' and 'objective,' Radtke,'Concepts in Literary Criticism,' pp. 118-9 ('*youwo*' and '*wuwo*,' '*kyakkanteki*' and *shukanteki*').

59.   Most of Yu Dafu's critics - including some Western ones - have avoided commenting on *Nanqian* - the longest novel in this trilogy - probably because of the numerous allusions to Goethe and the German romantics which often cannot easily be interpreted in the context of *Nanqian*.

60.   Yu Dafu was widely read and frequently referred to writers and philosophers such as Goethe, Sturm, Nietzsche, Rousseau, Turgenev, Huang Zhongze or Jiang Guangci (Li, Yongshou 'Yu Dafu wenyi guandian suotan.' *Zhongguo xiandai wenxue yanjiu congkan* 3 (1982), p. 67). Yu Dafu's use of quotations, allusions and straight references to foreign writers appear to be rather chaotic, and are often obviously out of touch with the originals referred to. He does, for instance, refer to Heine but his reference does not require the reader to become acquainted with the original; although he often includes even lengthy passages in the original language, he invariably includes the Chinese original (Chang *Yü Ta-fu*, p. 61). 'Such writers as Yu Dafu appear to have been quite impressed by Russian and European sources, and it should be apparent that "Sinking" and "Silver-gray Death" could possibly owe a large debt to Dostoevsky, for example. Such one-to-one relationships are difficult to prove, however, beyond saying that Yu was widely read in Western literature. To trace direct stylistic (as opposed to intellectual), relationships with Western authors is nearly imposible' (Egan 'Yu Dafu,' p. 323). See also Lee, 'Yü Ta-fu: Driftings of a Loner,' p. 112, and Zhang 'Yu Dafu he woguo xiandai shuqing xiaoshuo,' p. 157.

61.   Shimada, '"Denen no yūutsu kō,' p. 242.

62.   Shimada, op. cit., p. 254. According to Shimada, Satō's references to 'Fairyland' are based on a translation of John Oojii's 'Seeds of Light' which appeared in 1912. As he points out, however, Satō adapts the image in his own way without reference to the context in which it was used originally, (*Ibid.*, p. 242). Although Goethe obviously served as a source of inspiration for Satō's references to Goethe's Faust, Satō has moved into a completely different direction, (*Ibid.*, p. 217). Even Satō's reference to the sun as the source of life-power has little to do with the life-forces of Goethe.

63.   Shimada, op. cit., p. 254.

64.   Shimada further discusses phenomena like 'Doppelgänger' in purely literary terms; in the context of *Denen no yūutsu* the *psychological* function of this notif deserves further attention (Shimada, op. cit., p. 244).

65.   *Denen no yūutsu*, p. 29.

66. *Ibid*, p. 36.

67. Ishikawa Takuboku *Poems to Eat,* trans. Carl Sesar, Kodansha International, Tokyo, Pan Alto, 1966 c, 4th pr. 1970, p. 16; see also Tadtke, op. cit., pp. 109-110.

68. The term 'betsu sekai' (a differnt world) in *Denen no yūutsu* is ambiguous because it may refer to either the subjective fantasies of the protagonist or to a 'reality behind apparent reality.' 'Nanika - ningen o, kare jishin o subete no mono ga kono sekai to wa mattaku chigatta mono kara dekiagatte iru betsusekai e hikizusariagete yuku yō na, arui wa tada kare no me no mae e tarashinaku hirogerarete iru kono furui furui sekai o zenzen bekko no mono ni shite miseru yō na, arui wa sore o mattaku kontei kara kutsugaeshite mechakucha ni suru yō na, sore wa nan de mo ii, tada mō hijō na, subarashii nanmono ka ga, dō ka shite, doko ka ni arisō na mono da,' (*Denen no yūutsu*, p. 34).

69. *Denen no yūutsu*, p. 85. In another occurrence the term *hōetsu* is also explicitly linked with religion (*Denen no yūutsu*, p. 7: 'fukai nemuri! sore wa iwaba shūkyo teki na hōetsu da').

70. Hartley, *The Penguin Book of French Verse*, p. xxvii.

71. Morita, James R. 'Shimazaki Tōson' Four Collections of Poems.' *Monumenta Nipponica*, XXV, 3-4, p. 365, and McClellans discussion cited by Morita.

72. 'The river is spread out wide. It flows, sad and sluggish, and washes its banks. Above the barren clay of the yellow cliff ricks stand sadly in the steppe. O Russia! My wife! Our long road lies painfully clear ahead. Our road has pierced our breast with an arrow of the ancient Tatar power.' (*The Penguin Book of Russian Verse*).

73. *Denen no yūutsu*, 35.

74. Chang, *Yü Ta-fu*, p. 230. See also Wu Maosheng 'Langman zhuyi yingxiong? p. 138.

75. Wu Maosheng 'Langman zhuyi yingxiong?' p. 138. 'There is one central theme which runs throughout all of Yü Ta-fu's short stories and which describes the basic trait of his fictional characters: without exception, they are weeping heroes, effete and reluctant to help either themselves or their fellow men. They are imbued with a high degree of emotionalism and self-pity, and this makes their situations entirely hopeless.' Chang *Yü Ta-fu*, p. 50.

76. Turgenev's Rudin is a.o. characterized by 'notably his inability to give all of himself, whether to an idea or to a passion, and a certain aloofness about his presence in society,' (Waddington 'Introduction,' p. 26).

77. On the theme of the 'superfluous man' in Russian literature, see e.g. Waddington 'Introduction,' 26ff. The term has often been misused, and should not be equated with 'a useless hero.' 'A feeling of uselessness appears in several other stories, such as "The Superfluous Man" (Ling-yü-che), during this period.' (Chang *Yü Ta-fu*, 23). Due to lack of time I have been unable to check Wu Maosheng's assertion that there is a close similarity in diction between Turgenev's novel and *Chenlun*.

78. Waddington, 'Introduction,' p. 35.

79. Hartley, *The Penguin Book of French Verse*, p. xxx.

80. *Denen no yūutsu*, pp. 95ff.

81. There is, for instance, a clear reference to the well known image of the 'useless tree' in the Taoist text Zhuangzi (Sōshi) (*Denen no yūutsu*, p. 28). See also the use of the term 'muda' in another passage (*ibid.*, p. 39).

82. *Denen no yūutsu*, pp. 23-26. For further references to the image of 'man-made nature', see also *ibid.*, pp. 18, 23, 24, 25-6, 61-2.

83. Cf. Shimada '"Denen no yūutsu" kō', p. 230. *Denen no yūutsu*, in particular pp. 35, 39 and elsewhere. There is also a certain irony in the fact that the apparently serene landscape where the protagonist sought refuge contrasts with the landscape of his original home, so much more extreme and dramatic (*ibid.*, p. 6).

84. The most explicit reference to Goethe's Faust appears towards the end of *Denen no yūutsu* (pp. 95 ff.). In terms of aspirations and willpower alone it seems difficult to undertake a straight comparison between Faust and *Denen no yūutsu*.

85. 'We may interpret nature to be a mother figure for the young hero. When he lacks confidence, nature offers him security and approval.' Chang *Yü Ta-fu*, p. 54). See also *Chenlun*, p. 3: 'Zheli jiush nide binansuo.' It is quite correct to note the motif 'return to nature' in both novels. But it is not a return that emphasizes 'the joys to be found in nature,' as found in 'Wordsworth, Emerson, Thoreau, Heine and Gissing' (Chang *Yü Ta-fu*, pp. 53-4).

86. In *Nanqian* Tokyo is referred to in traditionalistic Buddhist clichés as a place of worldly desires (p. 14).

87. *Denen no yūutsu*, pp. 23, 47, 64; *Chenlun*, in particular p. 10. Although we cannot deal here with Satō's *Utsukushii machi* I should like to stress that Satō's 'beautiful city' has

functions that cannot be described by referring to the more common pairing of 'city' and 'nature' (or countryside).

88.   *Chenlun*, p. 10. 'Ernest Dowson and Huang Chung-tse have combined to conjure up one central image, that of a frail and lonely genius, frequently ill and melancholic, dissipating his life and talent in a society which alienates him.... Despite its Western borrowings, it is quite akin to the ts'ai-tzu prototype in traditional Chinese fiction.' (Lee, 'Yu Ta-fu: Driftings of a Loner,' p. 119).

89.   I refer to the role of the recluse in my study *Poetry of the Yuan Dynasty*, Canberra, 1984, pp. 23 ff.

90.   *Chenlun*, p. 18.

91.   *Denen no yūutsu*, pp. 6 f, p. 94. See also *Denen no yūutsu*, p. 6.

92.   His father died when he was three years old (*Chenlun*, p. 18). The relationship with his older brother is not further outlined (*ibid.*, p. 17 f). When he finally breaks off relations with his brother it may be simply the reaction to his feeling of betrayal by his brother who left him behind in Japan (*ibid.*, pp. 49 f). His early independence is one of the reasons for his difficulty in establishing normal relations with peers (*ibid.*, p. 1).

93.   *Ibid.*, p. 32; see also p. 3.

94.   *Nanqian*, p. 13.

95.   *Chenlun*, p. 19.

96.   *Chenlun*, p. 13.

97.   *Nanqian*, pp. 36, 78-9.

98.   Compared to the hero in *Chenlun*, the hero in *Nanqian* has a somewhat more relaxed attitude towards the other sex. But here, too, we find traditional Chinese attitudes concerning the corrupting influence of women on men (pp. 14, 24, 37, 55, 58-9, 68, 72).

99.   Shimada complains about the lack of characterization of the female side characters. Since all interest focuses on a protagonist who is unable to entertain human relations, and moreover because we are purposely left with hardly any comments from other persons in the novel concerning the protagonist, such criticism seems perhaps unfair (Shimada "Denen no yūutsu" kō,' 239-40).

100.   Chang 'The Cultural Context of Japanese Psychiatry,' 600.

101.   Itō Toramaru, 'Chinrin ron,' *Chūgoku bungaku kenkyū*, Nos. 1 and 3 (1961), quoted in Lee, 'Yü Ta-fu: Driftings of a Loner,' 111; the original article was inaccessible at the time I completed this paper).

102.   Zhang Enhe, *Yu Dafu xiaoshuo xinshang*, p. 62.

103.   *Ibid.*, p. 59.

104.   'On a more symbolic level, the protagonist's cycle of deliberate abuse of his body and guilt may be interpreted as his image of China. The feelings of guilt and personal unworthiness which follow each act of self-abuse parallel the shame which he feels for his country.' (Chang *Yü Ta-fu*, p. 59, and also p. 51).

105.   Lee 'Yü Ta-fu: Driftings of a Loner,' p. 91. Chang *Yü Da-fu*, p. 68, is perhaps more justified to ascribe certain nationalistic feelings to *Nanqian*. One may also add that the hero in *Chenlun* appears to deceive himself: 'Only then did he understand that his desire to compose poetry was not genuine, but his fleshly desires were' (p. 61). We are wondering whether the protagonist's professed love for a strong China is, at least to some extent, not also a device for self-deception: China's weakness is a scapegoat for his own inability to cope.

106.   *Chenlun*, pp. 23, 62.

107.   One may add that in *Nanqian*, the hero is introduced speaking English and Japanese, but not Chinese.

108.   The genesis of his psychiatric disorder is not clearly outlined (see, e.g. *Chenlun*, pp. 10 and 22).

109.   *Chenlun*, p. 13.

110.   *Chenlun*, p. 36.

111.   He clearly uses his professed love for his fatherland as a substitute for his failure in human relationships. *Chenlun*, pp. 64, 66, 72. Compared to the open ending of *Denen no yuūtsu* the death of the heroes in *Chenlun*, *Nanqian* and *Yinhuisede si* seems overly dramatic.

112.   On the topic of Yu Dafu's nationalism see also two recent publications on Yu's activities in Singapore during the war years (Yao Mengtong, *Yu Dafu lü -Xin shenghuo yu zuopin yanjiu*, Xinjiapo xinshe publ., September 1987, and Fang, Xiu and Lian, Qi comp. *Yu Dafu yiwenji*, Singapore, 1984.

113. Wu 'Langman zhuyi yingxiong?' p. 143. On his wavering attachment to the leftist cause, see Chang *Yü Ta-fu*, pp. 22 ff., 37 ff.
114. For an exception, see his rather forced interior monologue comparing the lot of Japanese and Chinese workers where the hero ridicules himself as 'having been affected by the socialism of the Japanese.' (*Nanqian*, p. 8; see also *ibid.*, p. 90).
115. *Denen no yūutsu*, p. 112.

BIBLIOGRAPHY: SATŌ'S AND YU'S NOVELS

quoted in this paper

I used the following editions of Satō's and Yu's novels:

SATŌ HARUO
Denen no yūutsu, Shinchōsha, 1973 [Shinchō bunko].
SATŌ HARUO
Tokai no yūutsu, Kaizōsha, 1927 [Gendai Nihon bungaku zenshū].
SATŌ HARUO
Utsukushii machi, Sōbisha, 1975 [Juniaban Nihon no bungaku].
YU DAFU
Chenlun, Nanqian, Yinhuise de si, Tianxia shudian, n.p., 1947.

BIBLIOGRAPHY

ARAKI TŌRU
'Rizumu (miitaa) ni tsuite no ichikōsatsu,' *[Kokubungaku] Kaishaku to kanshō* 534 (December 1976):121.
ASHITANI NOBUKAZU
'[Kunikida Doppo - hikaku bungakuteki kenkyū -] shohyō,' *Hikaku bungaku* (1982) Vol. 35, 64-67.
CHANG, RANDALL OLIVERS
Yü Ta-fu (1896-1945): The Alienated Artist in Modern Chinese Literature, Claremont Graduate School, Ph.D., 1974, [also: He Xin, Zhang Shengzhao trans. Chang, R. O. *Yige yü shi shuli de tiancai - Yu Dafu*, Taibei, Chengwen chubanshe, 1978].
CHANG, S.
'Correlations of Japanese Personality with its Art and Language,' *Folia Psychiat. Neurol. Jap.*, Suppl. 7 (1964):41-43.
CHANG, SUK CHOO
'The Cultural Context of Japanese Psychiatry and Psychotherapy,' *American Journal of Psychotherapy* 19 (1965):593-606.
CHENG, FANGWU
'Chenlun' de pinglun,' in He Yupo comp. *Yu Dafu lun*, Hong Kong, 1972 (reprint of the 1936 Shanghai Daguang shuju edition).
DOLEZALOVÀ, ANNA
Yü Ta-fu: Specific Traits of his Literary Creation, Bratislava - London - New York, 1971.
DOLIN, A. A.
'Stilistika romanticheskoj poezii novykh form,' *Teoreticheskie problemy izuchenija literatur Dal'nego Vostoka*, 1977:231-238.
FANG, XIU AND LIAN, QI comp.
Yu Dafu yiwenji, Singapore, 1984.
HARTLEY, A.
The Penguin Book of French Verse, 1968.
HE, YUPO comp.
Yu Dafu lun, Hong Kong, 1972 (reprint of the 1936 Shanghai Daguang shuju edition).
HIRANO KEN
'Tōson no buntai,' in *Shimazaki Tōson - Hito to bungaku*, 1960 [Shinchō bunko]:197ff.
KATO SHUICHI
A History of Japanese Literature. The First Thousand Years, London and Basingstoke, 1979.
ISHIBASHI MANABU
'Denen to hendo,' *Shin hihyō kindai Nihon bungaku no kōzō*, 1980 [Kindai Nihon bungaku no fudo, 3].
KAO, SHUHSI
'Structure et signification dans les nouvelles de Yu Dafu', *La littérature chinoise au temps de la guerre de résistance contre le Japon (de 1937 à 1945)*, Paris, 1982.
KAWAMURA MASATOSHI
'Satō Haruo,' *Kaishaku to kanshō* (July 1969):114-119.
KAWAMURA MASATOSHI
'Haruo. Ryūnosuke no bungakuteki shuppatsu,' *Kaishaku to kanshō* (September 1968):115-120.

KAWAMURA MASATOSHI
'[Utsukushii machi] shiron, - yūutsu no seishin kōzō o megutte -, *Nihon kindai bungaku* 3 (November 1965):41:56.
LEE, LEO OU-FAN
The Romantic Generation of Modern Chinese Writers, Harvard UP, Cambridge, Mass., 1973.
LEE, L. OU-FAN
'Yü Ta-fu: Driftings of a Loner,' in Lee, Leo Ou-fan *The Romantic Generation of Modern Chinese Writers*, Harvard UP, Cambridge, Mass., 1973.
LEE, L. OU-FAN
'Yü Ta-fu: Visions of the Self,' in Lee, Leo Ou-fan *The Romantic Generation of Modern Chinese Writers*, Harvard UP, Cambridge, Mass., 1973.
LI, YONGSHOU
'Yu Dafu wenyi guandian suotan,' *Zhongguo xiandai wenxue yanjiu congkan* 3 (1982):67-86.
MANN, OTTO PROF. DR.
Deutsche Literaturgeschichte von der germanischen Dichtung bis zur Gegenwart, Bertelsmann, 1964.
MAY, EKKEHARD
'Konstanten der modernen japanischen Erzählprosa und ihr Verhältnis zur literarischen Tradition,' Bochumer Jahrbuch zur Ostasienforschung 1981.
MIRSKY, D.S.
A History of Russian Literature, ed. and abridged by Francis Whitfield, London, 1964.
MORITA, JAMES R.
'Shimazaki Tōson' Four Collections of Poems,' *Monumenta Nipponica*, XXV, 3-4:325-369.
NAKAJIMA REISHI
'Doppo [Musashino] - sono kōsō to genbunitchitai no seiritsu -,' *Bungaku* 55.5 (1987):23-36.
'NASHIONARIZUMU TO BUNGAKU'
[*Kokubungaku] Kaishaku to kanshō* 451 (June 1971).
The Penguin Book of Russian Verse, Obolensky, D. ed., 1967.
RADTKE, KURT W.
'Concepts in Literary Criticism. Problems in the Comparative Study of Japanese, Chinese and Western Literature,' *Oriens Extremus*, Vol. 28 No. 1 (1981), 107-123.
RADTKE, KURT W.
Poetry of the Yuan Dynasty, Australian National University, Canberra, 1984.
RYAN, MARLEIGH
'Modern Japanese Fiction: "Accommodated Truth",' *Journal of Japanese Studies* 2 (1976).
SHIBATA RENSABURŌ
'Satō Haruo sensei to iu hito,' *Bungei shunjū* (March 1966):194-200.
SHIMADA KINJI
'"Denen no yūutsu" kō.' *Kōza hikaku bangaku* 2 (1973) [Tōdai shuppankai].
SUZUKI SHŪJI
Chūgoku bungaku to Nihon bungaku (1978).
TOMITA JIN
'Nihon ni okeru hikaku bungaku,' *Nihon kindai bungaku to seiyō* (1984):223ff.
TU, KUO-CH'ING
'The Introduction of French Symbolism into Modern Chinese and Japanese Poetry,' *Tamkang Review* Vol. 10 No. 3 (Spring 1980).
TURGENEV, I. S.
Rudin, Notes and commentary by Patrick Waddington, Bradda, 1970.
UCHIMURA, Y.
'Nihon Seishin Igaku no Kako to Shorai,' *Jap. J. Psychiat.* (*Seisin-Sinkei-gaku Zassi*):55:705, 1954.
WADDINGTON, P.
'Introduction,' in Turgenev, I. S. *Rudin*, 1970.
WU, MAOSHENG (XIANGGANG ZHONGWEN DAXUE)
'Langman zhuyi yingxiong? - lun Yu Dafu xiaoshuo li de lingyuzhe.' *Zhongguo xiandai wenxue yanjiu congkan* 4 (1982).
XU, ZIDONG
'Langmanpai? Ganshangzhuyi? Lingyuzhe? Sixiaoshuo zuojia? - Yu Dafu yu waiguo wenxue,' *Zhongguo bijiao wenxue* 1 (1985):200-232, 384.
YAO, MENGTONG
Yu Dafu lt-Xin shenghuo yt zuopin yanjiu, Xinjiapo Xinshe shuppan, 1987. (This study includes a very detailed bibliography).
YASUDA YOSHIAKI
'Kokyō to ikyō, - genzai kara hizai e -.' *Shin hihyō kindai Nihon bungaku no kōzō*, 1980 [Kindai Nihon bungaku no fudo, 3].
YOSHIDA SEIICHI
'Satō Haruo (VI),' *Kaishaku to kanshō* (August 1965):143-151.
ZHANG, ENHE
Yu Dafu xiaoshuo xinshang, Nanning, 1986 (2nd Ed.).

ZHANG, GUOZHEN
'Yu Dafu he woguo xiandai shuqing xiaoshuo,' *Zhongguo xiandai wenxue yanjiu congkan* 4 (1981):142-162.
ZHOU, ZUOREN
'Chenlun,' in He Yupo comp. *Yu Dafu lun*, Hong Kong, 1972 (reprint of the 1936 Shanghai Daguang shuju edition), [p. 101: (benwen zyh Beijing Chenbao fukan).

Chapter 15 BARBARA RUCH *Unheeded Voices; Winked-at Lives*

1. This Venice presentation focusses on two neglected areas of Japanese historical studies. The author has explored these and other related problems in a more extended context in 'The Other Side of Culture in Medieval Japan,' *The Cambridge History of Japan*, edited by Kozo Yamamura, Volume III, (Medieval Japan), Cambridge University Press, 1990, to which the reader is referred.

2. Nishikawa Kyōtarō, *Chinsō chokoku (Nihon no bijutsu)*, No. 123, Tōkyō: Shibundō, 1976.

3. To cite just a few: *Nihon rekishi daijiten* (Tōkyō: Kawade shobō shinsha, 1956; *Sanshū meiseki shi* XXI and *Fusō keika shi* II in *Shinshū Kyōto Sōsho* II and IX (Tōkyō: Kōsaisha, 1967); *Koji ruien* XLIV (Tōkyō: Yoshikawa kobunkan, 1969); *Dai Nihon jiin sōran* (Tōkyō: Meiji shuppan sha, 1917) and other works under entries for various relevant personal and place names. As of this writing no published accounts concerning Mugai's family should be taken as reliable. Even the most recent contain inherent inconsistencies and errors and many problems remain to be solved.

4. Mary Martin McLaughlin, 'Looking for Medieval Women: An Interim Report on the Project "Women's Religious Life and Communities, A.D. 500-1500,"' *Medieval Prosopography*, 8 (Spring 1987) pp. 62-63.

5. For an English translation of *Towazugatari* see Karen Brazell, trs., *The Confessions of Lady Nijō* (New York: Anchor Books, 1973).

6. Margaret Helen Childs, trs., in her 'Religious Awakening Stories in Late Medieval Japan: The Dynamics of Didacticism,' (University of Pennsylvania Ph.D. dissertation, 1983), p. 283. For the original see *Shichinin bikuni* in *Kindai Nihon bungaku taikei* (Tōkyō: Kokumin tosho, 1928) 1, pp. 224-225

7. From Letter to the *Corinthians*, 55, by Clement of Rome, referred to by Patricia Wilson-Kastner in 'Preface,' *The Lost Tradition: Women Writers of the Early Church*, (Washington, D.C.: University Press of America, 1981), p. ix.

8. Translated by Stanley Weinstein in 'The Concept of Reformation in Japanese Buddhism,' *Studies in Japanese Culture II* edited by Saburō Ōta (Tōkyō: P.E.N. Club, 1973), p. 82. For the original see *Shōbōgenzō* (Iwanami bunko edition, Tōkyō, 1939), Vol. 1, pp. 124 and 128.

9. Hōji-in is not a temple open to the public but a resident cloister. Sensitive and reverential inquiries made ahead of time, however, may make it possible for scholars to gain entrance in order to pay respects before Mugai Nyodai's *chinsō*. The address of Hōji-in is: Koromonotana, Teranouchi agaru, Kami-gyo-ku, Kyoto; tel: (075)441-4636.

10. One of the most seminal and revisionist works to date on medieval professional women including *kugutsu* entertainers is Wakita Haruko, 'Chusei ni okeru seibetsu yakuwari buntan to joseikan,' *Nihon josei shi - chūsei*, Tōkyō daigaku shuppan kai, 1983, Vol. 2, pp. 65-102. The origins of *kugutsu* remain clouded. Traditionally thought of as manipulators of puppets, *kugutsu* appear in medieval Japan in various other contexts as well. See particularly Wakita, pp. 69-70 and 94-95, and Amino Yoshihiko, 'Nihon chūsei no heimin to shokunin,' *Shishō*, Pt. II (No. 681, May 1980), pp. 81-84.

11. For the *Ryōjin hishō* songs and the *Kudenshū* about the songs and their singers as recorded by Emperor GoShirakawa see Kawaguchi Hisao and Shida Nobuyoshi, ed., *Wakan rōeishū; Ryōjin hishō* in *Nihon koten bungaku taikei*, Vol. 73, Iwanami shoten, 1970.

12. Mei was a *kugutsu* who had lived for years with Saigyō's maternal grandfather, Minamoto no Kiyotsune (fl. 1090s). He first heard Otomae sing when she was about 12 years old and urged Mei to teach Otomae seriously. When brought to the capital by Kiyotsune, Mei brought Otomae with her.

13. Confer *Nōsakusho* in Hisamatsu Sen'ichi and Nishio Minoru, eds., *Karonshū; Nōgakuronshū* in *Nihon koten bungaku taikei*, Tōkyō: Iwanami shoten, 1961, Vol. 65, pp. 470-471.

14. Leah Otis, *Prostitution in Medieval Society: An Urban Institution in Languedoc*. New York: Columbia University Press, 1980.

15. Theodore C. Bestor, 'Gendered Domains: A Commentary on Research in Japanese Studies,' *Journal of Japanese Studies*, Vol. 11, No. 1 (Winter 1985).

Chapter 16 BEN BEFU
Yūgen: Aesthetics and Its Implications in Global Communication
1.   Suzuki Takao, 'Mirage Effect and Xenophygia: Two Significant Consequences of Japan's Indirect Contacts with the Outer World,' *Orientation Seminars on Japan*, No. 25, 1-10. Text of seminar held on 14 May 1987, at the Japan Foundation.
2.   *Ibid.*, p. 5. See also Robert C. Christopher, *The Japanese Mind: The Goliath Explained* (New York: Linden Press/Simon & Schuster, 1983), p. 57.
3.   Suzuki, p. 7.
4.   Christopher, pp. 43-44.
5.   Nakamura Hajime, *Ways of Thinking of Eastern Peoples: India-China-Tibet-Japan* (Honolulu: East-West Center Press, 1964), p. 543.
6.   Edwin O. Reischauer, *The Japanese* (Cambridge: Harvard University Press, 1977), p. 386.
7.   Robert H. Brower and Earl Miner, *Japanese Court Poetry* (Stanford: Stanford University Press), pp. 265f. See also David Pollack, *The Fracture of Meaning: Japan's Synthesis of China from the Eighth through the Eighteen Centuries* (Princeton: Princeton University Press, 1986), pp. 78f.
8.   Brower and Miner, p. 269.
9.   *Ibid.*
10.   For Shunzei's and Teika's conceptualization of *yūgen*, see Ishida Yoshisada, *Fujiwara Teika no Kenkyū* (Tokyo: Bungadō Shoten, 1957), pp. 512-524; on Shunzei's *yūgen*, see also Kubota Jun, 'Yūgen to sono Shūhen,' in Sagara Tōru et al., eds. *Kōza Nihon Shisō* 5 (Tōkyō: Tōkyō Daigaku Shuppankai, 1984), pp. 53-82. The term *yūgen*, as used in *renga* and the *nō*, usually applies to the notion of beauty more closely approaching that of *yōen* 'ethereal beauty.' Much of the tonality of the *nō*, however, does reflect the concept of *yūgen*. For a discussion of *yūgen* in the *nō*, see Makoto Ueda, *Literary and Art Theories in Japan* (Cleveland: The Press of Western Reserve University, 1967), pp. 59f.
11.   Brower and Miner, p. 269.
12.   From Alan Turner's translation titled *The Three-Cornered World* (Rutland, Vt.: Tuttle, 1965), pp. 106-108.
13.   Masao Miyoshi, *Accomplices of Silence: The Modern Japanese Novel* (Berkeley: University of California Press, 1974), pp. 68-69.
14.   Kubota, op. cit.
15.   J. Thomas Rimer, *Modern Japanese Fiction and Its Traditions: An Introduction* (Princeton: Princeton University Press, 1978), p. 40.
16.   Translated by Thomas J. Harper and Edward G. Seidensticker. *In Praise of Shadows* (New Haven: Leete's Island Books, 1977).
17.   Makoto Ueda, *Modern Japanese Writers and the Nature of Literature* (Stanford: Stanford University Press, 1976), pp. 66, 70.
18.   Thomas J. Harper, 'Afterword,' in *In Praise of Shadows*, p. 45.
19.   Ueda, *Modern Japanese Writers*, p. 75.
20.   Reischauer, p. 386.
21.   John Hinds, 'Reader Versus Writer Responsibility: A New Typology,' in Ulla Conner and Robert B. Kaplan, eds., *Writing Across Languages: Analysis of L2 Written Text* (Reading, Mass.: Addison-Wesley, 1987), pp. 141-152.
22.   Hinds, pp. 143-144.
23.   I am reminded of an explanation I received when I was a schoolboy as to the reason why punctuation marks are customarily eschewed in personal letters. My teacher said their use presumes that the reader will not be able to understand or read the writing without the reading aids - an insult.
24.   Hinds, p. 144.
25.   *Ibid.*, p. 146.
26.   Slightly paraphrased and extracted from Bill Hosokawa's column, 'From the Frying Pan,' *Pacific Citizen*, 10-17 July 1987.

Chapter 17 ANTHONY H. CHAMBERS
Recognizing and Translating Covert Irony in Japanese Literature
1.   Wayne C. Booth, *A Rhetoric of Fiction* (Chicago and London: University of Chicago Press, 1974), p. 1.
2.   Booth, p. 72.
3.   Quoted by Booth, p. 106.
4.   p. 28.
5.   See Booth, pp. 120-123.
6.   The translation is by Paul Gordon Schalow, *The Great Mirror of Male Love*, (Stanford University Press, 1990), p. 310.
7.   Translation by Earl Miner, *Introduction to Japanese Court Poetry*, (Stanford: Stanford University Press, 1968), p. 91.
8.   Booth, pp. 222-227.
9.   Marian Ury, 'The Complete *Genji*', *Harvard Journal of Asiatic Studies*, 37:1 (June 1977), p. 189.
10.   Ury, p. 189, quoting Murasaki Shikibu, *The Tale of Genji*, translated by Edward G. Seidensticker (New York: Knopf, 1976), p. 498.
11.   Ury, pp. 189-90, quoting from Yamagishi Tokuhei, ed., *Genji monogatari*, Vols. 14-18 of *Nihon koten bungaku taikei* [NKBT] (Tokyo: Iwanami Shoten, 1965), III:131.
12.   Ury, p. 190.
13.   Ury, p. 193, quoting Seidensticker, p. 176, and NKBT, I:348.
14.   Northrop Frye, *The Sacred Scripture: A Study of the Structure of Romance*, Cambridge, Massachusetts and London: Harvard University Press, 1976. See especially Chapter 2.
15.   'Though parody is not ordinarily thought of as "irony," it is ironic in our definition.' Booth, p. 72.
16.   New York: Knopf, 1982, and Milano: Bompiani, 1970, respectively.
17.   *The Secret History*, pp. 89-90.
18.   Tanizaki Jun'ichirō, *Tanizaki Jun'ichirō zenshū*, 28 volumes (Tokyo: Chūō Kōronsha, 1966-70), XIII: 278.
19.   *Vita segreta*, p. 118.

Chapter 18 WILLIAM R. LAFLEUR
The Eccentric Tree: Kami and Gaki in the Botanical Imagination of the Medieval Japanese
1.   Carmen Blacker, *The Catalpa Bow: A Study of Shamanistic Practices in Japan* (London: George Allen and Unwin Ltd. 1975), p. 40.
2.   On the impact in the arts see William R. LaFleur, Masatoshi Nagatomi and James Sanford, eds., *Flowing Traces: Buddhism in the Arts of Japan* (Princeton University Press, in press).
3.   William R. LaFleur, 'Saigyō and the Buddhist Value of Nature' (in two parts) *History of Religions* 13:2 and 13:3 (Nov. 1973 and Feb. 1974), pp. 93-126 and 227-248.
4.   No. 3840 in Takagi Ichinosuke et. al. eds., *Manyōshū* in *Nihon Bungaku Taikei* (Tokyo: Iwanami shoten, 1962) Vol. 7, pp. 146-7; trans. mine.
5.   No. 608 in *ibid*, (1957) Vol. 4, pp. 276-7; trans. mine.
6.   See my *The Karma of Words: Buddhism and the Literary Arts in Medieval Japan* (Berkeley and Los Angeles: University of California Press, 1983), pp. 26ff.
7.   In India the restless *preta* could become a *pitri* or ancestor via ritual; see Diana L. Eck, *Banaras: City of Light* (Princeton: Princeton University Press, 1982), pp. 339-342 and pp. 267-8 for description of a tree in Banaras associated with such beings. Stephen F. Teiser, *The Ghost Festival in Medieval China* (Princeton: Princeton University Press, 1988) skilfully discusses the nexus in China between these Buddhist notions and ancestral rites. In Japan, at least, the features of the *preta* often seem to conflate with those of the *pishācha*.
8.   See my 'Hungry Ghosts and Hungry People: Somaticity and Rationality in Medieval Japan' in Michel Feyer, ed., *Fragments for a History of the Human Body*, 3 vols (New York: Zone Books) 1:270-303.
9.   The best reproduction of this is in *Rokudō-e* with photography by Kaneko Keizō and text in Japanese by Shimbō Toru (Tokyo: Mainichi Shimbunsha, 1977), plate 127, p. 155.
10.   *Ibid.*, plate 68, p. 86.

11. See *The Karma of Words*, pp. 52-54.
12. *Taishō shinshū daizōkyō* Tokyo, 1924-1932, Vol. 17: 92ab.
13. As translated by A. K. Reischauer, 'Genshin's Ojo Yoshu: Collected Essays on Birth into Paradise,' *Transactions of the Asiatic Society of Japan*, second series, No. 7, 1930, p. 48. (*Tokusa* may refer to a kind of reed or to the colour characteristic of such worms).
14. Miyeko Murase, *Emaki: Narrative Scrolls from Japan*, New York: The Asia Society, 1983, p. 62. See also selections from other scrolls mentioned above.
15. For more on this see 'Hungry Ghosts and Hungry People.'
16. On this see Aladair MacIntyre, 'Epistemological Crises, Dramatic Narrative, and the Philosophy of Science,' *The Monist* 60, 4:453-472, and *The Karma of Words*, p. 46.

Chapter 19 INAGA SHIGEMI
A European Eye on Japanese Arts and a Japanese Response to 'Japonisme' (1860-1920) A Transcultural Interaction between Visual Arts and Critical Discourses
1. A more complete French version is to be published in a special issue of *Word and Image*, for The First International Conference held in Amsterdam in April 1987.
2. Théodore Duret, *Voyage en Asie*, first published as 'feuilleton' in the Journal *Le Siecle* Sept.-Oct. 1873; Paris, Michel Lévy, 1874.
3. The first part is published as 'Les Peintres impressionistes' in May 1878 and the second as preface to Claude Monet's personal exhibition at the Gallery La Vie moderne in June 1880. Here quoted from Théodore Duret, *Critique d'avant-garde*, Paris, Charpentier, 1885, pp. 65-67; pp. 98-100.
4. Cf. William Leonard Schwartz, *The Imaginative interpretation of The Far East in Modern French Literature, 1800-1925*, Paris, Honoré Champion, 1927.
5. Théodore Duret, 'L'Art japonais, les livres illustrés, les albums imprimés, Hokousai,' *Gazette des Beaux-Arts*, 1882, pp. 211-212.
6. Cf. Siegfried Bing (1838-1905) remarks in 1891 this rediscovery of older prints among the later prints (*Exposition de la gravure japonaise*, Paris 1891, p. 40). Hayashi criticizes Duret's dubious authority on Hokusai books in one of his letters sent to Edmond de Goncourt on 8 January 1892 (*Correspondance des Goncourts*, Guerlin-Houbron, Vol. XLI, Nr. 107-108). As for Duret, Camille Pissarro writes to his son that 'terrible Duret' seems to have decided to sell all the prints he has collected until then, in order to attack 'ancient' ones (*Lettres à son fils Lucien*, 3 March 1893, ed. by J. Rewald, 1950, p. 299).
7. Mallarmé's collection of Japanese prints was partly exhibited in an exhibition; *Ukiyo-e prints and The Impressionist Painters. Meeting of The East and The West*, Tokyo, The Sunshine Museum, 1979-80.
8. Joris Karl Huysmans, 'L'Exposition des indépendants en 1880' reprinted in *L'Art modern*, Paris, 1883, pp. 89-90. Here Huysmans also criticizes the baselessness of Duret's apparently epistemological and scientific justification of Impressionist aesthetics.
9. Mori Ogai echoes Th. Duret in qualifying Kuroda's Violet School as Impressionism. *Mezamashigusa*, Vol. IV, April 1896. On Fontanesi see Iseki Masaaki, *Gaka Fontanesi*, Tokyo, Chūōkōron Bijutsu Shuppan, 1981. On the relationship between Raphael Collin and Kuroda Seiki, see an exhibition catalogue: *L'Académie du Japon moderne et les peintres français*, Tokyo, The Bridgestone Museum, 1983-84. For the quarrel between the Violet School and the Bitumen School, see Nakamura Giichi *Nippon Kindai Bijutsu Ronsoshi*, Tokyo, Kyūryū-dō, 1981, pp. 95-120.
10. Cf. Amano Shirō, 'Louis Gonse to Japonisme,' in Yoshida Mitsukuni (ed.) *Jūkyū-seiki Nihon no Jōhō to Shakai-hendō*, Kyoto, Jinbunkagaku kenkyūsho, 1985, pp. 333-356.
11. Oda Kazuma, 'Nihon no shizen to Hikari no kaiga honi,' *The Journal Asahi*, 23 February 1911. On this quarrel, see Nakamura Giichi, *op. cit.* (note 9) pp. 147-174.
12. Takamura Kōtarō, 'Midoriiro no Taiyō,' *Subaru*, April 1910.
13. Kinoshita Mokutarō, 'Futasu no tsugeoto' (obituary to R. M. Rilke and to Th. Duret), *Chūō bijutsu*, May 1927, pp. 81-86.
14. Cf. Tsuji Nobuo, 'Kobayashi Kiyochika' in *Kindai Nihon Bijutsu-shi I* (ed. by Sasaki Seiichi and Sakai Tadayasu), Tokyo, Yūhikaku, 1978, pp. 152-156.
15. Kinoshita Mokutarō, 'Kobayashi Kiyochika ga Tokyo Meisho Zue,' *Geijutsu*, Nr. 2, May 1913. Reprinted in *Kinoshita Mokutarō Zenshū*, Tokyo, Iwanami shoten, 1981, Vol. 8, pp. 144-46. 'Ko Kobayashi Kiyochika ō ga koto,' *Chūō bijutsu*, Feb. 1916, *Zenshū*, Vol. 9, pp. 70-82.

Chapter 20 LEON ZOLBROD
Communitas, Equality, Anti-Structure: Reading Buson's Painting and Basho's Prose Poem, 'The Broken Hammer'

1.   For English translation see Leon Zolbrod, *Haiku Painting* (Tokyo and New York: Kodansha International Ltd., 1982), p. 25 and fig. 2. For Japanese publication see Okada Rihei, *Haiga no bi: Buson, Gekkei* (Kyoto: Yutaka Shobō, 1973), p. 24, pl. 11 and pp. 167-168.

2.   Victor Turner, *Ritual Process: Structure and Anti-Structure* (Chicago: Aldine Publishing Co., 1969), pp. 96-97 characterizes 'communitas' as lowliness, sacredness, homogeneity and comradeship. He presents two models of human interrelatedness involving society 1) as a structured, differentiated and often hierarchical system, and 2) as an unstructured or rudimentarily structured, relatively undifferentiated communion of equal individuals who submit to the authority of ritual elders. 'He who is high must experience what it is like to be low.' See *passim*, pp. 97-129. Consult also Richard F. Hardin, 'Ritual in Recent Criticism: The Elusive Sense of Community', *Publications of the Modern Language Association*, 98, 5 (1983), 851 and *passim*.

3.   See Makoto Ueda, *Matsuo Basho* (New York: Twayne Publishers, Inc., 1970), pp. 113-124, 'The Haibun: Haiku in Prose.'

4.   Slightly different trans. from that in Zolbrod, *Haiku Painting*.

5.   Tansai, comp., *Sono kogarashi* (Kyoto: Izutsuya Shōhei, Genroku 14, or 1701).

6.   Kanji, comp., *Bashō kusen shui*. (Kyoto: Izutsuya, Hōreki 6, or 1756).

7.   Hisamatsu Shin'ichi, *Zen and the Fine Arts*, trans., Gishin Tokiwa (1971; rpt., Tokyo: Kodansha International Ltd., 1982), pp. 28-38, N.B. pp. 29-30. Originally published in 1957 as *Zen to bijutsu*.

8.   See Margaret H. Childs, 'Didacticism in Medieval Short Stories: Hatsuse Monogatari and Akimichi,' *Monumenta Nipponica*, 42, 3 (Autumn 1987), 253-288, for discussion of how didactic literature, in which the author has established a specific meaning, may also provide occasion for cognitive play and yield multiple interpretations.

9.   E.G., Peter Nosco, '*Man'yoshu* Studies in Tokugawa Japan,' *Transactions of the Asiatic Society of Japan, Fourth Ser.*, 1 (1986), 124. Ideology may be defined as an assertion about society that makes implicit evaluation and helps to legitimize the bearer's pursuit of interests. See also Ikuo Kabashima and Jeffrey Broadbent, 'Referent Pluralism: Mass Media and Politics in Japan,' *Journal of Japanese Studies*, 12, 2 (1986), 346, citing Norman Birnbaum *Toward a Critical Sociology* (New York: Oxford Univ. Press, 1971), p. 4.

10.   Ryusaku Tsunoda, *Sources of Japanese Tradition* (New York: Columbia Univ. Press, 1958), pp. 451-456, 'Haiku, the Democracy of Poetry.' B. S. Chamberlain's observation almost a century ago that, Comunitas, Chamberlain, *Things Japanese*, 1904 ed, 1971 rpt., 'The Japanese and Far Easterns generally are at bottom more democratic than Anglo-Saxons on either side of the Atlantic', 'a truth which the existence of an almost absolute government at first tends to conceal,' also deserves consideration in the present context. See *Things Japanese* (1904; rpt., Tokyo: Charles E. Tuttle Co., 1971), p. 383.

11.   Hirakawa Sukehiro, *Yōkyoku no shi to seiyō no shi* (Tokyo: Asahi Shinbunsha, 1975), pp. 245-249; citing Watanabe Shōichi, *Nihongo ni tsuite: kotodama no shiten kara*.

12.   Kanze Sakon, comp., *Atsumori*, in *Kanze-ryū yōkyoku zenshu*, Part One, p. 976, *Sore masaru o mo urayamazare, otoru o mo iyashimu na to koso miete sorae*.

13.   Otani Tokuzō, Okada Rihei and Shimasue Kiyoshi, comp., *Buson-shū: zen* (Tokyo: Shūeisha, 1972), 'Koten haibungaku taikei,' Vol. 12, p. 345.

Chapter 22 HERBERT PLUTSCHOW
Towards a Definition of Tama

1.   For a detailed discussion of *tamashii* see *Nihon Minzokugo Daijiten*, comp. by Ishigami Katashi (Tōkyō: Ōfūsha, 1983), pp. 797 cf.

2.   *Nihon Koten Bungaku Taikei*, Vol. 67, Part 1 (Tōkyō: Iwanami Shoten, 1967), p. 130.

3.   Perhaps it is the unrecognized 'double' or 'shadow' often believed to be an extension of one's personality in other ancient cultures, or the 'guardian angel' of Christian culture.

4.   *Kojiki, Norito* in *Nihon Koten Bungaku Taikei*, Vol. 1 (Tōkyō: Iwanami Shoten, 1958), p. 455.

5.   *Nihon Koten Bungaku Taikei*, Vol. 2 (Tōkyō: Iwanami Shoten, 1958), p. 105.

6.   Part 1, *op. cit.*, Vol. 67, p. 336.

7.   *Nihon Koten Bungaku Taikei*, Vol. 14 (Tōkyō: Iwanami Shoten, 1958), pp. 142-46.
8.   *Jikkinshō Shinshaku*, ed. by Okada Minoru (Tōkyō: Daidōkan Shoten, second ed., 1930), pp. 262-63. The story also figures in *Fukurozōshi, Toshiyori Kōden, Kokonchōmonjū, Sasekishū*, etc.
9.   See on this Nishitsunoi Masayoshi, *Kodai Saishi to Bungaku* (Tōkyō: Chūokōronsha, 1966), p. 331.
10.   *Origuchi Shinobu Zenshū*, Vol. 8 (Tōkyō: Chūokōronsha, 1955), pp. 244-49.
11.   Part 3, *Nihon Koten Bungaku Taikei*, Vol. 6 (Tōkyō: Iwanami Shoten, 1960), p. 287 (poem no. 3000).
12.   *Nihon Minzokugo Daijiten, op. cit.*, p. 793.
13.   For a pictorial representation of this legend, see *Kitano Tenjin Engi* in *Nihon Emakimono Zenshū*, Vol. 8 (Tōkyō: Kadokawa Shoten, 1959), colour plate 5 (section 4 of fifth scroll).
14.   *Yōkyokushū*, Part 2, *Nihon Koten Bungaku Taikei*, Vol. 41 (Tōkyō: Iwanami Shoten, 1963), p. 66.
15.   *Nihon Shoki*, Part 1, *Nihon Koten Bungaku Taikei*, Vol. 67 (Tōkyō: Iwanami Shoten, 1967), p. 310. Cranes, geese and other migratory birds were especially revered as *tama*-carriers, perhaps because they were believed to reach the other side of the ocean or mountains, realms which were often identified in the popular imagination with the beyond.
16.   *Nihon Minzokugo Daijiten, op. cit.*, p. 799.
17.   *Gunsho Ruijū*, Vol. 6, Kōji-bu (Tōkyō: Zoku Gunsho Ruijū Kanseikai, 1932), p. 550.
18.   *Ibid.*, p. 549. Quoted from the *Sendai Kyūji Hongi* (Kyūjiki), Vol. 3 *[Shintei Zōhō-] Kokushi Taikei*, Vol. 7 (Tōkyō: Kokushi Taikei Kanko-kai, 1936), p. 25.
19.   See on this Charles Haguénauer, 'La Danse Rituelle dans le Chinkonsai,' *Journal Asiatique*, Vol. 226 (Avril-Juin, 1930), pp. 318-19.
20.   Part 2, *Nihon Koten Bungaku Taikei*, Vol. 68 (Tōkyō: Iwanami Shoten, 1965), p. 71.
21.   *Manyōshū*, part 4, *Nihon Koten Bungaku Zenshū*, Vol. 7 (Tōkyō: Iwanami Shoten, 1962), p. 105 (poem no 3767).
22.   *Manyōshū*, Part 3, *Nihon Koten Bungaku Taikei*, Vol. 6 (Tōkyō: Iwanami Shoten, 1965), p. 313 (poem no. 3128).
23.   *Manyōshū*, Part 3, *op. cit.*, p. 189 (poem no. 2506).
24.   See on this Charles Haguénauer, *op. cit.*, p. 300 cf.
25.   *Kojiki, Norito, op. cit.*, pp. 81-83. See also Matsumae Takeshi, 'Heavenly Rock-Grotto Myth,' *Asian Folklore Studies*, Vol. 39, Part 2 (1980).
26.   See on this Charles Haguénauer, *op. cit.*, pp. 311-16.
27.   *Engi-Shiki-Procedures of the Engi Era*, Books I-V, transl. with introduction and notes by Felicia Gressitt Bock (Tōkyō: Sophia University, 1970), pp. 94-97. *Ryō no Shūge*, Vol. 40 *[Shintei Zōhō-] Kokushi Taikei*, Vol. 24 (1929), pp. 966-67.
28.   See also Charles Haguénauer, *op. cit.*, p. 308.
29.   See Charles Haguénauer, *op. cit.*, p. 308.
30.   Part 1, *Nihon Koten Bungaku Taikei*, Vol. 4 (Tōkyō: Iwanami Shoten, 1957), pp. 123-25 (poem no. 220-222).
31.   Part 4 (1962), pp. 163-65 (poem no. 3885).
32.   Part 1, *op. cit.*, p. 190.
33.   *Shindō Gobusho, [Shintei Zōhō-] Kokushi Taikei, op. cit.*, p. 46 cf. See also *Kōtai Jingū Gishiki Chō*, Vol. 1, Jingi-bu (Tōkyō: Zoku Gunsho Ruijū Kansei-kai, 1929), pp. 2-3.
34.   'Kokin Wakashū,' *Kokka Taikan* (Tōkyō: Chūbunkan Shoten, 3rd ed., 1942), poem no. 1084.
35.   Part 1, *op. cit.*, p. 9 (poem no. 1).
36.   Part 3, *op. cit.*, pp. 351-53 (poems no. 3253-4).
37.   *Pattern in Comparative Religion* (London: Sheed and Ward, 1958), pp. 19-23.
38.   Dr Friedrich Rudolf Lehmann, *Mana - der Begriff des 'ausserordentlich Wirkungsvollen' bei Südseevölkern*, (Leipzig: Verlag Otto Spamer, 1922).
39.   Part 1, *op. cit.*, p. 278.
40.   Although the Haori shake ritual objects to attract a deity or to prevent it from leaving or wander.

Chapter 23 TZVETANA KRISTEVA
'Sleeves' and 'Tears' in Classical Japanese Poetry and Lyrical Prose

1.   All quotations in English of *Kokinshu* poems are based on Helen Craig McCullogh's translation, *Kokin-wakashu*, Stanford Univ. Press, 1985.
2.   The English quotations of *Shinkokinshu* poems are based on H. H. Honda's translation, *The Shin Kokinshu*, The Hokusedo Press, Japan, 1970.
3.   Although I could not claim to be one of Derrida's fervent followers, I find some of his ideas, suggested in *Of Grammatology* (The Johns Hopkins Univ. Press, Baltimore and London, 1982), stimulating for the discovery of new referential modes of the text. One of my reasons to turn to his strategy of reading has been exactly the word *trace*, which happens to appear in a number of poems with the 'tear-wet sleeves' type of metaphors, and to be one of Derrida's key-words. In Derrida's concept, 'The trace is in fact the absolute origin of sense in general.... The trace is the difference which opens appearance and signification.' (p. 65). 'If the trace, arch-phenomenon of "memory"..., belongs to the very movement of signification, then signification is a priori written, whether inscribed or not, in one form or another, in a "sensible" and "spatial" element that is called "exterior".' (p. 70).
4.   Jonathan Culler, *On Deconstruction. Theory and Criticism after Structuralism*, Routledge & Kegan Paul, London, 1983, p. 81.
5.   My reading of the process of signification is based on Derrida's concept of 'the originary metaphor,' *op. cit.*, pp. 275-277.
6.   As Jonathan Culler has put it quite precisely, 'meaning is context-bound, but context is boundless,' *op. cit.*, p. 123.
7.   'There is nothing outside the text' is one of Derrida's largely quoted phrases (*op. cit.*, p. 158), and it is very important especially for the readers of classical literature, who often have little additional information 'outside the text' to rely on.
8.   I am using the comments made by H. Minemura according to the new Shogakkan edition, *Nihon-no koten*, Vol. 35, *Shinkokinwakashu* I, 1983, p. 407.
9.   Jacques Derrida, *op. cit.*, p. 93.

Chapter 24 LEONARD PRONKO
From Insularity to Internationalism: Kabuki in the Twenty-first Century

1.   Barbara Adachi, '"Super Kabuki" conquers Japan,' *Wall Street Journal*, 3 March 1986, 'Leisure and Arts.'
2.   Margaret Croydon, '"New Look" Kabuki', *New York Times*, n.d.
3.   Faith Bach, 'The Compleat Actor: A Portrait of Ichikawa Ennosuke III,' *International Friends of Kabuki* (Newsletter), March 1983, 'In the Spotlight,' p. 1.
4.   Suzuki Tadashi, *The Way of Acting*, tr. J. Thomas Rimer, New York: Theatre Communications Group, 1986, p. 76.
5.   A more detailed treatment of this production and of the entire problem of Kabuki productions in the West is found in Leonard C. Pronko, *Theatre East and West: Perspectives Toward a Total Theatre*, Berkeley and Los Angeles, University of California Press, 1967.

Chapter 25 GIOIA OTTAVIANI
The Shingeki Movement Until 1930: its Experience in Western Approach

1.   Iwata Toyoo, *Shingeki to watakushi*, Tokyo 1956.
2.   In English in the original text.
3.   Shimazaki Tōson, *Engeki zatsuwa*, quoted by Sugai Yukio, *Kaishaku, Osanai Kaoru engekiron zenshū*. Tokyo 1964, Vol. 1, p. 491.
4.   Yoshi Isamu, quoted by Sugai Yukio, ibidem p. 490. The composition was published in the 'Engeki Shinchō' in January 1925.
5.   Sugai Yukio, *Kaishaku*, ibidem p. 491.
6.   I would like to thank Prof. Adriana Boscaro for having kindly put at my disposition the translation of the chapter of *Seishun Monogatari* concerning the relationship between Tanizaki and Osanai Kaoru.

7.   'Civiltà Teatrale del XX secolo', ed. by Fabrizio Cruciani and Clelia Falletti, Bologna, Il Mulino, 1986, p. 104.
8.   Brian Powell, 'Shingeki and Modernization,' in *Studies in Japanese Culture*, J. Roggenford ed. Vol. 1, Tokyo, Japan P.E.N. Club 1973. And 'Japan's first modern theatre: the Tsukiji Shōgekijō and its company, 1924/1926,' *Monumenta Nipponica*, 1975, Vol. XXX, pp. 69/86.
9.   A. Horie Webber, 'Modernization of the Japanese Theatre: The Shingeki Movement,' in *Modern Japan*, ed. by W. G. Beasley, University of California Press 1975, pp. 147/165.
10. Komiya Toyotaka, *Shingeki Undō*, trans. in *Japanese Music and Drama in Meiji Era*, tr. Donald Keene, Edward Seidensticker, Tokyo 1956.
11. Thomas Rimer, *Kishida Kunio, Towards a modern Japanese theatre*, Princeton University Press 1974.
12. Hasegawa Saburō, *Zen'ei ga kaiga no shui*, quoted in 'Japon des Avant-gardes,' catalogue de l'exposition, Paris 1986, pp. 164/165.
13. Quoted by Thomas Rimer, *op. cit.*, p. 84.
14. Osanai Kaoru, cfr. *Osanai Kaoru engekiron zenshū*, Vol. II, pp. 48/50.
15. Osanai Kaoru, *Kyūgeki no mikata, Osanai Kaoru engekiron zenshū*, Vol. IV, pp. 312/314.
16. Hijikata Yoshi, *Enshutsusha no michi*, quoted by John Allyn, *The Tsukiji Little Theatre and the beginning of modern theatre in Japan*, Ph.D. Diss, UCLA 1970, p. 58.

PART 2: LINGUISTICS

Chapter 26 JEANNE JACOB *Rethinking Translation: The Role of Word Systems in the Translatability of Texts into Japanese*
1. Cf. Catford 1969, Nida and Taber 1970, and Steiner 1975 on the notion of intranslatabililty.

REFERENCES

Aphek, Edna, 1979, *Word Systems in Fiction: Reading in the Style of S. Y. Agnon*. Tel-Aviv: Dekel (in Hebrew).
Aphek, Edna and Yishai Tobin, 1981, 'S. Y. Agnon: Word Systems and Translation,' *Text* 1(4):269-277.
Aphek, Edna and Yishai Tobin, 1983, 'The Means is the Message: On the Intranslatability of a Hebrew Text,' *Meta* 28(1):57-69.
Catford, J. C., 1969, *A Linguistic Theory of Translation*. London: Oxford U. Press.
Cho Seung-bog, 1973, 'Some Linguistic Problems in the Translation of Japanese,' *Studies in Japanese Culture*. Tōkyō: Japan PEN Club.
Miner, Earl, 1961, 'On Translating Japanese Poetry.' Pp. 303-316 in Maurice Schneps and Alvin D. Coox (eds.) *The Japanese Image*. Tōkyō: Orient-West Inc.
Morris, Ivan, 1959 and 1964, 'On Translating from the Japanese Classics.' Pp. 327-335 in Maurice Schneps and Alvin D. Coox (eds.) 1965 *The Japanese Image*. Tōkyō: Orient-West Inc.
Nida, Eugene A. and Charles R. Taber, 1970, *The Theory and Practice of Translation*. Leiden: Brill.
Osgood, Charles E. and Meredith Martin Richards, 1973, 'From Yang and Yin to And or But,' *Language* 49(1), March: 380-412.
Saussure, Ferdinand de, 1959, *Course in General Linguistics*. New York: McGraw-Hill.
Seidensticker, Edward, 1963, 'Free versus Literal Translations.' Pp. 317-326 in Maurice Schneps and Alvin D. Coox (eds.) 1965 *The Japanese Image*. Tōkyō: Orient-West Inc.
Steiner, George, 1975, *After Babel*. London: Oxford University Press.

Corpus

Nishikawa Masatoshi and Ando Ichiro, 1952, (rev. ed. of 1940 ed.) *Watakushi Dake no Heya*. Tōkyō: Tōkyō Do Shuppan.
Woolf, Virginia, 1929, *A Room of One's Own*. New York: Harcourt, Brace and Co.

Chapter 27 KUMIKO TAKAHARA *The Changing Language in a Changing Society*

REFERENCES

Arlotto, Anthony, 1972, *Introduction to Historical Linguistics*, Boston: Houghton Mifflin Co.
Bynon, Theodora, 1977, *Historical Linguistics*, Cambridge: Cambridge University Press.
Davies, Peter, 1978, *The American Heritage Dictionary*, Paperback Edition. New York: Dell Publishing Co.
Hudson, R. A., 1980, *Sociolinguistics*, Cambridge: Cambridge University Press.
Oono Susumu, 1982, *Nihongo no Bunpoo*, Iwanami Shinsho 53. Tōkyō: Iwanami Shoten.
Oono Susumu, 1979, *Nihongo o Sakanoboru*, Iwanami Shinsho c.92. Tōkyō: Iwanami Shoten.
Morris, William, 1969, *The American Heritage Dictionary*, New York: The American Heritage Publishing Co.

Chapter 28 GÖTZ WIENOLD
How to Carry Something on Your Head in Japanese

1. In tune with Japanese ways of speaking, in the Japanese sentences the subject and/or topic will often be left out. Such a sentence can only be translated into English when one knows the context in which it is used. For convenience, the English equivalents of such subject-less sentences will mostly be written out as '(He/She).'

2. 'To lock s.th. (inanimate) up in s.th.' has a different translation than 'to lock s.o. or s.th. (animate) up in s.th.' In the latter case one would say *hito-o/dōbutsu-o heya-ni tōjikomeru* or *kankinsuru*. It is interesting to note that *tōjikomeru* actually also uses two verbs (*tōjiru* and *komeru*) but this time as a compound verb rather than a 'Verb *-te* plus Verb'-construction. The differentiation between animate and inanimate is also made in the distinctive use of *tsureru* 'taking along a person' vs. *motsu* 'taking along an object' in examples (4) and (5). Another interesting thing to note is that Korean which shares most of what can be said about Japanese in this paper also shares the distinction between animate and inanimate objects in the case of 'lock up s.o./s.th. in s.th.' Besides *saram-ŭl (koyani-rŭl) pan(an)-e(da)kaduda* 'to lock a person (a cat) in a room' we have *ton-ŭl sŏrab-e nŏh-ko camguŏssŏ* '(I) put the money into the drawer and locked it' = 'I locked up the money in the drawer.' Again, Korean shares the differentiation between animate and inanimate objects being taken along in *terida/ mosida* vs. *kajida*. (*kkomarŭl terigo wassoyo* '(I) came with the kids'; *c'aeg-ŭl kajigo wassŏyo* '(I) came with the book').

3. E.g.: *enter, exit, pass, descend, return, circle, cross, penetrate, transport, deliver, pierce, traverse, ascend, escape, elevate, elope, retract, recede, advance, proceed, infiltrate, insert, inject, eject, interpose, separate* (cf. Talmy 1985, 72; Gruber 1976, 24ff.; Miller 1972, 356f.).

4. As far as I can see with the exception of *heru* 'to pass through' and *saru* 'to leave.' Historically speaking, *saru* has a causative in *sarau* 'to take away/to make move away from,' but these verbs may not be related any more in the native speaker's mind.

5. The definitions of the meaning of the verbs in many cases do not use the standard entry of bilingual dictionaries. They are formulated in such a way that the essential path element is expressed.

6. The semantic element concerning the path of the movement can be said to be contained in the base morpheme independent of the precise way of stating the base, e.g. in the case of *noru* vs. *noseru*. That is whether we say that the base is *nor-* which changes to *nos-* in the case of the causative or whether we choose some other way, however that base is stated it contains the semantic element expressing the path 'to move on top of s.th.'

312

7. Actually, the matter is more complicated in that there are compound verbs like *ugokimawaru* 'to move about' or *miageru* 'to look up to s.th.' in great abundance next to the *-te*-constructions (cf. Ishii 1987, 58f.).

8. Of course, some of the expressions of English in this list are not prepositions but are complex expressions using a noun - like *front* or *side* - plus one or two other prepositions (*to, in, of*) and fulfilling the function which in other cases is fulfilled by a preposition.

9. Tatsuo Miyajima of the Kokuritsukokugokenkyūjō, Tokyo, kindly pointed out to me in a discussion that there is at least one aspect in which nouns like *ue, shita* and so on differ from other nouns, that is they can take adverbs like *chotto* or *skoshi, chotto ue, skoshi mae* and the like. Some Japanese informants allowed for sentences like:

(23) tsukue-no kitanai shita-o katazukete kudasai
    'Clean up the dirty place under the table'

or:

(24) mori-no utsukushii naka-o aruita '(I) walked through the beautiful interior of the forest'

instead of the usual:

(23a) kitanai tsukue-no shita-o katazukete kudasai 'Clean up under the dirty table'

or:

(24a) utsukushii mori-no naka aruita '(I) walked in (or: through) the beautiful forest'

But other Japanese whom I asked about sentences like (23) and (24), considered them to be quite strange. If this judgement should turn out to be the appropriate way of looking at the situation, this would present a second argument for saying the relational nouns differ from other nouns in certain distributional properties (and not only from a semantic point of view).

10. More precisely, there are some relational nouns that express other relations, e.g. cause: *tame*, time: *toki*. There are also some important other uses of such relational nouns, like *hō* in expressions of comparison or other ones like again *tame* and *toki*, but also *tokoro* and so on with verbal adjuncts. A discussion of this would lead into a different, very large chapter of Japanese grammar.

11. Again, a note of precision is in order. Besides *uma-ni notte hashiru* there exists the expression *jōba suru*, using a Sino-Japanese compound (*jōba*) plus the verb *suru*. But *jōba* is a compound of *jō* 'getting on' plus *ba* 'horse' and if we wrote that with Sino-Japanese characters we would see that we use the same characters for *uma* as for *ba*, and for *noru* as for *jō*. There are also *jōsen suru, jōkan suru* 'to get on a boat' and *josha suru* 'to get on train.' But these latter ones express only the action of getting on a vehicle and not the fact of riding, whereas *jōba suru* can be used to express the action of riding a horse. In the case of sail (cf. [7]) there is *hansō suru*, parallel to (16) there is *gyakuryū-o oyogu*, both again based on a Sino-Japanese compound.

I owe my thanks for a discussion to Professor Toshio Ohtaki of Kanazawa University, which made me include this note. I also have to thank Professor Takeshi Sengoku of Tokyo University for kindly discussing the contents of the paper with me and for organizing a group of colleagues to whom I could present an informal version of this paper at Tokyo University in August 1987.

12. English, in some respects, seems to be in a way similar to French or other Romance languages at least as far as the pattern of lexicalization of verbs of motion is concerned (cf. the list of verbs in fn. 3). For a more general point of this nature see Pisani 1966.

13. For this there is a wide range of expressions by a different compartment of Japanese grammar, that is adverbs, many of which are reduplicative and have an expressive value, combining with verbs as in *yochiyochi(to) aruku, tsutatsuta(to) aruku* and so on. This goes way beyond verbs of motion. Korean again is similar in this respect, if not even richer than Japanese.

14. Again, a more elaborate presentation of the Japanese lexicon would have to take account of Sino-Japanese compounds plus *suru*, in our case *tsūka suru* (combining the kanji for *tōru/tōsu* and *sugiru/sugosu*): *densha-ga eki-o tsūka suru toki-ni* 'when the train is passing through the station.'

15. Over the past half year or so I have had a series of discussions with Christoph Schwarze on the topic of motion verbs, syntactic properties associated with motion verbs, lexicalization patterns in French and Italian compared to Japanese and Korean and so on. Thus the paper owes more to these discussions than the one specific suggestion mentioned.

16. *ao* is, I take it, related to the verb *aogu* 'look upwards' *muke* is related to the path-verb *mukeru* 'to turn towards.'

REFERENCES

Döpke, Wilfried and Christoph Schwarze, 1981, 'Le rôle des prépositions locales dans la constitution sémantique de la phrase,' in: Christoph Schwarze (ed.), *Analyse des prépositions* (Tübingen: Niemeyer), 19-28.
Gruber, Jeffrey S., 1976, *Lexical Structures in Syntax and Semantics* (Amsterdam [etc.]: North-Holland).
Ishii Masahiko, 1987, 'Fukugodōshi-no seiritsujōken,' in: Hideo Teramura et al. (ed.), *Keesusutadinihonbunpō* (Tōkyō: Ōfusha), 56-61.
Iwasaki Eijiro, Haruo Nitta and Takashi Sengoku, 1984, 'Deutsche und japanische Wortbildungsmuster,' in: Tohru Kaneko (ed.), *Japanische Schrift, Lautstrukturen, Wortbildung* (Heidelberg, Groos), 108-224.
Miller, George A., 1972, 'English Verbs of Motion: A Case Study in Semantics and Lexical Memory,' in: Arthur W. Milton and Woodwin Martin (ed.), *Coding Processes in Human Memory* (Washington, D.C.: Winston and New York [etc.]: Wiley), 335-372.
Miyajima Tatsuo, 1984, 'Nihongo to Yōroppago-no idōdōshi,' in: *Kindaiichi Haruhiko Hakase kokikinenronbunshō* (Tōkyō: Sanseido), II, 456-486.
Nilsen, Don L. F. and Alleen Pace Nilson, 1975, *Semantic Theory: A Linguistic Perspective* (Rowley, Mass.: Newbury House).
Pisani, Vittore, 1966, 'Entstehung von Einzelsprachen aus Sprachbünden,' in: *Kratylos* 11, 125-141.
Rickmeyer, Jens, 1985, Morphosyntax der japanischen Gegenwartssprache. 2. Aufl. (Heidelberg: Groos).
Sakuma Kanae, 1983, *Gendainihongo-no hyōgen-to Gohō* (Tōkyō: Kuroshio).
Schwarze, Christoph, 1985, '"Uscire" e "andare fuori": struttura sintattica e semantica lessicale,' in: Annalisa Franchi de Bellis and Leonarda M. Savoia (eds.), *Sintassi e morfologia della lingua italiana d'uso: Teorie e applicazioni descrittive*. (Rome: Bulzoni), 355-371.
Schwarze, Christoph. In print. 'Lexikalische Bedeutung und Bedeutungskonstruktion: die Deutung der Präpositional-objekte von fr. *sortir*,' in: G. Lüdi, H. Stricker and J. Wüest (eds.), *Romania ingeniosa: Festschrift für Prof. Dr. Gerold Hilty zum 60. Geburtstag*.
Talmy, Leonard, 1985, 'Lexicalization Patterns: Semantic Structure in Lexical Forms,' in: Timothy Shopen (ed.), *Language Typology and Syntactic Descriptions. Grammatical Categories and the Lexicon* (Cambridge: Cambridge University Press), vol. 3, 57-149.
Tamamushi Sachio, 1979. 'Bemerkungen zur Bezeichnung räumlicher Verhältnisse in der deutschen und in der japanischen Gegenwartssprache,' Tōkyōdaigakukyōyō-gakubukiyōhikakubunkakenkyū 18. 133-171.
Teramura Hideo, 1982. *Nihongo-no sintakusu-to imiron I* (Tōkyō: Kuroshio), 182f.
Wienold, Götz, 1987, 'Strukturelle Zusammenhänge zwischen Lexikon, Syntax und Morphologie in typologischer Sicht: Englisch und Deutsch im Vergleich mit Japanisch und Koreanisch,' in: Rudolf Böhm and Henning Wode (eds.), *Anglistentag 1986 Kiel* 8, 327-349.
Wienold, Götz. In prep. 'Bewegung und Raumbezug im Japanischen typologisch betrachtet,' in: Roland Schneider (ed.), *Japanologentag Hamburg 1987*.

Chapter 29 TOSHIAKI TAKESHITA
On the Necessity of Contrastive Analysis of Japanese and Minor Languages of Europe

1. This is essential also for the compilation of dictionaries for the specific use, for example, of the Italians. It is not sufficient to substitute English for Italian in Japanese-English dictionaries prepared for the use of the Japanese. For further details see Nakamichi 1983.
2. Nomoto, 1982; NIRA 1985, p. 75, p. 162.
3. Teramura 1982; Satō 1980.
4. See note 3.

BIBLIOGRAPHY

Amato, Antonio, 1979-1980, Veicolarità e Linguaggio Scientifico, Analisi del Primo 'Progetto Italiano per Studenti Universitari Somali,' *Rassegna Italiana di Linguistica Applicata XI-XII 3-1*, Bulzoni Editore, Roma, pp. 61-115.
Itō Hanabusa, 1978, Bun no Jiten to Gogaku Kyōiku, *Kōza Nihongo Kyōiku 14*, Waseda Daigaku Gogaku Kyōiku Kenkyūjo, Tōkyō, pp. 1-9.
Nakamichi Makio, 1983, Nihongo Kyōiku no Kihongoi to sono Jiten, *Nihongogaku 6*, Meiji Shoin, Tōkyō, pp. 72-78.
NIRA/Sōgōkenkyū Kaihatsukikō, 1985, *Nihongo Kyōiku oyobi Nihongo Fukyūkatsudō no Genjō to Kadai*, Tōkyō.
Nomoto Kikuo, 1982, Nihongo Kyōiku to Nihongo Kenkyū, *Nihongogaku 1*, Meiji Shoin, Tōkyō, pp. 155-173.
Roncari, A. & Brighenti, C., 1968 (24th Edition). *La Lingua Italiana Insegnata agli Stranieri*, Edizioni Scolastiche Mondadori, Verona.
Satō Yōko, 1980, Doitsugo-ken ni okeru Nihongo kyōkasho ni tsuite, *Nihongo Kyōiku 40*, Nihongo Kyōiku Gakkai, Tōkyō, pp. 21-34.
Teramura Hideo, 1982, Taishōgengogaku to Nihongo Kenkyū, *Nihongogaku 1*, Meiji Shoin, Tōkyō, pp. 113-127.

Chapter 30 S. K. KAISER
Japanese Relative Clause Strategies

Andrews, Avery D. III, 1975/1985, *Studies in the Syntax of Relative and Comparative Clauses*. MIT Ph.D. thesis. Published 1985 (Outstanding Dissertations in Linguistics series. New York etc.: Garland).
Comrie, Bernard, 1981, *Language Universals and Linguistic Typology*. Oxford: Blackwell.
Ishigaki Kenji, 1944, 'Syukaku ga-zyosi yori setuzoku ga-zyosi e.' *Kokugo to Kokubungaku*, 221 & 222. Reprinted in Ishigaki (1955).
Ishigaki Kenji, 1955, *Zyosi no rekisi-teki kenkyuu*. Tōkyō: Iwanami.
Keenan, Edward L. and Comrie, Bernard, 1977, 'Noun Phrase Accessibility and Universal Grammar,' *Linguistic Inquiry*, 8/1:63-99.
Keenan, Edward L. and Comrie, Bernard, 1979, 'Data on the Noun Phrase Accessibility Hierarchy,' *Language* 55:333-51.
Kuno Susumu, 1973, *The Structure of the Japanese Language*. Cambridge, Mass.: M.I.T. Press.
Kuno Susumu and Wongkhomthong Preya, 1981, 'Relative Clauses in Thai.' *Studies in Language*, 5.2: 195-226.
Lehmann, Christian, 1984, *Der Relativsatz: Typologie seiner Strukturen; Theorie seiner Funktionen; Kompendium seiner Grammatik*. Tübingen: Narr.
Loetscher, Andreas, 1973, 'On the Role of Nonrestrictive Relative Clauses in Discourse.' Chicago Linguistic Society 9:356-368.
Mallinson, Graham and Blake, Barry J., 1981, *Language Typology: Cross-Linguistic Studies in Syntax*. Amsterdam etc.: North-Holland.
Platero, Paul R., 1974, 'The Navajo Relative Clause.' IJAL 40:3, 202-46.
Rodriguez, Joao, 1604, *Arte da Lingoa de Japam Composta Pello*. Nagasaki: Companhia de Iesu.
Seiler, Hansjakob, 1978, 'Determination: a Functional Dimension for Interlanguage Comparison.' In Seiler, Hansjakob (ed.), *Language Universals*. Papers from the conference held at Gummersbach, Germany, Oct. 4-8, 1976. Tübingen: Narr.

Steinthal, Heymann, 1948/1970. *De Pronomine Relativo Commentatio Philosophico-Philologica cum Excurso de Nomitivi Particula*. Berlin: Dümmler. Reissued in Steinthal 1970. *Kleine Sprachtheoretische Schriften*. Hildesheim, New York: Olms, 1-113.

ABBREVIATIONS OF TEXTS

EN: Engi Siki Norito; N. Aoki (ed.), *Norito*, honbun-hen. Oohuusya, 1975. K. Kuroita (ed.) *Sintei zooho kokusi taikei 'Engi Siki' (hukyuu-han)*. Yosikawa Koobunkan, 1977.[23]
GM: Genzi Monogatari; K. Ikeda (ed.), *Genzi Monogatari Taisei, honbun-hen*. Tyuuoo Kooronsya, 1957.
IM: Ise Monogatari; K. Ikeda. *Ise Monogatari ni tukite no kenkyuu, honbun-hen*. Oookayama syoten, 1933.
KKS: Kokinsyuu; K. Nisimoto (ed.), *Kokinsyuu koohon*. Kasama Syoin, 1977.
KM: Konzyaku Monogatari-syuu; *Konzyaku Monogatari-syuu*. NKBT Vols. 22-26. Iwanami, 1963.
SNS: Syoku-Nihongi Senmyoo; K. Kuroita (ed.), *Sintei zooho kokusi taikei 'Syoku Nihongi' (hukyuu-han)*. Yosikawa Koobunkan, 1977.
TN: Tosa Nikki; B. Hagitani (ed.), *Eiinbon Tosa Nikki*. Sintensya, 1975.
YM: Yamato Monogatari; T. Abe, *Koohon Yamato Monogatari to sono kenkyuu*. Enlarged edition. Sanseid, 1970.

NOTES

1. To illustrate this point, it is perhaps sufficient to point at the title of Steinthal's (1847/1970) Tübingen dissertation.
2. Following Lehmann 1984:48.
3. On this point, see Lehmann 1984:190f.
4. 'Proper' is not really the right adjective, as the very fact that they can be used in predication without the addition of a copula indicates their verb-like nature.
5. As distinct from 'minor' strategies, as for instance the difference in English between *The house that I bought* and *The house I bought*; Keenan/Comrie (1977) mainly discusses minor strategy differences.
6. See Comrie (1981:141).
7. See Andrews (1975:40).
8. See Andrews (1975:30) and Lehmann (1984:144).
9. See Lehmann (1984:144).
10. See Platero (1974:203).
11. These examples are taken from Platero (1974:205).
12. See Keenan & Comrie (1979:347).
13. See Schachter & Otanes, as quoted in Mallinson & Blake (1981:293).
14. In principle, Japanese prenominal relative clauses can of course be either restrictive or nonrestrictive (on this question, see for instance Kuno 1973:235).
15. See Lehmann (1984:197).
16. (29) is one rare instance of this.
17. See Seiler 1978:310.
18. See Seiler 1978:319.
19. See Lehmann, 1984:196.
20. See Kuno/Wongkhomthong (1981).
21. I am indebted to Professor Okazaki Masatugu of Kokugakuin University for drawing my attention to the implications this example presents (personal communication).
22. A development is generally assumed (for instance, in Ishigaki 1944) from the function of *ga* linking stacked circumnominal relative clauses into the conjunctive particle *ga*; that development in itself provides an important hint on the function of *ga* under discussion here.
23. For the *Norito Tuina maturi* from Vol. 16 of the *Engi Siki*, which is not contained in the other work.

Synchronic and Diachronic Approaches to the noda *Sentence*

1. In numerous theories on the matter proposed so far, a most comprehensive survey has recently been conducted by Tanomura Tadaharu of Kyoto University who also has presented a complete bibliography. 'Meidai shitei no NO no yōhō to kinō: Shosetsu no kentō,' *Gengogaku Kenkyū*, 5, Kyoto, Kyoto University Linguistics Circle, 1986, pp. 85-120.

2. Alfonso, Anthony, *Japanese Language Patterns: A Structural Approach*, Tōkyō, Sophia University, 1966.

3. For the difference between the two versions in sentences like: *Kyō wa doko e iku? Kyō wa doko e iku no?* see McGloin, Naomi H., 'Some observations concerning NO DESU expression,' *The Journal of the Association of Teachers of Japanese*, 15/2, 1980, p. 128. These sentences confronted with another pair of sentences like:

   Marco Polo wa doko de umaremashita ka?
   Marco Polo wa doko de umareta ndesu ka?

   will be discussed in my forthcoming paper.

4. For examples, see *Kōgohō Bekki*, Monbushō Kokugo Chōsa Iinkai, 1917, p. 294 and Nakayama Takashi, 'Juntai Joshi NO no Tsūjiteki Kenkyū,' *Nihon Bungaku Kyōshitsu*, 2, Tōkyō, Sōmeisha, 1950.

5. Yuzawa Kōkichirō, *Edo Kotoba no Kenkyū*, Tōkyō, Meiji Shoin, 1954, p. 419.

6. Yoshida Kanehiko, *Gendaigo Jodōshi no Shiteki Kenkyū*, Tōkyō, Meiji Shoin, 1971, pp. 465-6.

7. Nakayama T. ascribes the date as early as the An'ei and Tenmei eras, *art. cit.*, p. 22.

8. Yoshida K., *op. cit.*, pp. 380-1.

9. Mikami Akira, *Gendai Gohō Josetsu*, Tōkyō, Kuroshio Shuppan, 1953.

10. Tanamura T, *art. cit.*, p.96.

Intersection of Tense and Aspect in the Dynamic Predicate in Japanese

REFERENCES (in French)

1. Dubois, Jean, etc.: *Dictionnaire de Linguistique*, Larousse, 1982.

2. Grevisse: *Le Bon Usage*, Duculot, 1980.

3. Maës, Hubert: *Présentation Syntaxique du Japonais Standard*, Université Paris VII, Paris, 1976.

4. Mounin, Georges: *Dictionnaire de la Linguistique*, Presses Universitaires de France, 1974.

5. Lyons, John: *Linguistique Générale*, Larousse, 1970. traduit de l'anglais par F. Dubois-Charlier et D. Robinson.

(in Japanese)

1. Fujii Tadashi:"'Doshi+te iru" no imi' in *Nihongo dōshi no asupekuto*, Mugi Shobō, 1976.

2. Kindaichi Haruhiko: 'Kokugo dōshi no ichi-bunrui' in *Nihongo dōshi no asupekuto*, Mugi Shobō, 1976.

3. Kindaichi Haruhiko: 'Nihongo dōshi no tensu to asupekuto' in *Nihongo dōshi no asupekuto*, Mugi Shobō, 1976.

4. Kudō Mayumi: '*Shite iru* keishiki no imi no arikata' in *Nihongo-gaku*, 1982, Vol. 1, Meiji Shoin.

5. Kudō Mayumi: 'Asupekuto ni tsuite no oboegaki' in *Kokubun-gaku kaishaku to kanshō*, 1986, No. 1, Shibundō.

6. Matsushita Daizaburō: *Hyōjun nihon kōgo-hō*, Benseisha, 1977 (1st ed. 1930).

7. Mikami Akira: *Gendai gohō josetsu*. Kuroshio shuppan, 1973 (1st ed. Sukie Shoin, 1953).

8. Okuda Yasuo: 'Asupekuto no kenkyū wo megutte - Kindaichi-teki dankai' in *Kotoba no kenkyū, josetsu*, Mugi Shobō, 1984.

9. Okuda Yasuo: 'Asupekuto no kenkyū wo megutte' in *Kotoba no kenkyū, josetsu*, Mugi Shobō, 1984.

10. Onoe Keisuke: 'Gendai-go no tensu to asupekuto' in *Nihon-gogaku*, 1982, Vol. 1, Meiji Shoin.

11. Sakuma Kanae: *Gendai nihongo no hyōgen to gohō*, Kuroshio Shuppan, 1983 (1st ed. 1936).
12. Suzuki Shigeyuki: 'Gendai nihongo no dōshi no tensu' in *Bumpō to bumpō shidō*, Mugi Shobō, 1982.
13. Suzuki Shigeyuki: 'Nihongo no dōshi no sugata (asupekuto) ni tsuite - *suru* no katachi to *shite iru* no katachi' in *Nihongo dōshi no asupekuto*, Mugi Shobō, 1976.
14. Suzuki Shigeyuki: 'Nihongo no dōshi no toki (tensu) to sugata (asupekuto) - *shita* to *shite ita*' in *Nihongo dōshi no asupekuto*, Mugi Shobō, 1976.
15. Takahashi Tarō: *Gendai nihongo dōshi no asupekuto to tensu*, Kokuritsu Kokugo Kenkyūjo, Shūei Shuppan, 1985.
16. Teramura Hideo: *Nihongo no shintakusu to imi*, Kuroshio Shuppan, 1984.
17. Teramura Hideo: '*Ta* no imi to kinō' in *Ronshū nihongo kenkyū 7 - Jodōshi*, Yūseidō, 1979.
18. Teramura Hideo: 'Tensu, asupekuto' in *Nihongo no bumpō* Vol. 1, Kokuritsu Kokugo Kenkyūjo, Ōkurashō Insatsukyoku, 1978.
19. Teramura Hideo: 'Tensu, asupekuto no koto teki sokumen to mūdo teki sokumen' in *Nihongogaku*, 1982, Vol. 1, Meiji Shoin.
20. Yoshikawa Taketoki: 'Gendai nihongo dōshi no asupekuto no kenkyū' in *Nihongo dōshi no asupekuto*, Mugi Shobō, 1976.

Chapter 34 LONE TAKEUCHI
On Predicate Nominals in Japanese

1. The notation in capital letters is meant as a shorthand to capture characteristic forms of bundles of dialects ignoring minor differences between them. Details on individual dialects are provided in the notes in the transcription of the reference. The observations on dialects are based on available descriptions of two KA-dialects, the Tanegashima dialect in Uemura 1984 and the KA-dialects of Miyako shotō in Hirayama 1983; and of three SA-dialects, the Shuri dialect in Okinawago jiten 1969 and Nakamatsu 1973, Tarama dialect of Miyako shotō in Hirayama 1983 and the Yaeyama dialects in Miyara 1933. The conclusions are necessarily tentative as the available descriptions of dialects are fragmentary on syntactic structures, e.g. valence and semantic distinctions, status of variant forms.
2. E.g. the Shuri dialect shows SA consistently, although Okinawago jiten: 86 note 16 also reports of I-adjectives, which are said to be used for emphasis; the adjective paradigm of Tarama dialect of Miyako shotō (Hirayama 1983:201) has -sja in all forms, e.g. ´akasjaEr 'is red.'
3. The adjective paradigm of Tanegashima (chūbu) dialect (Uemura 1984) has KA, e.g. ha'jaka 'is early, fast', with the qualification that the conjunctional form is derived by ku-onbin, e.g. ha'joE (hajaku); the adjectives of the KA-dialects of Miyako shotō (Hirayama 1983) have completely KA(RI) based paradigms, and the sentence-final form -ka´i echoes the sentence-final form -ta´i of the perfect (cf.**3.2.1**).
4. The open class of adjectival nouns (this term from Martin 1975:754) have attributive forms in **na**, reflecting the Classical Japanese (CJ) copula nar-i that preceded da(<nite ar-i). Some Western dialects retain na-forms extensively, e.g. some Tottori dialects have a paradigm based on CJ **nari**, alongside da-forms (Hōgengaku kōza).
5. See for instance Yamaguchi 1981.
6. For instance, ?irana **si** kusa kajuN 'cut grass with a sickle' (Shuri dialect, Nakamatsu 1979:57). For details on other dialects, see note 34. Cf. also **site** in Classical Japanese.
7. For instance, 'ora basu**kara** 'juQkuri 'ikaE 'I will go leisurely by bus' (Tanegashima dialect, Uchima 1984:5o5). The immediately apparent KA cognates in Miyako shotō dialects (Hirayama 1983) enter largely governed and non-controlled relations: locative goal **kari**; indirect object **kai**. The latter has circumstantial functions, too. It is perhaps to be analyzed as **n** + **kai**, where **n** is cognate with **ni** in the central dialects. In Tarama dialect of Miyako shotō, which is a SA dialect, **ke:** comprises both the above-mentioned functions. In Shuri dialect (Nakamatsu 1973), both governed and circumstantial functions can be expressed by forms which are likely KA cognates, or alternatively, by combinations of KA and NI: **nakai, Nkai, kai** are labelled locative goal, existential locative, passive agent and indirect object; **kara** labelled actional locative, enters circumstantial functions only.
8. DA cognates are reported sporadically in KA and SA dialect areas, e.g. **zje** in Tanegashima (Uemura 1984).

9. This particular construction is reported only in Hachinohe dialect in Tōhoku, e.g.: mattja asunbi **sa** egu 'goes to town to play' (Hirayama 1982:252). It is consistent with the morphological configuration in question inasmuch as there is extensive evidence for SA in Tōhoku: in Hachinohe dialect, **sa** seems possible in most if not all functions of **de** and **ni** in the NI dialects; in Akita and Aomori it is somewhat less central (Hirayama 1982); further to the south, on Hatijōjima and Aogashima, **sjan** and **gee** alternate to indicate locative goal (Hirayama 1965). In some of the Tōhoku dialects at least, there is no evidence of CJ **nar-i** or **ni** (**ar-i**), as the nouns and the adjectival nouns show **DA**-reflexes only, suggesting perhaps that the adjective conjugation is a recent borrowing. The adjective forms (-I) are similar to those of the other central dialects, except that they show no traces of combination with existential verbs.

The dialects on the northern fringes of traditional Japanese territory therefore broadly align with the Ryūkyū dialects with the result that an overall wave pattern emerges.

10. Nohara (1986:62) mentions that this function of KA is found in Omorosōshi, and it is reported from all present-day Kyūshū and Ryūkyū dialects. Examples are: 'o'iga soEdaNsji **kaE** kuru 'I am going to talk to someone' (Uemura 1984:505); jama Nkai tamuN tuiga ʔicabitaN 'he went to the mountain to gather firewood' (Nakamatsu 1973:50); tt   kai **ga** ʔndzan 'goes to welcome someone' (Yonakuni dialect in Uchima 1984:410); asobii **ga** itsun 'goes to play' (Nohara 1986:62).

11. Examples include two conjunctors in Miyako shotō KA dialects: one is a coreferential conjunctor **gadii** 'while' (glossed by **nagara**), the other **tigaE** 'if' (glossed **nara**) is free, in the sense that it is neutral to switch-reference of subjects in the conjoined clauses. Both have voiced consonantism in common with the actional goal **ga** of these dialects. The Tarama dialect has a conjunctor **ke:n** glossed **nagara**, which requires coreferentiality of subjects. The assumptive verbal ending of that dialect is **ge:ra** glossed **deshō**. Note that the Yaeyama dialects which form the actional goal construction by **na**, have a cognate assumptive verb ending **ne:ra**.

12. Such a faculty for a particular structure does of course not preclude the possibility that more than one kind of change is responsible for the implementation of a given instance of the structure.

13. Nichols 1981:8ff.

14. *Ibid*:8. Note that in this approach, the copula is merely a particular case of predicate nominal, in which the equational relationship is expressed by a surface predicate.

15. Okutsu 1978 (:89-111) demonstrates the predicate-like characteristics of the actant marked by **ni** in sentences such as boku wa **unagi ni** natta and Takesh o **gunjin ni** shita, e.g. inability to function as head for the clause, e.g. *boku ga natta unagi, etc.

16. **site** was presumably more common in instrumental function.

17. To the conditions under which CJ **te** allows switch-reference mentioned in Akiba 1977, should be added instances of loss of control, where the upper clause indicates the unforeseen or inevitable outcome of the event in the **te**-clause, e.g. Mina fito, kareifi no ufe ni namida **otosite** fotobinikeri. (Ise Monogatari, sect. 9) 'Everyone **dropped** tears on top of the dried rice, and it **swelled**.'

18. See Saeki 1956:5 and Takeuchi 1987:167, note 8.

19. CJ data allow plenty of scope for speculations on recurrent fomations, CJ **nari** parallels the just mentioned CJ unlimited perfect, if i in **ni** is related to i of the conjunctional form of the verb. The CJ adjective and past **-ki/-si** endings would represent yet another, older formation.

20. Under this assumption, one would expect CJ or post-CJ newly formed adjectives (mostly of Sino-Japanese origin) to show no delimited/non-delimited distinction. In Russian a similar lexical condition accounts for differences in the use of nominative and instrumental case in predicate nominals, see Nichols 1981, chapter 3.

21. In this connection, it is noteworthy that there exists a trend in modern Japanese for narrowing of **ni**, as **kara** appears to take over some of the direct, governed functions of **ni**, viz. the variation between N **ni** kiku and N **kara** kiku 'asks somebody,' or N **ni** kiite morau and N **kara** kiite morau 'has N ask.'

Another question is whether the innovation of **kara** is related to the popularity of the so-called periphrastic adjectival form **-kari** in post-CJ literary language. If so, one would like evidence that **kara** supersedes **yori** in texts where **-kari** adjectives are frequent, such as the Bakin texts surveyed by Suzuki 1965. Perhaps these adjective forms and **kara** both represent influence from non-central dialects?

22. This reminds of the CJ clause particle **ni** which may well have undergone a similar loosening of its coreferentiality conditions: strict coreference still being required only in the actional goal construction (3) and CJ intensive verb form, e.g. **yuki ni yuku** 'goes and goes.'

23. See Li and Thompson 1977, Nichols 1979 and Frajzyngier 1986.

24. An alternative course of development in other sentence types would result in specific subject or agent functions, as these actants are presumably focused more often than others.

25. The information on pronominal systems is from Nakamoto 1983, in particular 173ff.

26. **Te** of **te**-accretion, at first glance, would seem to deviate from this course of derivation. However, I have suggested elsewhere that CJ **-te** might be derivable from a verb meaning 'to come' and therefore belongs to the category of shifters (Takeuchi 1987:217-38). Published too late to be useful in the writing of this article is Z. Frajzyngier: 'From verb to anaphora,' in: **Lingua 72** (1987):155-16, in which it is proposed that one of the deictics in Chadic languages is to be derived from the verb 'to come.' Ultimately, the relation between the categories of deictics and motion verbs should be considered.

27. Cf. later developments of distal pronouns, such as **sonata** or **anata**, to refer to the addressee.

28. **Kara** certainly seems less well entrenched in OJ than **nite**. A closer look at CJ **site** and **nite** might reveal that **site** was in competition with **nite** in certain functions such as instrumental.

29. On the whole, the function of **ga** is more restricted in southern dialects. The condition is primarily semantic. In Tanegashima dialect, **ga** can mark a human subject and a human possessor, except the 2nd person (pronoun). It is also found with low transitive objects, e.g. **kaki ga naru** 'is able to write.' **no** is used elsewhere. In the KA dialects of Miyako shotō **ga** is used with human subjects only and the oblique **ga** is possessive rather than attributive.

In Shuri, **ga** attaches to personal pronouns and human beings only, and is further limited to affirmative statements. Finally in the Tarama dialect, **ga** is largely confined to personal pronouns. Note that in Yaeyama dialects where **ga** is not found at all, the conjunctor **na** in the actional goal construction is a NI cognate, e.g. pana mii **na** du paru 'goes flower-viewing.'

30. I have no information on the forms of the copula predicates in Tanegashima dialect. In Shuri, noun predicates are formed by what Okinawago jiten takes to be a contraction of the particle **ja** (glossed **wa**) and **ʔaN** (glossed **aru**) (although **ni aru** or even **nite aru** might be equally likely sources?) with an alternative (emphatic and delimited?) structure formed by the focus particle **du**. In Miyako-shotō and in Yaeyama dialects, the copula is either unmarked or formed by the focus marker **du**. The conditioning factor seems to be tense: non-past predicates use the noun on its own, and past and other auxiliary denotations are formed by **du** and the appropriate form of the existential verb, e.g. past **du atai/atar**. Interestingly, **du** **'ar** is reported with adjectives in Miyako shotō, e.g. **'akasja du 'ar** 'is red,' however, without mentioning of any specific denotation.

31. For instance, uja **ga dun** wuree siwaa saNsiga 'If my parents had been here, I wouldn't have been worried' (Nakamatsu 1973:29) or ujaga ï ku tu **nu du** ssana 'I don't understand what my parents say' (Hirayama 1983:223).

32. The below scheme represent trends rather than rules. It ignores many problems not covered by the available descriptions, such as whether subduing/highlighting (**wa/mo**) is optional or not, whether subject marking is optional, etc.

33. The presence of **no** as marking subject in these dialects and thereby available for further development in predicate nominal constructions, as found in the NI dialects, could conceivably be another old feature.

34. In the Shuri dialect, **saani, saai, sai** and **si** are reportedly variants. They enter circumstantial relations only. Nakamatsu describes their functions as instrumental and degree, using **de wa** to gloss them. The Tarama dialect is similar to Shuri with some phonetic variation. Thus, **si:** enters circumstantial relations only, primarily as instrumental. In the Yaeyama dialects, instrumental **sa:r** and **s'i** are clearly cognate with the adjective ending. These particles enter only circumstantial relations.

Only Tanegashima dialect has a SA cognate **sanaE**, labelled locative goal, which enters governed relations with motion verbs, e.g. 'oEkazjaE nisjis**anaE**'iki'oru 'The typhoon is moving westwards' (Uchima 1984:5o4).

35. E.g. the KA-dialects of Miyako shotō.

36. In Shuri dialect, both governed and circumstantial functions can be expressed by forms, which seem likely KA cognates, or alternatively, combinations of KA and NI. Thus, **nakai,**

Nkai, kai are labelled locative goal, existential locative, passive agent and indirect object. In Tarama dialect, the KA cognate *ng* **ke**: comprises governed relations, such as goal, indirect object. It is similar to N, glossed **ni**. In Yaeyama dialects, a conspicuous pair of particles occur in governed and in some controlled relations, locative goal **nanga** and locative existential **nangatee** or **nanga**.

37. In Shuri and Tanegashima dialects. **ni** (with allomorph **i** following a vowel) is reported to have functions similar to the ones of NI dialect **ni**.

38. The extent of voicing varies considerably among dialects. Kagoshima dialect has voiced adjective forms, and the question particle too is reported as **ga** rather than **ka**.

39. Cf. Frajzyngier 1986 for an example of similarly alternative existential and focus copula formations in the Chadic languages.

BIBLIOGRAPHY

Akiba Katsue, 1977, 'Switch reference in Old Japanese,' in: *Proceedings of the Third Annual Meeting of the Berkeley Linguistics Society*: 610-19.

Akiba-Reynolds Katsue, 1982, 'Reconstruction of *nu - A hypothesis for the origin of Japanese,' in *Papers in Japanese Linguistics* 8:1:1-22.

Frajzyngier Zygmunt, 1986, 'From preposition to copula,' in: *Proceedings of the Twelfth Annual Meeting of the Berkeley Linguistics Society*: 371-386.

Harries-Delisle, Helga, 1978, 'Contrastive emphasis and cleft sentences,' in: *Universals of Human Language Vol. 4*, ed. by J. Greenberg: 420-486.

Hirayama Teruo (ed.), 1965, *Izu shotō hōgen no kenkyū*. Tōkyō: Meiji shoin. - 1982. *Ōshū hōgen kiso goi no sōgō-teki kenkyū*. Tōkyō: Ōfūsha.

- (ed.), 1983, *Ryūkyū Miyako shotō hōgen kiso goi no sōgo-teki kenkyū*. Tōkyō: Ōfūsha.

Hōgengaku kōza, Vols. 2, 3. 1961. Misao Tōjo (superv.) Tōkyō: Tokyōdō.

Ishigaki Kenji, 1955, *Joshi no rekishi-teki kenkyū*. Tōkyō: Iwanami Shoten.

Li, Charles and Sandra A. Thompson, 1977, 'A Mechanism for the Development of Copula Morphemes,' in: *Mechanisms of Syntactic Change*. Austin & London, Texas UP:419-444.

Mackenzie, J. Lachlan, 1978, 'Ablative -Locative Transfers and their Relevance for the Theory of Case-Grammar,' in: *Journal of Linguistics 14*:129-56.

Martin, S. E., 1968, 'On the Forms of Japanese Adjectives,' in: *Glossa* 2.1:46-69.

- 1975, *A Reference Grammar of Japanese*. New Haven: Yale UP.

Miller, R. A., 1971, *Japanese and the Other Altaic Languages*. Chicago & London: University of Chicago Press.

Mills, D. O., 1974, *A Historical Linguistic Study of the Copula in the Japanese Language*. Ph.D. dissertation, University of Michigan.

Miyara Tōsō, 1930, *Yaeyama goi*. Tōkyō: Tōyō bunko.

Munro, Pamela, 1977, 'From Existential to Copula: the History of Yuman BE,' in: Charles Li (ed.) *Mechanisms of Syntactic Change*, Austin & London, Texas UP:445-489.

Nakamatsu Takeo, 1973, *Okinawago no bunpō*. Naha: Okinawa gengo bunka kenkyūjo.

Nakamoto Masatie, 1981, *Nihongo no genkei: Nihon rettō no gengogaku*. Tōkyō: Kinkeisha.

- 1983, 'Ninshō daimeishi no keisei to hatten,' in: *Ryūkyū goi-shi no kenkyū*. Tōkyō: Mizusu shōbō:154-186.

Nichols, Johanna, 1981, *Predicate Nominals: a Partial Surface Syntax of Russian*. Berkeley: University of California Press. (= University of California Publications in Linguistics, Vol. 97).

Nohara Mituyoshi, 1986, *Ryūkyū hōgen joshi no kenkyū*. Tōkyō: Musashino shoin.

Okinawago jiten, 1969, Kokuritsu kokugo kenkyūjo (ed.) Tōkyō: Ōkurashō insatsukyoku.

Okutsu Keiichirō, 1978, 'Boku wa unagi da' no bunpō. Tōkyō: Kuroshio shuppan.

Saeki Umetomo, 1956, '"Ni ari" kara "de aru" e,' in: *Kokugogaku* 26:1-6.

Serafim, Leon, 1985, *The Prehistory of a Northern Ryukyuan Dialect of Japanese*. Tōkyō: Honpo Shoseki Press.

Suzuki Tanjirō, 1965, 'Bakin no bungo: keiyōshi -KARI katsuyō no baai' in: *Kokugogaku* 60:62-73.

Uemura Yūtarō, 1984, 'Tanegashima chūbu hōgen bunpō no kijutsu-teki kenkyū,' in: Hirayama Teruo hakase koki kinenkai (ed.) *Gendai hōgengaku no Kadai*, Vol. 2, Tōkyō: Meiji shoin:481-524.

Unger, J. Marshall and Yoko Ito Tomita, 1983, 'The Classification of Old Japanese Adjectives,' in: *Papers in East Asian Languages* 1:52-65.

Uchima Chokujin, 1984, *Ryūkyū hōgen bunpō no kenkyū*. Tōkyō: Kasama shoin.

Yamada Minoru, *Ryūkyūgo keiyōshi no keitairon-teki kōzō*. Tōkyō: Ōfūsha.

- 1979, *Ryūkyūgo dōshi no keitairon-teki kōzō*. Tōkyō: Kokusho kankōkai.

Yamaguchi Yoshinori, 1973, 'Keiyōshi katsūyo no seiritsu,' in: *Kokugo to kokubungaku* 50.9:22-36.

- 1981, ''Keiyōdōshi no seiritsu,' in: *Kokugo to kokubungaku* 58.5:1-17.

INDEX

328